DRAWING FROM COVER OF ORIGINAL EDITION (SEE PAGE 373).

André & Sleigh, Ltd.

THE DALAI LAMA AS A GOD.

From a painting in Potala.

Lhasa and Its Mysteries

With a Record of the British Tibetan Expedition of 1903–1904

by

L. Austine Waddell

DOVER PUBLICATIONS, INC.
New York

Published in Canada by General Publishing Company, Ltd., 30 Lesmill Road, Don Mills, Toronto, Ontario.

Published in the United Kingdom by Constable and Company, Ltd., 10 Orange Street, London WC2H 7EG.

This Dover edition, first published in 1988, is an unabridged republication of the work originally published in 1905 by John Murray in London and E. P. Dutton and Company in New York under the title *Lhasa and Its Mysteries: With a Record of the Expedition of 1903-1904*. In the present edition, some of the illustrations have been moved to new places in the book; the three illustrations and one map originally in color appear in black and white; the three original foldout maps appear as double-page spreads; and the seals on p. 448 appear in black instead of red. Incorrect cross-references to illustrations and maps have been tacitly corrected wherever noticed.

Manufactured in the United States of America
Dover Publications, Inc., 31 East 2nd Street, Mineola, N.Y. 11501

Library of Congress Cataloging-in-Publication Data

Waddell, L. A. (Laurence Austine), 1854-1938.
Lhasa and its mysteries : with a record of the British Tibetan expedition of 1903-1904 / by L. Austine Waddell. — Dover ed.
p. cm.
Reprint. Originally published: New York : Dutton, 1905.
Includes index.
ISBN 0-486-25763-0 (pbk.)
1. Tibet (China)—Description and travel. 2. Waddell, L. A. (Laurence Austine), 1854-1938—Journeys—China—Tibet. I. Title.
DS785.W2 1988 88-16150
915.1'5043—dc19 CIP

PREFACE.

THE following pages give an account, inadequate no doubt, yet I would fain hope, so far as it goes, intelligible and authentic, of Central Tibet, its capital, its Grand Lama hierarchy, and its dreamy hermit-people, as they appear to one who has had exceptional advantages for making their acquaintance.

It is now nearly a quarter of a century since I paid my first visit to the mystic land beyond the Himalayas. Soon thereafter, on my return from the war in Burmah (1885-86), where I had had an opportunity of examining the primitive Buddhism of King Thebaw's late subjects, I was stationed for some years at Darjeeling on the borders of the Forbidden Land, where there was a floating colony of several thousand Tibetans, Lamas and laity, fresh from the sacred city, and in daily communication with it. The curiosity naturally aroused by the sight of these strange people, with their picturesque caravans and encampments, was farther stimulated by echoes of the theosophist belief that somewhere beyond the mighty Kanchenjunga there would be found a key which should unlock the mysteries of the old world that was lost by the sinking of the Atlantis continent in the Western Ocean, about the time when Tibet was being upheaved by the still rising Himalayas. Here more obviously and indisputably must lie the key to many unsolved problems in the ethnology, natural history, and geography of the "Roof of the World." At Darjeeling also I made the acquaintance of several of the Survey spies, those brave men who, carrying their lives in their hands, are engaged in what Kipling calls "The Great Game," the exploration of the most savage and least known parts of the Trans-Himalayan valleys, and I heard from their lips the stirring narratives of their adventures.

To turn these hitherto neglected opportunities to best account, I set about learning the Tibetan language and collecting information wherever available. Awaking from my first surprise at finding how little is certainly known as to the religion of the country, and how unlike it is to the Buddhism of Burmah, from which I had freshly come, I undertook a comparison of the Tibetan beliefs and rites with those which pass under the Buddhist name in other lands, devoting much of my holiday leave to the prosecution of the enquiry in Ceylon, China, and Japan; whilst, with a view to acquire information of a more secular character, I tramped many hundreds of miles along the mountain tracks of the Tibetan frontier, at various points from Garhwal and Nepal in the west, to Assam in the east, where the valley of Central Tibet ends in that of the Brahmaputra River, often at great altitudes, sometimes sleeping in caves to evade the frontier guards, and on several occasions penetrating some days' journey into the territory of the Lhasa Government, eliciting information about the tribes,[1] topography, and natural history[2] of those regions. Although my attempt to reach the mystic citadel in disguise in 1892 failed, yet during these years of preparation I had accumulated such accurate pictures of the land that my ultimate entry into its capital, when it came, seemed but the realisation of a vivid and long-cherished dream.

The reader will, I trust, excuse these personal references, which are made in no boastful way, but merely to explain the somewhat peculiar position in which I found myself as a member of the advance column of the recent historic expedition to Lhasa. The circumstances enumerated opened to me an intercourse with the Lamas, native chiefs, and people met with on the journey, which would have been impossible to one not similarly prepared beforehand, and put into my hands a means of interpreting much symbolism, custom, and myth which would have been quite incomprehensible to the uninitiated.

Amongst the wealth of photographs of this book, all taken by myself, with one or two exceptions, are some unique ones, direct from Nature, by the "colour-process," which give vivid and truthful pictures of the marvellous colouring of the originals.* The clever sketches by Mr Rybot, a member of the Expedition, after the style of the Bayeux tapestries, will be appreciated.

[1] *Tribes of the Brahmaputra Valley*. Calcutta, 1900.

[2] My large collection of the birds of the South-Western Tibet borderland is now in the Hunterian Museum, Glasgow University, and is analysed by me in the *Gazetteer of Sikhim*, pp. 198-234. Calcutta, 1894.

* In black and white in the present edition.

An unusually full Index has been added for convenience of reference.

I take this opportunity of expressing my great indebtedness to my friend Dr ISLAY BURNS MUIRHEAD, and to Mr JOHN MURRAY, for much-valued assistance in revising the proofs.

L. A. W.

LONDON, *9th February* 1905.

CONTENTS.

CHAPTER I.

LHASA THE FORBIDDEN.

CHAPTER II.

THE GRAND LAMA AND HIS EVOLUTION AS THE PRIEST-GOD OF LHASA.

CHAPTER III.

HOW THE BRITISH MISSION CAME TO BE SENT.

CHAPTER IV.

FORWARD! THE PEACEFUL MISSION BECOMES AN ARMED FORCE.

CHAPTER V.

INVASION OF THE CHUMBI VALLEY ACROSS THE JELEP PASS AND OCCUPATION OF PHARI FORT.

CHAPTER VI.

ADVANCE TO TUNA ON THE TIBETAN PLATEAU, ACROSS THE FORMIDABLE TANG PASS.

CHAPTER VII.

WINTERING IN TIBET.

CHAPTER VIII.

ON TO GURU, WITH BATTLE AT THE CRYSTAL SPRINGS.

CHAPTER IX.

THE TIBETAN ARMY AND ITS LEADERS.

CHAPTER X.

DASH ON GYANTSÉ, PAST THE LAKES RHAM AND KALA, WITH FIGHT IN THE GORGE OF THE RED IDOL.

CHAPTER XI.

GYANTSÉ—ITS FORT AND TOWN.

CHAPTER XII.

TEMPLES, PRIESTS, AND CONVENTS OF GYANTSÉ AND NEIGHBOURHOOD, WITH VISIT TO THE CAVES OF THE ENTOMBED HERMITS.

CHAPTER XIII.

BESIEGED AT GYANTSÉ.

CHAPTER XIV.

RELIEF OF GYANTSÉ AND STORMING OF THE JONG.

CHAPTER XV.

GYANTSÉ TO LHASA, PAST THE YAMDOK SEA, AND ACROSS THE TSANGPO VALLEY.

CHAPTER XVI.

LHASA, "THE SEAT OF THE GODS."

CHAPTER XVII.

TEMPLES AND MONKS IN THE HERMIT CITY: THE LAMAS' HOLY OF HOLIES.

CHAPTER XXI.

PEACE NEGOTIATIONS AND SIGNING OF THE TREATY.

CHAPTER XXII.

RAMBLES ROUND LHASA.

CHAPTER XXIII.

THE RETURN JOURNEY—EXPLORATION OF THE TSANGPO VALLEY, AND SNOW-BOUND AT PHARI.

APPENDICES.

SCIENTIFIC RESULTS OF THE EXPEDITION AND NOTES TO THE TEXT.

LIST OF ILLUSTRATIONS

*In Colours.**

In Half-Tone.

* In black and white in the present edition.

In Text.

MAPS AND PLANS.

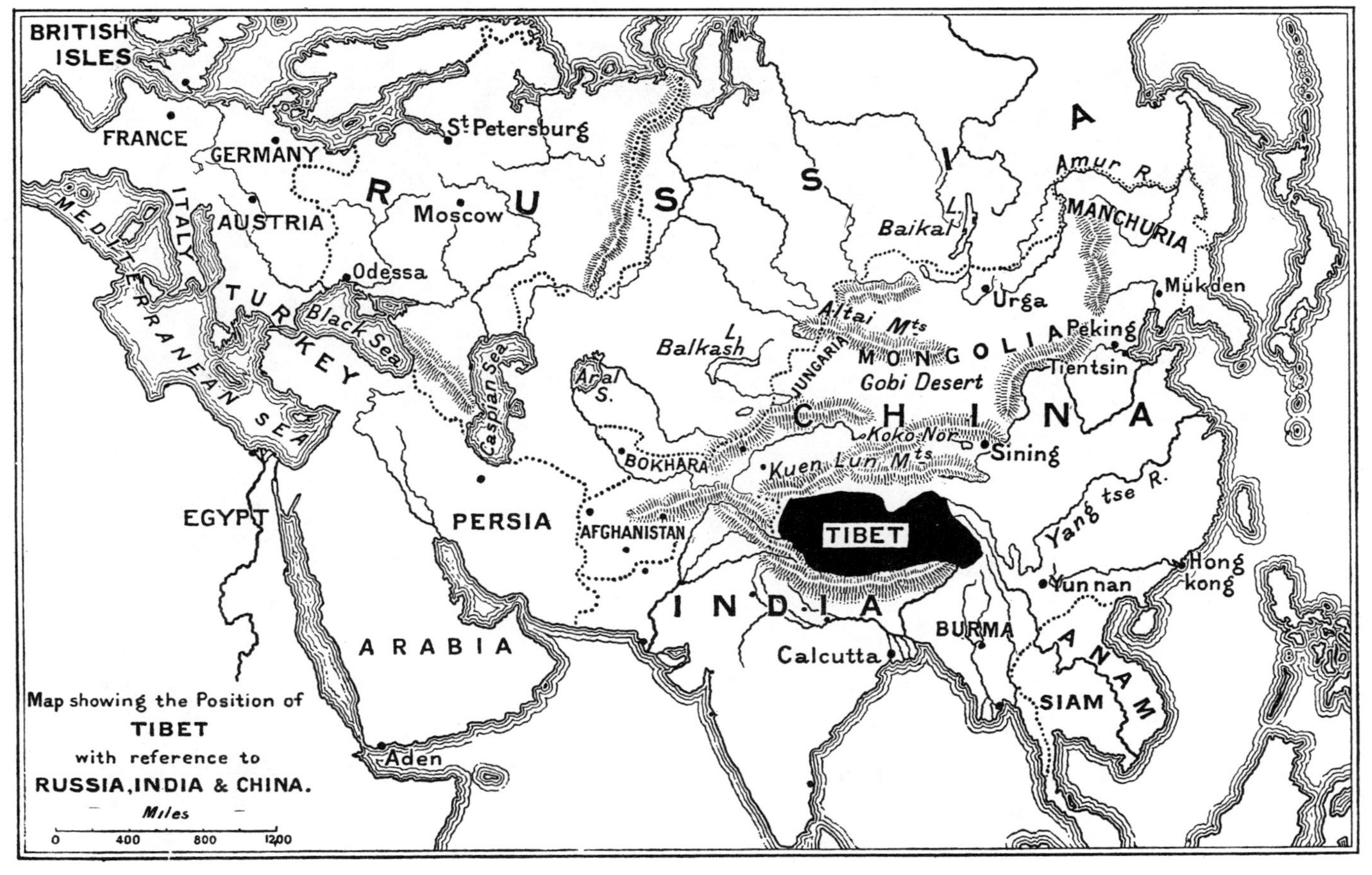

Map showing the Position of
TIBET
with reference to
RUSSIA, INDIA & CHINA.

André & Sleigh, Ltd.

PALACE OF DALAI LAMA ON POTALA AT LHASA

LHASA AND ITS MYSTERIES.

CHAPTER I.

LHASA THE FORBIDDEN.

"*In the heart of Asia lasts to this day the one mystery which the nineteenth century has still left to the twentieth to explore—the Tibetan oracle of Lhasa.*"—CURZON.

"*In the year of the Wood-Dragon* [1904 A.D.] *the first part of the year protects the young king;* [*then*] *there is a great coming forward of robbers, quarrelling and fighting, full many enemies, troublous grief by weapons and such-like will arise, the king, father and son will be fighting. At the end of the year a conciliatory speaker will vanquish the war.*"—TIBETAN PROPHECY from Almanac for the Wood-Dragon Year [1904 A.D.].

WREATHED in the romance of centuries, LHASA, the secret citadel of the "undying" Grand Lama, has stood shrouded in impenetrable mystery on the Roof-of-the-World, alluring yet defying our most adventurous travellers to enter her closed gates. With all the fascination of an unsolved enigma, this mysterious city has held the imagination captive, as one of the last of the secret places of the earth, as the Mecca of East

Asia, the sacerdotal city where the "Living Buddha," enthroned as a god, reigns eternally over his empire of tonsured monks, weaving their ropes of sand like the schoolmen of old, or placidly twirling their prayer-wheels, droning their mystic spells and exorcising devils in the intervals of their dreamy meditations. But now, in the fateful Tibetan Year of the Wood-Dragon, the fairy Prince of "Civilisation" has roused her from her slumbers, her closed doors are broken down, her dark veil of mystery is lifted up, and the long-sealed shrine, with its grotesque cults and its idolised Grand Lama, shorn of his sham nimbus, have yielded up their secrets, and lie disenchanted before our Western eyes. Thus, alas! inevitably, do our cherished romances of the old pagan world crumble at the touch of our modern hands!

How the astrologers of Tibet were able to predict this distressful storm which was in store for their country, so long before it happened, and to specify that it should occur exactly in this very year, is amazing. Certain it is, that the prophetic words heading the foregoing page, and here reproduced from their original, were copied out by myself, about a year before our expedition was ever heard of, from a Tibetan manuscript almanac for this ill-starred year of the Wood-Dragon, of the fantastic calendar of the Lamas.[1] In view of this adverse prophecy staring them in the face, the poor Tibetans, so deeply influenced at all times by superstition, are much to be admired for their patriotism and fanatical loyalty to their priest-god, in desperately rushing headlong upon a conflict which, even in their ignorance

[1] This calendar, with its grotesque symbols and terms, is compounded of the twelve zodiacal beasts, mythological and other, coupled on to the five Chinese elemental bodies, all of which are implicitly believed by the Tibetans to exercise a powerful influence on man's destiny during the year. See Appendix I.

of our overwhelming strength, they knew was already doomed by their own oracles to be a hopeless contest, in which Tibetan exclusivism was fighting its death-struggle.

The inaccessibility of Lhasa has been due in part to the well-nigh unsurmountable natural barriers

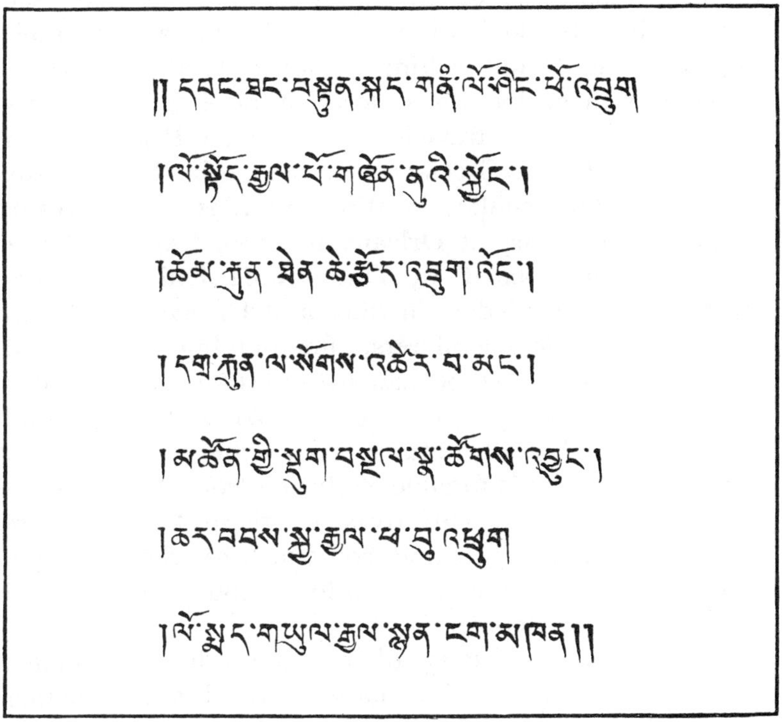

༎ དབང་ཐང་བསྟུན་སྐད་གཉིཾ་ལོ་ཤིང་པོ་འབྲུག

།ལོ་སྟོད་རྒྱལ་པོ་གཉེན་ནུའི་སྐྱོང་།

།ཆོམ་རྐུན་ཐེན་ཆེ་རྫོད་འབྲུག་འོང་།

།དགྲ་རྐུན་ལ་སོགས་འཚེར་བ་མང་།

།མཚོན་གྱི་སྡུག་བསྡུལ་སྣ་ཚོགས་འཁྲུང་།

།ཆར་བབས་སྐྱུ་རྒྱལ་ཕ་བུ་འཕྲུག

།ལོ་སླད་གཡུལ་རྒྱལ་སླན་ངག་མཁན།།

FACSIMILE OF THE PROPHECY.

which seclude that city behind the most stupendous mountains in the world, and to the extreme difficulty of journeying within the country of Tibet itself, owing to the enormous elevation, averaging 12,000 to 15,000 feet above the sea-level, and the absence of all facilities for travel. But the chief cause has been the political barriers raised by its monks, the Lamas, who are at the same time the rulers, the priests, and the merchants of the country; and who, prompted by their own commercial and clerical self-interest, and their dread of losing their advantageous monopoly by the introduction of Europeans and their methods, have struggled and striven by every means in their power to preserve their isolation. Suspicious of all strangers, and ever on the alert, they blocked all avenues of approach to their country, and unflinchingly opposed all intruders, repelling them by armed force if necessary. In this way, such daring travellers as Colonel Prjevalsky in 1872-1879, Count Szechenyi in 1880, Mr Rockhill, the great Tibetan scholar, in 1889 and 1892, M. Bonvalot and Prince Henry of Orleans in 1889, Captain Bower in 1891, the ill-fated M. Dutreuil de Rhins in 1893, Mr and Mrs Littledale in 1895, and Dr Sven Hedin in 1901—all of these explorers, after braving unparalleled dangers in the attempt, had to confess to having failed to penetrate beyond the mere outskirts of the central province, and not within a week's journey of Lhasa. As a result of this forcible exclusion from the populous central tracts, the narratives of these travellers are mainly geographical, and contain, with the exception of Rockhill's, little information about the life and notions of the people.

Nor was the jealousy of the Lamas directed against Europeans only. All natives of India, whether Buddhists or not, except a few well-known merchants from Nepal and Ladak, were equally excluded and prevented from crossing the frontier, in accordance with the standing order of the Emperor of China, as conveyed to the missionary M. Huc half a century ago, which prescribed that "no Moghul, Hindostani (Indian), Pathan or Feringhi (European)" should be admitted into Tibet.

It resulted from this exclusive policy that when the British Government wished, in view of possible contingencies, to get a trustworthy map of the great unknown territory of the Land of the Lamas which for so many hundreds of miles marched with the frontiers of India, it had to employ as its secret surveying spies, for the most part Tibetans, who had settled on our side of the Himalayas as naturalised British subjects, and whose Mongoloid features assisted in their disguise. Of this class were the famous surveying "Pundits"[1] Nain Sing and "A-K," trained and sent out into unknown Tibet by Colonel Montgomery of the Indian Survey in 1866 and subsequently; and to these survey spies we are indebted for most of our knowledge of the map of Tibet. These gallant exploring pundits, both of them naturalised Tibetans from the North-western Himalayas of Kumaon, after being thoroughly trained to survey-work—to the use of the prismatic compass, to plot out routes, understand maps, read the sextant, recognise the fixed stars, use the boiling-point thermometer for altitudes, etc.—they proceeded, in the guise of merchants, risking their lives in the event of detection, to traverse Tibet in all directions and map it out in secret. In this adventurous enterprise they displayed wonderful courage and resource in evading and overcoming suspicion.

The former pioneer explorer, Nain Sing, disguised as a merchant of Ladak, reached Lhasa through Nepal in 1866, and was the first to fix the latitude and longitude of the Forbidden City. Again, eight years later, in 1874, he revisited that place from Ladak by way of the great gold-mine region, in both cases making wide traverses and curves across the country. He did most of his surveying under cover of his prayer-wheel and rosary. When he saw anyone approaching he at once began to twirl his prayer-wheel, and as all good Buddhists whilst doing that are supposed to be absorbed in religious thoughts, he was very seldom disturbed.

[1] An Indian word meaning "learned men."

His prayer-wheel, instead of the usual prayer-scrolls, contained long slips of paper for recording the compass-bearings of places, and the number of paces between towns, etc. ; and afterwards, as it was always exempt from customs-house examination, it secreted a compass. His rosary, instead of the usual one hundred and eight beads, was made up of one hundred as counters for his paces—at every hundred paces he dropped a bead. On his visit to the Grand Lama, in a batch of pilgrims, he was much exercised lest His Holiness, who is credited with knowing the secrets of all hearts, should penetrate his disguise; but the pundit put on a bold face and passed this ordeal successfully.

The latter explorer, Krishna, who is a well-educated gentleman and a personal friend of mine, is officially known as "A-K" by reversing the initials of his name. He did even better work, the best of all these native explorers. He, too, visited Lhasa twice, the second time in 1878, and cross-quartered Tibet, up to the borders of Mongolia, China, and Burma, with such remarkable accuracy that, when his figures were calculated out in Calcutta, they fitted in almost exactly with those of the Russian observer, Colonel Prjevalsky, at their points of contact in Mongolia, this agreement being the more surprising when we consider that their routes extended across many hundreds of miles of the most difficult country in the world. Captain Ryder of the Royal Engineers also informs me that he recently tested several of A-K's road-measurements in South-eastern Chinese Tibet by wheel-cyclometer and found that A-K's measurement by paces was marvellously accurate. The other most famous Tibetan surveying spies are Lama Ugyen Gyatsho and Küntūp, both naturalised British Tibetans of the Sikhim or Darjeeling border of Tibet.

Even such men were repeatedly stopped as suspects, and as they procured this geographical information at the risk of their lives, they have mostly been rewarded with pensions and grants of land.

The geographical knowledge thus bravely procured by these Tibetan agents of the British Government, combined with the route-surveys across the outer ranges by Mr Rockhill and the few Europeans above-named, has already filled up most of the map of Tibet, the basis of which was the old "Lama Survey" of the Jesuits, under that most active of Chinese Emperors, Kangshi, in 1717.[1]

A very few Indians also have gained entry into Tibet, during the past century, and even into its sacred capital, in the guise of Tibetans, which their swarthy skin renders somewhat easy. Thus Babu Sarat Chandra Das of Bengal contrived to get into Tibet from our frontier town of Darjeeling, over a quarter of a century ago, in disguise as the Tibetan companion of the surveying Lama, Ugyen Gyatsho; and he was also smuggled into Lhasa for a few days as a feigned Tibetan monk by a Lama friend of Ugyen Gyatsho. The terrible penalty, however, paid by Ugyen's old Lama friend for being a party to the impersonation by which this Bengali procured entry into Lhasa is horrible to relate, and throws a lurid light on the savage inhumanity of Buddha's so called vice-regency on earth. I heard the story several years ago from eye-witnesses, and from the lips of my friend the Tibetan governor of Lhasa himself, who shed tears of emotion as he related it to me. This beloved old Lama

[1] This emperor having employed the Jesuit Fathers Regius and others in constructing a remarkably accurate map of China, more accurate than most of the maps of Europe in those days, asked them to make a map of Tibet. For this purpose two Lamas were trained as surveyors by the Fathers at Peking, and sent to Lhasa and the sources of the Ganges; and their results were plotted out by the Jesuits, and form the first map of Tibet, which was published by D'Anville in Du Halde's work of 1735. See Markham's *Narrative of the Mission of Bogle and Manning*, lxi., for details.

was one of the chief monks of the western capital of Tibet at Tashilhumpo, who have practically nothing whatever to do with the political government of the country, which is in the hands of the Lhasa Lamas. He bore the high title of "Minister" or *Seng-chen*. As he was anxious to learn the language of India, the native country of Buddha, he asked Ugyen Gyatsho, on the occasion of one of his visits to Tibet, to bring with him next time he returned an Indian to teach him this language, and he would arrange to have him passed secretly through from the Darjeeling frontier. In this way Sarat C. Das, who happened at that time to be at Darjeeling as a vernacular teacher in the school there, got to Tashilhumpo, and after a few months there he begged the Lama, in return for his services, to get him a sight of Lhasa. After much importunity the Lama consented, and persuaded his nephew, the governor of Gyantsé, to whom he disclosed the Babu's disguise, to take the Babu there for a few days in the retinue of his wife. When, over a year later, it leaked out at Darjeeling that this good-hearted old Lama had assisted an Indian to get into Lhasa, even for a few days, notwithstanding his high position, next in rank only to the Grand Lama himself, and of such sanctity that he was esteemed to be an incarnation of a divinity, and the bodies of his predecessors for three generations were all enshrined in gilded tombs in the Grand Lamasery, where they were objects of worship by swarming pilgrims—nevertheless, when it transpired that he had assisted Sarat Chandra to get into Lhasa, he was denounced from Lhasa as a traitor, he was dragged from his high office by the fanatical Lamas of Lhasa to that sacred city, and there beaten daily in the public market-place, and afterwards ignominiously murdered, with his hands tied behind his back. His body, denied its place amongst his predecessors,

PRIME MINISTER OF TIBET—THE SHATA SHAPÉ.

PHALA MANOR, DONGTSÉ.

was thrown into a river to the east of Lhasa,[1] and his reincarnation was abolished for ever by the Grand Lama, who exercises dominion over the soul as well as the body,[2] although, curious to relate, a child which was born immediately after the murder, and who is now an inmate of one of the monasteries, bears on his body the peculiar mark of being a re-incarnation of this Lama, namely, the absence of a left knee-cap, which is an extraordinarily rare abnormality. The ruin thus brought about by the Babu's visit extended also to the unfortunate Lama's relatives, the governor of Gyantsé (the Phala Dahpön) and his wife (Lha-cham), whom he had persuaded to befriend Sarat C. Das. These two were cast into prison for life, and their estates confiscated,[3] and several of their servants were barbarously mutilated, their hands and feet were cut off and their eyes gouged out, and they were then left to die a lingering death in agony, so bitterly cruel was the resentment of the Lamas against all who assisted the Babu in his attempt to spy into their sacred city, which resulted in practically no addition to our knowledge of that city beyond what was already recorded by the native survey explorers.

Of Asiatic outsiders, other than Indians, a few Russian survey spies, of late years, have added considerably to our knowledge of the Forbidden City. One of the best known of these is M. Tysbikoff, who brought back, in 1902, photographs of that city. The last of all these Asiatic foreigners who contrived to

[1] The Kongbu river at Shoka fort-prison.

[2] This case is not without precedent. In the *Peking Gazette* of 31st May 1877 a Tibetan incarnate Lama, who was denounced by the Chinese political resident at Lhasa for having carried off the seals of office, was declared by The Son of Heaven, under his celestial powers, that "his soul should not be allowed to transmigrate at his decease."

[3] They were imprisoned at Chukya fort to the south of Chetang where the Dahpön died.

enter Lhasa was the Japanese priest, Kawaguchi, and he had to flee for his life in May 1902, when his disguise and nationality were discovered. In revenge, several of his friends amongst the monks in the Sera monastery where he lodged in Lhasa have been imprisoned, and some, it is reported, had their eyes gouged out by order of His Holiness the Grand Lama.

Contrary to the general popular belief, quite a number of Europeans succeeded in reaching Lhasa in former days during the past three centuries; and, though never welcomed, they were permitted to reside there for varying periods of months and years. Most of them were devoted Roman Catholic missionaries, and the meagre accounts they have left us, industriously collected by Sir Clements Markham merely served to whet our curiosity for more.[1]

The first European to set foot in Lhasa seems to have been Friar Odoric, who is believed to have reached that sacred city about the year 1330 A.D. on his way overland from China. Nearly three centuries elapsed before another European followed him, this time also from the China side. The Austrian Jesuit, Grueber, accompanied by the Belgian Count Dorville, made his way from China to Lhasa on foot in 1662, and remained there for two months and passed out by Nepal; the only extant sketch of the Grand Lama's palace, until a few years ago, was made by the former of these two travellers. They did not see the Grand Lama, as they refused to prostrate themselves before him. They were followed, in 1706, by the Capuchin Fathers Joseph de Asculi and Francisco de Tour, and, in 1716, by the two Jesuits Desideri and Freyre, who travelled from Delhi *viâ* Kashmir and Leh. Desideri undertook this daring journey and settled at Lhasa in the hope of converting the Tibetans to Christianity. He

[1] Published by Kircher; see my *Buddh.*, p. 229.

remained there thirteen years, when he was recalled by the Pope and prevented returning on account of complaints made against him by Capuchin monks who had found their way to Lhasa shortly after him from Patna in India *viâ* Nepal, and established there a rival mission. The chief of these Capuchins was Horace della Penna, with no less than twelve others, of whom at least four reached Lhasa *viâ* Nepal in 1719, and established there a mission[1] which lasted more or less continuously for *nearly half a century* in that city. They were, in 1724, allowed to build a chapel in Lhasa, which the Grand Lama, who held many friendly arguments with these fathers, himself visited, and was deeply impressed by what he saw there. Horace returned to Rome in 1735 for reinforcements, and the Pope sent out with him, in 1738, nine more, *also letters to the Dalai Lama*, the Grand Lama of Lhasa. They reached that city in 1740, and remained there for twenty years more,[2] when they were expelled through the influence of the Chinese political Resident, and were forced to retire with their converts to Nepal. From here, driven out a few years after by the barbarous Goorkhas at their cruel invasion of that country, they settled in British territory at Bettiah in Bengal on the borders of Nepal, where I visited this mission in 1880, and heard for the first time of its chequered and romantic history. Its Tibetan work was not abandoned, and thus has given rise

[1] At Sachen Naga. About 1730, whilst these missionaries were settled in Lhasa, a young Dutch traveller, Van de Putte, reached that city in disguise, and after "a long residence" there travelled to Peking in the guise of a Chinese mandarin, and finally returned to India through Lhasa, thus being the only European who has completed the journey from India through Lhasa to China up till now. See Markham, lvi. etc.

[2] One of them, Beligatti, has left a journal of which most of the information is incorporated in George's *Alphabetum Tibetanum*, Rome, 1762.

to the paradox that the "Vicar Apostolic of Tibet," who is still nominated at Rome up to the present day, unable to find a footing in Tibet, is forced to live on the borderland in China to the east, or in British territory in the Darjeeling district to the west of the closed land.

No Englishman ever saw Lhasa up till the present year, except one, about a century ago, if we do not admit the doubtful case of Moorcroft.[1] This one was Thomas Manning, of the Chinese branch of the old East India Company's Service. He was a friend of Charles Lamb, himself also of the same Company's office in London. Manning, fascinated by the romantic accounts of China and its mysterious dependency Tibet, determined to devote his life to exploring these regions. His friend Lamb tried to dissuade him from what he termed "foolish" purposes. "Believe me," writes Lamb, "'tis all poets' invention. Pray try and cure yourself. Take hellebore. Pray to avoid the fiend. Read no more books of voyages, they are nothing but lies." But Manning was resolved, and entered the Chinese branch of the Company's service to acquire the Chinese language and the knowledge of the customs of the people necessary for his plan of travel. After three years at Canton he proceeded to Calcutta, in 1811, for official assistance in his enterprise; but the red-tapeism of those early days, discouraging the employment of anyone outside its own clique, however specially fit, denied him help of any kind, and would not even grant him any credentials. Depressed by this official neglect, he nevertheless bravely set out alone; and in the guise of a Chinese physician, enduring endless hardships, made his way through Bhotan to Lhasa. He resided in that city some months, and had several friendly interviews with the Grand Lama there till he was finally arrested by

[1] See, for doubtful case of Moorcroft, p. 16-17.

the Chinese and deported back to India. Thence he returned to China by the way he came; but disgusted with his official treatment he withheld the report on his travels, and even related his experiences to no one, and left only a few jottings in a rough diary.[1]

Manning's first interview with the Grand Lama is recorded in some detail, and the glimpse thus obtained lent some colour to the popular belief in the supernatural character of this sacred personage, who just before Manning's visit had "transmigrated" into the body of a princely young child.

"This day (17th December 1811) I saluted the Grand Lama! Beautiful youth. Face poetically affecting; could have wept. Very happy to have seen him and his blessed smile. Hope often to see him again," and Manning goes on to relate:—

"The Lama's beautiful and interesting face and manner engrossed almost all my attention. He was at that time about seven years old, had the simple and unaffected manners of a well-educated, princely child. His face was, I thought, poetically and affectingly beautiful. He was of a gay and cheerful disposition, his beautiful mouth perpetually unbending into a graceful smile which illuminated his whole countenance. . . . He enquired whether I had not met with molestations and difficulties on the road, to which I promptly returned the proper answer. I said that I had had troubles, but now that I had the happiness of being in his presence they were amply compensated, I thought no more of them. I could see that this answer pleased both the Lama and his household peoples." On Manning being asked if he had any request to make: "I begged of the Grand Lama to give me books respecting his religion and ancient history, and to allow me one of his learned Lamas who understood Chinese to assist and instruct me." This request was only very partially complied with, a promise being made that copies would be prepared and delivered afterwards.

[1] These are published by Markham, *op. cit.* clix., etc.

This unfortunate child died a few years afterwards, assassinated, it is believed, by his regent[1] in his intrigues to retain the sovereign power for some time longer in his hands.

Previous to Manning, only two parties of Englishmen had ever set foot in Tibet, though neither of them reached Lhasa. They were the emissaries of Warren Hastings, the first and greatest of our governor-generals of British India. This far-sighted administrator, who did so much to transform the trading East India Company into a sovereign power and source of strength to England, had strong geographical instincts. In the same year in which he assumed office, he caused a survey of his territory to be made, resulting in the celebrated map of Rennel, the first fairly correct map of India. In the same year he tried to bring the Land of the Lamas into friendly and commercial intercourse with the plains of Bengal. For this purpose he established a great fair under the mountains at Rangpur, below Bhotan, and taking advantage of a letter he received from the Grand Lama of Western Tibet, interceding for Bhotanese raiders,[2] he despatched, in 1774, a mission to the Grand Lama, consisting of Mr Bogle, a magistrate, and Dr A. Hamilton of the Indian Medical Service, in the hope of opening up new trade. This mission was well received in Western Tibet, but was not allowed to go on to Lhasa; nor did it succeed in negotiating any commercial treaty. Still, it was a great thing to have opened up amicable relations with Western Tibet, and to cement the friendship

[1] Named Si-fan.

[2] The Bhotanese, in 1772, invaded Cooch Behar, a dependency of the East India Company, and carried off the Raja prisoner. The Company sent a force which retook Cooch Behar, and would have severely punished the Bhotanese, but Warren Hastings forgave them on the intervention of this Grand Lama.

still further, Warren Hastings established a Tibetan temple at Howrah in Calcutta,[1] and he seized the opportunity of the death of this friendly Lama of Tashilhumpo in Western Tibet to send another mission to congratulate the new Lama upon his "reincarnation" — for the Tibetans believe that their great Lamas never die, but on their apparent death merely transmigrate into the body of a newly-born child. This mission of congratulation was despatched in 1783, under Captain Turner, a relative of Warren Hastings, as Bogle had meanwhile died. Captain Turner seems to have been not a little impressed by the halo of supernatural dignity and decorum surrounding this infant, though one cannot help feeling that the irony of the following passage of diplomatic history is at least as remarkable as its official adroitness.

"On the morning of the 4th December (1783) the British envoy had his audience and found the child then *aged eighteen months* seated on a throne with his father and mother on his left hand. Having been informed that though unable to speak he could understand, Captain Turner said: 'The Governor-General on receiving the news of your decease in China was overwhelmed with grief and sorrow, and continued to lament your absence from the world until the cloud that had overcast the happiness of your nation was dispelled by your reappearance; and then, if possible, a greater degree of joy had taken place than he had experienced grief on receiving the first mournful news. The Governor anxiously wished that you might long continue to illumine the world by your presence, and was hopeful that the friendship which had formerly subsisted between

[1] The temple for the use of Tibetan traders visiting Calcutta was endowed by Bogle's friend, the Grand Lama of Tashilhumpo with Tibetan books and images. The building was rediscovered in 1887, with its books and some of its images, which latter are now worshipped as Hindu gods. It bears the name of the "Tibetan Garden" (*Bhot bagan*).

us would not be diminished, but rather that it might become still greater than before; and that by your continuing to show kindness to his fellow-countrymen there might be an extensive communication between your votaries and the dependents of the British nation.'

"The infant looked steadfastly at Captain Turner with the appearance of much attention, and nodded with repeated slow motions of the head as though he understood and approved every word. His whole attention was directed to the envoy, and he conducted himself with astonishing dignity and decorum. He was the handsomest child Captain Turner had ever seen."[1]

But this mission also failed to reach Lhasa, or to secure any commercial treaty, owing to the hostility of the Chinese Resident at Lhasa, who, it was alleged, caused the following letter to be sent by the Regent of Lhasa to the friendly Lama of Western Tibet. He had heard, he wrote,[2] "of two Feringhis [Europeans] having arrived in Tibet with a great retinue of servants; now the Feringhi were fond of war, and after insinuating themselves into a country raised disturbances and made themselves master of it; and as no Feringhis had ever been admitted into Tibet he advised the Tashilhumpo Lama to find some method of sending them back"; and the Emperor of China, he added, forbade the admittance of all Feringhis.

Another Englishman, Dr Moorcroft, is alleged to have reached Lhasa in 1826 and to have remained there for many years, although another account asserts that he died in 1826 before reaching Lhasa. Dr Moorcroft had a remarkable career. He devoted himself to the commercial exploitation of Ladak and North-Western Tibet, chiefly as a source of breeding horses for the Indian Government, but, as in the case of Manning, his request for official recognition in

[1] Turner's *Embassy to the Court of the Teshoo Lama*, pp. 335-6.

[2] This referred to Mr Bogle.

dealing with these far-off countries, was rigorously refused. Even when, undeterred by his want of official standing, the chiefs of Ladak, whose confidence he had won through his unique intimacy with the people, made him their medium of an offer of their allegiance to the Indian Government, this offer was peremptorily refused, with the result that the Sikhs took over Ladak, and it afterwards passed with Kashmir to the Raja of the latter country and so was lost to us. Moorcroft disappeared soon after, and the story which M. Huc heard in Lhasa from the lips of Moorcroft's servant, and also from several Tibetan officials, of his master's long residence in that city in the disguise of a Kashmir merchant, is quite possible.

"The servant's story, which was confirmed by other people in Lhasa, was: Moorcroft arrived from Ladak at Lhasa in the year 1826 with his Ladak servant; he wore the Musulman dress and spoke the Persian language, expressing himself in that idiom with so much facility that the Kashmirians of Lhasa took him for one of their countrymen. He hired a house in the town, where he lived for twelve years with his servant Nishan, whom he had brought from Ladak, and who himself thought that his master was a Kashmirian. Moorcroft had purchased a few herds of goats and oxen, which he confided to the care of some Tibetan shepherds in the gorges of the mountains about Lhasa. Under the pretext of inspecting his herds, the feigned Musulman went freely about the country, making drawings and preparing his geographical charts. At last, having dwelt for twelve years at Lhasa, Moorcroft took his way back to Ladak, but whilst in the province of Nari (or Hundesh in North-Western Tibet) he was attacked by a troop of brigands, who assassinated him. The perpetrators of this murder were pursued and arrested by the Tibetan Government, who recovered a portion of the property of the English traveller, among which was a collection of geographical designs and charts. It was only then, and upon the sight of those objects that the authorities of Lhasa found out that Moorcroft was an Englishman."[1]

The last Europeans to enter Lhasa were the two French Lazarist priests MM. Huc and Gabet. They went, in 1845, to inspect the new diocese of the Vicar Apostolic of Mongolia, which the Pope had just created. They arrived in the sacred city on 29th January 1846, and sojourned there about a month, when they, like the missionaries before them, were expelled by the Chinese resident Minister, who cunningly persuaded the Lama that their spiritual power would be overthrown by the rival creed of the Christian missionaries; though the real reason was believed to be retaliation for China's defeat at that time in the opium war.

There is, indeed, no doubt that China has all along persistently exercised her suzerainty over Tibet to encourage the Lamas to exclude Europeans from the country, lest her own commercial advantages and political prestige should suffer. China's suzerainty dates only from 1720 A.D., when she stepped in with an army, on the invitation of one of the rival factions of monks at Lhasa, to put down a civil and religious war there. On restoring order, the emperor Kangshi established at Lhasa for the first time two Chinese mandarins as political agents or *Ambans*[2]—of whom we have heard so much lately—with large powers[3] and a suitable force for their protection. Up to this time Tibet, though paying nominal tribute to China, was practically independent. As an indemnity,

[1] Huc's *Travels in Tartary*, etc., ii. 202. Huc fully discusses the conflicting statement of Moorcroft's prior death, which is suggestive of a possibility of mistake.

[2] It is a Manchu word, and all Ambans are Manchus and bear the title of "Imperial Associate Resident in Tibet and Military Deputy Lieutenant-Governor."

[3] See p. 34, footnote.

China also retained a large slice of the richest part of Eastern Tibet[1] (see map).

Still tighter did China draw her hold over Tibet to the express exclusion of Europeans, when the Emperor Chenlung (famous for his artistic porcelain) had to send an army to drive the Goorkhas out of Tibet in 1792. In that year the freebooting Goorkhas attracted by the reports of the immense riches of the great monastery of Western Tibet which Bogle and Turner had visited, sent an expedition to plunder it. The panic-struck monks appealed to the Chinese emperor, whose army routed the Goorkhas, drove them over the Kirong Pass (about 16,000 feet above the sea), and pursuing them into Nepal, inflicted on them a humiliating defeat near their capital (Kathmandu).[2] As the Chinese general reported that the Goorkhas had been assisted by British officers (which, however, was not a fact), China thereupon established the forts at Phari and other places along the Indian frontier to bar all ingress from that side.

Since our Sikhim-Tibet war of 1888, the Chinese have aided the Tibetans in making exclusion still more absolute.

My own private attempt to reach Lhasa from the Nepal side, in the summer of 1892, in the disguise of a Tibetan pilgrim, with surveying instruments secreted in prayer-wheels, hollow walking-sticks, and false-bottomed baskets, was frustrated by the unfortunate circumstance that the Raja of our protected Himalayan

[1] The districts of Dartsendo (Ta-tsien-lu), Lithang with its silver mines, Bathang and Amdo, all now incorporated in Sze-chuan province.

[2] An amusing reference to this Chinese army is made by the then Amban at Lhasa in a letter translated by Mr Rockhill :—"At present (1791) the wild Gorkhas have everywhere shown their deceitfulness ; the Imperial forces are advancing against them, and they no more can escape than fish at the bottom of a cauldron, so easy will be the task of putting out the flames of revolt and restoring order"—(*Jour. Roy. As. Soc.* xxiii. 22). And the Amban proved to be quite correct.

state of Sikhim, to the east of Nepal, on his intrigues with the Tibetans having been discovered, escaped with all his valuables into Tibet, at the very time and by the very same track, *viâ* Tashiraka, which I had selected. Thereupon that track, thus favoured by the Raja in his unplanned excursion, the only one at all promising for my purpose, was so rigorously watched by both Nepalese and Tibetans that my small party was detected. In the passes remote from the central province I found it was possible to evade the frontier guards so as to march for several days in the interior, always shifting camp after dark to circumvent spies and robbers. In this way on two occasions I penetrated to the source of the Sutlej river in North-Western Tibet, but when discovered and stopped I had of course to return to avoid political complications.

To escape detection was well-nigh impossible for a European, as every headman of every village in Central and Western Tibet has for many years been held responsible by the Lhasa Lamas, under penalty of death, that no foreigner should pass through or receive shelter in his village. The headman passed on this threat and responsibility to each villager. Thus every Tibetan watched and pryed so keenly into the personality of all travellers, that our Tibetan survey spies were constantly stopped on suspicion. Even the Mongolian-featured Kawaguchi was frequently suspected—"You are not what you pretend to be," said one of his inquisitive companions; "I am inclined to think you are an Englishman in disguise. If you are not actually English, I am sure you are a European of some sort." Nevertheless, as there was an off-chance of escaping detection, I was willing to take it, notwithstanding that my movements at Darjeeling were watched by resident Tibetan spies, and a description of my appearance sent to Lhasa. In this latter was the reference to blue eyes, which puzzled Dr Sven Hedin as to why his Tibetan captors should search for this particular feature in his face.

The almost insuperable obstacles thus raised against entry to any part of Tibet proper, even far outside the charmed Lhasa, seems to have led many European travellers of late years to extend the limits of the magical term "Tibet" so far northward as to include the whole of that vast uninhabitable desert the "Changthang" (see map, p. 41), which lies between inhabited Tibet and the Kuen Lun wall of the lofty plateau overlooking the lowlands of Central Asia; although neither this no-man's-land itself nor its approaches are held by the Tibetans, nor by anyone to "forbid" the way for hundreds of miles. One result of this has been to convey the false impression to the public that Tibet is a vast desert plain, bleak, barren and treeless, which we shall see is widely different from the reality.

This isolation of Lhasa, maintained for so many centuries, has resulted in that city becoming the centre of the most extreme form of priest-government the world has ever seen, and has led its esoteric priest-king, in his luxurious, self-centred leisure, to arrogate to himself the position of a divinity. He is adored as a manifestation of the Divine Being who has taken an undying form upon the earth—a supernatural condition which has exercised over European minds a weird fascination.

CHAPTER II.

THE GRAND LAMA AND HIS EVOLUTION AS THE PRIEST-GOD OF LHASA.

"*Om! ma-ni pad-me Hung!*"
"Hail! The Jewel [Grand Lama] in the lotus-flower!"

To understand the circumstances which led up to the despatch of the British Mission to Lhasa, it is necessary to refer somewhat more in detail to the earlier history and traditional legends of the country.

The Tibetans were once a very warlike people under their own chiefs and kings, who were chosen for their great personal strength and success in war. This was before they knew anything of Buddhism or owed any suzerainty to China, and when they were still fierce savages without any written language.

In those days, 400 to 600 A.D., the Chinese describe their Tibetan neighbours as "ferocious barbarian shepherds," divided into small clans which were continually at war with one another. Each year they took "a little oath" to their chief, when they sacrificed sheep, dogs and monkeys. Every three years, they took "the great oath" and *sacrificed men*, horses, oxen and asses. Having no written language, they made use of notched pieces of wood, and of knotted cords. The still current common deed of agreement by the broken stone, like our lovers' broken sixpence in which each contracting party keeps a half, is a survival of this early period.

THE COMPASSIONATE SPIRIT.
Incarnate in the Grand Lama.

The origin which these Tibetans fondly claim for themselves, would have delighted the heart of Lord Monboddo who forestalled Darwin in his hypothesis of the descent of man. They claim as their first parent a monkey which crossed the Himalayas and there married a she-devil of the mountains. The young progeny of apes ate some magical grain given to them by the Compassionate Spirit of the Mountains (who afterwards became the Grand Lama); and wonderful were the results which then happened. Their tails and hair grew shorter and shorter and finally disappeared. They began to speak—they were men! and noticing the change, they clothed themselves with leaves. Thus also they account for their chief traits of character and disposition—from their father's side they say they have got their love for piety (and mummery, they might have added), whilst from their mother they have inherited their roughness, cruelty, ferocity and deceit.[1]

In the early part of the 7th century A.D., just as they emerge on the misty horizon of history, the Tibetans overran Upper Burma and Western China, and forced the Chinese emperor to a humiliating peace. As part of the terms of this peace with China in 640 A.D., the king of Tibet, Srongtsan Gampo, then aged twenty-three years of age, received a Chinese princess in marriage.

The details recorded in the Chinese annals of that time are interesting:—The Tibetan king "had erected for her a palace built [on Potala hill] with ridge-poles and eaves (in Chinese fashion). The princess disliking the reddish-brown colour put on the faces of the people, he ordered the practice to be discontinued. Moreover, he himself put on fine silks and brocade *instead of felt and sheepskins*, and gradually took to Chinese customs. He sent the children of the chief men to the national schools [of China]. . . . He asked for silkworms' eggs, for stone-crushers, and presses for making wine, and for paper and ink makers. Everything was granted, together with an almanak.[2]"

This Chinese princess, like the Nepalese wife of the king was an ardent Buddhist; so these two ladies speedily converted their young husband to their faith, and prevailed upon him to introduce their religion into savage Tibet. Thereupon he became a zealous patron of Buddhism, devoting his wealth and resources to its establishment and endowment throughout his dominions. He sent for Buddhist priests from India, where Buddhism was still flourishing, and got them to reduce the Tibetan language to writing in the Indian alphabet, which then became

[1] Rockhill's *Life of Buddha*, etc., p. 205. Also my *Buddhism*, p. 19, etc.

[2] Rockhill, *Jour. Roy. As. Soc.* xxiii. 191.

and has continued till now to be the written character of Tibet; and into this new written language of the country he caused to be translated several of the more important Buddhist books from India and China.

This new religion, thus forced upon the people by the king to please his favourite wives, proved rather a mixed blessing to the country. Ultimately it became a disastrous parasitic disease which fastened on to the vitals of the land. The form of Buddhism which was introduced, already impure, became a cloak to the worst forms of oppressive devil-worship, by which the poor Tibetan was placed in constant fear of his life from the attacks of thousands of malignant devils both in this life and in the world to come, and necessitating never-ending payments to the priests of large sums to avert these calamities. Its priests, or "Lamas" as they are called in Tibetan, multiplied rapidly under the princely patronage of this Charlemagne of Tibet and his successors. They soon usurped the substance of authority in matters of State; and after a struggle with the old nobility for supremacy they gained the ascendancy and made mere puppets of the kings. Latterly they threw aside the kings altogether and openly assumed the kingship.

Priest-kingship in Tibet, as in other lands, proved a retrograde movement. The Lamas ruled the country entirely in their own interests. They were not even ecclesiastics; they never preached or educated the laity, but kept the latter in ignorance and servitude, with the result that the Tibetans have become the most priest-ridden people in the world, and, sapped of their vigour and spirit, have gone steadily down as a nation ever since.

The first priest-king of Tibet was the high-priest of the red-cap Lamasery at Sakya in Western Tibet. Already the petty king of his own part of Tibet, he was raised to the kingship of the whole of Tibet in

1252 A.D. by the great Mongol Emperor of China, Kublai Khan, in return for becoming the official consecrator and coronator of the emperors of China, just as the Christian Pope having anointed Charles the Great Emperor of the West received in return a large accession of spiritual authority throughout the imperial dominions. Kublai Khan, the son of the famous Genghis Khan, as we know from the accounts of his servant, Marco Polo, and others, was a most enlightened ruler, and employed talent wherever he found it, whether amongst Europeans or Asiatics. In searching about for a religion to weld together the more uncivilised portions of his new empire, he called to his court the most powerful Lamas as well as representatives of the Christian and several other faiths. After investigation he ultimately fixed upon Lamaism for himself and his people, as having more in common with the popular faiths already prevalent in China and Mongolia than had Confucianism, Mahomedanism or Christianity.

His conversion to Buddhism is made miraculous. He is said to have demanded from the Christian missionaries, who had been sent to him by the Pope, the performance of a miracle, as a proof to him of the superiority of the Christian religion, while if they failed and the Lamas succeeded in showing him a miracle he would adopt Buddhism. In the presence of the missionaries, who were unable to comply with Kublai's demands, the Lamas caused the emperor's wine-cup to rise miraculously to his lips. On this the emperor adopted the Lamaist religion, and the discomfited missionaries declared that the cup had been lifted by the devil himself, into whose clutches the king had now fallen. Kublai conferred on this Grand Lama or Pope of Sakya monastery, royal honours, a jade seal, and a Chinese title.

On the downfall of the Mongol dynasty in China,

its Kalmuk princes fled to outer Mongolia on the border of Siberia, where cut off from Tibet, as they now were, they set up for themselves a new Grand Lama of their own, who, at the present day, has his capital at Urga, near the great Lob Nor lake (see map, p. 41), where he is in close political relations with a resident Russian official.

Deprived in this way of the patronage of the Mongol dynasty, the Sakya Pontiff and his successors nevertheless continued to be kings over the greater portion of Tibet for nearly four centuries, although the new Chinese dynasty, to curb the Sakya power, gave jade seals and royal titles to the head-priests of the chief monasteries of the rival orders. In 1641 A.D., some marauding nomad Tartar tribes from the north tried to overthrow this old-fashioned Lama rule.

Seizing advantage of this invasion and the waning power of the Sakya Pope, an ambitious high-priest of the vigorous young rival sect of Lamas, the "yellow-caps," or so-called "virtuous order" (*Geluk-pa*) snatched the temporal rule out of the hands of the red-caps. Himself of a princely family, he persuaded his patron, the Tartar prince, Gushi Khan, to overthrow by an armed force the Sakya Pontiff, and to raise him to the kingship instead. In return for this favour, Gushi and his successors were made military commanders at Lhasa, with the title of "Kings"; whilst the *de facto* king and absolute monarch was this yellow-cap high-priest. His surname was "Vast as the Ocean" (in Tibetan, *Gyatsho*), which in the Mongol language of his Tartar patron is "Dalai," hence came the title of "Dalai Lama" (or vulgarly "Ta-le") by which the priest-kings of Lhasa are best known to Europeans.[1] The first Dalai Lama was not known to

[1] This title of "Dalai" was actually used by the Mongols to two of his predecessors who also bore the same surname, as Mr Rockhill has shown.—*Jour. Roy. As. Soc.* xxiii. 286.

the Tibetans as such, but as "The Precious Protector, or Victorious Lord" (*Gyal-wa* or *Kyab-gon Rim-po-che*). I shall, however, use the former title, "Dalai," in referring to him hereafter, as being now the more familiar English title of the Grand Lama of Lhasa. On gaining the throne, he visited the Manchu Emperor of China, who had just overthrown the Ming dynasty, and, offering him his fealty, was confirmed in the sovereignty of Tibet.

This Tibetan Cardinal Wolsey, the first of the pope-kings or sovereign Dalai Lamas of Lhasa, was named Lobzang-the-Eloquent. He was a born diplomatist, and the most masterful figure which has ever passed across the stage of Tibetan history. It was he, as far as I can ascertain,[1] who invested himself and his successors with the halo of a divine origin and a supernatural ancestry in order to consolidate his rule, and secure firmer hold upon the superstitious reverence of the poor Tibetans. The manner in which he contrived to do this seems to me to have been as follows:—

He was the fifth of the series of chief abbots of the new yellow-capped order of celibate Lamas, who had adopted for their high-priest or chief abbot Buddha's title of the "Victor or Conqueror of Life" (*Gyal-wa* in Tibetan and *Jina* in Indian). For these five generations of abbots the succession had been regulated on the fiction of supposed reincarnation of the spirit of the first abbot, who on dying was believed to be immediately reborn again and again into the world, in the body of a newly-born infant, for the good of his monastery and his order of yellow caps.

Availing himself of the received theory, that he himself was a reincarnation of the first abbot, this new Grand Lama enlarged the theory on the principle of the *Divine* right of kings to rule, so as to make it

[1] For details see my *Buddhism of Tibet*, pp. 39-40, 229, etc.

appear that both he himself and the first abbot were reincarnations of the most powerful and most popular king of Tibet, namely Srongtsan Gampo; and also that the latter in his turn was an earthly incarnation of the Compassionate Spirit of the Mountains who had given the early Tibetans the magical food which transformed them from monkeys into men. This compassionate spirit was identified with the most popular of all the divinities of the later Buddhists, namely, the "Lord of Mercy" (*Avalokita*, in Tibetan *Chän-rä-zi*), who is supposed to be a potential Buddha who relinquished his prospect of becoming a Buddha, and of passing out of the world and existence into the Nirvana[1] of extinction, in order to remain in heaven and be available to assist all men on earth who may call upon him to deliver them from earthly danger, to help them to reach paradise and escape hell. All of these three great objects are, the Tibetans believe, easily secured by the mere utterance of the mystic spell of this Lord of Mercy, namely, "*Om! ma-ni pad-me Hung!*" "Hail! Jewel [Lord of Mercy,] in the Lotus-Flower!" (See frontispiece, also on page 23, for figure of this god within a lotus-flower.) It is not even necessary to utter this spell to secure its efficacy. The mere looking at it in its written form is of equal benefit. Hence the spell is everywhere made to revolve before the eyes, it is twirled in myriads of prayer-wheels, incised on stones in cairns, carved and painted on buildings, as well as uttered by every lip throughout Tibet, Mongolia, Ladak and the Himalayan Buddhist States down to Bhotan, and from Baikal to Western China.

In this way, this Dalai Lama converged upon himself the most popular legends and traditions of the Tibetans, and appropriated the most popular of all the mystic spells—"*Om! ma-ni pad-me Hung!*" On these lines he constructed for himself a super-

[1] Strictly *Parinirvana*.

natural genealogical tree, and to prove its truth he "discovered" a book of "revelations," in which all this was purported to have been written down prophetically a thousand years before by King Srongtsan Gampo himself.[1]

Supported by such convincing proof, the majority of the poor Tibetans, priests and laity, immediately accepted the supernatural origin and character which the crafty Dalai Lama ascribed to himself. Those incredulous Lamas of the other rival sects who dared to refuse to accept this story were cruelly killed, at the sword's point, by this unscrupulous despot posing as the earthly incarnation of the gentle Buddha, and their monasteries were forcibly converted into convents of the now dominant State Church, the yellow-cap order. The Jesuit Grueber, who visited Lhasa at this time, about 1656 A.D., calls this Draconian Buddhist monk, that "*devilish God-the-Father who puts to death such as refuse to adore him.*" And so this fiction of the priest-god at Lhasa, invoked by the mystic *Om! ma-ni pad-me Hung!* has continued up till now.

The only other person whom this Grand Dalai Lama permitted to share to some extent these divine honours with him was the abbot of the large monastery of his own yellow-cap order at the western capital—Tashilhumpo (or Shigatsé). This abbot had the privilege of examining and approving newly-born candidates for the Lhasa Grand Lamaship, and of ordaining the one selected for the new reincarnation; whilst the same offices were performed for him by the Grand Lama of Lhasa. For this monastery of Tashilhumpo, which had been built about 200 years previously, had also begun to regulate its succession of high priests by the method of the reincarnation theory. Its abbot was now raised by the Lhasa Dalai Lama to the dignity of a Grand Lama, who, it was

[1] My *Buddhism*, pp. 19, etc.

now alleged, was an earthly incarnation of that fictitious Buddha which the depraved latter Buddhists of India had created out of one of the titles of Buddha, namely the "Boundless Light" (*Amitabha*).[1] This Buddha-god, whose earthly reflex is thus placed at Tashilhumpo, seems to me to incorporate a sun-myth. He is figured with a glowing red complexion, and is made to reside in a dazzling heaven in the West, to which all the suns seem to hasten. This Western paradise is the popular heaven which every lay Tibetan hopes to enter in his future life, and here also the Lamas place their "Coming Buddha" or Messiah. In consequence of the latter belief, the Lamas, although opposing the entry of Westerns into their country, are ever on the outlook, with anxious eyes, for the appearance of a Buddhist from the West. For this reason they attributed my, to them, inexplicable knowledge of their religion to my being a reflex from this Western paradise; and the Russian Lama Dorjieff is said to have urged the present Grand Dalai Lama to accept the Tsar as suzerain on the pretext that the Russian emperor was a reflex from this fabled paradise in the West. This popular god of paradise was made out to be the spiritual father of the Lord of Mercy, who is incarnate in the Grand Lama of Lhasa; and to show the relationship, the image of the latter is frequently figured with the flaming red head of this solar Buddha seated in his hair. The Pontiff of Tashilhumpo is known to Europeans as the "Tashi" (vulgarly "Teshu") Lama, after his place of residence. It was this dignitary who was seen by Bogle and Turner. As he has practically no temporal duties to distract him, beyond those of supervising the estates handed over for the endowment of his monasteries, he devotes himself more absorbingly to spiritual matters than his brother Grand Lama at Lhasa. In consequence of this he has a superior reputation for piety and learning,

[1] See my *Buddhism* for details, pp. 141, etc.

so that he is given the title of "Great Gem of Learning" (*Pan-chen Rimpo-che*).[1]

Ruffian though he was, the first Sovereign Dalai Lama of Lhasa patronised art and learning; and he built for himself a new palace on the hill of Potala outside the city, where miraculous legends grew up rapidly around his life.

After reigning as Pope-king of Tibet for thirty-five years and firmly establishing his pretensions to divinity, he retired in his declining days into hermitage, and on his abdication in 1676 A.D., he handed over the sovereignty to his natural son Sangyä Gyatsho as Regent (*Desrid*), with absolute political power. The son, masterful and as full of intrigue and as ambitious for power as his father, concealed the death of the latter for sixteen years, ruling capriciously. He afterwards set up on the throne as Grand Lama a dissolute youth who so outraged everyone's feelings by his profligate life that, in 1706, the Regent was murdered by the military commander or "king" of Lhasa, Gushi Khan's great grandson. His protégé, this vicious young Dalai Lama, not mending his ways, was with the consent of the Chinese Emperor deposed, exiled, and shortly after murdered,[2] notwithstanding his professedly divine nature.

After the last assassination the priesthood, scandalised at the results of this method of succession by the fictitious theory of rebirths, revolted. They threw

[1] In Mongolian this is "*Irtini*" or "*Erdenni*." Bogle was much impressed by the grand character of the Tashi Lama whom he met: "He is possessed of much Christian charity, and is free from those narrow prejudices which next to ambition and avarice have opened the most copious sources of human misery. . . . One catches affection by sympathy; and I could not help, in some measure, feeling the same emotions with the Lama's votaries; and I will confess I never knew a man whose manners pleased me so much; or for whom upon so short an acquaintance, I had half the heart's liking."

[2] Officially it is recorded that he died of dropsy in exile.

over the reincarnation theory and elected one of themselves as Dalai Lama, an aged priest from the medical school of Lhasa, into whom they alleged, as if to save their conscience, the *breath* of the former Dalai had passed, though not his *life*; and this election was confirmed by the Chinese Emperor.

A rival faction of monks, meanwhile, harking back on the discarded theory of rebirths, procured a young child, born shortly after the murder of the dissolute Dalai, and brought it forward as the genuine claimant to the throne.

This new claimant was kept by his patrons at Sining in China, on the border of Tibet, until matters ripened. He received considerable popular support, and the conflict between the rival factions resulted in civil war, during which a band of Eleuth Tartars from Jungaria (see map, p. 40), under Tse Wang Rabdan, on the pretext of restoring religion swept down on Tibet from the north, took Lhasa by storm in 1710, pillaged the city and committed great havoc, sacking and burning the Grand Lama's palace of Potala, levelling to the ground the "pagoda" of the great Dalai Lama, Nagwang, destroying monuments, and killing the Lamas, and the commander or "king," the successor of Gushi Khan. (For details, see Appendix V.) This successful invasion of Lhasa by an undisciplined army mounted on camels, from the plains of Turkestan on the north, is not without interest at a time when so many writers are declaring that this is an impossible feat even for Russia's modern army.

The people implored the Emperor of China for aid, and the Emperor Kangshi sent an army 10,000 strong to restore order. After taking Lhasa and slaying the Tartar usurper, he restored the succession by rebirths, installing as Grand Lama the young claimant approved by the people. But he curtailed his power, vesting in him only spiritual rule; whilst he appointed an old

Prime Minister to the temporal power with the title of "king," though nominally subject to the Grand Lama. Kangshi now, in 1720 A.D., formally assumed suzerainty over the country, and located two Chinese mandarins at Lhasa as political residents or Ambans with very large powers[1] and to commemorate this restoration he set up a large inscribed stone in Lhasa below Potala Castle, facing the city, in the 60th year of his reign.

The new Dalai Lama ungratefully had his Prime Minister or "king" murdered in 1727. On hearing this the Chinese Emperor sent another army to Lhasa, cast the sacred person of the Dalai Lama into prison, slew the other conspirators and appointed as Regent an old respected monk named Kisri, but deprived him of all temporal power, which he transferred to a mayor of the palace named Polhané Miwang with the title of "king." For these stirring events we have as eye-witnesses the Jesuit and Capuchin missionaries, who, strange to say, were residing in Lhasa through them all.

While the sacred Dalai Lama was languishing in prison, in Potala, for his crimes, the Regent displeased

[1] "The Amban will consult with the Tale Lama or Panshen Rinpoche on all local questions brought before them on a footing of perfect equality. All officials, from the rank of Kälon (minister) down, and ecclesiastics holding official positions must submit all questions to him for his decision. He must watch over the condition of the frontier defences, inspect the different garrisons, control the finances of the country, and watch over Tibet's relations with the tribes living outside its frontier." "Addresses which the tribes have for presentation to the Tale Lama, they must first submit them to the Amban who will have them translated and will examine them. Later on the Amban and Tale Lama will conjointly prepare replies which will be given to the envoys. . . . Should the tribes write to the Kälons (ministers) these latter must forward the letters to the Ambans, and he, acting in concert with the Tale Lama, will prepare answers, but the Kälon may not answer them directly."—Chinese State Records translated by Rockhill, *Jour. Roy. As. Soc.* xxiii. pp. 7-11.

the Chinese Ambans, and was murdered by them in 1750. The people then flew to arms and massacred the Chinese, whereupon another punitive Chinese army was sent, this time by the great Emperor Chenlung.

On Chinese ascendancy being thus restored, the influence of the Ambans was so enormously increased that they kept the appointment of Regent in their own hands. Originally appointed to "protect" the Grand Lama, they became his "old man of the sea." They were the wire-pullers behind the throne, and the real driving power of the machine of State behind the figure-head of the time-serving Regent. They even regulated the selection of new Dalai Lamas, if not actually privy to the policy of assassination of the old which now began.

From this time onwards it is remarkable that the poor Dalai Lama was made to transmigrate very rapidly. He always died young. He never succeeded in attaining his majority, but always remained a minor and died a minor. No sooner did the unfortunate young Dalai reach the age of eighteen, the age of majority in the East, than he invariably died in a mysterious manner, thus necessitating the accession of a new-born infant, and so prolonging the term of office of the Regent. In this way there was always a Regent in charge of the government, and he worked in collusion with the Chinese Ambans. The limit of life of the last four Dalai Lamas has been eleven, eighteen, eighteen, and eighteen years respectively; these figures speak for themselves.

The present Dalai Lama of 1904 has been permitted to become an exception to this rule, through the influence of the national party which has risen up in Tibet in veiled revolt against the excessive interference by the Chinese in the government of the country. This national party saved the young Dalai from the tragic fate of his predecessors, and they rescued him and the Government out of Chinese leading-strings by a dramatic *coup d'état*.

When in 1894 he reached the tragic age of eighteen years, which from experience of the ill-fate of his predecessors had come to be regarded as the limit of a Dalai's life, his friends by a stratagem obtained the seals of office from the Regent, whom they then imprisoned in a monastery, where he shortly after died. Having become possessed of the seals, the Dalai Lama seized the reins of government, and deprived the Chinese Ambans of any say in the State. The discomfited Ambans procured a peremptory edict from Peking ordering the seals to be returned and the Regent to be reinstated in office. Meanwhile, with the Regent dead or murdered, a new Amban had come to Lhasa, and he was bribed heavily to let matters remain as they were. So he suppressed the edict, never delivering it, whilst leading Peking to believe it had been complied with.

Afterwards, the opportunist young Dalai, profiting by China's loss of prestige from her defeat by Japan in 1895 and by the allied armies in 1900, openly refused to be guided by the Chinese, who now have to admit the decline of their power in Tibet, and the undisguised contempt in which the Tibetans have come to regard their authority, which is reduced to an empty farce, the shadow of a shade. So much had this become the case two years ago that the Chinese viceroy of the western province of Sze-chuan, which adjoins Tibet, asked the Peking authorities to send an army to Lhasa to make Chinese power respected.

The present young Dalai Lama bears the title of "The Eloquent Noble-minded T'ūb-dän." Temporal sovereign of Tibet, his spiritual sway extends through Tibet, along the Himalayan Buddhist States from Bhotan to Ladak, and thence to Lake Baikal, to Mongolia, and a great part of China as far as Peking.

His appearance in 1902 was thus described by the Japanese priest Kawaguchi, who in the guise of a Chinese physician had several interviews with His Holiness.

"He was a young man of about twenty-six years of age with a fine intelligent countenance. He was seated in a chair, wearing the yellow Tartar hood, or priest's cowl, and robes of yellow silk and red wool, with many under-robes of parti-coloured silks. He held his rosary of *bodhi*-tree beads in his left hand. Although the Dalai Lama possesses incredible stores of gold and jewels, and rosaries of every precious material, he carried only this simple rosary of the priests on each occasion of my seeing him. The attendants brought tea in handsomely carved silver teapots, and extending my wooden tea-cup, which everyone in Tibet carries with him, I drank in his presence. 'You must cure my priests,' was his frequent remark, but we discussed many other things."

Other hearsay reports from Lhasa merchants alleged that His Divinity is very proud and headstrong and subject to violent fits of temper, so it would seem that he is not entirely free from the failings of humanity.

His court and counsellors consist of a number of Lamas from the chief yellow-cap monasteries around Lhasa, a sort of priestly aristocracy, with a very few laymen in addition; and all these are divided into factions quarrelling amongst themselves for chief power. The party in favour, for the time, influences the Dalai Lama.

He is, indeed, to be pitied on his uneasy throne, in this heated atmosphere of faction. Still young, barely thirty years of age, without any personal experience whatever of the outer world, he is surrounded by counsellors almost as ignorant as himself, who mislead him grossly, unwittingly or for their own ends, and present everything to him in a perspective so false that it becomes practically impossible for him to detect or to act upon really sound advice. No wonder, then, that he is apt to be misled by scheming men. Such indeed has proved to be the case, and has been the cause of this British Mission.

On his escape from Chinese influence the unlucky young Dalai soon fell deeply into Russian clutches, through the influence of his favourite tutor, the Lama Dorjieff. This Lama is a Mongolian Buriat from the shores of Lake Baikal, and therefore a Russian subject by birth. He grew up and received his education in Russia,[1] and afterwards, when thirty-five years old, settled in Lhasa, in Dä-pung (or De-bung), one of the great convents there twenty years ago. There his learning procured him the title of "Honorary Professor,"[2] and he won favour with the court of the Dalai, especially as he was the agent through which the Peter's pence of the Tartars of Baikal were made over to the Lhasa exchequer. He is a well-educated man, a member of the Russian Geographical Society, and has travelled over India several times on his way to Odessa and St Petersburg. Latterly he has been in charge of the arsenal at Lhasa. On getting the ear of the young Dalai Lama he poisoned his mind against the English, and induced him to believe that the White Tsar is his friend, and not England.

Acting upon this advice, the Dalai Lama, by making repeated overtures to Russia, whilst insolently refusing all communications from us, and aggravating his misdeeds by fiercely attacking our political Mission, has caused such a storm to burst over Tibet that the results of it are difficult yet to foresee, and he has made his own position precarious. His sham pretensions to divinity did not shield his sacred predecessors from

[1] In the monastery of Azochozki in Trans-Baikal Russia. His full name is Go-mang Lobzang Dorjieff.

[2] *Khan (po)-de-phyi-ka*, or *Tsannyis Khanpo.*

being deposed, imprisoned, and even murdered by their own people, when it suited the convenience of the Lamas or the suzerain Chinese, and they are not likely now to protect him and his hosts of vampire priests from the results of his present hostile policy.

Will this Leviathan of the mountain-top weather the storm of this epoch-making year of the Wood-Dragon? Who can say what is woven into his destiny; but it is curious to find that so long ago as 1866, that is ten years before he was born, the surveying pandit, Nain Sing, recorded that it was then a popular saying in Lhasa that the Grand Lama will transmigrate only thirteen times. Now it is noteworthy that the present Lama *is* the thirteenth.

"*Om! ma-ni pad-me Hung!*"
"Hail! The Jewel [Grand Lama] in the lotus-flower!"

CHAPTER III.

HOW THE BRITISH MISSION CAME TO BE SENT.

"*What handling will do for other weeds will not do for the nettle.*"
—TIBETAN PROVERB.

IT was no mere light-hearted curiosity to see the Forbidden Land which led to the despatch of the armed British Mission to Tibet in December 1903, but the aggressive hostility of the Tibetans themselves, aggravated by the alarming intrigues of Russia for supremacy at the great politico-religious centre, the Rome of Buddhist Asia, and for the possession of its mountain plateau, which commands the eastern passes to India.

The exasperating hostility and insolence of the Lamas had been going on for a long series of years to the detriment of our trade and prestige, and although several attempts had from time to time been made to grapple with this standing question, successive viceroys had always let it drift, so that the last mission, that to Khamba Jong in 1903, might also have been abandoned and the *impasse* suffered to go on for some years longer. The discovery, however, in 1903, of Russia's avowed intrigues for establishing her influence at Lhasa, so long suspected, but now openly admitted, compelled England to advance in self-defence, without delay, in order to prevent this important geographical position, so near and so capable of being utilised for

PRIME MINISTER OF TIBET AND SUITE.
The Shata Shapé.

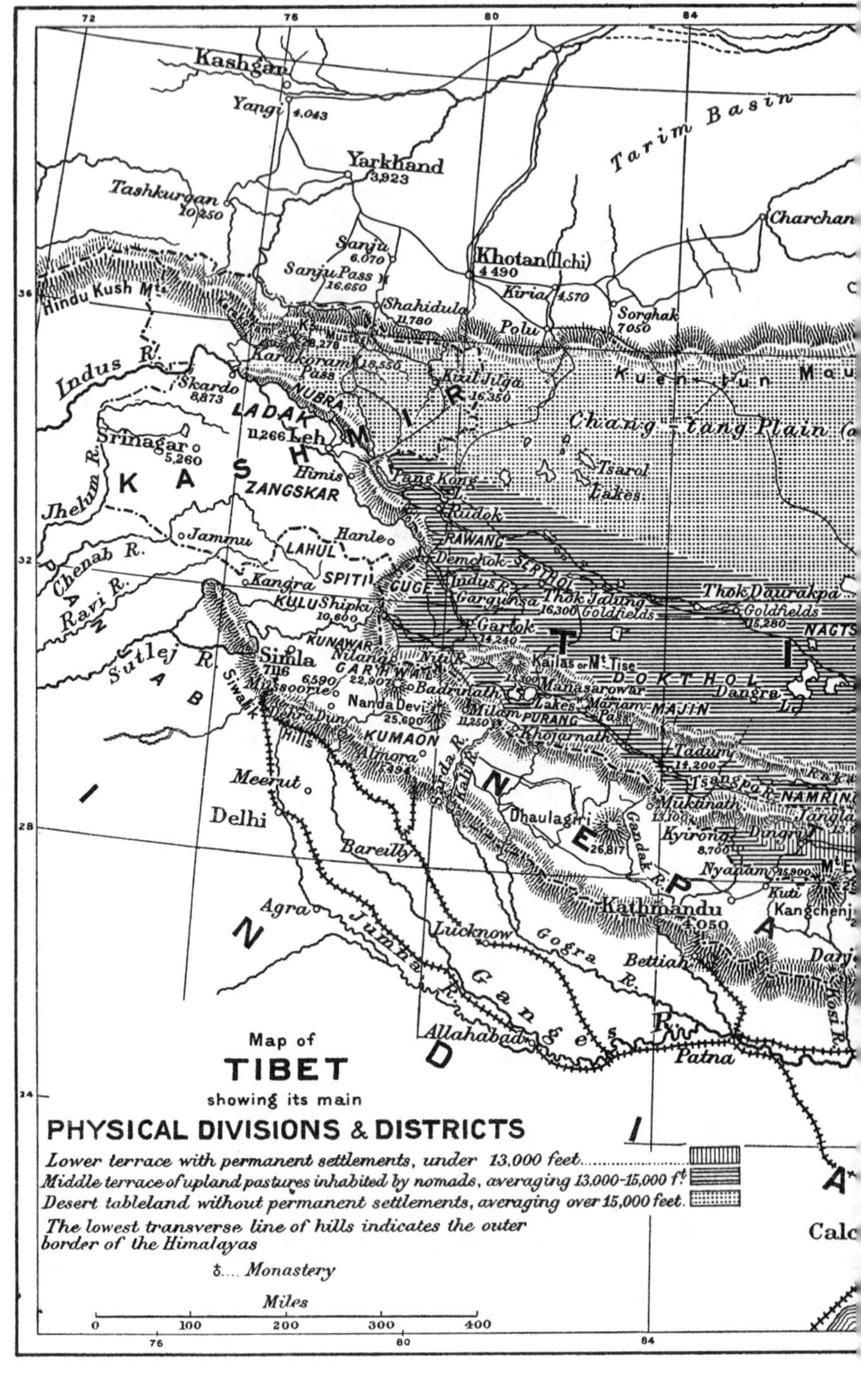
Map of
TIBET
showing its main
PHYSICAL DIVISIONS & DISTRICTS
Lower terrace with permanent settlements, under 13,000 feet
Middle terrace of upland pastures inhabited by nomads, averaging 13,000-15,000 ft.
Desert tableland without permanent settlements, averaging over 15,000 feet.
The lowest transverse line of hills indicates the outer border of the Himalayas
Monastery
Miles
0
100
200
300
400
72
76
80
84
36
32
28
24
Kashgar
Yangi 4,043
Tarim Basin
Yarkhand 3,923
Tashkurgan 10,250
Charchan
Sanju 6,070
Sanju Pass 16,650
Khotan (Ilchi) 4,490
Kiria 4,570
Sorghak 7,050
Hindu Kush Mts.
Shahidula 11,780
Polu
Kuen-Lun
Karakoram Pass 18,550
Indus R.
Skardo 8,873
NUBRA
LADAK
Kizil Jilga 16,350
Chang-tang Plain
Leh 11,266
Srinagar 5,260
KASHMIR
Himis
Pang Kong
Tsarol Lakes
Jhelum R.
ZANGSKAR
Rudok
Jammu
Hanle
LAHUL
RAWANG
Chenab R.
Demchok
Ravi R.
Kangra
SPITI
GUGE
Indus R.
KULU
Shipki 10,600
Gargunsa
Thok Jalung 16,300 Goldfields
Thok Daurakpa Goldfields 15,280
Gartok 14,240
PANJAB
Sutlej R.
KUNAWAR
Simla 7,116
Nilang
GARHWAL
Kailas or Mt. Tise
DOKTHOL
Mussoorie 6,590
22,903
Badrinath
Manasarowar Lakes
Dangra
Siwalik Hills
Nanda Devi 25,600
Milam 11,250
PURANG
Mariam Pass
MAJIN
Dehra Dun
KUMAON
Khojarnath
Almora 5,494
Tadum 14,200
Tsangpo R.
NAMRING
Meerut
Sarda R.
Kali R.
Muktinath 13,100
Delhi
Dhaulagiri 26,817
Gandak R.
Kyirong 8,700
Dingri
Bareilly
NEPAL
Nyanam 15,900
Kuti
Agra
Kathmandu 4,050
Kangchenj
Jumna R.
Lucknow
Gogra R.
Bettiah
Ganges R.
Kosi R.
Allahabad
Patna
INDIA
Calc

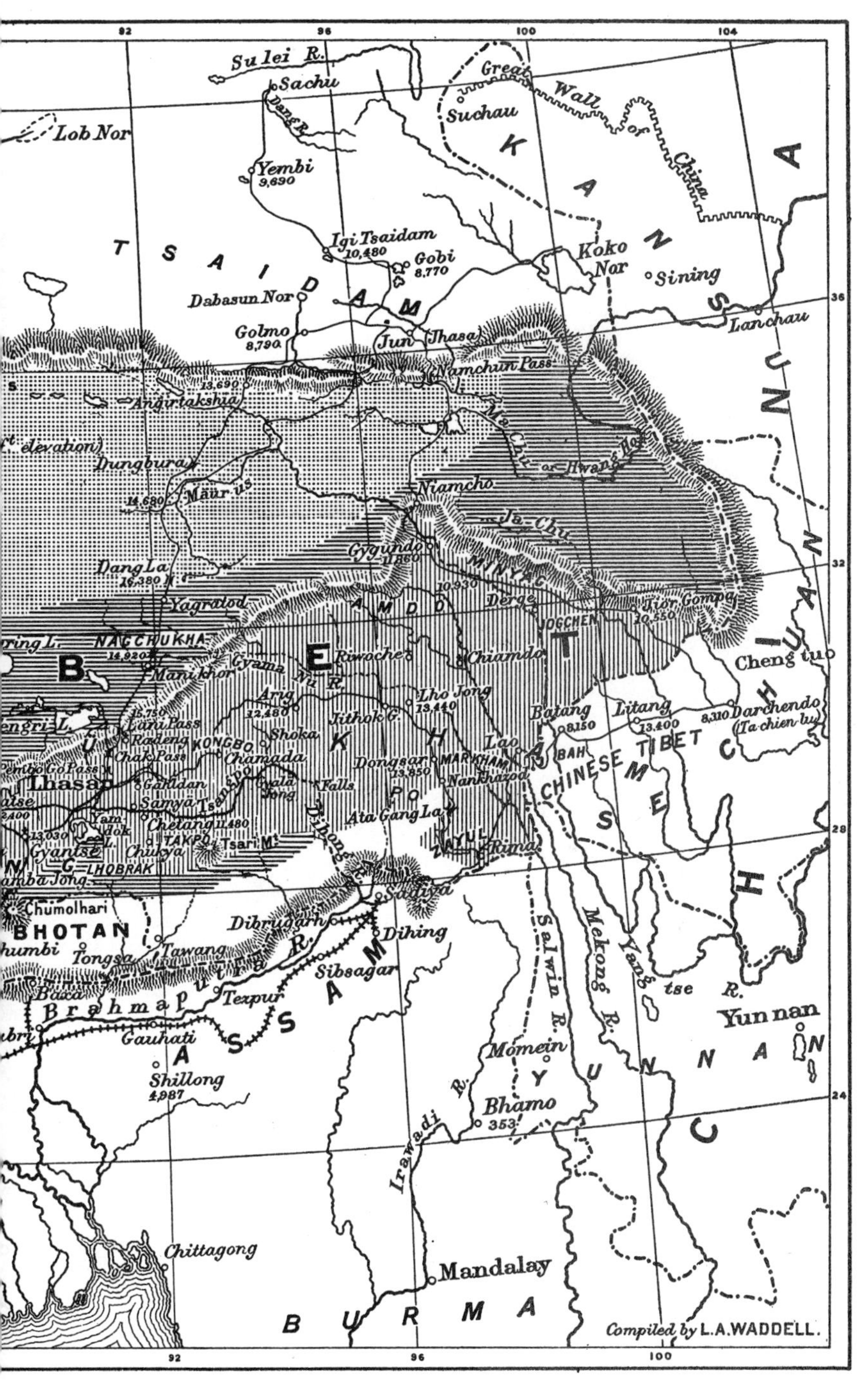

Su lei R.
Sachu
Great Wall of China
Lob Nor
Suchau
K A N S U
Yembi
9,690
Igi Tsaidam
10,480
Gobi
8,770
Koko Nor
Sining
T S A I D A M
Dabasun Nor
Golmo
8,790
Jun (Jhasa)
Lanchau
Namchun Pass
13,690
Angirtakshia
Ma Chu or Hwang Ho
Dungbura
14,680
Mäur us
Niamcho
Ja Chu
Gygundo
11,860
MINYAG
Dang La
16,380
10,930
Derge
Yagralod
A M D O
JOGCHEN
Jior Gompa
10,550
NACCHUKHA
14,920
T I B E T
Riwoche
Chiamdo
Cheng tu
Mani khor
Gyama Nu R.
Arig
12,480
Lho Jong
13,440
Batang
8,150
Litang
13,400
8,310
Darchendo
(Ta chien lu)
Lani Pass
Radeng
Chak Pass
KONGBO
Chamada
Shoka
Jithok G.
K H A M
Lao
BAH
CHINESE TIBET
S E C H U A N
Lhasa
Gandan
Samya
Tsangpo
Gyala Jong
Falls
Dongsar
13,850
MARKHAM
Nankhazod
Yam dok L.
Chetang
11,480
TAKPO
Tsari Mt
Ata Gang La
Gyantse
13,030
Chukya
LHOBRAK
ZAYUL
Rima
Chumolhari
Dihong
Sadiya
BHOTAN
Dibrugarh
Dihing
Tongsa
Tawang
Brahmaputra R.
Sibsagar
A S S A M
Tezpur
Salwin R.
Mekong R.
Yang tse R.
Yun nan
Gauhati
Shillong
4,987
Momein
Y U N N A N
Irawadi R.
Bhamo
353
Chittagong
Mandalay
B U R M A
92
96
100
104
36
32
28
24
Compiled by L.A.WADDELL.

attacking India, from gravitating definitely into the orbit of Russia.

For, notwithstanding the magnificent defence which the Himalayas afford to India on the east, it is not the Himalayas but the vast and lofty plateau to the north of them and of Tibet, the great desert wall of the Kuen Lun plateau (see map) which forms India's scientific frontier against the great rival Power in the Central Asian lowlands, namely Russia. This vast and stupendously high plateau of Kuen Lun is indeed an effective barrier between the two great rival empires of mid-Asia.

This immense desolate icy plateau, the *Chang-tang*[1] no-man's-land, which is unfit for human settlement, where without water, the traveller, "oppressed constantly

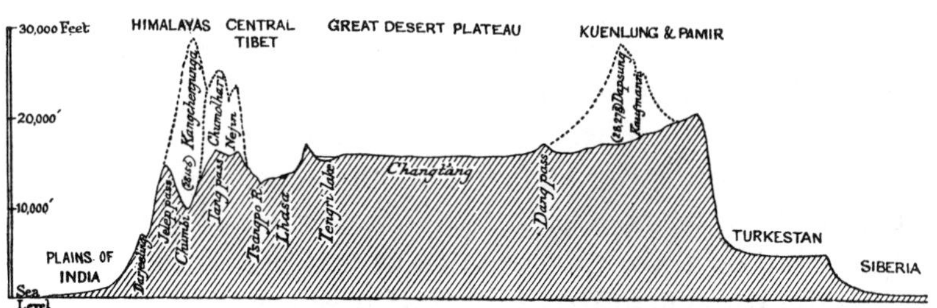

PROFILE SECTION ACROSS TIBET FROM INDIA TO SIBERIA.

[1] This vast lofty desert, the *Chang-tang* or *Jang-tang* stands at an elevation of 15,000 to 16,000 feet above the sea-level. It is about 1500 miles long with an average width of about 500 miles, tapering to 100 miles at its northern end to 350 miles at its eastern border. The area of the desert is about 480,000 square miles, or about three and a half times as much as Great Britain and Ireland. It is unfit for permanent settlements, but its surface in the summer months from May to August is covered by sparse grass, which attracts from the lower plateaux herds of wild yak, wild goat, sheep, antelope, and wolves which prey upon them. Tibet proper lies to the south of this Chang-tang, and in area is not much over 200,000 square miles, and not much larger than twice the size of Great Britain. This is inclusive of the Thok goldfields but exclusive of Chinese Tibet.

by an altitude of more than 5,000 metres, drags along for more than two months in the wind and snow without seeing a single human being or a single tree between the plains of Eastern Turkestan and the first encampment of the Tibetan shepherds 150 or 200 kilometres to the north of Lhasa," is practically impossible for any army, whereas Tibet is a near and accessible neighbour of India. As Prince Henry of Orleans used to say—"*Il n'y a qu'un pas de l'Inde au Tibet.*" This step is over the Himalayas no doubt, but it is accomplished in a few days' time; Darjeeling is nearer to Lhasa (330 miles) than it is to Calcutta, from which it is less than one day's rail. And as the present expedition proves, the journey to Tibet from the Indian side can be accomplished, either way, by a considerable army, even in mid-winter. A Chinese army of 70,000 men crossed the Himalayas from Tibet into Nepal on the Indian side, in 1793, by the Kirong Pass of about 16,000 feet, and inflicted a crushing defeat on the Goorkhas near their capital. It is no wonder therefore that England does not mean to allow this important and penetrable frontier of India to be acquired by a hostile Power.

Were Russia to establish herself in the rich valley of Lhasa, or make her influence supreme there, this would have far-reaching political effects all along our eastern frontier for over a thousand miles, from Ladak and Kashmir on the north end, to Nepal and Assam on the south, leading to combinations against us among the many Himalayan States, and whilst endangering our hold on our great Dependency would entail enormous outlay in fortifying our eastern frontier along its length, and in maintaining in Bengal a standing army of tens of thousands of men, as large as we have in the Punjab, and even more expensive.

The inevitableness of this forward movement to Tibet, on these same grounds, was recognised several years ago by some of us who were familiar with the facts, and represented the necessity for it so long ago as 1888 and in 1895, and the imperativeness of throwing over the Chinese intermediary and dealing directly with Tibet. Again, more particularly, we advocated this forward movement in 1898, receiving for this a good deal of abuse from a section of the English press in India; but in 1903 it became an accomplished fact.

How extremely long-suffering England has been over her relations with Tibet is evident from a brief survey of the causes leading up to this mission, which also illustrates the tortuous and evasive policy of the Chinese to an almost comical degree.

Our first relations with Tibet arose out of raids by the Bhotanese, in 1772, into Bengal. The Grand Lama of Tashilhumpo then sent a letter to our Governor-General, Warren Hastings, interceding for the Bhotanese, and the outcome was Bogle's commercial mission of 1774.

The acquisition by us of the Himalayan State of Sikhim, adjoining Bhotan and containing the sanitarium of Darjeeling, famous for its snow views of Everest and Kanchenjunga, brought us into more direct relations with Tibet, as Sikhim was spiritually subject to Lhasa and its frontiers marched with Tibet for over a hundred miles, and, indeed, it was the question of these Sikhim boundaries and the trade across them which led to the present mission. The manner in which we secured suzerainty over Sikhim forms an interesting portion of English history, and is of importance in our case against Tibet.

On the break-up of the Moghul empire in the beginning of the 19th century, when petty prince adventurers and marauding bands were carving for themselves short-lived principalities out of the moribund empire, a small tribe of Goorkha soldiers of fortune seized Nepal, and, establishing themselves there, overran the whole stretch of the Himalayas from the Sutlej river to Bhotan, and then began to intrigue with the Mahratta princes of India against us for the mastery of India and for the expulsion of the English from the country. At that critical time in 1815, the year of Waterloo, when our rule was trembling in the balance, General Ochterlony (whose great pillar of victory is now rightly the most striking monument in the capital of India) saved the empire. He defeated the Goorkhas in 1816 and drove them out of the northern Himalayas of Kumaon (Naini Tal), and Garhwal (Mussoorie), and also ejected them from Sikhim on the south-east.

Permanently to cripple these aggressive little Goorkhas, to confine them to Nepal, and wedge them in there against any further expansion, the tracts on either side of Nepal were then either taken over and held by us or restored to their former rulers. In this way we reinstated the Raja of Sikhim under British suzerainty. Some years later, in 1830, when a hill sanitarium was required for Calcutta, a tract on the outer Sikhim hills as far as Darjeeling was leased from the Sikhim Raja, and this was opened by Dr A. Campbell of the Indian Medical Service, regarding whose achievement Dr Hooker wrote: "He [Dr Campbell] raised British Sikhim from its pristine condition of an impenetrable jungle tenanted by half savages and mutually hostile races to that of a flourishing European hill-station and a rich agricultural province." He also introduced the tea industry, which has since assumed such vast dimensions. When, in 1849, Dr Campbell and Dr (afterwards Sir Joseph) Hooker were travelling in the Sikhim Himalayas, they were captured and imprisoned by the Raja at the instigation of his rabid Tibetan prime minister, "the mad *diwan*," Namgyal.

As a punishment for this outrage all outer Sikhim,

including the station of Darjeeling, was annexed as a British district. The Lhasa Lamas, taking advantage of their spiritual influence over the Buddhist Raja and his Tibetan wife,[1] excited him to hostilities. When these were suppressed, in 1872, Mr (afterwards Sir John) Edgar, the magistrate of Darjeeling, seized the opportunity to try and establish friendly communication with the Tibetans, for the first time since Warren Hastings' attempt a century before, partly in the hope of opening up new trade—for the shortest of all existing trade-routes to Lhasa from the outer world pass through Sikhim—and partly to be in good political and neighbourly relations with the religious head of some million of Lamaistic Buddhists who now are British subjects in our Himalayan States, from Ladak on the north to Bhotan on the south-east. Mr Edgar effected, in 1873, an interview with the petty Tibetan magistrate of the adjoining Chumbi Valley of Tibet, but failed to open up any communication with Lhasa.

In 1884, Mr Colman Macaulay, a secretary of the Bengal Government, which has its summer headquarters at Darjeeling, impressed there by the trade possibilities of Tibet with India, effected a meeting with the Tibetan magistrate of the frontier fort and customs station of Khambo on the north of the Sikhim boundary; and enlisting the interest of Lord Randolph Churchill, then Secretary of State, in his scheme, obtained from Peking, as suzerain of Tibet, a passport to visit Lhasa with a trade mission. When this mission was organised in 1886, and on its way to cross the Sikhim frontier into Tibet, the Chinese objected to its proceeding, notwithstanding that they had given the passport; and Lord Dufferin, acting under the orders of Lord Salisbury, who held the then current but exaggerated notions of the enormous military strength

[1] The present wife of the Raja is the daughter of an inferior officer of the Grand Lama's court at Lhasa.

of China—the Yellow-Terror colossus whose feet of clay it was left for the Japanese a few years later to reveal—and not caring to oppose her wishes, ordered the abandonment of the mission.

This decision proved a most unfortunate one, as it gave the impression of weakness on our part, for which we were despised accordingly. Emboldened by this apparent weakness, the Lamas became actively hostile. They invaded our tributary State of Sikhim in 1886 with an armed force, and advanced to within sixty miles of Darjeeling, causing a panic in that European sanitarium. Their wave of fanatical hatred to Europeans thus excited, swept across Tibet to the other side, where the Lamas expelled the Roman Catholic missionaries from their long-established home at Batang in 1887, burned their mission-houses to the ground, and massacred many of their converts. The Lamas also forced the Sikhim Raja to sign a treaty declaring that Sikhim was subject only to Tibet. After fruitless negotiations with China, as the Tibetans refused to withdraw from Sikhim, we had to expel them by force of arms in the costly little expedition of 1888 under General Graham. Their entrenchments were stormed, and the Tibetans, "showing great courage and determination," were driven out and pursued by our troops over the Jelep Pass into the Chumbi Valley.

Farce now succeeded comedy. The envoy of His Celestial Majesty the Emperor of China appeared immediately on the scene and haughtily ordered the Western Barbarians to withdraw, notwithstanding that China had just declared herself unable to control the Tibetans or induce them to evacuate Sikhim. In deference to these fresh demands of the dreaded Chinese, the then Viceroy of India ordered the instant recall of our troops from Chumbi, and they were withdrawn the very same day they got there. Our immediate compliance with this demand, coupled with the fact that not only did we not annex this desirable Chumbi Valley as a sanitarium, but exacted no indemnity whatever for the cost of this little war—about a million sterling and our casualties[1]—which the Tibetans had thrust upon us, confirmed both the Chinese and Tibetans in the belief that we were afraid of them.

Two years' negotiations with the Chinese after the Sikhim War of 1888 now followed for the settlement of the boundary on this Sikhim frontier, and a treaty was then signed on the 17th March 1890 by the Chinese Amban of Lhasa for the nominal suzerain of Tibet on the one hand, and by Lord Lansdowne as Viceroy of India on the other. In this treaty the Lamas, in addition to arranging for the settlement of boundary disputes, agreed to facilitate trade across the frontiers, and to the appointment of a joint commission to give effect to this. This was in 1890, but the Lamas afterwards refused to acknowledge this treaty, and imposed still more vexatious taxes and obstructions on Indian trade than before.

After three more years of negotiations with China, so long dragged out by her usual evasiveness, the British and Chinese commissioners, namely, Mr Paul, the magistrate of Darjeeling, and Mr James Hart of the Chinese Customs, and the Chinese Amban[2] met on the 5th December 1893 and signed a set of trade regulations under the treaty. This included the opening to all British traders of Yatung in the Chumbi Valley of Tibet, as a trade-mart, and specified that no duty was to be imposed on Indian goods

[1] The British loss was one officer killed, one officer and three men wounded; the Tibetans lost about 200 killed, 400 wounded, and 200 prisoners.

[2] Sheng Tai, a brother of the present Amban of Lhasa, and a Manchu of the royal house.

for five years, except on arms, salt, and a few other things, and that Indian tea was to be admitted after five years on a tax not exceeding that imposed on China tea imported into England. This arrangement had some personal interest for me, as I was to have been the resident British officer at this mart.

Unfortunately our commissioners missed this excellent opportunity of making the Tibetans a party to this treaty, and so probably preventing further trouble. Notwithstanding that the Tibetans had sent all the way from Lhasa to Darjeeling, in the suite of the Chinese, one of their highest officials, their prime minister-elect, the Shata Sha-pe, of an old noble family, he was not associated in the negotiations, nor was he recognised in a way befitting his high rank. Happening to be at Darjeeling at the time, and being keenly interested in Tibet, I paid him several visits, and found him to be a most refined and well-informed gentleman, and very well disposed towards the English. As a hereditary ruler he was anxious to learn something about how we ruled India, and he begged me to give him a summary of our criminal, police, and civil codes. For said he, as he had nothing to show politically for his visit of many months to Darjeeling, he should like to be able to take back to Lhasa some useful information by which his countrymen might improve their government by imitating portions of our Indian system, the superiority of which had much impressed him. I complied with this request, and in handing him the translations, indicated their general contents. He was much struck with our practice of not compelling an accused person to testify against himself, and exclaimed, "Why, we, following the Chinese, do the very opposite, for we torture the accused until he confesses to the crime!" He also asked me for a list of officials in order of precedence, and for several kinds of medicines, all of which I gave him. Offering to take him down to the plains to see Gaya, the holiest place on earth to a Buddhist, the spot where Sakya Muni became a Buddha, he thanked me effusively, but explained that, while personally nothing would give him greater pleasure, he was an official, a servant of the Grand Lama, who had permitted him to go only as far as Darjeeling, and that were he to go further on to India he might, on returning to Lhasa, be disgraced and lose his position and influence, on the ground of having been too friendly with the English. He hoped, however, to take back a favourable report and be allowed to return with permission to make the pilgrimage to Gaya. Just before he left Darjeeling he was much incensed at the rude treatment his clerk received at the hands of some hot-headed young British "subs," who pulled him off his horse and hustled him on the public road because he did not salaam to them. So this friendly Tibetan nobleman, who came specially in connection with the treaty, was allowed to return to Lhasa without having been associated in it.

The treaty thus concluded between the Chinese and British was repudiated by the Lamas, who, with some reason, refused to acknowledge it, on the plea that they had not been a party in the making of it. The Lamas effectually neutralised the opening of Yatung by preventing any Tibetan traders from coming to or settling in it, and by barring the valley beyond by building a strongly loopholed wall across. It is an open secret that the Chinese were at the bottom of this stratagem, to give the Tibetans a proof of their diplomatic skill and show them that while they were forced to open Yatung, they were clever enough to evade this concession by the erection of this block-house.

This strangled the trade by the most direct of

all the routes to Lhasa; and the Chinese officials, both in Lhasa and Chumbi, were given a monetary interest in stopping all trade this way by the Chinese viceroy of Sze-chuan, the province of China bordering on Tibet, who exerted himself to divert the trade which had hitherto flowed by this short Indian route into the long and difficult route *viâ* Eastern Tibet through his own province, in order that he himself might reap the tolls and other profits on Chinese tea, and European goods from the Lamas and Tibetan merchants. He is the same unpatriotic viceroy who negotiated for Russia the secret treaty with China, by which the latter transferred her suzerainty of Tibet to the former, for which services part of the price was to be a monopoly for him of all the traffic with Central Tibet. All trade was therefore to be made to pass through his hands, through his province, and none by the Chumbi route.

In addition to blocking Indian trade through the Chumbi valley, the Lamas threw down the boundary pillars erected under the treaty, made further encroachments in Sikhim, and carried off from there several British subjects against their wills into Tibet. All attempts to obtain redress either from Peking or Lhasa failed entirely.

Communication with the Dalai Lama by letter was attempted in 1900 and 1901. These letters from our Government to the Dalai Lama were sent by the hands of a Bhotanese chieftain, Ugyen Kazi, a British subject (see photo, p. 84).

"The first of these letters was despatched in August 1900 from Ladak by our political officer there, who travelled as far as Gartok, several weeks' journey within Tibet, to deliver the letter to the Tibetan governor or *Garpön* of that district for transmission to Lhasa. This official, however, returned it a few weeks later with the message that he dared not forward it as promised. In June 1901 a second letter was sent from Darjeeling along with the returned one by Ugyen Kazi, who was proceeding on a complimentary errand to the Dalai Lama from the Raja of Bhotan with presents of two elephants and a leopard. This emissary reached Lhasa in August 1901. His account of his efforts to present the letters was as follows in his own words:—'I told the Chamberlain Abbot that I brought a letter from His Excellency the Viceroy. He reported this to the Dalai Lama. On the fifth day after my arrival I gave his Excellency's letter to the Dalai Lama. The Chamberlain went with me, but left the room, and there was only a servant present, who was serving tea. On this servant leaving the room the Dalai commenced to talk about things concerning Bhotan, and then about the government of India. Regarding the letter, he said he could not take it without consulting the council and the Amban, and, as he knew they would not agree he did not wish to call them, as he said he was afraid the Chinese Amban would make a fuss and probably create a disturbance, in which case he could not be responsible for my life, and, he added, he was precluded from writing any letter to any foreign government. . . . I then pointed out that this letter was written by the greatest official under the king. To this he replied that the agreement precluding him from receiving it was not made by himself but by his predecessors, and that he was sorry he could neither receive a letter nor send an answer. . . . "Your government must not be angry with me, I have never done it any harm. I allow my subjects to trade in the products of this country, but if any of the subjects of your big government come in here I am afraid disturbances will follow." I pointed out that allowing our merchants in would do no harm, to which he replied that that might be, but he doubted it, and pointed to the manner in which the Chinese and Nepalese were already making trouble.'"

Whilst these letters were insultingly returned unopened,[1] it transpired that the Dalai Lama, on the

[1] The address was:—"To the Illustrious Dalai Lama Nay-wang Lo-sang, *Theedan Gyarso Gyon Rimboochay*, Supreme Pontiff of the Great Buddhist Church."

other hand was sending autograph letters by special envoys under the Lama Dorjieff all the way to the Tsar in St Petersburg in 1900, and in 1901, as the following official Russian notifications show:—

Extract from the Journal de Saint-Pétersbourg *of 2nd Oct.* 1900.

"Sa Majesté l'Empereur a reçu le Samedi 30 Septembre, au Palais de Livadia, Aharamba Agvan Dorjiew, premier Tsanit-hamba près le Delai-lama du Tibet."

Extract from the Odesskia Novosti *of 12th June* 1901. (*Translated from the Russian.*)

"Odessa will welcome to-day an Extraordinary Mission from the Dalai Lama of Tibet, which is proceeding to St Petersburg with diplomatic instructions of importance. The *personnel* of the Mission consists of eight prominent statesmen, with the Lama Dorzhievy at its head. The chief object of the Extraordinary Mission is a *rapprochement* and the strengthening of good relations with Russia. At the present time Tibet is, as is well known, under the protection of China, but the conditions of this protectorate have never been clearly defined. . . . The present Embassy has been equipped by the Dalai Lama, and despatched to His Imperial Majesty, and the Envoys *carry autograph letters and presents* from the Dalai Lama. . . . This Extraordinary Mission will, among other things, raise the question of the establishment at St Petersburg of a permanent Tibetan Mission for the maintenance of good relations with Russia."

The composition of this mission was detailed in the *St Petersburg Gazette* with Agwan Dorshieff as Head; the Secretary of the Dalai Lama, Chambo Donid (or Hambo Donir) Lubson Kaintchok; the Captain of a district of Tibet Sombou Tsiduron Pundzok (or

Djantsan Zombon Tsitong Puntsok); Dorshieff's secretary and translator, Owshche Norsunof; and the Chief Shigshit Gaszonof.

Extract from the Messager Officiel *of 25th June* 1901.

"Sa Majesté l'Empereur a recu le Samedi 23 Juin, au Grand Palais de Peterhof, les Envoyés Extraordinaires du Dalai-Lama du Tibet; Hambo Akvan Dorgéview et Loubsan Kaintchok Hambo Donir. Après la réception des Envoyés a l'honneur d'être présenté à Sa Majesté l'Empereur le Secrétaire de la Mission Djantsan Zombon Tsitong Puntsok, Chef de l'Arrondissement du Tibet."

Extract from the Messager Officiel *of 1st December* 1901.
(*Translated.*)

"On the 28th November the Envoy of Tibet, Hamba-Achvan-Dorjew had, the honour of being presented to Her Majesty the Empress Alexandra Feodorowna."

The political character of these Missions is even more evident from an article in the *Novoe Vremya* of 18th June 1901, which stated that Dorjieff wrote for the information of the Russian Government a pamphlet in which the customs of Lhasa, and the intrigues surrounding the Dalai Lama, are described. This newspaper goes on to say that "the news of the defeat of China, the Russian victories in Manchuria, etc., have penetrated to the Lama of Tibet. Under these circumstances, a *rapprochement* with Russia must seem to him the most natural step, as Russia is the only power able to counteract the intrigues of Great Britain, who has so long been endeavouring to obtain admission, and only awaits an opportunity to force an entrance." Those envoys with Dorjieff at their head were escorted back to Tibet, so the Russian newspapers stated, by a "scientific mission," which included officers of the intelligence branch of the Russian army.

This suspicious interchange of missions with Russia, combined with the sullen hostility and deliberate discourtesy and rebuffs received by us from such a weak and semi-barbarous Power as Tibet, was the last straw on the patience of our Government. Strong pressure was therefore applied at Peking by our minister in 1902, with the result that China agreed to a British political mission proceeding to Khamba Jong within Tibet; and she promised that the Chinese Amban from Lhasa, accompanied by certain high Tibetan officials, would meet the British Commission there to discuss disputed matters with a view to their settlement; and China made a display of so far modifying her policy of obstruction as not only to instruct her resident Amban, in Tibet, to cease from further opposition to the admission of British agents, but also to publish in the *Peking Gazette* a report from him describing his urgent remonstrances with the "Councillors" of the Dalai Lama, against any further incivility to British Envoys. There must, he says, be conciliation, for "if hostilities occurred, the consequences would pass conception, and the intervention of the Imperial Resident would be of small avail." In doing this, however, the Chinese Government was evidently merely making an empty pretence of shifting responsibility from itself on to the Lamas, whom it scornfully terms "our barbarian vassals"; for, when the Amban at Lhasa urged the Lamas to acquiesce in what he termed "the very just demands of the British," he was impeached as a traitor by the Chinese and immediately recalled, and it is believed the unfortunate man committed suicide.

Meanwhile, the British Commission was organised. Major F. E. Younghusband, of the political department, was chosen as Envoy, with the Resident of Sikhim, Mr J. C. White, as assistant, Mr E. C. Wilton of the Consular Service as Chinese interpreter, and Captain W. F. O'Connor, Royal Artillery, as Tibetan interpreter and secretary. In July 1903 this peaceful Mission, with a small escort of 200 Sikh pioneers, crossed the frontier to Khamba Jong as had been arranged, travelling at considerable expense, on account of having to carry its own provisions and transport all the way from the Indian plains. On arrival at Khamba Jong, 20 miles within the Tibetan frontier and across a pass over 16,000 feet above the sea-level, the Mission found no one to meet it, neither Chinese nor Tibetan. An enquiry, addressed to Peking, asking why the representative of the Son of Heaven had not arrived, elicited the reply that the new Amban had started from Peking, but had succumbed to the hardships of the journey, and that another Amban had left Peking in December 1902 and was still on his way, and, meanwhile, a very high Tibetan official had left Lhasa for Khamba Jong. This individual arrived after several weeks' delay, but turned out to be a person of very low rank, so that the British Commissioner properly refused to enter into any relations with him.

In this deadlock Colonel Younghusband's Mission waited wearily for four months for envoys who never came. On the contrary, an army of 3000 Tibetans was drawn up in front of the Mission camp, and threatened to attack it if the Mission did not withdraw.

At the time of this hostile demonstration by the Tibetans there are grounds for thinking that a secret treaty was arrived at between Russia and the Dalai Lama, in which the former assumed the suzerainty of Tibet and protectorate of the Lamaist religion. Russia, on being taxed with this, denied the treaty, but admitted that she was establishing interests in Lhasa, and in her usual menacing way, by which she has so successfully extended her empire in Asia, indulged in veiled threats, which only showed all the more our need for immediate action. Indisputable evidence was received that Tibet was preparing for war against us. The Nepalese Raja (see portrait, p. 112) informed our Government that the Dalai Lama had asked him for armed assistance in expelling the Mission; and there was ample proof that Russian breech-loading rifles and ammunition had been imported into Tibet. This was common talk amongst the Tibetans in the Darjeeling Bazaar, to which Lhasa news quickly filtered, and it was confirmed by the Japanese priest, Kawaguchi, who on his return from Lhasa, in 1903, reported that two hundred camel-loads of rifles were received by the Lamas in Lhasa, in 1902, from the Russian Government. In September 1903, it was ascertained that Dorjieff was combining with his professional Buddhist labours the business of supervising the war preparations in the Lhasa Arsenal.

With the interests of India thus vitally threatened by Russia, the immediate advance of our Mission became an imperative necessity; for, as Lord Curzon explained, we could not afford to tolerate hostile influences on our Indian frontiers, and that while we had no wish ourselves to occupy the territory of other tribes or countries, and were quite content to let such territory be occupied by our allies and friends, the Government could not allow rival and unfriendly influences to creep up to our frontiers and lodge themselves under our very walls.

At last, therefore, on the 6th November 1903, His Majesty's Home Government decided (1) that our Mission must advance, without delay, as far as the large market-town of Gyantse, in the heart of Tibet, 130 miles from the British frontier, and 145 miles from Lhasa, accompanied by a sufficiently large escort to force its way there, if necessary, and insist on the Tibetans fulfilling their treaty obligations; (2) that the Chumbi Valley should be occupied to show we were in earnest; and (3) that the expedition was to withdraw as soon as reparation should be exacted from the Lamas.

(*From the Modern Bayeux Tapestry by Rybotte de Jersey.*)

CHAPTER IV.

FORWARD! THE PEACEFUL MISSION BECOMES AN ARMED FORCE.

"*Beat a Chinaman enough and he will speak Tibetan.*"
—TIBETAN PROVERB.

THUS it happened that this time our entry into Tibet was not to be in the character of suppliants begging for admittance, nor as a small party of travellers sneaking undignified past an insolent and barbarous frontier guard. It was now to be the advance of the representative of a superior Power, unclandestinely in a peaceful manner, yet with a sufficient force to compel an opening of the door if it were found closed. The situation was deliciously hit off with blunt frankness in *Punch's* cartoon on the subject, where the Grand Lama, in protesting to John Bull, the peddler, that he does not want the proffered blessing of Free Trade, is told "You've got to have it!"

When, therefore, in October 1903, it was decided that the British Mission must force its way forward into the heart of Tibet, against armed opposition if necessary, the precaution was taken of increasing the strength of the escort up to a brigade of troops, so as to secure the safety of the Mission against all risks, and bear down all probable opposition. This brigade,[1]

[1]
23rd Sikh Pioneers .	700
32nd Do. .	700
8th Goorkhas . .	700
1 Coy. Mounted Infantry	100
1 Coy. No. 3 Bengal Sappers.	
1 Coy. No. 4 Madras Sappers.	

2 Guns, No. 7 Mountain Battery
Machine Guns, Norfolks.
Engineers, Field Rank.
5 Sections, Field Hospitals.
Supply and Transport Departments.

GENERAL SIR JAMES R. L. MACDONALD,
C.B., R.E.

SIR FRANCIS E. YOUNGHUSBAND, I.A.

CHART OF THE ALTITUDES
TRAVERSED.

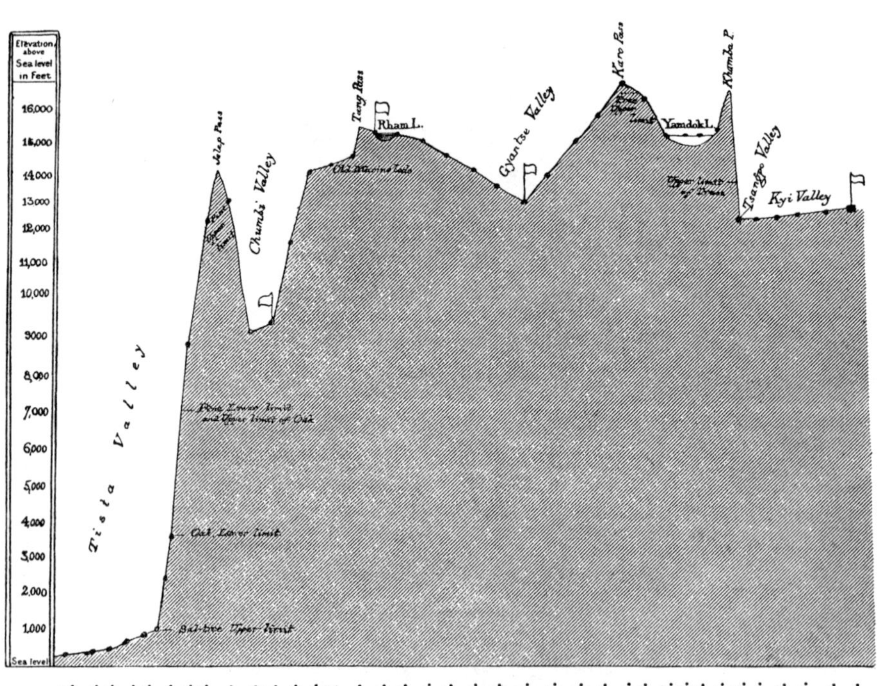

SILIGURI.
Sivok.
Riang.
Tarkhola.
Rorotang.
Lingtam.
Jeyluk.
Gnatong.
Langram.
Rinchengang.
New Chumbi.
Tongshong.
Kamparab.
Phari
Chugya.
Tuna.
Dochen.
Kala Tso.
Samada.
Kangmar.
Saogang.
GYANTSÉ.
Kotang.
Taklung.
Ralung.
Karo La.
Zara.
Nagartsé.
Yasig.
Palté.
Tomalung.
Partsi.
Chaksam.
Jang.
Nam.
Toilung Bridge.
LHASA.

numbering about 2800 rifles, was placed under the command of Brigadier-General J. R. L. Macdonald, C.B., R.E., of Uganda fame, with instructions to advance on peaceful lines, and act strictly on the defensive in protecting the Mission during its advance in Tibet as well as in the occupation of the Chumbi Valley.

Never before in military history had the army of any civilised Power been called on to conduct a little war—for that is what it had now become—at a height of over 15,000 feet above the level of the sea—on

EXERCITVS : TRANS : MONTES : ITER : FECIT.

YE : GENERAYLE : WITH : A : RYGHTE : GOODLYE ANDE JOYOVS COMPAGNIE : CROSSES : YE : MOVNTAYNES.

a level with the summit of Mont Blanc. The task thus allotted to General Macdonald might well have awed most leaders. The advance in the face of such physical difficulties had to be made on the shortest notice, without any preparations whatever having been previously made, and, owing to the lateness of the season, it had to be made in the depth of winter, with its intense cold to be endured by the Indian troops in the face of unparalleled difficulties in mountain transport, and with the probabilities of armed opposition in the strong natural defences by the way.

General Macdonald selected as the line of his

advance into Tibet the easiest route, namely, the ordinary trade route over the Jelep Pass by Chumbi, which was all the more desirable as the Chumbi Valley was to be occupied by us. So, whilst his troops and their transport were being mobilised, and food and other supplies being collected at the base, at the foot of the mountains, he arranged for the withdrawal of the Mission and its small escort from Khamba Jong back to the Jelep route, and to give up the former route. This decision was a wise one, as it placed the lines of communication on a better basis for the advance of the large body of troops which it was now decided to send. The long and difficult Lachen route, little better than a goat-track, with its pass over 16,000 feet, and very little firewood by the way, was thus given up in favour of the Chumbi route, with its pass nearly 2000 feet lower, and affording considerable firewood and grazing for the transport animals.

Food supply and its transport—those bugbears of the traveller as well as the general of an army—were soon found to be the especial difficulty of this expedition, and associated with these was the construction and improvement of the mountain tracks for the passage of this transport along the most difficult line of communications in the world. For, in addition to the carriage of tents, bedding, ammunition, and other stores, up the mountains, there was the infinitely greater difficulty that all the food supply for the troops, and for the still larger army of followers, had to be brought up the mountains from the Indian plains, as practically no food supplies were obtainable within the mountains. The daily food supply for an army, consisting chiefly of grain-eaters as ours was, mounts up to an incredible number of loads, and the question of how to push on the greatest number of these loads in the quickest possible time up the many scores of miles of bad mountain tracks at enormous elevations—was the problem which General Macdonald and his Chief of Supply, Major Bretherton, had to tackle. It was soon solved. Almost every conceivable form of transport and baggage animal suited for the work was impressed, and soon the whole track was filled by a toiling, moving mass of baggage animals and coolies. From the base at Silliguri, where the shrieking locomotives dumped down their hundreds of tons of food and other stores daily

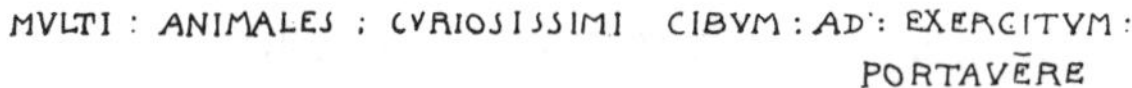

MANIE : STRAVNGE : BEASTES : BRINGE : PROVENDERE : FOR : Y^e : ARMIE : MANIE : ALSOE : DOE . DYE : OF : A : GREEVOVS : MVRRAYNE .

from Calcutta, some camels and thousands of bullock-carts with their yoke-oxen, brought all the way from Bombay and Madras, carried the loads along the cart-road winding up the Tista Valley for 45 miles, and when the road became too steep for the oxen, draught-mules replaced the bullocks in the carts. Where the cart-road ended, pack-bullocks carried the stores up the goat-tracks, which the sappers and pioneers had enlarged into mule-paths in surprisingly quick time. When the track became steeper, pack-mules and ponies were used, and when too steep for laden mules, several thousands of coolies "humped" the loads on their backs. These coolies were a great army in themselves, and were a motley lot drawn from all parts of the Himalayas, even 1000 miles distant. There were Baltis from beyond Kashmir, Garhwalis from beyond Mussoorie and Naini Tal, a dozen different tribes from Nepal (which the Raja of that country lent for the occasion), the local Lepchas and Bhotiyas from Sikhim, Bhotanese from the east, and a considerable number of friendly Tibetans.

When everything was cut down in this way by considerations of difficult transport our personal kits did not escape. Already on the very light field-scale, they were still further reduced to under 80 lbs. for officers and 40 lbs. for men, inclusive of tents and everything—an alarmingly meagre outfit for the almost arctic regions into which we were to plunge.

The starting-place and base of operations of our force was at Silliguri, the terminus of the plains railway. It lies at the foot of the Himalayas at an elevation of only 397 feet above the sea-level.

On stepping out of the train at Silliguri on the 6th November 1903, we found ourselves on the trail of an army in the field. Within the railway station were busy khaki-clad military men, and outside the station yard, amongst little mountains of piled-up stores of various colours—according as they consisted of sacks of grain, flour, sugar, salt, boxes of provisions, bundles of clothing—stood ranged some hundreds of bullock-carts, mules and ponies with their drivers, and of coolies loading them up with the food for our army. At one side stood the transport ready waiting for our particular unit. I also found awaiting me my two trusty old Tartar servants from Darjeeling, Küntūp, the famous survey explorer and Achum my cook, both of whom have been my faithful companions during many years' travel among these Eastern Himalayas, carrying gun and camera, and improvising shelters and appetising meals on the shortest notice. Whilst our baggage was being loaded, several of us made for the railway refreshment-room to enjoy a civilised meal once more before plunging into the wild mountains.

The start-off from the scorching Indian plains, with their hot copper skies and roasted dust, for the cool hills, always so exhilarating to the European exile in India, was especially so on this occasion, bound as we were for the mystic land beyond the snows. These snowy ranges were already to be seen far away, towering high above the dark ramparts of the outer Himalayas, and glittering in the sunshine, cold, relentless, and menacingly, the gleaming white fangs of India's icy sentinels, over 20,000 feet above us.

Heading our shaggy little hill ponies along the road, which struck straight for the deep gap in the outer ranges through which the Tista river bursts out into the plains, we pass through some bare open plain which the Tartar Koch tribe of these parts (Cooch Behar) has reclaimed from the forest of the Terai, as this swampy tract at the foot of the mountains is called. Our progress is at first blocked occasionally by bits of the army, companies of marching soldiers, mule-corps, and slow-travelling trains of commissariat bullock-carts. On passing these, we enter at about the fifth mile the great belt of *Sal*-tree forest, through whose tall depths our road cleaves for us a cool shady avenue several miles long. In this forest, almost the only other tree besides the stately *Sal* is the *Khair* or Catechu, an acacia-like tree with a pleasantly acid fruit suggestive of a gooseberry, which now was ripe and proved refreshing. Suddenly we emerge at the gorge of Sivok or "The Cleft of the Winds," and are now in British Sikhim, whilst across the Tista river is British Bhotan,[1]

[1] "Bhotan," the Indian name for this country means "The end of (*Bhot*) or Tibet." The people themselves call their country "*Dūk*" in the "Land of the Thunder-Dragon," which is very appropriate, as it is the most thundery part of all the Himalayas.

that slice of Bhotan which was annexed in 1866 on account of persistent raiding and outrages by the Bhotanese on the Indian plains[1]; its outer undulating tract under the mountains is the Duars, or Dooars,[2] now a tract of flourishing tea-gardens.

This deep-slit gorge where the turbulent Tista river pierces the mountains is very well named by the native Lepcha tribe, "The Cleft of the Winds," for through it pours a ceaseless stream of mist and rushing wind, as through a mighty funnel or chimney, blowing a gale down the valley in the daytime and up it at night; and with unquenchable thirst it sucks up all night the fever-laden mist and rain-clouds from the swampy Terai plains below, and so contributes towards making this country of Lower Sikhim one of the dampest in the world. In the morning the bottom of the gorge is usually filled, for a mile or so up its sides, with a gauzy stream of mist, rushing up the valley like a river of smoke. It is this too which gives this place its notorious reputation as the most malarious spot in all this deadly Terai swamp. Certainly, this place is pestilentially poisonous in the rainy season. At present, November, it is less so, and as no other convenient halting-stage is available, we pitched our camp here on a clearing on the bank of a small

[1] Eden's mission, in 1864, to prevent further raids, was subjected to the grossest outrage, the leaders being imprisoned and spat upon. This resulted in the war of 1865, and the annexation the following year of Kalimpong down to the plains, whilst a subsidy of Rs.50,000 was to be paid yearly to the Bhotanese if they kept the peace. Independent Bhotan extends from Kalimpong away to the east for about 200 miles, with a width of about 90 miles from the Tibetan frontier to the Indian plains. In 1838 Dr Griffiths of the Indian Medical Service, who accompanied Captain Pemberton's mission in 1838, made a very extensive tour within Bhotan by himself, which he described in his *Journals* (3 vols.), and collected a large number of plants, which are arranged at Kew by Mr Oliver.

[2] Literally the "doors" to the hills.

tributary stream, opposite the huts of a small bazaar of hillmen, who encamp here with their families in the winter months, bringing down oranges, walnuts, and other produce of the mountains for sale. They obtain most of their own food and utensils from the adjoining jungle; and even their cooking pots and pitchers are waiting to be cut off the bamboos. Here, though no mosquitoes were noticeable, I took the precaution of dosing everybody with quinine, and of seeing that they protected themselves against this chill blast blowing through the gorge, laden with the exhalations of the rank tropical forest.

A BAMBOO PITCHER.

Although so unhealthy, this gorge is grandly beautiful. Here the impetuous waters of the mighty Tista in their exit from their mountain home, no longer hemmed in by the rocks, and tired with their mad rushing down from the crags, seek the pervading languor of the plains, and stretch themselves out lazily in a broad network of sluggish channels which creep along through the dense jungle to the distant horizon. The river's low banks and islets are covered by a dense and almost impenetrable tangle of the rankest and loftiest tropical forest, in whose deep recesses lurk almost every kind of wild beast, from tiger downwards, and the game on which they prey. Here, if provided with sufficient elephants to beat through the jungle, you may meet almost any game from quail to wild elephant; so we were not surprised that one of the bullock-drivers here complained that a tiger had killed and carried off one of his huge bullocks during the night.

Beyond the gorge, the journey next day up the rock-bound valley of the winding Tista, covered with dense green jungle to the water's edge, carries you through some of the most magnificent river scenery in the world, with ever-changing views at every turn, an endless succession of perfect pictures.

In the foreground, from dank, shady corners here and there along the road peep up the picturesque huts of the few of the sturdy hill people who, braving the unhealthiness of the valley, come here for a few weeks in the cold weather to trade, or to pick up a livelihood as woodcutters or otherwise. Most of them are immigrants from the adjoining hills of Nepal, the men with *Kukri* knives stuck in their belt; a good many are Lepchas, the aborigines of these Sikhim hills, and a few are Bhotiyas or naturalised Tibetans.[1] Traders from the Forbidden Land also may be seen, accompanied by huge mastiffs and leading shaggy ponies laden with a little wool which they have managed to smuggle over from Tibet despite the trade restrictions. All these tribes are more or less picturesquely dressed, especially their womenfolk, and all are bright and good-humoured; their alert, frank style is refreshing after the obsequious languor of the

[1] The Tibetans call their country *Bod* and themselves *Bod-pa*. Our European name for the country, namely "Tibet," is adapted from the Kashmir *Tibbat* or Tebet, a corruption of the word for Upper Tibet or *Tö-bod*, the name for the high-lying portion of Tibet which adjoins Kashmir and Ladak, which was the part first known to Europeans. The Indians, on the other hand, have corrupted the native name of the country from *Bod* into *Bhot*, and call the inhabitants *Bhotiya*, which is the current name for Tibetans now in this part of the Himalayas. See my *Among the Himalayas* for further details.

LEPCHAS OF SIKHIM.

NEPALESE AND LEPCHAS SELLING ORANGES.

ACROSS SNOW SLOPES AT LINGTU.

"PRAYER-WHEELS" FOR TWIRLING THE MYSTIC SPELL.

The one on the right has its cover removed to show its roll of paper inscribed with the mystic sentence,

Om! mani padmé Hung!

plains people. In front of most of their huts are exposed for sale piles of "the golden fruit" (*Sonalu*)—delicious oranges, the best of all the fruits of Sikhim, and so abundant is the supply that they sell eight to twelve for a halfpenny. As I have already in my book, *Among the Himalayas*, exhaustively described and illustrated the many interesting Tartar tribes of Sikhim, with their quaint customs, and the marvellous variety of scenery of this country, including the route by which we are now going from Silliguri up to the Jelep Pass, I shall here describe, as far as that Pass, only the fresh military features introduced by our present expedition, and refer the reader to my above-mentioned book for fuller details.

This cart-road up the Tista Valley, towards Tibet, is really a military road which was aligned in 1888, out of an old track, for General Graham's expedition of that year to drive the Tibetans out of their encroachments in Sikhim back over the Jelep Pass. It is a fine, well-engineered road, but the heavy traffic during the past few weeks of several thousands of laden carts daily passing over it has cut it up badly in places. Averaging about 16 feet wide, it winds along the bottom of the gorge about 100 feet above the river, across many precipices, where it is hewn through the cliff-side of solid rock. The more dangerous places are where it crosses the numerous landslips and ledges of gravel banks undermined below by the river floods, which rise as much as 80 feet. At such places the roadway is often supported only by stakes horizontally or vertically thrust into this loose soil to form an insecure bracket or shelf for the road. The geological formation here is particularly unsafe for carrying a roadway. It is a crumbling shale,[1] liable to be torn down by the torrential rains of these hills, so that this road becomes impassable from

[1] The "Daling" Shales of Indian geologists. See Appendix XII.

the landslips in the rainy season (June to September), when whole stretches of the road disappear into the river. Even at this season it is surprising that so few of the transport animals fall over the many narrow bits at dangerous precipices, many of which are not fenced in. Looking over the edge at such places, I only saw evidence of two or three animals having fallen recently, where the great vultures had collected round their carcasses in the rocky river-bed far below.

At these constricted and landslippy places overhanging the precipices, our passage on the rut-worn road was frequently blocked by carts and animals coming from the opposite direction. In trying to pass one another under such circumstances it is amusing to see how the instinct of self-preservation makes everybody and every beast alike struggle for dear life to keep to the inner or safe side of the track and obstinately retain it. Most of these carts, which had gone up with food-stuffs, were returning laden with logs of the valuable *Sal* timber, which the forest department, seizing advantage of this returning empty transport, in this way gets conveyed from the recesses of the forest to the railway at cheap rates, to the benefit also of the military department—a very business-like arrangement.

Following up the right bank, and crossing the Kali Jhora or "Black Stream," black with coaly shale, not far from the coal mines of Daling, we encamp on a terrace above the river at Riang, under the Government Cinchona plantations. Here on these hot, damp hills the Cinchona plant finds a home like its own in Peru, and enables Government to manufacture for distribution throughout India tons of quinine —that divine drug which makes life possible in the malarious tropics; and by the roadside are stacks of barrels of petroleum ether, the cheap spirit by which the quinine is extracted.

At Tista Bridge, where the road crosses to the left bank, we are about 718 feet above the sea-level. The bridge has now been widened to permit carts to cross over without being taken to pieces. This was the terminus of the old cart-road, whence a pony track winds up the hill out of the gorge for 4 miles to the sanitarium of Kalimpong, where the thriving Scotch Mission, under the Rev. J. A. Graham, has just established several orphanages on the Barnardo system for the slum Anglo-Indian and half-caste children of Calcutta. No nobler piece of humanitarian work could have been conceived. By these "Homes" the poor little waifs are rescued from the squalor and vice of the city gutters, and trained to wholesome and useful lives in these healthy hills. A few miles from the "Homes" is the small chapel of the devoted French Catholic missionary, Father Desgodins, who has been working here for a quarter of a century, after an equally long period in eastern Chinese Tibet.

The cart-road from here has now been prolonged up the Tista Valley for about 40 miles further, towards the great passes beyond the capital of the Raja of Sikhim, and we continue along it, past the picturesque junction of the Rangit with the Tista, to a stagnant, stifling clearance in the forest (Tarkhola), where we encamp; and the following day crossing the Rongli rivulet, we enter the post of Rangpo which is in Native Sikhim, and is the advanced base depôt for this expedition; for here our road to Jelep Pass leaves the cart-road and strikes up the steep mountain bridle-tracks.

Rangpo is therefore a place of great importance for our expedition. Stores are being piled up into little mountains, lines of sheds are being run up, and a large bazaar has already been formed where a week ago there was only a single hut. Its proper name is "Ram-pu" or "the twisted spurs," which here force the river into a U-shaped curve, within the bend of which lies the post on a little flat on the bank, deeply set in the ravine; and as it is only 800 feet above the sea, amidst semi-tropical forest, it is very malarious. To escape this we encamped in a grove of orange trees on a plateau higher up. At this busy post everyone was overworked, and perhaps the hardest worked of all was the Bengali clerk at the post-office who sleepily handed out letters with one hand as he clicked off a telegram with the other, doing the work of four men.

This depôt outfits all the men of the various units with the special warm clothing for the arctic regions, now to be seen towering high above us, so we halt here for a few days to get this clothing and collect local hillmen as coolies and bearers for ambulance stretchers. Warm clothing was issued free to the men, both troops and followers, on a most generous scale, to protect against the cold and frost-bite. In addition to the ordinary winter scale of clothing, which included a Balaclava cap, heavy flannel-lined warm coat, woollen drawers, thick boots, waterproof sheet and blankets, each man also received—

1 sheepskin coat (*Poshtin*) with long sleeves.
1 thick quilted cotton rug.
1 pair thick woollen gloves.
1 pair fur-lined bag gloves.
2 thick lambswool vests.
1 pair quilted cotton overalls.
1 heavy woollen comforter.
1 pair felt knee-boots ("Gilgit-boots").
1 pair woollen socks.
1 pair of goggles against snow-blindness.

Each of the coolies also received practically the same scale as this, so that there were about 10,000 sets of each of these articles issued.

During the halt here, I designed some ambulance

chairs for the transport of our sick in the mountains; to be carried by the hill coolies in the same way as they carried their own loads, namely, on their backs with a forehead band. The Lepcha coolies in a few days made up forty of these basket chairs from the bamboo[1] and cane of the adjoining jungle, and whilst they were so engaged their prince, the Raja's son and heir-apparent, paid us a visit.

Resuming our advance from Rangpo up the mountains, we ascend the Rongli river towards the Jelep by the mule-track newly made by the Madras sappers. Now we see why it is that the majority of

A : ROAD : IS : BVILDED : AMONGE : Ye : MOVNTAYNES :

our force consists of pioneers and sappers. This excellent riding path by which we are winding in and out up the mountains and passing across cliffs, was made during the past few weeks; and notwithstanding the large amount of blasting which had to be done is already a capital track, with several working parties

[1] The best and toughest bamboo for basket-work is the *Po* or *Pa* (*Dendrocalamus hamiltonii*); this is the largest of all the bamboos, as much as a foot in width, and its stem cut into segments is used as pitchers. The other, growing side by side with it, the *Zhu* or *Mahlo* (*Bambusa nutans*), although strong for uprights, cracks if it is bent.

of the Muzbi Sikh pioneers giving it its finishing touches. At the tenth mile we cross the river by a substantial bridge also thrown across by the sappers, below some copper mines where the green ore is worked by Nepalese lessees; after 8 miles more of gradual ascent, we strike the old track of 1888 from Kalimpong, by which I ascended to the Jelep in the Tibetan expedition of that year.

What a change has been wrought over this part of Sikhim since then! This fine valley, which at that time was one vast primeval forest with scarcely a single inhabitant, is now a well-peopled country-side with thriving villages and little farms dotted all over the cleared hillsides. And so it has been with most of the other lower valleys. This opening up of the country has been wrought by Mr White, an engineer of the Public Works Department, who was appointed as Political Resident in Sikhim. Most of this industrious new population had to be imported by Mr White from Nepal, as the unenterprising aborigines would not respond to the strong inducements he held out to them to open up this new land.

The Sikhimese accompanying me considered that this was a great grievance to their people, and they lost no opportunity of loudly saying so. One can scarcely however sympathise with them in this. To the Sikhim State the result of the active development has been that Mr White has already increased the Raja's revenue tenfold, while the agreeable result to us travellers is that now we are able to purchase along the road, eggs, fowls, and other provisions, and obtain coolies where previously all was an uninhabited wilderness.

From Rongli, or "The Lepcha's Hut," which gives its name to the river, we now commence to mount the great staircase of the Himalayas. Here we are as yet only 2700 feet above the sea-level; but in the next 15 miles we rise about 10,000 feet higher and pass right up through the heart of the range. From the semi-tropical forest of giant bamboos, figs, cinnamon, etc., we zigzag up the steep spurs of the higher ranges, passing rapidly through the cooler zones of temperate oak, chestnut and maple, ashes and elms, with undergrowth of raspberry and barberry, into open snow-sprinkled pine forest at Jeyluk. Above this frozen snow are the rhododendrons and junipers of Lingtu, and beyond them open undulating stretches of alpine pastures with patches of snow and wide views of the snowy mountains. In these few miles we have passed at one bound from scorching midsummer into midwinter!

Puffing and panting up this stupendous winding stairway comes, slowly struggling along, our motley crowd of fighting men and followers, all now attired in their heavy warm clothing. The hill coolies, with their loads on their backs and sticks in their hands, plodding patiently and painfully upward, stand aside on the edge of the road to let the files of soldiers pass by—and very straggling files they are, and fearfully and wonderfully clad. Every man now has his head muffled in a Balaclava cap tied round with a woollen cravat; his thickly-wadded figure is befurred with sheepskin coat and gloves; his eyes are sheathed by green goggles, and, with his rifle on his shoulder, he digs his short alpenstock into the slippery frozen ground at each step. Yet despite all this outward disguise, there is no mistaking the tall, stolid, bearded Sikh, the squat, little snub-nosed Tartar Goorkha, the dark-skinned, lank Madrassi sapper, and the British "Tommy Atkins"—the last most at home of all in this climate, and ever ready with a cheery jest or jibe to his fellows on passing events.

Just below the shoulder of Lingtu (12,617 feet) where the Tibetans in their invasion of 1888 built a rude stone fort, the remains of which are still visible from below, I was interested in passing this time to look again at a tree upon which I remembered having seen in the 1888 war the dead bodies of two Tibetan soldiers, who had formed part of an ambuscade in the forest, and when discovered, as they would neither descend nor surrender, but fired at our party, were shot in their high perch.

At Lingtu our great climb is over. The almost level track beyond this leads over the undulating downs of a flat ridge past coppices of rhododendron bushes to the frontier post of Gnatong, on an old moraine with its glacier lake set amongst black pine forest. Snow began to fall ere we sighted Gnatong, the first snow-storm that the majority of our Indian troops had ever seen, and fierce gusts of chill wind swept over our track, already dangerously slippery with old frozen snow. Benumbed and blue we all were when we reached Gnatong, 12,030 feet above the sea-level, on the 5th December 1903. But in the shelter of the old wooden barracks, and refreshed by a hot cup of tea, we all, Indians and every one else, soon forgot our discomforts before a blazing log-fire.

At Gnatong a halt was made for a few days to allow all the troops to concentrate for the advance in force to the Jelep Pass, 10 miles distant. This has hitherto been the highest cantonment of any civilised Power. The old barracks, built by the Derbyshire regiment in 1888, and afterwards occupied by the Connaught Rangers, have been mostly burned down or become dilapidated since this outpost was abandoned in 1895. They are now fast being repaired, and new sheds being run up of pinewood from the forest near at hand.

The scenery here is very grand, and even now at this inclement season is full of colour, although wanting its bright carpet of alpine flowers. The lake is a great resource in itself for boating in summer and skating in winter under the dark pine trees silhouetted against the sky. The snow views towards the south are exceptionally wide and grand, far more extensive than the views from Darjeeling. From this greater elevation Kanchenjanga with its glaciers seems much more massive, as also does the distant shoulder of the Everest range beyond. From here one can realise how this stupendous projecting mass of the Himalayas should so disturb the symmetry of the earth's attraction as to pull the sea-level in the Bay of Bengal some distance up its sides, so that in sailing to Calcutta you sail somewhat up hill! Since I unearthed this interesting subject in 1899[1] I am glad to see that my remarks have induced the Survey of India to take up the question and institute observations to determine the exact amount of this disturbance.

It must also be gratifying to all interested in the identification of the peaks of the highest mountains in the world to notice that another Survey officer (Captain Wood, R.E.) has just been deputed to Nepal to report upon another question regarding these mountains to which I drew attention at the same time, namely, the proper name of Mount Everest, and the impossibility that this king of mountains could, as generally believed, be the peak called "Gaurisankar" seen from Kathmandu in Nepal. The great peaks of the Himalayas were at first measured by the Survey officers many miles off, 70 to 100 or more miles, from points in the Indian plains below, where their native names were usually unknown. When the peak, now known as "Everest," was first measured in 1854, and was thus ascertained to be the highest known summit on the globe, it was called "Peak XV" in ignorance of its native name, and afterwards was christened "Everest" in honour of the name of the Surveyor-General of India

[1] *Among the Himalayas*, pp. 34 and 432.

who had instituted the survey of the Himalayas, which had led to the discovery of this surpassing summit of the earth's surface. The then Resident in Nepal, Mr Hodgson, informed the Royal Geographical Society that this peak was seen from Kathmandu, where it was called "Devadhunga" by the Nepalese; whilst the Schlagintweit brothers, in 1862, also declaring that it was visible from Kathmandu, alleged that it was the "Gaurisankar" of the Nepalese. This latter name was generally accepted and printed on the continental maps. In 1898, in bringing forward evidence to prove that Everest was not visible from Kathmandu, I showed[1] that this giant peak was worshipped by the Tibetans, who paint its portrait as a picture-map, and call it "Jomo Kangkar," or the "White Lady of the Glaciers," and that its outer glacier-passes are called "Lapchi Kang." As a result of his observations, Captain Wood now reports[2] that: "The name Gaurisankar is given by the officials of Kathmandu to Survey Peak XX," which is about 78 miles distant from their city, and not in the Everest group at all; whereas Mount Everest, which is Survey Peak XV, is not visible from Kathmandu, and from the Kaulia range several miles above that place it "is an insignificant point just visible in a gap in the main range." This is as I had anticipated.

On the 10th December 1903, all our troops having arrived at Gnatong, and six days' provisions having been lifted up thus high, it was ordered that the column escorting the Mission should start the following morning to cross the Jelep Pass into the Chumbi Valley, and so complete the first stage of our invasion of Tibet.

[1] *Among the Himalayas*, p. 345; and *Geog. Jour.*, p. 564, etc., 1898.
[2] Calcutta, 1904.

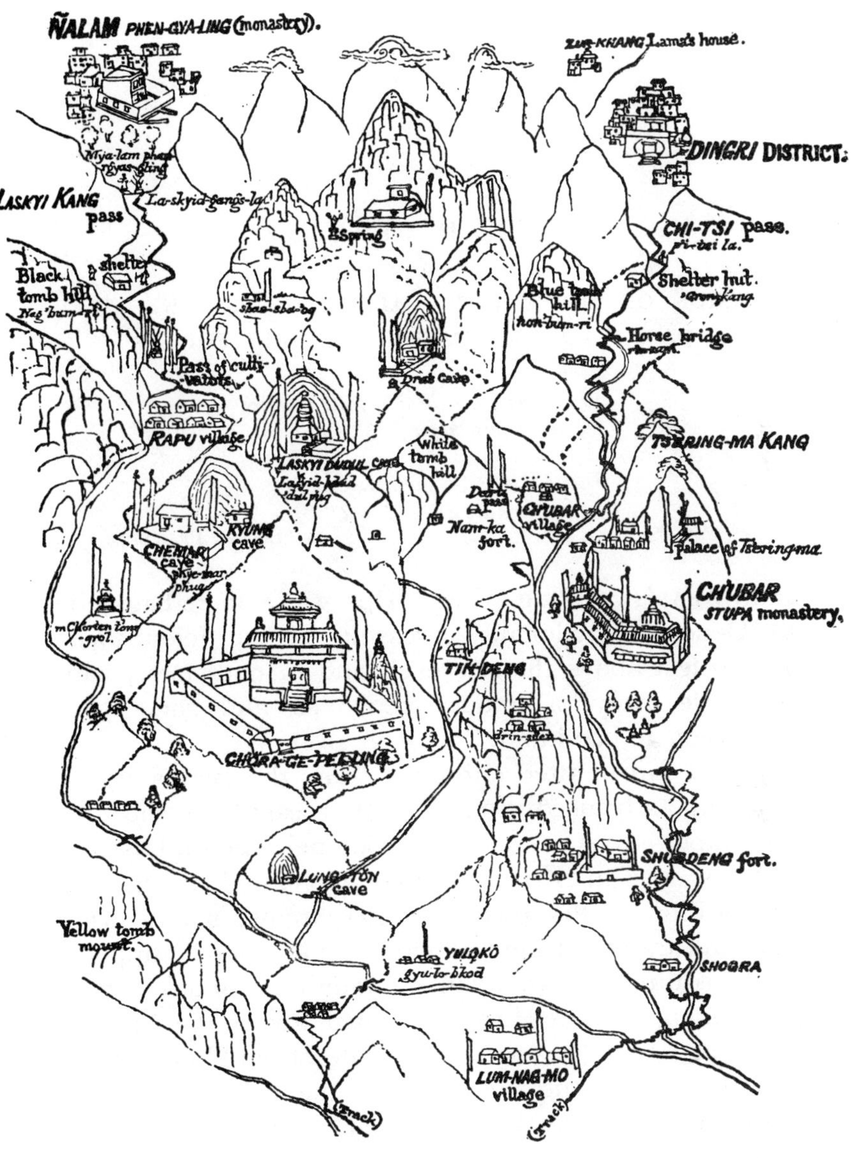

PICTURE-MAP OF MOUNT EVEREST.

From a Tibetan Drawing.

CHAPTER V.

INVASION OF THE CHUMBI VALLEY ACROSS THE JELEP PASS AND OCCUPATION OF PHARI FORT.

"*India will be ruined by false scruples,*
Tibet by false hopes."

. . . .

"*Words are mere bubbles of water,*
But deeds are drops of gold."

— TIBETAN PROVERBS.

HANNIBAL'S crossing of the Alps was a mere bagatelle to General Macdonald's crossing of the Jelep Pass, 14,390 feet above the sea-level, and in midwinter, with his little army of about 3000 men and some 7000 followers, 10,000 in all.

This force, after climbing from the plains up to Gnatong, advanced from the latter camp on the 11th December 1903, escorting Colonel Younghusband and his mission Staff, each man carrying his own food in addition to his own full accoutrements and load; and the transport department carrying food supplies, camp equipment, abundant ammunition, and a supply of cooking firewood, as we halted above the limit of trees, at *Kuphu* (13,200 feet), 5 miles from Gnatong and 4 miles below the pass. Here the cold during the night fell to minus 2° Fahrenheit, or 34° F. below the freezing-point.

Early next morning we advanced guardedly up to the Jelep Pass, as it was reported that the Tibetans would probably dispute our crossing; but no opposition was offered here, for the reason, as it afterwards transpired, that the Tibetan troops were still encamped in front of our small dummy decoy escort at Khamba Jong, and were unaware of our approach by this route, the whole movement across these strongly defensive positions having been kept profoundly secret by General Macdonald. Even without any human opposition, the crossing of this formidable pass in the rarefied air and cold of such a high elevation was extremely trying to everyone, man and beast. Our column, winding like a snake up the steep zigzag track to the pass, was over 4 miles long, and seemed to crawl along up amongst the bleak black rocks almost at a snail's pace, as everyone, oppressed by the rarefied air, had to stop for breath every few yards. Scarcely anyone, even those who rode most of the way, escaped having aching temples and eyeballs; many suffered from actual mountain sickness, and several of the transport animals succumbed on the roadside. A good deal of the delay was due to frequent halts to readjust fallen loads. Fortunately there was no snow, and very little wind.

Our swift-winged link of communication with the world below us, namely the field telegraph-wire, kept advancing with us in such rapid strides that the line of telegraph-posts reached the top almost as soon as we did.

On gaining the summit of the pass, which is a knife-edge in a narrow cleft through the great mountain spur thrown off by the main chain of the Himalayas towards the Indian plains, we found it was swept by a merciless icy blast, which cut painfully like a knife, snatched away our breath, and pierced through our thickest garments as if they were mere gauze. This made it impossible to stand on the top for more than an instant. In that instant we caught a glimpse of a sea of wild hill-tops in front of us, dashed here and there with snow, above which towered far on our left the graceful horn of Chumolhari; and from our feet a stony track sank rapidly down into a deep ravine of dark pine-trees far below us, in which the Kargyu monastery seemed a mere white speck. Diving down this slope, we got out of the wind almost immediately, and then sliding and slipping down the loose shoot of frost-splintered rocks which here formed our track, along which the heavily-laden coolies stumbled foot-sore and weary and bruised by the rocks, we passed a small frozen lake of green ice; thence descended some 2000 feet more, and across frozen side-torrents, now solid ice, till we reached the black pine-forest. Here on the banks of the half-frozen rivulet we encamped on a springy bed of pine-needles amongst fallen pine-trunks, which latter were soon converted into welcome log-fires, and afforded us a hot cup of tea until our baggage animals came up and were unloaded and tents pitched, by which time it was getting dark.

Just then the fact that we had entered a part of the Celestial Empire was vividly brought home to us by the appearance of a procession of Chinese soldiers coming up the valley escorting some dignitaries, each of whom had a huge umbrella of honour carried over him. These were the Chinese mandarins, and the Tibetan governor of the Chumbi Valley, who, having heard of our advance, had come to ask Colonel Young-husband to go back with all our force. They were of course told that that was now impossible; whereupon they quietly disappeared down the glen into the darkness.

Early next morning, the 13th December, we were all up and off by daybreak from this camp (Langram, 12,100 feet) in eager hopes of seeing the long-looked-for Chumbi Valley. The night's rest had rid everyone of headache. The air was deliciously crisp and dry, the temperature during the night having fallen to

TIBETAN OFFICIALS OF YATUNG.

Dargyä.

CHINESE BLOCK-WALL AT CHORTEN KARPO, CHUMBI.

22° F. or 10 degrees below freezing. Resuming our descent, the rough track wound steeply down through a forest of silver firs, crossing many frozen hill torrents which were now sloping sheets of solid ice, which, filling up the hollows, formed literal "death-slides" where the mules and baggage animals slid at every step. In this northern shade everything was frozen up, and no signs of life were anywhere except an occasional flight of snow-pigeons bound for some sunny thawing spot. Descending further, the sunshine became less chilly, and we reached in a clearing in the forest the much discussed and forlorn "trade-mart" of Yatung.[1] It lies landlocked in the chill bottom of this narrow gorge, shut in by high hills, an impossible site for a trade-mart, and, as we have seen, it was used by the Chinese to check trade from entering Tibet, instead of encouraging it; and they employed as Tibetan representative an outlaw and notorious criminal from Darjeeling named Dargye (see photo attached).

The gate in the Chinese block-wall, that was built here as a barrier across the valley, had been left open, but just as Colonel Younghusband was entering it a Chinese soldier rushed forward and seized his horse, and there followed a little altercation. The Tibetan governor of the Chumbi Valley, who, from his residence at the castle of Phari is styled the Phari Depön, a big, lusty, well-bred youngish man, of a good family at Gyantse called Kyi-bu, came forward and urged our Commissioner to wait here for two or three weeks until he could write to Lhasa and get back a reply from the Grand Lama. The Chinese officers supported him by declaring that they had just received a letter from the Amban, stating that he would be arriving at Yatung very soon. In reply, Colonel Younghusband

[1] Its proper name, as it is called by the Tibetans, is "Na-dong," or "The Ear," probably with reference to its being an outpost for the hearsay intelligence of frontier news.

said that it was impossible to discuss matters at this place, or with anyone but the proper representative persons. Then these crestfallen Tibetan and Chinese officials retorted that as they had formally protested against our advance, they could do no more in view of our overwhelming force.

After this theatrical performance, when our force began to stream through the narrow gate in the barrier wall, Colonel Younghusband and his Staff were invited to a sumptuous lunch by the hospitable resident officer of the Chinese Customs post here, Captain Parr, for this place is technically one of the treaty ports of China. When the European dishes had been discussed, Chinese delicacies — shark's fins, birds'-nests soup, putrid black eggs, etc.—were brought in, and we were then joined by the two Chinese mandarins and the Tibetan governor, who were duly introduced, and with whom we began on the choice Chinese morsels — which mercifully it was not rigorous etiquette that we should eat — and drank healths all round, clinking glasses, and smiling in the most friendly way. The Tibetan governor wore in his left ear a gold earring, 4 inches long (see photo, p. 80), jewelled with pearls, and a long pendant of turquoise. He retired rapidly up the valley to his fort at Phari immediately after we left. The little cottage of exile in this wilderness now occupied by Captain Parr possessed for me a personal interest, as it was built, in 1894, for a British resident officer, an appointment intended for me, when at that time high hopes were still entertained of the trading possibilities of Yatung.

Tracking on down the ravine from Yatung for 2 miles, we emerged at the flourishing village of Rinchengang on to the famous Chumbi Valley. This slice of Tibet, wedged in between Sikhim and Bhotan, lies on the southern slopes of the Himalayas, like

Sikhim itself, so geographically it is outside Tibet proper.

The charming valley, here about 9530 feet above the sea-level, is truly alpine, recalling the beautiful valleys of upper Kashmir. Craggy mountains rise on either side into jagged snow-streaked peaks banded by dark pines, and between, the clear green waters of the Mo river wind noisily in their shingly bed through grassy meadows and fields. The meadow here is a quarter of a mile broad, and its turfy terraces, sprinkled with the frosted remains of last year's wild-flowers—primulas, anemones, wood-sorrel, celandines, wild strawberries—are dotted freely over with fine large houses, two- and three-storeyed in the Swiss chalet style, with widely-projecting eaves and wooden balconies carved and gaudily painted.

The village of Rinchengang consists of about forty of these handsome houses, much superior to any native house in Sikhim or even at Darjeeling. They are closely clustered between narrow lanes, and all are picked out in bright colours, giving an air of prosperity and comfort.

Crowds of the excited inhabitants, including many red-robed monks, stood by on the roadside, staring in open-mouthed astonishment at our invasion of their valley. Although overawed by the strength of our force, their demeanour could not be called oppressively respectful. They did not, for instance, put out their tongues, the respectful salutation of these parts, nor did any even salaam; but we took no notice of this want of civility. These people are the middlemen traders between the Tibetans of the plateau above Phari on the one hand, and the Darjeeling and Calcutta markets on the other, and having a monopoly of this carrying trade (see p. 477), they are not overjoyed to see a mission which avowedly is going to establish traffic direct with Phari and the upper Tibetan plateau, and so destroy their monopoly. They dress generally like the Tibetans at Darjeeling. They are not pure Tibetans, but a blend evidently with the Bhotanese, and they call themselves "*Tomo*," after their name for the valley. There are also some pure Bhotanese from the adjoining valley[1] on the east.

Fortunately, our entry did not cause any general panic. A few had run away, taking their women and valuables; but the great majority remained, and they began at once to bring into camp large quantities of corn, fodder, and other supplies, for which they were well paid in rupees. To secure their goodwill all our men received the strictest injunctions from the General not to molest the village in any way, under the severest penalties, for as the Tibetan proverb says, "To get milk and eggs you must not frighten the cow and hen."

Next day (14th December) a reconnoitring party having reported that the road was clear, we marched up the valley, to the village of Chumbi, which has given the valley the name by which it is known to Europeans, though its natives call it "*To-mo*," or "The Wheat Country," evidently in contrast to the adjoining land of Sikhim, which the Tibetans call "The Rice Country."

This was a delightful march along the river-bank by a good and almost level road, through magnificent scenery. Every turn of the river revealed ever-changing pictures, with peeps of snowy peaks, both up and down the valley, beyond the variegated masses of birch and pine. Our road at first was like a country lane hedged in from the river by clumps of willow trees, wild-rose and red-currant bushes, which fringe the crystal waters of the Mo as they rush over pebbly strands, or narrow into deep green pools, the haunt of trout, or swirl in white foam around the great bleached boulders of pink granite or gneiss fallen from the cliffs

[1] Ha-pa.

VILLAGERS OF CHUMBI.
The bare-headed figure in the foreground is the Bhotanese chief, Ugyen Kazi.

LINGMO PLAIN, CHUMBI.

UPPER CHUMBI.
(Note the Tibetan Saddle.)

above, or split into two arms to encircle islets of alder and pine.

In the fields, walled off by stone dykes, and now bare of their crops of wheat, barley, potatoes, turnips, etc., flocks of finches and red-legged crows were foraging, with larks overhead whose joyous notes awoke memories of home; flights of snow-pigeons shot swiftly by; whilst the bark of a silver fox on the hillside suggested pheasants and other game in the uplands.

Underneath the Kargyu monastery, perched on a cliff against the sky-line about a mile away, our road led past several watermills for grinding corn. By the roadside were many sacred cairns, or "*chortens*," solid domed funereal monuments (see photo, p. 231) sometimes enshrining the relics of departed saints; also *mandongs*[1] or short dykes of stone or squat pillars of masonry faced by carved stones bearing the mystic legend of the Grand Lama, "*Om! ma-ni pad-me Hung!*" each syllable painted in a different colour, and bordered by the tall poles of the "Prayer-flags," which are the favourite perches of redstarts and hoopoes. At some of these villagers occasionally were seen devoutly circumambulating the holy cairn, twirling their prayer-wheels and droning out the mystic formula under the flags which flutter in the breeze.

These prayer-flags are luck-compelling talismans. They are called "Dragon-horses," and bear in their centre the figure of a horse with the mystic "Jewel" on its back, and surrounding it are spells which combine Indian Buddhist mysticism with Chinese myth, and are intended to invoke the aid of the most favourite divinities of the Lamas upon the person who offers the flag and whose name or year of birth is generally inscribed thereon. The divinities invoked are (1) He who conveys wisdom (*Manjusri*); (2) He

[1] Literally "faced with the *Mani* legend."

who saves from hell and fears (*Avalokita* incarnate in the Dalai Lama); (3) He who saves from accident and wounds (*Vajrapani*); (4) He who cleanses the soul from sin (*Vajrasatwa*); and (5) He who confers long life

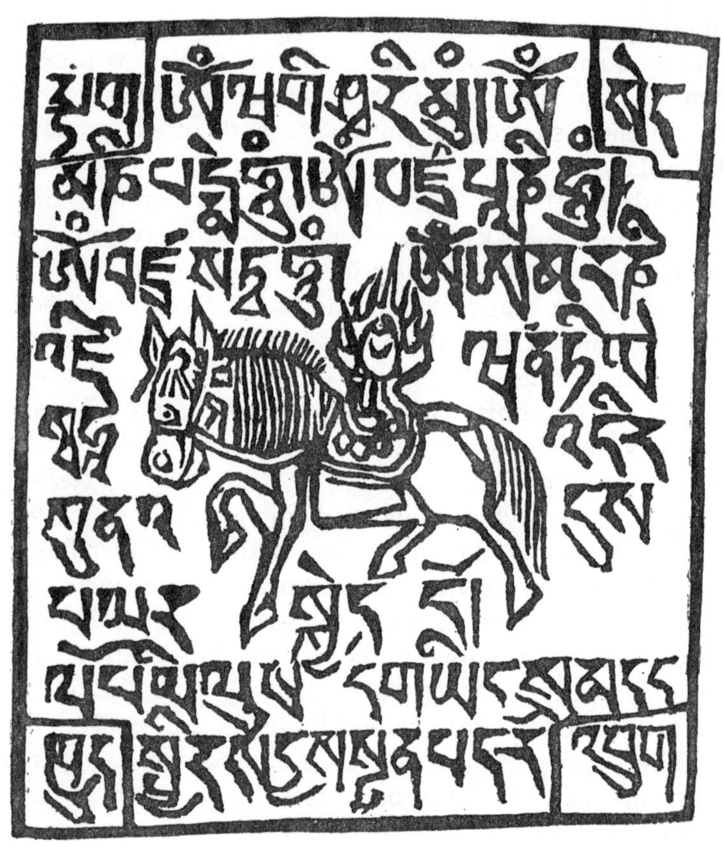

PRAYER-FLAG.

(*Amitayus*). I reproduce here one of these "flags," and give a translation of it.

A turn of the road, where a rocky spur dips sheer into the river, brings into view the pretty village of Byema,[1] or "The Sandy," nestling on the sandy bank

[1] Sometimes pronounced "Chema."

of a torrent from the rugged glen above. Its houses, with their finely carved and painted beams, are quite the most artistic in the whole valley. Beyond this rocky point the gorge opens out again, and here we met a party of Chinese officials and soldiers, the latter in yellow blouses emblazoned on the back with three large Chinese letters in black, all hurrying down the valley. Just beyond this, we come upon the village of these

TIGER. **LION.**

"Hail! *Wagishwari mum!*[1]
Hail! to the Jewel in the Lotus! *Hung!*[2]
Hail! to the holder of the *Dorje* (or thunderbolt)! *Hung!*[3]
Hail! to the Diamond Souled one![4]
Hail! *Amarahnihdsiwantiye swahdh!*

[The above is in Sanscrit; now follows in Tibetan.]

Here! Let the above entire collection [of deities whose spells have been given] prosper . . . [here is inserted the year of birth of the individual], and also prosper—
the *Body* (*i.e.*, to save from sickness),
the *Speech* (*i.e.*, to give victories in disputes),
and the *Mind* (*i.e.*, to obtain all desires);
of this year holder [above specified]
and may Buddha's doctrine prosper!"

PHŒNIX. **DRAGON.**

TRANSLATION OF PRAYER-FLAG.

people, a bit of real China-land transplanted thus far west. Entering the gateway under the Chinese tablet, bordered by ferocious leering dragons, you are in a truly Chinese street. On either side are the shops with their swinging signboards, on the window-sills are neat flower-pots with a marigold, daisy, or balsam in bloom, an unexpected luxury in mid-winter; and the fostering care bestowed by the Chinese on such things,

[1] Spell of Manjusri.
[2] Avalokita's spell.
[3] Vajrapani's.
[4] Vajrasatwa's.

and on their caged song-birds, cannot fail to have some civilising effect upon the wild Tibetans. Inside the shops, behind the counters, are the pigtailed shopkeepers, placidly smoking their opium-pipes beside a teapot and saucer. In the street in front of the Courthouse or *Yamen* little baby John Chinamen are playing about with their Tibetan mothers dressed in celestial costume. A few lantern-posts stand up like dove-cots. Even the unwholesome lean pigs are here, routing amongst the garbage and scurrying off at our approach. Many celestials find here a last resting-place; for outside the village a top-heavy arch covered with inscriptions bestrides the entrance to their small cemetery with its votive tablets. This post is said to have been established since the treaty of 1893, for the express purpose of blocking trade and neutralising that treaty. Some of the Chinese officials have a quiet dignified appearance. They look at the Tibetans with unconcealed contempt, and at us Western Barbarians quite uninterestedly, as if our entry was an everyday occurrence and in no way concerned them.

Above this village the hills approach on either side and give the valley a bare rocky look for about a mile, till we cross a cliff by a solid stone embankment of remarkably well-built masonry, when the ravine again opens out at the foot of a prettily wooded glen, round the bend of which stands up boldly the Sikhim Raja's old summer palace in his private estate ot Chumbi, or "The Bend of the Waters," in an amphitheatre of receding hills.

This palace is a great square, three-storeyed house of stone, surmounted by a glittering gilt cupola, and overtopping the dwellings of the Raja's serfs, some twenty houses, which cluster round it. It is in a dilapidated state, having been deserted since 1892, when the Raja, on his recapture, was forbidden to come here, in order to stop intrigues with the Tibetans, of which this had been a hot-bed. Some remains of good frescoes cover the walls of certain of the rooms, and Chinese influence is seen in the framework of the papered windows. In the small chapel I found a set of the Tibetan translation of the Indian Buddhist scriptures[1] in a hundred bulky volumes. The watch-dogs chained up at the doors of the houses gave us a fierce reception. They are huge Tibetan mastiffs—"the mastiff dogs" of which Marco Polo writes, "as big as donkeys, which are capital at seizing wild beasts."[2]

Strategically, Chumbi was declared by the General to be unsuitable for the headquarters post of this valley; so a halt was made for a day, and an exploring party ascended the valley for some miles in search of a better site. A more defensible spot was found a mile and a half higher up, at the junction of the Khangbu Valley with this one. This position, selected 9780 feet above the sea level, was christened "New Chumbi," and we moved there the following day, crossing to the left bank by a fine cantilever bridge, with a guard-house at one end. Below our camp is the pretty village of Eusaka, amidst willows and pines, and beyond it the small monastery of Bakcham on a terrace above the river; and towering nearly 7000 feet above it on the west, is the Tangkar Pass, which after Hooker I was the first European to visit. The defect of the spot as a permanent camp (as it is to be the headquarters of the Civil officer of the Mission, Mr E. Walsh, who has been deputed to the charge of this newly occupied or annexed district) is that it is so windy and overshadowed by high cliffy ridges that it receives very little sun in the winter-time.

This new station of Chumbi, however, was not General Macdonald's objective, but the fort of Phari, 28 miles higher up, at the apex of the horse-shoe

[1] *Kahgyur.* [2] Yule's edition, ii. 41.

basin of the Mo river, on the edge of the great plain of Tibet proper, and commanding the traffic of the Chumbi valley route. For the speedy occupation of the Phari fort, a flying column of 800 rifles, with Maxims and 4 guns, was got ready to start within two days, so soon as the six days' provisions necessary for this enterprise had been hurried up from the Indian plains, for we were at present forced literally to live from hand to mouth.

When the timid Sikhimese coolies, the Lepchas and Bhotiyas, heard that a move up the valley to the dreaded Tibetan stronghold was about to take place, they were so terror-struck that they deserted during the night, almost to a man, under their headman, the grandson of that "mad minister" who had imprisoned Dr Hooker, and who now had been given this opportunity of retrieving the lost character of his family by assisting the British Government; but he proved hopelessly disloyal at the very outset. It is quite remarkable to see how terribly overawed all these semi-savage border tribes are at the mere mention of the word Tibetans. In their silly fear they thought that we should all be annihilated by the Tibetans, notwithstanding that many of these men have lived at Darjeeling for years, and have even visited Calcutta, where they should have been impressed by our superior strength. But they are not impressed by it. Their wholesale desertion when barely outside their own frontier compels us to reconsider the too favourable character which we are apt to give them on seeing them in their own forests. They lose heart immediately they leave their jungle home a few miles behind, and they now have proved themselves hopelessly untrustworthy for work even a short distance outside their own narrow zone of the lower forests. It was this radical defect of character which compelled Mr White in despair to give them up in his attempt to open Sikhim, and to import plodding Nepalese for the work in their stead; so if these more aboriginal Buddhist natives of Sikhim are now being swamped in their own country by immigrated Hindus from Nepal, they have themselves and their own effeteness only to blame for it.

The Phari flying column left Chumbi on the 18th December, the second day after our arrival there. The upper valley of the Mo, through which we were now threading our way, had never before been seen by European eyes. It was very picturesque but too steep and rocky for cultivation, except in the alluvial flats below the finely variegated forest, above which, in the upland pastures, yaks were grazing. At the third mile, where an almost vertical cliff about 1000 feet high, "The Vulture's Fort" (Gab-jong), juts into the river-bed and bends the valley round at right angles, contracting it to a narrow gorge and making it a position of enormous natural strength, the Chinese have built another barrier wall across the valley, blocking the passage most effectually. The only path is through a gateway in the rampart, and a mere handful of determined riflemen on the cliffs could annihilate a whole column. Commanding this wall, on a terrace above it, is a fortified post for the Chinese troops, who, to the number of about a hundred, are here under the command of a Chinese colonel, whilst Tibetans man the Vulture's Fort across the river. Fortunately they had taken the precaution of leaving the gate in the wall open for us. Had this place been held against us, it could not have been stormed without the loss of many lives on our side.

A steeper climb over a rocky track for a mile more brought us to the large flourishing village of Galingk'a (10,800 feet), on a sunny terrace surrounded by fertile fields. The headman of the village came out and respectfully greeted the General, doffing his hat and putting out his tongue in his most polite way, and presenting a ceremonial silk scarf.[1] From here no less than five monasteries[2] are visible across the valley mostly perched eyrie-like on almost inaccessible spots 1000 to 4000 feet above the river-bed.

Now we had to zigzag up the face of a mighty landslip, fallen from the mountain on our left, which some few hundred years ago blocked the valley, forming a dam about 1000 feet high, over whose remains the river still tumbles in a series of cascades. On reaching the top, therefore, I was almost prepared to see the magnificent plain which then burst into view. The vast landslip had dammed the waters of the upper valley into a great lake, which in course of time had become silted up by the mud deposited from its torrent-feeders, until it formed the present wide grassy meadow, flat like a billiard-table, and about 3 miles long by half a mile broad, through which the limpid stream, unfrozen except at its margins, winds silently in curving links, narrowing into turquoise pools, where the speckled trout can be seen even at this winter season. In the shallower pools a few wild duck and other water-fowl are wading. Some startled blood-pheasants and tragopan disturbed in their wanderings escaped into the open pine-woods encircling the meadow, where the great stately stag of Chumbi, the "*Shao*," has his home.

In this restful meadow of Lingmo, which combines the beauties of the Alps with the grandeur of the Himalayas, we encamped on the green sward amid the scent of the pines at an elevation of 11,200 feet above the sea, where, sheltered by the encircling pine-

[1] The scarf is about a yard long and is called *Khatag*. No Tibetan, however poor, would dream of approaching a big man for a request, or paying a visit without one. They are also used to envelop letters.

[2] The most conspicuous is "The White-faced" (*Dong-Kar*).

clad hills, which rose up boldly into graceful snow-peaks, it was much warmer than at Chumbi, nearly 2000 feet below us. I felt at once that this beautiful meadow seemed destined in the near future to be a great sanitarium for Bengal. Its delightfully crisp and exhilarating air and beautiful surroundings fit it to be an Indian Nordrach for the open-air treatment of consumption, so alarmingly on the increase in India. In this belief, I went around and selected sites for hotels and hydropathic establishments, with graduated exercises in walking and climbing through the woods above the golf-links in this delicious alpine air. The beauties of its restful glades are worthy of being idealised by brush, pen and song.

Next day's track was about the worst possible. It led over great masses of sharp-cornered rocks which bruised the feet and bodies of both men and the struggling animals. It also took us over the slippery bergs of ice on the edges of the frozen streams. The valley now became very bold and wild; great over-hanging naked cliffs of blackened granite swept up in unbroken beetling masses for 1000 feet or more, on each side of the narrowed gorge, meeting frown with frown. The trees, now limited to thin fringes in the ledges, became more and more stunted, and finally ceased at an elevation of 13,350 feet, the silver birch, creeping above the pine, and shrubby rhododendron some few hundred feet higher, till we emerged from the rugged ravines on to the open, bare, wind-swept uplands, furrowed into bright red and ochrey yellow and purple streaks from the shaly formation of the Tibetan plateau, which surges thus far down this valley. A trudge over these undulating grassy slopes for about a mile more brought us to the bleak frozen plain of Do-t'ak, or "The Rocky Stones," about a mile long by a quarter of a mile broad, where we encamped amidst the frosted stems of deadly aconite, opposite a frozen waterfall, over 100 feet high, which King Frost had made solid from top to bottom in a twinkling.

This icy plain was bitterly cold beyond all belief. The sun had just dipped behind the hills, and the cold even then, at 4 P.M., was the intensest we had yet experienced in the daytime; already it was minus 11° Fahrenheit, or 43° F. of frost, and in the icy wind which then sprang up it became positively painful. Our tents did not arrive till nearly dark, and the supply of firewood we brought with us, owing to want of transport, was barely sufficient to warm a little food, and left none to warm us. The terrible intensity and penetration of the cold of this wind was excruciating; it seemed as bitter in our tents as outside; our felt boots gave no warmth to our benumbed feet, and none of us, shivering as we were in our sheepskins, could sleep during that awful night. The poor chilled troops and followers, huddled cowering together for warmth in their tents, kept up around us a chorus of coughs and sneezes till day broke. It was a marvel that no one died, except a few of the mules, and that there were so few cases of frostbite. At last the day dawned in this arctic region, the wind died down, and we began to venture out in the sunlight. A comical sight we were, as, wrapped up in our furs with livid blue faces, we stamped about for warmth, our breath falling in snowflakes, or frozen into long icicles on our moustaches and beards —for everybody had by this time grown a beard, or tried to grow one, as a protection against the cold.

No better testimony to the paralysing intensity of the cold could be had than the effect it had on our hardiest sportsmen. When at daybreak it was discovered that the cold had driven down a herd of wild blue sheep near to our camp, even this exciting news failed to interest our keenest sportsmen, who

UPPER CHUMBI.

PHARI FORT.

OUTSIDE THE WALLS OF PHARI FORT.

ordinarily would climb 4000 feet on the mere chance of sighting this game.

In the reviving sun, we soon forgot the misery we had suffered during that awful night, and struck camp and started off again up the valley. The pleasures of this nomadic life, however, did not seem to appeal to our Asiatic fellow-travellers, though they plodded on faithfully and uncomplainingly. There was very little more climbing in store for us. Winding ahead three miles through the bare hills above the frozen rivulet, we arrived at the edge of the plain of Phari at the ford of Khangbu (Khangbu-rab), and from here our progress became quite easy. The great plateau of Tibet throws a wave into the head of this valley to form the plain of Phari. On the grassy open downs of this plain, about 3 miles broad, our long winding thread of a column massed up into a broad front, with the mounted infantry a mile off on either flank. In this order our little army advanced across the plain, bounded on either side by round-topped bare hills, above which towered, only about 12 miles away, the snow-capped chaste Chumolhari,[1] or "The Mountain of the Goddess Lady," which lifts her horn in the angle of meeting of the three countries of Tibet, Bhotan, and Chumbi. On the plain, several gazelles (*Ga-wa*) were quietly grazing within shooting distance, but were safe from us, as no shooting was allowed on the march; and on the hills a glimpse was got of the wild blue sheep (*Barhal*, or, as the Tibetans call them, *Na-wa*). A good deal of this plain is a peat-bog, yet, strange to say, the people, although under great privations for want of fuel, do not use the peat for this purpose. Our track was crossed by several broad frozen streams coming down from the low hills, the ice of which is so thick as to bear our weights, and also the laden animals.

[1] Properly "Jo-mo-lha-ri."

Phari fort loomed suddenly into view about 4 miles off on turning a corner of the plain. It seemed to be nestling at the very foot of the great white peak of Chumolhari, with the black huts of the town clustering round it; and on our right was the low pass from Bhotan adown which had come, a century or more ago, Bogle, and Turner, and Manning; so that now we had struck a track over which Europeans had been before us, though long ago.

As we approached Phari we could see that there was great commotion amongst the people, who were buzzing about like bees, and a deputation of the towns-folk came out to meet General Macdonald and begged him not to enter the fort or the town. Neither the governor, that is our friend of Yatung, the Depöno, nor the two joint magistrates of the fort (*Jong-pön*) came out, however, one of the latter excusing himself on the plea of illness and the other as absent. But when the General considered the occupation of the fort necessary, for military reasons, and after his mounted infantry reported that there were no Tibetan troops in the fort, and two companies of our Goorkhas occupied it, and hoisted the Union Jack on its top-most tower, these *Jong-pöns* made a remarkably quick recovery; for one of them came into our camp almost immediately to pay his respects to the General, who permitted them both to remain in the quarters in the fort, and told them to continue to perform their duties under his protection. Reassured, they at once began sending into camp large quantities of fodder and fuel and a few available provisions, such as turnips, for all of which they received full and prompt payment. The resident Bhotanese commercial agent here[1] seemed especially friendly, and exerted himself in getting in supplies for us. The following day, the 21st December, the Depön, accompanied by the

[1] The Ka-tso Tsong-pön or "Master Merchant."

Chinese colonel, Chao, and the two *Jong-pöns*, paid the General a visit in camp, who explained to them that he had come to prepare the way for the Mission, and they need fear nothing so long as they remained friendly. Colonel Chao volunteered the information that he had received a letter from the Amban saying that he was *starting from Lhasa that day*.

This bloodless victory of General Macdonald was a great achievement. By a swift and secret swoop he was able to seize this great mobilisation centre of the Tibetan troops, with its tons of gunpowder and bullets, without firing a single shot, as all its large garrison were still at Khamba Jong in ignorance of our advance. By this rapid movement we had now got possession of that fortress which dominates the great trade-route to India, and had obtained peaceful possession also of the almost invincible lower ravines, which, if held by the Tibetans against us, could not have been captured without very much bloodshed on both sides. Any idea of retreat, therefore, which our withdrawal from Khamba Jong may have led the Tibetans to entertain, has been much more than dispelled by our rapid reappearance at Phari in greater force than before, with the strong fort of Phari itself also in our hands.

This fortress of Phari looks like a mediæval castle in Europe. It stands upon a hillock about 60 feet high in the middle of the bare mountain-girt plain, and towers up with its turrets over 70 feet above this, in front of the pass into Tibet on the north, over which it keeps watch and ward. It has an appearance of great massiveness and strength owing to the thickness of its stone-built walls, their inward tapering slope, as in the Egyptian style, and the fewness of its windows, though it is freely slit by loopholes.

Inside, when you enter to explore it, it is less imposing. Stepping within the massive gateway, we see the courtyard strewn with old lumber, chain-armour, iron helmets, spears, swords, matchlocks, and miscellaneous rubbish. When passing across the courtyard you enter the main door of the building—the charm is at an end. You feel as if you were down the dark hold of a ship. Steep ricketty ladders of rough-hewn logs lead up and down through mazes of dark narrow passages to malodorous dingy cabins, kitchens, larders, etc., and everywhere the undersized lintels rudely remind your head of their limited door-space. On the ground floor are stored cakes of yak-dung fuel and grain; in the middle storey are the barracks of the troops, with stores of gunpowder and bullets, thrown by us into the river. In this flat is a chapel, with a set of the Tibetan version of the Buddhist Scriptures in 100 volumes, of which the British Museum has not a copy.

On the upper storey is the citadel with the residential rooms of the two joint governors, the *Jong-pöns*[1] and their offices. These were the best rooms in the building, and were occupied afterwards by the officers of our small garrison holding the fort, and by the Head-quarters Staff. The *Jong-pön's* room, in which I was quartered, had its walls decorated with rude frescoes. But even these, the best of all the rooms, are miserably adapted for keeping out the arctic cold of this place. They have no glazed windows, but doors which have to be kept shut to keep out the wind, and usually no chimney whatever. When there is a hole in the roof for the latter purpose, the acrid smoke of the yak fuel, refusing to take advantage of it, fills the room with suffocating fumes, and irritates the eyes insufferably. Even with a small stove of this fuel in the room, the cold was so intense that the thawed ink froze on our pen, boiled eggs crunched in ice-spangles

[1] One is in charge of the eastern half of the district, and the other the western.

GATE OF PHARI FORT.
(14,700 feet above sea-level.)

VACATING PHARI FORT FOR THE BRITISH.
Note the head-dress of the women.

in our teeth, and some kerosene oil which I had brought froze solid and had to be thawed before it could be poured into my lantern. At this great height, on the top of the castle, the wind was terrific, and sweeps down the pass from the tableland and the glaciers of Chumolhari, blowing gales all day long, such as never blew at sea.

How this old fort holds together is a marvel. Many of these high-perched rooms are quite unsafe, owing to the walls being badly cracked, and having even fallen out of the vertical. The unsafest room of the lot had been selected for our messing, when I discovered that it was a death-trap supported 60 feet in the air by a mere thin shell of the inner layer of the wall, bulging and badly cracked, so that the mere vibration of walking across the floor was enough to precipitate us to the bottom. Closer inspection showed that the fort walls are built of two outer shells of stone and mortar, the interval between which is packed with loose stones and mud. That such a badly-built and cracked building continues to stand favours the local statement that earthquakes are unknown in these parts.[1] On the flat roof of the citadel, from whose highest turret flies the British flag, and where a gale is always blowing as on a hurricane-deck, magnificent bird's-eye views are obtained of the surrounding country, completely encircled by snowy peaks, from the jagged "Hill of Heroes" (Pawori) on the northern ranges of Sikhim, round by the snows of Bhotan on the south to the Chumolhari group from the east to the north. The upper parapets and balconies are all of peat-sods pinned together by wooden spikes, so as to lessen the weight of this superstructure, on the ricketty supporting walls. This band of purple peaty turf is bordered below, on its supporting rafters, by a

[1] An earthquake occurred at Tuna, 18 miles north of Phari, in February 1904.

strip of red ochre, which helps to bring out boldly the detailed form of the building, as the rest of the walls are whitewashed.

Before we occupied these rooms an attempt was made to remove some of the accumulated garbage of ages, but it took many days before an army of several hundreds of the villagers, carrying off basketfuls of stuff all day long, made any impression on its dirt.

The date of building of this fort I have as yet been unable to find out with certainty; but it was enlarged, if not rebuilt, in 1792, under Chinese advice, as a defence against the British, when it was alleged that we had assisted the Nepalese in their invasion of Tibet. Previous to this it was called "The Victorious White One";[1] then its name was changed to "The Fort of the Sublime Mountain," or Phag-ri, the Phari of our maps — which is a title of Chumolhari which overtops it as a background. It is kept directly under Lhasa in view of its important relations with India.

The dirty town of Phari consists of about two hundred mean, low-roofed, windowless huts, built of black peat sods cut from the plain, and huddled round under the southern side of the fort, with a population of about two thousand. It is appallingly foul and dirty, possibly the dirtiest and foulest town on the earth. Its benumbed villagers for generations have been throwing all their refuse immediately outside their doors into the streets, where this accumulated dirt of ages has raised the level of the streets so high that the dingy rooms now seem subterranean cellars, entry to which is got by digging steps down through the layers of this garbage. It is indeed a vast barrow in a muck-heap, with an all-pervading foul stench everywhere, the source of the smell often being visible to the eyes.

[1] Gyal-kar.

The people of Phari-the-Foul, this first outpost of real Tibet, are in thorough keeping with the squalor and filth amidst which they live. They are sunk in almost the lowest depths of savagery. They are as inferior to their relatively clean and better-featured near neighbours of the Lower Chumbi Valley as are their wretched hovels to the fine lofty houses of the latter—though it must be said in excuse for the poverty of their dwellings, that there is not here the bountiful supply of wood which makes building easier at lower levels.

The great majority of the inhabitants at the time of our arrival were women, doubtless the wives of the soldiers and militia of the fort, who were still at Khamba Jong, opposing as they imagined our mission there, unaware of our rapid change of front. These women were more like hideous gnomes than human beings, and the men were no better. Clothed in greasy rags and sheepskins, their ugly flat features scourged by the cold and seared by the frost, begrimed and blackened like a chimney-sweep's with the deeply ingrained dirt and smoke of years, they were indeed repulsively hideous. Yet no "lady" in Phari society with any pretensions to good manners, it is said, would be so indiscreet as to wash her face or hands, for she would at once be considered not quite respectable or something worse were she to do so. Despite this repulsive coating of material dirt, both men and women cover themselves with jewellery. The married women wear a wonderful piece of headgear, a large hoop like the framework of a tall crown, suggestive of the Norwegian bride's hat, and set with a wealth of turquoise, coral, etc. No doubt this thick coating of dirt does protect to some extent against the cold, and almost any sacrifice of conventional appearances would be justified could it reduce the suffering inflicted by the cold of this most miserable spot of the earth. Even our own officers after a time, bearded and begrimed, seated around a reeking yak-dung fire, began to acquire an almost Tibetan aspect and complexion. In the distance, sufficiently far off to avoid disenchantment, these women looked picturesque enough as they trooped out carrying wooden pails to draw water or chipped ice from the frozen stream running past our camp. To obtain it they dig a hole in the thick ice and ladle up the water with a wooden cup. Their clumsy, uncouth figures were also seen in camp, where they drove a thriving trade in selling to our men, turnips, dried fish, cheese, butter, and, what was most in demand, basketfuls of cake-fuel.

The trade of these people is to carry merchandise, wool, salt, borax, gold, etc.,[1] from Tibet proper to this place, and exchange these here for imports from India, which they carry back to Tibet. At Phari the exports from Tibet change into the hands of the Chumbi carriers who ply with their mules between here and Darjeeling (109 miles) and Kalimpong (87 miles) for the markets of India. No grain whatever except barley grows on this bleak spot, and that even does not ripen, but only yields seedless ears, so that it can only be used for fodder. The people, therefore, have to obtain their food grain by barter—rice, for the few rich from Bhotan on the south, and barley from the lower-lying parts of Tibet, in the Gyantse Valley on the north; whilst their flocks of sheep and yaks supply them with meat, clothing, and fuel. The revenue of this fort, which is one of the chief Customs barriers in Tibet, is derived mainly from a ten per cent. toll imposed on all goods, both exports and imports, passing this way.

Speaking of crops, I elicited here a local proverb, which runs, "When rice grows at Phari, the foreigners will reach Lhasa." This is of course supposed to

[1] See Appendix No. X.

imply an impossibility, like the Shakespearian reference to the Dunsinane Woods. Nevertheless, in view of the absurdly superstitious nature of the Tibetans, I suggested that capital might be made out of this legend to justify in the eyes of these natives our advance to Lhasa, in the exceptional year of the Wood-Dragon, were our garrison here to cultivate a little rice this year, by forcing it in a box, which was quite possible.

A curious illustration of the monetary value of fuel in this arctic region, where the only available material, namely, yak-dung, is a life necessity, came to light, when, owing to our telegraph wire having been cut near Phari, a fine was inflicted on the town of dried yak-dung fuel, as this was badly required by our troops. A fine of fifteen tons of cakes of this material was imposed, which at local barter rates represented in money about £15 sterling. So effectual was the fine, in this local coinage of the country, that they willingly paid half of it in Indian rupees, to escape parting with this invaluable article, and the line was never cut again. Without this commodity all human life in this barren part of Tibet would be impossible. As it is, the Tibetans seldom warm themselves at fires, but trust to thick clothing and animal food to keep themselves warm, and use fuel only for cooking. The yaks are indeed a god-send in these barren regions. They are never given any food by their owners, but are sent adrift to forage for themselves, yet in return they work as beasts of burden, give milk for butter, and their own flesh for food, and also bestow this indispensable fuel daily. This arrangement recalls the extensive use of a similar article for the same purpose in India, where firewood is scarce, and where its substitute is gratefully called by the Indian peasantry "the gift of the cow" (*go-bar*).

Our troops, encamped on the plain outside the fort

of Phari, spent a miserable existence for two days and nights in the biting icy wind, which blew all day in gales, literally icy dust-storms, full of flying grit and gravel, blinding to the eyes. Phari is notorious for its terrible dust-storms. The cold here was little less than at our frozen camp of Do-ta'k, and even at mid-day the temperature was below the freezing-point, and at night it fell to 41½ degrees below freezing. This dry and terrible cold shrivels up, wrinkles, and chaps the skin and cracks the nails; and it so benumbs the limbs that scarcely anybody could move outside his tent until the sun rose. At Phari we are only twelve marches from Lhasa, and express couriers do the journey in two and a half days.

But Phari, after all, although politically part of Tibet, is not geographically within Tibet at all, but lies on the Indian or southern side of the Himalayas. As our Mission had received orders to proceed without delay to the large market-town of Gyantsé within Tibet, the immediate objective of General Macdonald therefore now became the nearest village within Tibet proper, which was Tuna, on the great plateau, 18 miles distant. To conduct the Mission to Tuna, however, necessitated the immediate return of our flying column down the valley again to Chumbi, in order to save consumption of the precious rations brought with such difficulty so far up the line of communications, and also to hurry up and escort back a store of food from the Indian plains for the advance to Tuna. So leaving the small garrison of 200 Goorkha rifles with all the food we had brought up, except one day's rations to take us back to Chumbi, the General, on the third day after our arrival at Phari, hurried back again to Chumbi, doing this return march in two days. Travelling lightly, and unwilling to suffer again the agonising cold of the frozen camp of Dotha, we scurried past it, down into the tree zone, and soon had blazing camp-fires at Gaut'ang, "The Meadow of Gladness," a name which very well expresses how it gladdens the eye with its delightful green forest, and affords warmth and agreeable shelter to anyone descending as we had done from the cruelly cold and inhospitable uplands.

The following forenoon saw us back in Chumbi, and it was surprising to see how much the track had been improved in these few days by the pioneers and sappers, whose blasting operations now boomed and echoed through the hills.

Back at Chumbi again, the General and Major Bretherton wrestled with the mighty problem of food supplies, for our advance and for the garrison left at Phari and on the road between, as well as for the consumption of the force in the lower valley. This task is immensely more difficult than it would seem at first sight; for all the food for both men and animals of the force, except some of the fodder for the animals, has to be brought up all the way from India, as we have already seen, and by a long line of the most difficult communications, now extended to about twenty marches. This would be a comparatively easy matter, putting aside the difficulties of the track, were transport unlimited, and were it a mere question of carrying a given number of loads from the railway at Silliguri up the mountains, and having them delivered bodily at Chumbi. But the facts are very different. Each of the coolies and the transport animals eats up a great portion of his load as he goes on the way. Thus a coolie on a single stage would eat up by himself a whole load in a month; so that thirty coolies carrying their loads up one stage would deliver only twenty-nine loads to be passed on; and so the loads go on rapidly dwindling at every stage of the journey, until there is comparatively little left to deliver at Chumbi to keep the garrison there in food, let alone the storing of any for our advance. Mules are even worse offenders than coolies in this respect, for a mule eats four times the weight of grain that a coolie does, and only carries twice the load of a coolie.

As it was found that the Jelep Pass route, even when worked to its fullest extent, with continuous lines of coolies and mules threading its difficult track, could not deliver at Chumbi nearly sufficient to provide for our advance, it became necessary to open another pass to supplement it. For this, the Nathu Pass (14,250 feet), a goat-track, 10 miles to the north of the Jelep and over the same ridge, was opened out by Mr White. This tapped the cart-road higher up at Gangtok, and soon brought in nearly as much as the Jelep route, the total of the two amounting to about 40,000 lbs. daily, carried with immense difficulty by coolies and mules and ponies over tracks often wrecked by snow and rain, and at an elevation where any exertion is almost painful.

This transport difficulty brings prominently forward the radical mistake of all these passes through Sikhim to the Chumbi Valley; for the natural and easy way into this valley from India is not through Sikhim at all, but up the lower valley of the Chumbi river from its outlet as the Torsha river, in the plains of Bengal, thus avoiding all passes whatsoever. The very circuitous routes through Sikhim, by which the traveller, after being compelled to climb needlessly more than 14,000 feet over roads constructed at great expense, only to dip down 5000 feet to reach his destination, must inevitably be given up, and their cost lost, in favour of the direct route. The proper ingress to the Chumbi Valley was first pointed out over thirty years ago by Mr (afterwards Sir Ashley) Eden; and when it was afterwards lost sight of and other costly roads continued to be made in the same old wrong direction, with their needless ascents and descents, the necessity for this natural alignment was repeatedly urged by some of those possessed of sufficient local knowledge.

A great step towards the realisation of this project comes as the immediate result of General Macdonald's occupation of Phari fort; for, whilst Phari is the key to the Chumbi Valley, it also commands one of the chief passes from Tibet into Bhotan, that by which Bogle and Manning travelled. No sooner was Phari occupied by us, and our military strength displayed in the Chumbi Valley, than the Bhotanese at once consented to the proposed road running through the narrow strip of their territory which separates the valley from the Indian plains. One of our native surveyors was then sent down the valley, on 27th December 1902, to the Indian plains, and followed by a British officer. Their reports, whilst showing that the existing map of this track is most inaccurate, make it appear that below Posha monastery the river flows between steep but by no means precipitous cliffs, which are not impracticable for the proposed road. Meanwhile another road is being aligned, not up the Chumbi or Torsha Valley, but from an existing railway station at the foot of the hills east of the Tista, whence it will pass up another valley, namely, the Dichu, and cross into the Chumbi Valley over a pass 9000 feet high. There seems to be some strange fatality about the roads into the Chumbi Valley from India. One after another, they are constructed at great expense in a wrong direction, to be inevitably abandoned, and even now the direct one seems still postponed. In any case the new one up the Dichu Valley, although ever so much better than the existing lines, cannot be completed in time to benefit the present expedition in any way.

The delay in aligning the new road up the Chumbi Valley from the Indian plains may also postpone the inevitable railway from India to Chumbi. This small steam-tramway, like the one to Darjeeling, whilst connecting with our new frontier post of Phari, and drawing a paying traffic from the wool, tea, cloth, and other Tibetan imports and exports,[1] should also whisk the passenger or tourist from Calcutta up to Chumbi within about twenty-four hours, through most picturesque river scenery into magnificent alpine country, where, no longer perched on a mountain-top, as in other Himalayan hill-stations, the visitor may wander on the level amongst the mountain streams and wooded glades, drink in the divine air, and enjoy abundant fishing and shooting, or golf on the Lingmo plain, and then be sped away comfortably back to civilisation, all the way by train.

To return to the present. Our occupation of the Chumbi Valley, with the fort of Phari at its head, marks the first stage in the progress of our Mission to Tibet, which fortunately has been accomplished without bloodshed.

[1] See Appendix No. X.

CHAPTER VI.

ADVANCE TO TUNA ON THE TIBETAN PLATEAU, ACROSS THE FORMIDABLE TANG PASS.

"*The goal will not be reached if the right distance be not travelled.*"
—TIBETAN PROVERB.

ENERGETIC transport arrangements had their reward, so that by the 4th January 1904 sufficient stores had been pushed up to Phari by the General to enable the force to advance to Tuna and establish the Mission there, within the threshold of Tibet proper. On that date the Mission, escorted by the General with all his available force, left Chumbi for Tuna.

The track by this time had been so immensely improved by the pioneers that it was now quite a good mule-path the greater part of the way; fresh tracks had been hacked out in the worst places. It was remarkable how the ice had increased in size and in height within the previous fortnight, owing to the rivulets flowing over their frozen surface in the day-time and then freezing up again at night, thus raising their level several feet in these two weeks and flooding the paths with long stretches of slippery ice.

As we were passing the Chinese fort at the "White Cairn" barrier (Chorten Karpo), Colonel Chao, the Chinese commander of the troops in the Chumbi Valley, invited the General and his Staff in for some refreshments. He is a *Tungling*, corresponding to a colonel in our army, and wears the coral button of a mandarin of the second highest grade. He is a courteous old gentleman, and chatted pleasantly about various things. He gave some recent information about Dorjieff in Lhasa, a Chinese courier having just arrived from that city after performing the journey hither in three days. He reported that the Tibetans, relying on Russian support promised by Dorjieff, were openly taunting the Chinese and saying that they now had a greater Power than China upon which to depend for assistance. I handed him my Chinese visiting-card, and mentioned that I had stayed for several months in one of the imperial palaces at Peking, in 1900, which seemed, however, to revive in his mind unpleasant memories of China's late humiliation, so that I immediately changed the subject. Before we left, he stated that he had been superseded in his command here by a major coming from Lhasa, because he had failed to keep us out of Chumbi; and for the same reason the four great Secretaries of State at Lhasa, the Shapés, had all been imprisoned by the irate Dalai Lama; the senior one, my friend the Shata Shapé (see photo, page 48), had been banished to a fort in South-Eastern Tibet,[1] a recognised prison for political offenders, and the Horkang Shapé had committed suicide by jumping into the Kyi river at Lhasa, on hearing his sentence by the Dalai Lama's secret tribunal.

CHINESE VISITING-CARD OF AUTHOR.

The beautiful meadow of Lingmo, where we again encamped, was more wintry-like than before, owing

[1] Sangnak Cho in Tsa-rong.

to the freshly-fallen snow which had crept down its encircling pine-forests to the plain, where it lay in patches. Our ponies, as they went, snatched mouthfuls of the soft snow crystals, and ate them with great relish.

The frozen plain of Do-t'ak was less painfully cold this time, for fortunately no fierce wind blew during the night. But Phari was as before, with its insufferable cold and icy dust-storms blowing all day long.

Great droves of yaks, laden with our stores, were now conspicuous on the plain of Phari. These shaggy, uncouth beasts have somewhat the appearance of small Highland cattle, but with much longer hair, which almost sweeps the ground. The commonest colour is a jet black, with bushy white tail, and a white spot on the forehead. Though looking so clumsy, these animals cross the most slippery frozen streams with the greatest ease, carrying their heavy loads. Most of them were locally hired by our transport department, and their wild Tibetan drivers, as they went, glanced furtively at us, energetically twirled their prayer-wheels, and fingered their beads to neutralise the evil results of working for us, foreign infidels, against the orders of their priest-god at Lhasa. A very few of these yaks were survivors of the 3000 procured for us by the Raja of Nepal several months ago, and of the 500 presented by that prince, amongst which rinderpest and anthrax broke out, killing hundreds daily, until now some two hundred only remained. This Raja of Nepal, Chandra Sham Sher Jang,[1] who succeeded his brother on the latter's death two years ago, has rendered the expedition

[1] He is technically Prime Minister, though bearing the title of Maharajah. The hereditary king, with the title of "Primordial King" (Adiraja), is a mere puppet, and is given no part in the government.

much assistance; he sent several thousands of his peasantry as coolie porters. He also sent several letters to the Dalai Lama, urging him to come to terms with the British; showing how his own relations with the Indian Government had benefited his country, and warning him of the consequences of his obstinate policy. Thus the Dalai Lama has received advice and information from more than one outside source, from Nepal and from Bhotan.

THE RULER OF NEPAL. MAHARAJA CHANDRA SHAM SHER.

At Phari, several high Lhasa and other Tibetan officials had arrived a few days previously, and were living in the town. Amongst them were one of the two Lhasa generals, namely, the Lheding Depön; a commander of troops, called the Honourable Teling, a grandson of the "mad minister" who imprisoned Hooker (see p. 44); the Master of Horse of the Tashi Grand Lama, and three monks representing the three great ruling yellow-cap monasteries of Lhasa, namely, Däpung, Sera, and Gahldan, which are collectively spoken of, from the first syllables of their name, as the "Dän-se-gah-ni" or the "Sen-dä-gah."

As these officials had by means of threats induced the Phari villagers to stop selling us any more supplies of grain, fodder, etc., Captain O'Connor was sent to invite them to come and see the General with

YAKS ON THE SLOPES OF CHUMOLHARI.

TIBETAN GENERALS IN COUNCIL.
The one on the right is the Leding Depön of Lhasa.

BRITISH FLAG CROSSING PASS (15,200 FEET) UNDER CHUMOLHARI PEAK.

CHATSA MONASTERY, PHARI.
(Where Captain Turner's Mission lodged in 1783.)

reference to their interdict. On his entrance he found them all assembled in a room, with the Lhasa General seated on a cushion at the top, and the monks squatting apart by themselves. They all rose and returned his greeting, except the monks, who remained seated and scowled sulkily, and evidently were men of low birth, with coarse repellent features. In reply the Lhasa Depön, or general, said he had no wish to see General Macdonald about supplies, but that he and the Lamas had been deputed from Lhasa to discuss the disputed frontier questions at Yatung, and could only do so there and not here. This Depön (see photo, p. 112) is about thirty-five years of age, tall and stout, with a pleasant, well-bred manner.

Next day, as these Tibetans were still preventing the villagers from selling supplies, General Macdonald sent them an ultimatum that (1) they must come and see him about this stoppage of supplies, and bring a written declaration that they would not interfere with the people selling to us; or (2), if they did not do this, he must request them to quit Phari within three days. In reply, they refused either to come or to write anything, and the monks were especially rude in their snarling and snappish refusal, and used disrespectful language, whilst the others employed the polite honorific forms of expression. As to the notice to quit, they made no reply, but seemed vexed and nonplussed about it; what they decided to do will appear presently. A Chinese major, Li, called on the General, and informed him that he had been sent to supersede Colonel Chao in command of the troops in Chumbi, because the latter had failed to keep us out of the valley.

We left Phari for Tuna on the 7th January, doing the distance of 18 miles in two stages. The first march was only 4 miles along the plain to the small village of Chugya, or "The Pearly White Water," a series of frozen pools and marshes, glancing white in the sun at the foot of the Tang Pass. Our little army, advancing with its broad front of four columns, followed by our 2000 baggage animals, looked most imposing and seemed to fill the plain.

On our way we met a wild-looking Lama, with piercing eyes, long matted locks, and straggling beard flowing in the wind, riding under a battered yellow umbrella, with a single attendant who ran by his side. I recognised him as the same monk who had visited our camp at Chumbi about ten days before, and who introduced himself as a restorer of temples and shrines.[1] In this work he travelled a great deal to collect subscriptions, and frequently saw the Dalai Lama, who was a personal friend of his; so that he wished to take a friendly message to the Dalai in the endeavour to settle our disputed questions. Colonel Younghusband, anxious to avail himself of every means to effect a settlement, took the trouble to inform this wandering monk of our case against Lhasa, and he thereupon set off, promising to convey the information to the Grand Lama in person. Now, however, he was already coming back with some important news, which caused his large eyes to flash with emotion as he asked me excitedly for the secretary to the Mission. I directed him to this officer, to whom he quickly made his way, and looking furtively about to see that he was not overheard, whispered hoarsely, "*War! —War! They mean War!*" After being calmed a little, he explained that pursuing his way to Lhasa he reached the neighbourhood of Gyantsé, but every day's travel only showed the more how the Tibetans

[1] Shik-so-pa is the title of such a person. He is a Bhotanese named Yun-den Norbu, and says he is an incarnation of the Indian hermit Kara.

everywhere were actively preparing for war, so that he returned to give us this news, and warned us that 2500 Tibetan warriors were collected a few miles beyond Tuna.

THE FOUNDER OF LAMAISM. ST. PADMA SAMBHAVA.

During this stage also, I visited the monastery of Chatsa on the flank of Chumolhari, where Turner of Warren Hastings' Mission had lodged one hundred and twenty years before, and passed by Manning a few years later, since which date no European has been here (see photo here). It is a branch of the great Tashilhumpo convent; but I found that its monks were woefully illiterate, and, though professing to be reformed Lamas, that is of the yellow-capped order, they were giving the first place in their most popular temple to a gaudily painted image of the deified wizard priest Lo-pön Rimboché,[1] whom I have shown to be the founder of the earliest form of Lamaism, which is a debased devil-worship rather than Buddhism. Near this monastery I saw a herd of gazelles (*ga-wa*) grazing quietly within gunshot, and started several hares; but all shooting, even for the pot, was as usual strictly forbidden, for military reasons, during our advance. We encamped on a grassy stretch amidst gentians and wild rhubarb. The cold during the night was terrible here; the thermometer fell to minus 25° Fahr. or 57 degrees below freezing, but the chill wind bit worse than the frost.

The ascent of 5 miles to the top of the pass next morning took us about five hours, including occasional halts to recover our breath, though most of us now had become acclimatised and suffered little from distressed breathing. At one of these halts it was discovered that the intense cold had so frozen the Rangoon oil lubricant of the rifle locks that the triggers did not work until rubbed warm, and the Maxims were unworkable until thawed—a serious predicament in case we were attacked here; but this we were not, nor did we see a single soul.

This lofty pass, called the Tang La,[2] or "Clear Pass," from its being so seldom snowed (15,200 feet), was the highest our little army had yet crossed, and nearly as high as the top of Mont Blanc. It is a

[1] Or Padma Sambhava, the "Lotus-born One," figured on p. 115.

[2] Spelt *Dvangs*.

rounded, saddle-like depression in the main axis of the Himalayas, in the chain of the highest peaks, of which one, Chumolhari,[1] lifted her snowy head over 8000 feet above us only a few miles to our right, and seemed to overshadow us. The summit of the pass is marked by a line of cairns; otherwise it would not be easy to see when you had reached the actual top, so very gently curving is the gradient. At the cairns, our Tibetan servants and mule-drivers stopped, and turning towards the sacred Chumolhari, or "Mountain of the Goddess Lady," doffed their hats and reverently placed a stone on the cairn, exclaiming in a shrill voice: "Take! take! [this offering] given to the gods! The gods have conquered [our difficulties for us]! The devils are defeated!" (*Kī! kī! so! so! lha gyal lo! dud pam-bo!*) We, too, shared their thankfulness at having successfully gained the summit, for it was a severe trial of endurance for everyone, both man and beast, and a great triumph for our Indian companions, natives of the plains, to have reached such an altitude.

From this point of view, it was curious to see that our British flag, in passing under Chumolhari, seemed to be reflected on the face of that mountain, which, as seen foreshortened from here, has cross-like ledges in its strata (see photo here).

Turning our eyes from this great mountain, we now see stretching out in front of us, to the north, and only a few hundred yards below us, the great plain of Tibet, the great trans-Himalayan tableland. So we now have crossed the Himalayas to their other side!

The Indians applied the name "Himalayas," or the "Abode of Snow," in a general way to this great belt of snowy mountains which separated their plains of the Ganges from Tibet. The limits of this mountain-chain

[1] Properly Jomolhari.

at either end were not defined, nor can they easily be determined owing to the chain being continuous with that of Afghanistan on the west and of China on the east. Our geographers now restrict the term "Himalayas" to that portion of the range which lies between the gorge of the Indus on the north-west, where the Karakorum Mountains bend into the Hindu Kush, on the one hand (see map, p. 40), and the gorge of the Tsangpo or Dihong river, where it pierces the chain to enter Assam, as the south-eastern extremity on the other. The geologists, however, extend the term to include the parallel range to the east in Tibet, calling that the "Tibetan zone" of the chain; and it consists largely of an old sea-bottom of marine fossiliferous rocks thus raised up with the uplifting of the Himalayas. They restrict the zone of the Himalayas proper to that on which we now stand, the line of the highest peaks restricted to, down to the outer hills up which we have come, composed mainly of crystalline quartz, granite and gneiss in their upper parts and unfossiliferous slates and sedimentary beds of detritus in their lower; whilst they call that parallel range which lies outside the foot of the Himalayas, on the Indian plains, the "Sub-Himalayas," or "Siwaliks," formed by the alluvial deposits from the early Himalayas in the glacial period, which deposits have been pushed southward and elevated into hills by the rising of the main axis to their north. The crumpled inner ends of these strata of the Siwalik hills, consisting of sandstone and a conglomerate of boulders, abounding with the fossil remains of the mastodon and other large mammals, show that the Himalayas rose to their surpassing height so late as the tertiary period of geological time, and that they are still rising, or have only recently ceased to rise.[1]

[1] *The Geology of India*, by R. D. Oldham, pp. 459, etc., for details.

CROSSING THE GREAT PLAIN OF TUNA.

TUNA, WITH CHUMOLHARI IN THE DISTANCE.
The Mission walled post is seen on the right.

On the Tibetan face of the Himalayas may be discerned two chains of peaks parallel to the great range, thus making with the latter three parallel ranges. In pointing out this, Mr Trelawny Saunders has drawn attention[1] to the remarkably close analogy which exists between the Himalayas and their great rival chain in the western hemisphere, the Andes. Both consist of three parallel chains, and in both the great rivers have their source in the inner chain, and force their way through the outer two.

So this is the great tableland of Tibet! But why are there so many hills on the tableland? This was my own impression the first time that I saw Tibet many years ago, and it is, I find, the invariable exclamation and question of most people on seeing the Forbidden Land for the first time. The popular misconception, that it is flat like a vast billiard-table, is to be attributed, I think, to the accounts of travels in the great desert plateau to the north of Tibet proper. For Tibet is not a flat, but a very uneven tableland; indeed, so freely intersected is it by mountain ranges that it might rather be defined as a mountainous country with lofty flat-bottomed valleys several miles wide, fingering away up between the hills, and stony in their upper reaches.

The Tibetan landscape, on which we looked down from the Tang Pass, was nearly as high as the pass itself, and gave the impression of vast rolling downs, so very small and softly rounded were the outlines of most of its treeless hills, after the stupendous and sharply upstanding peaked mountains, slashed with deeply-cut, narrow, rugged ravines on the southern side of the Himalayas, up which we had just passed. The colouring had a weird unnatural look; fiery-hued, bare, rocky hills, of a baked ochrey yellow, streaked with dull red and cindery purple, set in snow and

[1] Markham, *op. cit.* xli.

ice, with a broad flat strip of barren plain in between, stretching out to what seemed an arm of a blue sea in a bay amongst the recesses of the distant ranges, the great Rham Lake. The plain was bounded on our right by a spur of snowy peaks from the great ice-bound mass of the Goddess Lady Mountain, ending in a few graceful white cones, but the snows seemed to dwindle in the distance into unsnowed summits on the farthest horizon.

On this hill-girt plain, 10 or 12 miles wide, no habitation was visible, but our guide pointed to the eastern shoulder of a reddish hill streaked with light ochre rising out of the plain, and he said that Tuna lay at its foot, although invisible from here. This hill, for which we now made a bee-line, seemed to be only about 3 miles away in this deceptively clear atmosphere, but it proved to be about 12.

Passing along under the flank of Chumolhari, we found that the apparently bare desert plain, as we traversed it, was freely studded over with clumps of grass and weeds between the pebbles, for the plain was thickly strewn with loose pebbles and sandy gravel like the dried-up bed of a sea or lake; and this loose gravel was very trying to walk on and for the transport animals, as it wore out their shoes and lamed them.

Browsing on this scanty herbage, which curiously included many thistles, were hundreds of large wild asses, the *kyang* of the Tibetans, in troops of tens and twenties or more. At first we mistook them for detachments of Tibetan cavalry, the wild horsemen of the Changtang, as they came galloping along in a whirlwind of dust, then executed a perfect wheel-round, then extended out in line at regular intervals, and advanced again; and as if at the word of command reformed into close order and came to an instant halt.

Several of them galloped towards us and stood looking at us, out of curiosity, as near as 300 yards away, and a few trotted through the lines of our baggage-mules, doubtless recognising their family relationship. They are pretty animals, more like ponies than asses, and move with great grace. They are about the size and shape of zebras, but with better heads. Their general colour is a rich golden brown with jet-black points and stripes. When I was in North-Western Tibet, evading the frontier guards, I have seen these colours form startling kaleidoscopic varieties of tints in the bright sunshine, at one time bright sandy yellow, almost white, changing to golden chestnut and deep black, giving the appearance of a caravan of black-coated men moving amongst light-coloured laden animals. The Tibetans say that these animals are untameable, but they do not look so very wild. I cannot help thinking that here, in the home of these large wild asses, we have a great field for breeding mules for the Indian army, the supply for which never can meet the demand; and to obtain these insufficient numbers we have yearly to ransack the whole world, sending agents to Persia, Spain, Italy, China, Yunnan, and America, at enormous cost.

As we march on and on across this great plain, with nothing to relieve the dulness but these herds of roving *kyang* and the encircling hills beyond, the eye wearies of the stretches of loose gravel with its stunted tufts of withered grass, and the monotony of it all oppresses the spirits. The wind, which we had fortunately escaped on the pass by getting over it so early, now began, and even at midday pierced through our clothes. Later on it died down, leaving an impalpable dust which, quivering suspended in the sunshine, created a mirage, in which we fondly thought we saw the houses of Tuna; but this dim vision would vanish as you gazed at it.

As we still march on across the dreary expanse of plain, about the seventh mile, and yet see no signs of Tuna, although it was now 2 P.M., we began to think that our guide had mistaken his distance, if not direction, and that we should be benighted on the parched stony plain, before we could reach water and a suitable place to encamp. But at the eighth mile we caught a glimpse of the top of the highest whitewashed house of Tuna, showing above the horizon about 4 miles away, like the top of a mast at sea; for this bit of plateau was so absolutely flat that owing to the earth's curvature we could see no further than in a little boat at sea.

The village of Tuna,[1] where about thirty inhabitants extract from their stony surroundings a wretched livelihood, consists of three small clusters of poor houses, a dozen in all, at the southern sunny foot of a bare stony hill on the plain, at an elevation of about 15,000 feet, considerably higher than Phari. It evidently in former times stood on the bank of the great Rham lake, which has now shrunk back, as seen from the hill above, to a blue streak about 10 miles further down the plain, leaving hummocky clumps of a rough bent grass of poor value for pasture. The hill of yellow sandstone streaked with purply-grey limestone runs into the plain at right angles to the length of the latter, and so cuts off the view northwards, to see which we have to climb the hill about 200 feet or so.

As the villagers reported that Tibetan troops were in the neighbourhood, although our mounted infantry scouts failed to see them, we encamped near a spring about 2 miles from the village. The cold here fell so low at night that none of our thermometers could register it, our lowest record not going below -25° Fahr., or 57° below the freezing-point.

[1] Spelt Dus-na.

Next day, the 9th January, we moved to the village, and the best defensive position there was occupied, entrenched, fortified, and surrounded by barbed wire, and the Mission was installed there, in a walled enclosure, with an escort of 400 rifles, 2 guns, 2 Maxims, abundant ammunition in case of attack, and a three weeks' supply of food and fuel. A reconnaissance by the mounted infantry under Captain Ottley during the day, to the north-west, discovered the Tibetan camp in a valley about 5 miles off, covered with patches of brushwood fuel. Its scouts fell back without firing, on the approach of our party, who estimated the number of Tibetan soldiers at about 2000, which confirmed the news brought by our wild hermit Lama friend. We received news from Phari, by Captain Parr, that after our departure yesterday those five Tibetan officials, including the three hostile monks, acted upon the ultimatum they had received and were leaving Phari. Lieut. Grant, the officer on duty there, requested them to delay their departure in order to see our commander of the fort, whereupon one of the monks shouted an order to his attendant, who felled Lieut. Grant senseless to the ground by a stone. A Tibetan then rushed forward and picked up the rifle of the stunned officer, and the Lhasa Depön and the others galloped off furiously across the plain to the Tibetan camp, before our guard of Goorkhas could stop them. This was the first hostile act of the expedition, and the Tibetans were the aggressors.

The following morning, the 10th January, some of us who climbed the hill above our entrenchments saw several hundred Tibetan soldiers moving from their tents northwards to near the village of Guru, where they encamped about 5 miles off across the road to Gyantsé, for the purpose, as the villagers reported, of blocking the progress of our Mission to that town. It seemed somewhat threatening for the Mission, with its small escort, to be left so near this Tibetan army, and so far out of touch with our reserves in the Chumbi Valley. Our small garrison, however, feeling confident of their safety, General Macdonald left the same day with his flying column and the empty transport for Chumbi to push up more supplies from the Indian plains for the Mission and its escort, and for the advance to Gyantsé. Travelling so lightly, we marched through to Phari over the Tang Pass in one day.

Crossing the pass underneath cold, relentless Chumolhari, several of our transport followers, buffetted by the pitiless icy wind, lay down, and would have died in the frozen clutches of the Goddess Lady, had they not been roused up and helped along, staggering like drunken men. All of us had the skin peeled off our faces by the biting wind, and nearly all suffered from loss of voice for some days.

During our two days' halt at Phari I climbed the flanks of Chumolhari to a height of about 19,000 feet, where its south glaciers run down to meet the plain, and in those solitudes shot three gazelle bucks, with fine horns averaging 13 inches long, a golden fox (*wa-mo*), a woolly hare (*ri-gong*), and saw tracks of snow-leopard and musk-deer (*la-wa*). Another party who crossed into the Khangbu valley, 12 miles to the west of Phari, reached the hot-springs, of which there are about a dozen, possessing a great reputation for their medicinal virtues. The water is said to be sulphureous, and is so hot that it requires cooling by admixture with cold water. Here a soldier from Lhasa was taking a course of the baths, and had been occupying one of them for several days. They are roofed in and walled round to protect bathers from the cold. They seem to be similar to the adjoining sulphureous springs of Yumtang, 10 miles to the west, in the Lachung Valley of Sikhim, the temperature of which I found to be 132° Fahrenheit, and an analysis of which was published.[1]

With the establishment of the Mission on the great Tuna plateau another important stage in our advance into Tibet has been reached.

[1] In my *Among the Himalayas*, p. 434.

CHAPTER VII.

WINTERING IN TIBET.

"*Eat according to the height of your meal-bag,*
And walk according to the width of your track."
—TIBETAN PROVERB.

OUR enforced halt for the winter in outer Tibet was for the double purpose of filling up our "meal-bags" with sufficient food for the advance of the force across the hundred miles of plain from Phari and Tuna to Gyantsé, and of widening and improving the tracks for our advance. It served to harden us to the rigorous grip of the Tibetan winter with all its discomforts and positive suffering. It also enabled some of us to climb the mountains to explore their recesses and glaciers, whilst General Macdonald was engrossed in keeping open the long lines of communications, and, trusting nothing to chance, was with minute prevision arranging for every contingency, and exhausting every conceivable device in pushing up from the Indian plains, through freezing winds and driving snow, the "sinews of war," the all-essential food supplies — the fuel for generating that energy which our fighting men were to display in the heart of Tibet, for political purposes.

Fortunately the winter was an exceptionally mild one for Tibet, so the natives said, though to us its uncommon cold recalled memories of Nansen in his arctic regions, the temperature falling frequently

GENERAL MACDONALD AND STAFF WINTERING AT CHUMBI.

Front Row—Major Bretherton, D.S.O., Chief of Supply; General Macdonald, C.B.; Major Iggulden, Chief Staff Officer; Lt.-Colonel Waddell, C.I.E., Principal Medical Officer.
Back ,, Captain Elliott, R.E., Field Engineer; Orderly Officer; Lt. Manson, Brigade Transport Officer.

SPRINGTIME IN CHUMBI.

to 40° Fahrenheit below the freezing-point.[1] The snowfall undoubtedly held off much longer than usual, to the intense alarm of the superstitious Tibetans, whose Lamas conceived that it was kept off by the devilish spells which our heliographs flashed over the mountain tops, so that some of the Tibetan peasantry actually came into our camp and besought us to allow a little snow to fall, to feed the springs and save their crops in the incoming summer. The supernatural power with which they credited their white invaders certainly contributed to overawe the superstitious Tibetan.

In December and the early part of January, until the bitter winds set fully in, the lower part of the Chumbi Valley was quite pleasant during most of the day. A bright cloudless sky, with a few hours of genial sun, and fresh bracing air in which, after our work for the day was over, we could occasionally wander along the river and up the hillsides after game or photographing or sketching, made life quite bearable in these wilds, though every night we were almost frozen in our tents.

At Phari and Tuna, however, our people, freezing in furs, led a miserable existence, tormented by the fumes of their argol fires, and stung by the cold and the icy wind, which blew almost without intermission all day long. Those who had to cross the upper passes, the Tang and the Jelep, especially the former, had their faces peeled by the pelting hurricanes of icy dust, grit and gravel, which caused also loss of voice and hoarseness for several weeks. So general indeed was hoarseness that the voices of most officers in giving their orders sounded more like the gruff shouts of an ancient mariner in a gale.

Living in tents in this arctic weather, we had to resort to various expedients to keep out the cold, whose

[1] See Appendix IV. and Chart, p. 139.

icy breath descended on us through the roof, entered by the door, and every chink and eyelet-hole. Even when all the latter were sewn up, the cold struck upwards from the frozen ground and poured through the meshes of our cloth walls, undeterred by the dykes of turf or stone we had built outside to keep away the wind. To escape part of the icy wind, which was more painful than the mere cold, some dug deep pits in the frozen ground inside their tents. The best kind of tent to keep out the wind we found to be the bell shaped, in spite of their thinness, for having no erect walls nor sharp corners to catch the wind, like our "Kabul" ones, they deflected the blast up over the sides. The Tibetan kinds, too, have mostly sloping walls, apparently for this purpose.

No one could indulge in any artificial means of warmth inside his tent. No stove could be brought up on account of its weight in transport, even had suitable fuel been obtainable and an argol fire was insufferable. We had therefore to depend on extra clothing for warmth, instead of fires inside our tents. Even at Chumbi, everyone went about muffled up in furs, and the men in sheepskin coats, Balaclava caps to keep the temples warm, and shod in long felt boots.

Your difficulties began at daybreak, when the poor shivering servant unlaced the door of your tent, and brought in, with a gush of chill air, the morning cup of hot tea, which he had painfully concocted out in the cold. It then required quite a mental effort on your part, deep in a sleeping-bag, with only the tip of your almost frozen nose projecting from a Balaclava, and moustache glued to the pillow by the icicles of your frozen breath, to stretch a hand from under your blanket-bag out into the chill air to take hold of the cup immediately it was brought. For if you hesitated even for a few moments you lost the hot cup of tea, and in its stead there remained only a cup of brown ice. Knowing this by experience you nerved yourself up for the venture, and darted out a hand. When warmed a little by this hot draught, you then pulled yourself quickly out of your bag, and hastily threw on some more clothes, which, with the thickest overcoat and muffler and gloves, completed your dressing, as no one thought of using water at his toilet until the sun was well up and his frozen basin thawed. The sun did not reach us at Chumbi until about 9 A.M., as our camp was pitched under a high mountain-spur.

After breakfast, at 8 A.M., the work of the day began; in office this was done with frozen ink and benumbed fingers. About noon the wind would spring up and, gathering strength and chilliness, would nearly every day sweep hurricanes of dust up the valley, penetrating everywhere, coating your food, entering your eyes and peppering your face, and painfully smarting your chapped fingers, and continuing till near sunset. Then, after an early dinner, came the great social event of the day, when everybody, each bringing with him his own camp-stool, gathered round a big log-fire, if the camp was within the wood-zone; and here, underneath the sparkling stars, a ring of stalwart warriors, browned and bearded—as everyone had long since given up shaving—spent a pleasant half-hour in light-hearted talk and banter, the fitful gleams of the fire lighting up their faces, peeled and blistered by the icy blast. Some of the messes built huts of turf or stones, and thatched them over with brushwood to enjoy the luxury of a fire during the day, and labelled their abodes "The Emerald Bower"—not because it was green, but in honour of the Dublin men inside—"The Cave-dwellers," or such like title; but the fire-place being at one side, fewer could congregate around it than at the log-fires outside. The increasing cold by 9 P.M. would then drive nearly everyone off to seek his tent in the dark. On the way you would usually receive the sentry's challenge, "Who goes there?" and the answer "A friend," and reply "Pass, friend; all's well!" would still be ringing in your ears as you reach your tent. There, stamping off the clogging snow, and entering, you strike a match, light your scrap of candle, lace up the door, and with scarcely any undressing beyond exchanging boots for sheepskin socks, drawing on your Balaclava, and seeing that your sleeping-bag lies open, you blow out your precious inch of candle (which must still last you a week longer), and creep, shivering and with chattering teeth, into your sleeping-bag; for those who had not brought a Jaeger's bag had improvised one by sewing up their blankets. A bag was a real necessity, for no matter how you rolled yourself up in the blankets, you could not avoid leaving some chinks, and the slightest movement in your sleep, by displacing your wraps and exposing a hand or foot or your chest, might mean frost-bite or pneumonia. Even within your bag, with blankets all round you, and buttoned close up to your neck, and no open chink anywhere, it often was impossible, on account of chilled feet, to sleep for hours. Such was the daily routine of most of us for many long weeks.

The silence of this blighting reign of the killing frost was sad. In the wooded copses and glades away from the noisy river you missed the lap and splash of the smaller streams, now silent in ice. All nature seemed asleep. No hum of insect life was heard, nor the sound of many birds or beasts. Almost the only birds to be seen were occasional cheery redstarts, which took the place of the robin redbreast, a few perky red-legged choughs, a soaring eagle, and the pale slatey snow-pigeons which swooped up the valley back to their rocky nests as the sun sank behind the hills, leaving an afterglow of swift-changing colours, crimson and opal staining the weatherbeaten stones rosy-purple, and fading fleetly to cold steely-grey in the chilly twilight.

The freaks of King Frost added many charms of their own to the landscape. Outside our tents his troops of frost fairies decorated with their icy fingers the dead burnside flowers and ferns and stems of the grasses with dainty new flowery forms and tracery of sparkling gems, which revealed more than before the graceful outlines of the grasses and the curves of the leaves. They transformed the pine and juniper needles into sprays of diamond dew-crystals, and the trailing briars and rosebushes and the rhododendron scrub into shining plumes, with a delicate lacework of beaded pearl fringes and star spangles of fleeting frost jewels which changed their form in the sunshine even as you gazed at them. These frost sprites, when stopped in their wanderings by the running streams, which they, like all other wraiths, are unable to cross, bridged the leaping cataracts by breathing on them, and froze them solid into those ribbons of white ice which everywhere streaked up and down the rocks and hillsides around us. Yet on crossing some of the larger frozen streams, you could still hear the gurgling murmur of trickling water burrowing its way underneath.

The long-deferred snow did not fall until the end of January. It was heralded by a chill mist, which crept up the valley and hid the mountain-tops under a canopy of storm-clouds. Preceded by heavy thunder and lightning, the snow began to fall heavily, and was welcomed by us all as an agreeable relief from the irritating dust-storms; it also reduced the cold perceptibly. It fell several feet deep on the passes and for a long way below us into the pine-forests, where it split many of the branches; and it extended down into the very bottom of the valley, mixed there usually with drizzling sleet, yet wrapping the landscape in its white sheet for days together. It never stopped the traffic, however, for more than one or two days, even over the passes, as relays of coolies shovelled it off the track or trod it down. It actually improved some parts of the more rocky parts of the path by clogging over the spaces between sharp-cornered stones. When it fell on the running river it froze into masses where the current was not rapid, and, clogging over obstructions, made flimsy snow-bridges or causeways, doubtless the first step to the freezing of the river. Some heavy hail which fell, with several large flat "stones" about an inch in diameter, was regarded by the villagers as a sign of their demon's displeasure, whilst they rejoiced at the snow. I crossed the Jelep on the 1st February in a snowstorm, and the Nathu (14,300 feet) in a small blizzard on the 24th February. For two marches below the latter pass, the thawing snow formed a muddy, freezing slush nearly knee-deep, through which men and mules struggled painfully and benumbed. A few days later this slushy track was "corduroyed," that is, ribs of logs were laid closely side by side across its icy mud, to afford a firmer footing. Nearer the pass the tracks along the precipices were sheets of ice, which had to be notched and hacked with hatchets.

We had real English February weather in the Chumbi Valley, with torrents of sleet, turning often in March into drenching downpours of rain with storms of hailstones coming up one after another and whipping our tents viciously. At these times, we took a melancholy pleasure in telling each other that the temperature is so-and-so, or was so-and-so at such a place, and that the snowfall that morning on the Jelep was 33 inches; or in the evening we would trudge over with lanterns across the slushy snow to the Field Post Office tent, to enquire whether the post had arrived. For it was one of the few luxuries we enjoyed, that, owing to the admirable arrangements of the Post Office under Mr Tulloch, we received letters daily every evening in Chumbi (and the following morning at Phari) in two and a half days from Calcutta, and weekly in eighteen days from London, notwithstanding the enormous physical difficulties of the track along which the postal runners ran night and day covering the hundred miles from Silliguri up the mountains and over the Jelep Pass, often over snowdrifts and along precipices in the dark. Yet, so much was all this taken as a matter of course, that not a few used to complain if the mail arrived ten minutes late! The telegraph, too, under Mr Thuringer, connected Chumbi and Phari and all the military posts down along the line with India, bringing us within a few minutes of Calcutta, and within one hour or so of London, and the line was being pushed on in spring over the Tang Pass to Tuna on the great plain. To protect against the inclement weather at the higher posts along the line of communication, comfortable huts were quickly run up as hospitals and barracks by Mr Green of the Public Works Department; and wooden sheds at Chumbi to shelter the stores of flour, etc., from the rain and snow. Our gratitude was also earned by the enterprising firm of Calcutta merchants, Madan & Co., who opened grocery stores at Rangpo, Gnatong, and Chumbi.

After the middle of March less snow fell, but great masses of fog-clouds rolled overhead, blurring the outlines of the mountains. When these fogs lifted, curling themselves up in the wind like a grey curtain of smoke, or dissolved in thin showers, they disclosed the trees and uplands covered with a fresh coating of ice-crystals from their freezing vapours. These ice-spangles went on growing in size from day to day under cover of the passing fog-clouds, like the growing of large crystals in a strong salt solution, till they resembled knife-blades and lance-heads or scales of giant fish. The snow used to clear off the lower mountains with marvellous rapidity and theatrical effect. A fairly heavy snowfall during the night, showing in the morning as a spotless sheet of white stretched over the hills, would often, as the sun rose, become hid for a few minutes under a gauzy veil of mist, which quickly curled itself up from below and rolled away up the hillsides and thence rose into the sky, exposing again the sombre black outlines of the mountains devoid of a speck of snow, except in the ravines, in place of the white mantle of a few minutes before.

The game of the uplands and passes were driven down by the snow, in considerable numbers, from the passes to lower levels within reach. As the Tibetan saying goes—

> "You know the depth of the snow on the pass
> By the cry of the snow-cock below."

This induced some of us to climb the pine-forests to the haunt of the great Tibetan stag, the *shao*, which had never before been seen or shot by any European; and which was reported to be found here, the Chinese general Chao having sent a present of its venison and its feet as delicacies to General Macdonald. For this I secured the services of a native hunter of musk-deer of the valley, who knew the mountain tracks well and the haunts of the game, and arranged to start on a particular morning. When all was ready, my hunter-guide, dressed in a shaggy skin-coat, rushed up in an excited state and declared that we must not go that day; "for," said he, "just as I was starting, the first person I met was a ragged old woman carrying an empty basket, and this is the most unlucky of signs," and he begged to postpone the journey till the following day. As I was not pressed for time, and knew from experience that these people are as deeply influenced by portents and omens as any superstitious hind in Europe in the Middle Ages, and that once they are disheartened by what they believe to be ill-fate your outing is spoiled, I decided to humour him, and consented to this postponement to a more lucky day. On asking him why a person with an empy basket was unlucky, he then recited in a sing-song chant the

OMENS OF GOOD AND BAD LUCK IN A JOURNEY.

"*Take heed of all signs when you travel!*

"If on setting out you meet anybody, man or woman, dressed with fine ornaments; or carrying a full vessel, or grain, grass, or firewood, or erecting a prayer-flag; or clashing cymbals; or a well-dressed woman carrying a child, or milk, or curds, water or oil; or a woman who salutes you with kind words; or any one riding, or dressed in a new suit of clothes, or carrying a corpse, *then it is a good omen!*

"But if you meet any person with bad ornaments; or old dress or worn-out boots; or carrying an empty vessel or empty scabbard; or going empty-handed, or with empty saddle; or a poor man or a beggar, or any one asking alms or demanding debts, or speaking uncivil words, or bad language, or with hands tied behind back, *these are all of bad omen!*

"If you meet any one carrying weapons, or clad in armour, or see any quarrelling, fighting, conflagration, or any one carrying a torch, or a piece of flesh, these are signs of a law-suit or dispute in store for you.

"If you meet a deaf, or blind, or lame, or imbecile person, your sick will die.

"Seeing any one mourning, weeping, or tearing their hair, it is bad if you are a widower or widow.

"Meeting your enemy or a wild animal is bad.

"Wind, snow, or rain means loss of food and property.

"Seeing an ugly-faced boy is bad.

"If a priest pursues, you will be cursed and bewitched by evil spirits, and be despoiled by robbers.

"To see any murder, or wild animals chased by a dog, or to pass a dead body lying on the ground, is bad.

"Meeting any one carrying stones, bringing a bride, or any animal under a yoke, or any one suffering from goitre, means mischief and loss; the king of devils will injure your familiar good spirit, so *spit at him!*

"If you meet any animal which goes from your left to the right, it is good luck; if it goes from right to left, this is middling unlucky; if it is seen at the bottom of a valley it is bad.

"If a crow caws on your right, or on a wall, or river-bank, or tree, or in a desert where four roads meet, your journey will be good.

"If a crow caws behind you when you are well on your way, it is good.

"If it flaps its wings and caws, great danger awaits you.

"If it pecks at its feathers and caws, this is a sign of death.

"If it pecks food and caws, you will get food on the way.

"If it caws from a thorny bush, your enemies are making mischief.

"If it caws from a fine house, you will find a good lodging.

"If it looks in at the door and caws, you will suffer harm.

"If it sits on a plough and caws, it is a sign of death.

"If it caws from a housetop with a white thread in its mouth, the house will be burned.

"Many crows gathering in the early morning mean a gale.

"If a crow caws at sunrise, you will obtain your wishes."

The portent varies with the stage of the journey:

"A good omen is best at the beginning of a journey, less good, though not harmful, at the middle, and better near the end.

"A bad omen seen in the beginning of the journey

weakens the good luck, but this ill luck may be counteracted by meeting good omens later on, or by the aid of the priests.

"*Take heed of all signs when you travel!*"

Next day's signs proving more auspicious, we started off, taking care as we went along the bit of public road to evade meeting any of the above unlucky portents. We soon left the road, and, crossing a frozen stream, turned up a narrow glen into the solitudes of the dark pine-forest, mounting the steep slopes by pulling ourselves up by means of the knotted roots and creepers. As we ascended, we found numerous tracks of the great stag, where it came down to the river to drink, some of them quite fresh; and we startled a few blue *monal* pheasants, which swept down the forest calling lustily, also several blood pheasants, and saw the snares set for the latter by the hillmen. These consisted of low hedges of plaited sticks placed across their runs and meeting at an angle, where an opening is left, in which are placed several nooses by which the birds are strangled or caught by the feet in passing through. On reaching an altitude of about 13,000 feet, or over 2000 feet above where we started, the steep slope ceased, and, like Jack after climbing his beanstalk, we came out on to a new country — a magnificent alpine world of undulating open forest of birch, rhododendron, juniper, and pine, broken at intervals by stretches of grassy downs and pastures, with the frozen remains of the wildflowers which carpet it in summer. On every side are wide views over occasional pools, now frozen over, and above some bold pine-clad cliffs there shoot majestically into sight several pure snow-capped peaks. This was the beautiful home of the *shao*. In these open glades, free from tangled forest, these great horned animals can freely roam. We followed some fresh tracks in and out amongst the patches of its favourite food—the graceful, feathery, dwarf bamboo grass, the *Ringal* (*Dendrocalamus hamiltonii*), the reedy quill-like stems of which are in great demand by the Lamas for making pens. We were not so fortunate as to sight any of them at that time. The herd had evidently gone on to the Lingmo meadow some miles distant, for within the next few days a fine stag was shot there by Major Wallace-Dunlop of the Pioneers, who thus earned the distinction of being the first European to shoot one—previous heads having been obtained only by native hunters. Some weeks later a herd of hinds came into the camp of the mounted infantry on Lingmo plain, of which two were captured. This magnificent stag, about twelve hands high, is somewhat like the Kashmir species, but has larger and finer horns, measuring over 4 feet, while their flattened beams suggest some approach to the elk and wapiti. Although it has been called the "Sikhim stag," it is not found in Sikhim, and erroneously got this name merely because some horns were obtained there. Its western limit is Chumbi Valley, whence it extends eastwards through the upper valleys of Bhotan to the Tibetan border of China, where it has been recorded by the Abbé Desgodins as being found near Darchendo, the "Tachienlu" of the Chinese. Its young are said to be born in Chumbi in April.

On the way down to camp I shot several blood pheasants, which were very common between 11,000 and 12,000 feet. They receive their name from the male bird having large deep crimson splatches over the delicate pale green of its breast. This colour scheme is admirably calculated to protect the bird from notice in its favourite surroundings, namely, the granite rocks covered with a pale greenish lichen, interspersed with patches of a dull crimson fungus. They seldom take to wing, but run quickly and hide amongst the

Chart of Weekly Mean Minimum & Maximum Temperatures in

TIBET 1904.

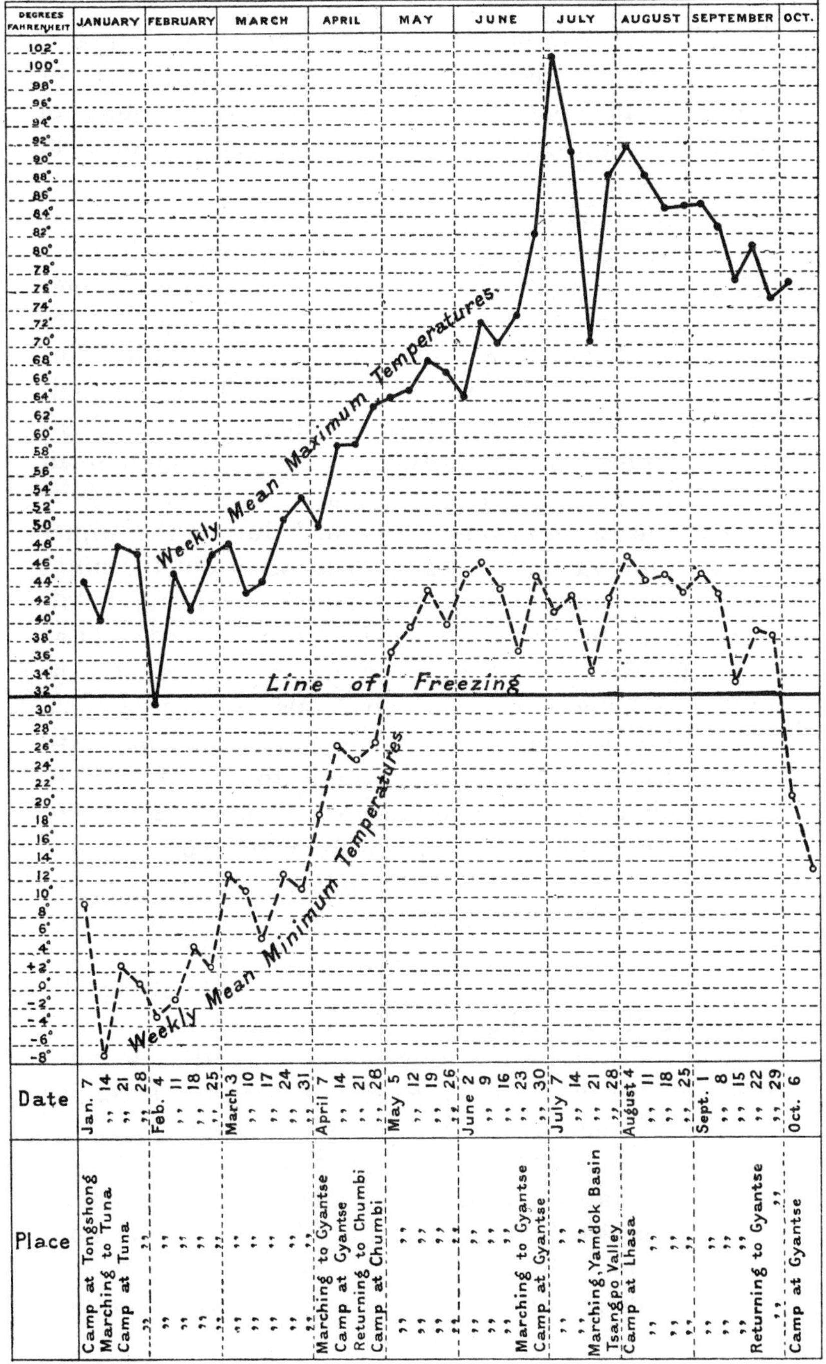

rocks. Lower down near the river-bank I got a fine, white-spotted, horned chestnut pheasant or tragopan, the *Bap* of the Tibetans. It is a bird of the tree jungles, and seems less common here than in Sikhim.

Several ducks, geese, gosanders, and other water-fowl began passing up the Chumbi Valley in the end of February, migrating from the Indian plains to their breeding-grounds in Tibet. They loitered by the way on pools on the river and on the Lingmo plain, thus showing that winter was drawing to a close, although on the 11th March the cold at Chumbi and at Phari still registered respectively 31° and 46° Fahrenheit below the freezing-point.

The lowest temperature recorded during the winter was at Chugya on the Tang Pass, when on the night of the 7th January the temperature registered below −26° Fahrenheit, or 58° Fahrenheit of frost, and at Tuna on the following night, when 17° was registered, and 15° at Phari (see accompanying chart, also Appendix III.). These very low temperatures were found, as in North China, to be quite bearable until the wind set up, when, although the temperature rose slightly according to the thermometer, the pain from the cold became intense. This is doubtless owing to the living body surrounding itself in calm weather with a protective cushion or envelope of warm air, which when the cold wind blows is removed, whereupon the cold strikes the body directly and stings it painfully.

The general health of nearly everybody, notwithstanding the continuous exposure to this excessive winter cold, and the rarefied air of these high altitudes, ranging from 10,000 to over 15,000 feet above the sea, kept remarkably good. The men were, of course, specially selected to start with, the obviously unfit having been eliminated by a medical examination before leaving India, then by a process of natural selection the weakest soon fell out, and those who remained represented the survival of the fittest.

On arrival from the plains in these cold altitudes the men, most of whom had never experienced cold before, seemed for a few days shrivelled up and semi-paralysed. They soon became hardened when they did not knock up altogether. Although still feeling the cold, they went about doing their work, and endured their sufferings heroically. Daily the convoys and their escorts did their long round of marching over the wind-swept passes, the Madras and Bengal Sappers and Miners—the "Suffering Miners" as they called themselves—daily shouldered their picks and shovels and marched off to their bridge- and road-making, assisted by the Sikh Pioneers ; the sentries and pickets performed their rounds of duty, beaten by the weather all through the bitter night, but not a murmur passed the lips of any one.

The results of this exposure to the cold and altitude were chiefly pneumonia, frostbite, and mountain-sickness. *Pneumonia* occurred mainly and most fatally in those exposed to night sentry and picket duty when the cold was most intense. Although the rarefied air of the high altitude predisposed to this specific disease, owing to the lessened atmospheric pressure permitting the blood to come nearer to the surface of the lung and thus favouring congestion of the lungs, whilst the latter were forced to work more rapidly on account of the lessened oxygen in a given bulk of air, still it was found that it was actual exposure to the cold air which was the chief predisposing factor in this disease. As a person attacked by pneumonia dies mainly from want of oxygen, tubes of this gas were sent for from India for the treatment of the cases. *Frostbite* was not so frequent or severe as would have been expected. The cases were mostly mild ones of fingers and toes, and chiefly amongst followers who neglected to carry out the medical orders issued for its prevention. Only two fatal cases occurred, one of them in a postal clerk who sat at a desk all day, and so cramped up the circulation that he died of gangrene of the legs. Paradoxical as it may seem, most of the cases of frostbite were due to burns, consequent upon thrusting the frozen limb close up to a fire. *Snow-blindness* caused very little trouble, as all the men were provided with green and smoked glass goggles. As this affection is due to an intense congestion of the conjunctiva or membrane over the eyeball, the treatment practised by Captain T. B. Kelly of the Indian Medical Service is worth recording, namely, by the application of adrenaline, which is so constringent as to blanch at once the most congested surface. *Hoarseness and sore throat* every one suffered from more or less. It was generally temporary, but in those exposed to the cold of the high passes and the acrid smoke of the argal fires, the hoarseness lasted for several weeks after leaving those places. *Mountain-sickness* was experienced by nearly every one more or less at the high altitudes, in the form of headache and nausea, with occasionally retching and vomiting. The mechanical effects of lessened atmospheric pressure on the living body have been ascertained by physiological experiment in the laboratory to be little more than an alteration of the volume of the gases contained in the blood, and do not perceptibly affect the respiration and circulation while the person is at rest.[1] It is probably, therefore, the lowered temperature of the atmosphere, and the effects on the blood-pressure of excessive exertion in the rarefied air which produce the headache and sensation

[1] "Experiments have been repeatedly performed on men and animals showing that a rapid change from 760 mm. to 400 mm. or even 300 mm. (equal to about 14·18 inches' and 18·12 inches' fall in the barometer respectively) can be endured while at rest with very little change in the respiratory and circulatory mechanism and without the appearance of any symptoms."

of muscular fatigue at high altitudes. Experiments were made to ascertain any dilatation of the chest, by a large series of measurements of plainsmen before entering the mountains and afterwards. Mountain-sickness is undoubtedly induced by indigestion, hence probably the custom for hill-men to chew cloves or ginger when crossing high passes. The remedies we found most efficacious were phenacetin with brandy and purgatives, and to get down to a lower altitude in the more obstinate cases. *Indigestion*, which was

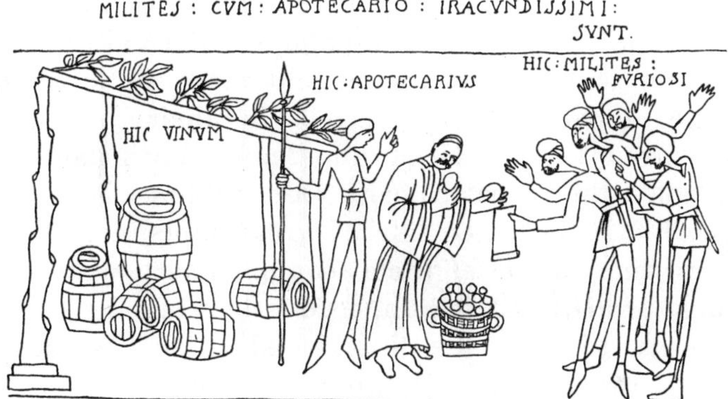

YE : MASTER : APOTHECARYE : REFVSETH : WINE : TOE : YE : SOLDIERS. YE : MEN : MAKE : GREATE : COMPLAYNTE. HE TRYETH : TOE : APPEASE : THEM : WYTH : FRVITES BVTTE : INNE : VAYNE.

widely prevalent, was largely due to bad cooking arising partly from hurry but chiefly from insufficient fuel, and the lowered boiling-point of water, which, falling about two degrees for every thousand feet of ascent, was often reduced to near 180° Fahrenheit, a temperature insufficient to burst the starch grains of rice, potatoes, and peas. Even flesh meat required boiling for a longer period than usual to soften its fibre, which, indeed, proved too often an utter impossibility, so that it well deserved its title of "*sinews* of war." There was no *scurvy* at all, notwithstanding that fresh vegetables were often not procurable, and the lime-juice or orange issued as a ration was frequently evaded by the men, who clamoured for rum instead. This absence of scurvy under such circumstances was doubtless owing in great measure to the large issue of fresh flesh-meat throughout the campaign. As to food, there was an undoubted craving for an extra amount of sugar, and of fat in the form of butter; the ordinary rations of these had therefore to be increased on medical grounds for the men in the coldest posts.

One curious result of the cold should be mentioned here, namely, its effect upon the speech of the people. A peculiarity of the language of the Tibetans, in common with the Russians and most arctic nations, is the remarkably few vowels in their words, and the extraordinarily large number of consonants: for example, the Tibetan name for Sikhim is "*Hbras-ljongs.*" Indeed, so full of consonants are Tibetan words that most of them could be articulated with almost semi-closed mouth, evidently from the enforced necessity to keep the lips closed as far as possible against the cutting cold when speaking.[1]

The severity of the winter began to abate with the opening of the Tibetan new year, which coincides more nearly than our own with the natural division of the calendar. It begins almost with the opening of spring when Nature is awakening to her new-found life after her long winter sleep. This year it fell in the middle of February, and its festivities lasted for ten days. It was made the occasion of great rejoicing and a carnival of bright colours and dissipation, which attracted the villagers from all the hamlets, and, dressed in their best, they indulged in a revelry of dance and song, and a saturnalia of drinking.

[1] Some of the initial consonants have not this origin, but serve the purpose of distinguishing roots of a similar sound though different meaning, and to indicate differences of tone.

Some of the women actually washed their faces at this season, when it was discovered that most had rosy cheeks. New prayer-flags for good luck were erected on their poles tipped by tufts of fir-tops, crimson-dyed yaks' tails and wool. Amongst games, shooting with the long bow at targets 50 to 80 yards distant was practised with considerable skill. A few black tent nomadic herdsmen, *Dogpa* or *Drugpa*, came into these fairs. Their large tents of yak hair-cloth accommodated twenty to thirty persons, their boxes being ranged around inside, and in the centre of the floor on a stand was a small shrine with some images.

Almost immediately this festival ceased the weather became milder and spring-like, and the people commenced to plough and sow their fields in the Chumbi Valley, although slight snow continued to fall at intervals. This change to spring was accompanied by violent thunderstorms, in one of which two of our people were killed by lightning near the Jelep Pass, and another lightning storm set fire to the forest and burned up one of the large sheds, with much of our valuable food-stuffs.

By the middle of March, the shrubs and trees, as far up as Lingmo plain, had burst into bud and blossom, but the change was so gradual as scarcely to be noticeable at first; as the Tibetans say:—

> "Summer comes gently in like a mother,
> Winter comes fiercely like a foe."

This advent of spring soon led us to forget most of the winter hardships we had suffered, and to congratulate ourselves on the splendid endurance of our troops. Most of these men were natives of the scorching plains of India who had never seen snow in their lives before. Yet they plodded on, as we have seen, up the highest mountains in the world, in wind and snow and sleet, often having to rest every few yards with purple faces gasping for breath, yet with a determined look in their eyes, pushing on, fighting the spirits of the cold and altitude, and doing this when on convoy duty, day after day, whilst the hill tracks up which they came were strewn with the skeletons of the transport animals which had succumbed to the hardships of the journey. How often, when benighted above the wood-zone, and too cold to cook outside with the few faggots available, many of these poor Indians crept supperless to huddle in a corner of their frozen tent, and pass a sleepless night in untold misery! But now, after paying some tribute to the inexorable Ice King, they have escaped his clutches, and, crossing the highest passes of the Himalayas in the depth of winter, and in the teeth of the snow-storms, they have penetrated these ice-bound regions to their further side.

This bloodless victory over physical dangers of a kind hitherto unparalleled in the history of warfare, and secured by such dogged endurance and tenacity, should gain for our troops engaged in it as much credit as the most glorious achievement of British arms.

Having conquered the arctic cold and winds and freezing altitudes, which had hitherto been Tibet's chief protectors, we now advanced into the less forbidding regions of this Forbidden Land.

CHAPTER VIII.

ON TO GURU, WITH BATTLE AT THE CRYSTAL SPRINGS.

"*Beware
Of entrance into quarrel, but being in,
Bear't that the opposer may beware of thee!*"
—Polonius in Shakespeare.

At last! After a wearisome wait of about three months, and a painfully rigorous winter in outer Tibet, General Macdonald was able, at the end of March, to give the welcome order to advance to Gyantsé, the large market-town in the interior of the country.

By this time it was evident that our occupation of the Chumbi Valley, and of the post of Tuna on the great plateau beyond the Himalayas, had not in the least influenced the Lhasa monks towards making any effort for a settlement; on the contrary, they refused all Colonel Younghusband's requests for an interview with proper representatives. The only answer from Lhasa was the muster of a large army at Guru, a few miles beyond the Mission camp at Tuna, which threatened to attack the Mission if it did not withdraw to Yatung. Every week this Tibetan camp was strengthened by new arrivals of armed men, until in March the Tibetan force there numbered about 5000 warriors, half of whom blocked the road to Gyantsé, and the other, a few miles off, the road to Lhasa.

The whole attitude of the Lamas grew daily more and more hostile. On the 12th January, the Lhasa

General, called the Lheding Depön, asked for an interview, but refused to come into our camp, being, as he said, too suspicious of us; so an officer went out and met him, but all he had to say was: "Go back to Yatung." He was informed that this was not possible, and that the Commissioner required as representatives on the Tibetan side the Amban and one of the ministers of the Lhasa council. So inferior in rank were this Tibetan General and his associates, that the petty chief of Bhotan, who came to Tuna about this time to receive the annual British subsidy for his Raja, could not visit them, but summoned them to his presence, and they promptly complied with his order.

Notwithstanding this, Colonel Younghusband, thinking that something might be gained by explaining matters fully to these people in an informal way, rode over next day, the 13th January, to the Tibetan camp, with a very small escort, at great personal risk. He was received by the Lhasa and Shigatse Generals, and by three monks from the capital. These soldiers were all geniality and politeness, but the monks, who were "as surly and evil-looking as men well could be," preserved a frigid demeanour bordering on insolence. "Back to Yatung!" was their constant cry when any mention was made of negotiations or treaties. "They protested that they had nothing to do with the Russians; that there was no Russian near Lhasa at the present time; and that Dorjieff was a Mongolian, and that the custom of Mongolians was to make presents to the monasteries, and they asked me not to be so suspicious." At one period the discussion became somewhat acrimonious, and the position of the British officers unquestionably perilous.

"So far," continued Colonel Younghusband in his report, "the conversation, in spite of occasional out-

MISSION RECEIVING HEADMEN.

APPROACHING GURU, BEFORE THE BATTLE.

bursts from the monks, had been maintained with perfect good humour; but when I made sign of going, and said that I hoped they would come and see me at Tuna, their tone suddenly changed, and they said we must go back to Yatung. One of the Generals said, though with perfect politeness of manner, that we had broken the rule of the road in coming into their country, and that we were nothing but thieves and brigands in occupying Phari fort. The monks, using forms of speech generally addressed to inferiors, loudly clamoured for me to name a date for our retirement from Tuna before I left the room; the atmosphere became electric; the faces of all became set, a General left the room; trumpets outside were sounded, and attendants closed round us. It was necessary to keep extremely cool under these circumstances. I said that I would have to obey whatever orders I received from my Government, just as they had to obey orders from theirs; that I would ask them to report to their Government what I had said, and I would report to my Government what they had told me—that was all that could be done at present. The monks continued to clamour for me to name a date, but a General relieved the situation by suggesting that a messenger should return with me to Tuna to receive my answer there. The other Generals accepted this suggestion, and the tension was removed."

The following week, the Lhasa General who always seemed friendly visited the Commissioner at Tuna, and after the invariable refrain, "Go back to Yatung!" the conversation became general, and at points rather amusing.

"I asked him," writes Colonel Younghusband, "why it was that while Tibetans went down to India without hindrance, travelled there as long and as far as they liked, traded there, resided there, and saw their sacred places duly respected and protected by us, not a single Englishman or native of India was allowed into Tibet. This did not appear to me either a very hospitable or a very fair arrangement. What was the reason of it? The General said the reason was the difference in religion. I told him I could not accept that, for I had carefully studied their religion and found that it inculcated the brotherhood of man and hospitality and generosity to strangers, not exclusiveness. The General then said that the Tibetans were the 'inner' people, implying that they were above the rules applying to the rest of the world. I asked him if he would do me the favour to have their sacred books searched and send me any text sanctioning inhospitality to strangers. He replied that there was no text sanctioning exclusion, but that there was an agreement or covenant of the whole people that strangers should not be admitted to Tibet. I said in that case the matter was very simple, all that had to be done now was for the people to make a fresh agreement more in accordance with the spirit of their religion and admitting instead of excluding strangers. The General laughed at this, but said that the agreement once having been made could not be altered. I told him I could understand a disagreeable people wishing to keep to themselves. What was so aggravating was that a pleasant and genial people like the Tibetans wished to debar the rest of the world from the pleasure of their society."

On the 7th February the Tibetan leaders sent a peremptory message asking whether Colonel Younghusband wanted peace or war; if the former, then he should return at once to Yatung. In reply the Colonel sent a letter, but they refused to receive it, and returned an insolent message by two sergeants, stating that their commanders at Guru were pressing the Lhasa Lamas to be allowed to fight. An attack on our Tuna camp was arranged for the night of the 2nd of March, but fell through on account of some unlucky portent. A few days later an alarm was sounded of an attack on Tuna, but the long line of advancing Tibetans wheeled round, and was found to be only a detachment of their ragged army scouring the plains in search of argols for fuel. On 16th March a party of Lamas was sent, like Balaam, to curse our force; and for full three days in a solemn service they cursed the British Mission by all their devils.

By this time General Macdonald had accumulated sufficient food at Chumbi for the advance, also the necessary transport to carry it on to Gyantsé; for amongst other expedients on the breakdown of the yak corps he had hit upon the happy idea of getting up pony-carts, or *ekkas*, for use on the plateau of Phari and beyond, and so made the advance possible thus early. These carts, which had to be got from India,

as no wheeled vehicle is used in Tibet, were carried in pieces up over the mountains on coolies' backs and shoulders, along the narrow precipitous tracks above Gangtok, past Changu lake (12,000 feet), and over the Nathu Pass (14,300 feet) to Chumbi, where they were pieced together, greatly to the astonishment of the natives who had never seen a cart before.

We left Chumbi on the 24th March in a slight snowstorm. As we ascended the valley the snow on our track, melted by the sun, was churned by the thousands of feet of our men and animals into a slushy freezing puddle over ankle-deep the greater part of the way to our first camp in the pine-forest at Gaut'ang beyond the meadow of Lingmo. At this latter pretty spot, while halting to munch some dry biscuits as lunch, we were tempted by the successful fishing of numerous waterfowl in the shallow backwaters of the stream to catch for ourselves, in one of our servants' turbans improvised as a drag-sheet, a lot of trout-fry, which made an excellent dish of whitebait for our meagre dinner.

Next morning the mud of yesterday having frozen hard as iron rendered our progress much easier at first, though higher up, where the track led across sheets of ice, it had to be hacked and strewn with gravel, and frequently the mules had to be led by the hand singly across. This time we hurried past the frozen Do-t'ak meadow, of unpleasant memories, and camped at the ford of Khangbu on the edge of the Phari plain amongst snowdrifts, but now like the terminus of a railway, from the rows of the pony-carts or *ekkas* all packed there in line ready waiting for the loads which the coolies were bringing up. This place was renamed the "Camp of Frozen Haddocks"; for the tinned haddocks we happened to have for breakfast arrived on the table frozen hard, although only carried a few yards from the fire, where they had been frying hot a minute before. They were sent back to be heated up afresh three times, with the same result; however, as they appeared on the table frozen into solid chunks of ice, and eating our frozen doughy bread, insufficiently baked through want of faggots, was like tackling a cannon-ball.

The following day, whilst the force went on to Phari by the old track across the plain, I went up the left-hand valley after some gazelle which were wanted for the pot. At the head of the valley, some 10 miles up, I came upon a line of Tibetan sentries watching this valley from the hill-tops, this being a possible line of advance for us to take the Tibetan camp at Guru in the rear. On seeing them about half a mile off I crossed over a ridge 2000 feet higher to Phari, passing down through snow-drifts to the plain, and thence across some marshes, where ruddy sheldrakes or Brahmany ducks were breeding.

As we left Phari on the 28th March, in brilliant sunshine, the housetops of the town were crowded by excited Tibetans witnessing the advance of our little army, which, with the mounted infantry on the flanks, about 6000 transport animals, and the *ekka* carts, seemed to fill the plain and formed a magnificent spectacle. We halted for the night in a sheltered hollow near the top of the lofty Tang Pass, at an elevation of about 15,100 feet, Captain Ryder having now reduced the pass to 15,200 feet. From here I climbed up the sides of Chumolhari to about 18,000 feet, and had a magnificent view of the glaciers and plain of Tuna, with its encircling hills, and got two gazelle and some snow-pigeons.

Early next morning our force crossed the Tang Pass to Tuna, and press correspondents now for the first time crossed with us. The mist was so thick that the four columns, marching abreast about 100 yards apart, were entirely hidden from one another until we reached the summit and entered the great plain, when the mist rolled itself up around the majestic Chumolhari and hung there, shrouding her from our view as if that coy virgin goddess, the guardian of the great plateau, wished to hide our intrusive passage from her own view by this misty veil. The telegraph had now crossed the pass, and stretched away across the many miles of plain in a bee-line, straight as an arrow, and serving as a good guide to the village of Tuna. As we approached this post, Colonel Younghusband and his Staff rode out to meet the force with evident relief after their long and close confinement for nearly three months. Although the winter was now over, the thermometer during the night registered 24° Fahrenheit.

A halt was made at Tuna next day (30th March); its height was now reduced to 14,700 feet by our Survey officers. Climbing the stony hill above our post to see the Tibetan camp at Guru, and sheltering myself from the battering wind behind the cairn at the top, I could see with the naked eye the Tibetans moving about, and with my glasses, the stone entrenchments (*sangars*, as they are called in India), about 16 miles away, which they had built on the plain across the Gyantsé highway at the springs, and on the hills above for the purpose of preventing our advance. I could see also bodies of their troops moving between these points, and others crossing over the plain to a similar position on the right, where they blocked the short road to Lhasa along the further bank of the great Rham lake, gleaming in the sunshine as blue as the Bay of Naples.

As the village of Lhegu immediately opposite Tuna, on an old moraine on the flank of Chumolhari, was still held by the Tibetan soldiers and threatened to cut our line of communications, a detachment of the mounted infantry was sent to order them to retire, which they did very reluctantly. At the same time notice was also sent to the Tibetans at Guru that General Macdonald was going the next morning to establish there a depôt for our food-supplies and fodder; but the Tibetans refused to receive the letter, and warned off threateningly the mounted infantry picket which approached their wall.

On the morning of the 31st March, the Mission, escorted by General Macdonald's force,[1] moved out from Tuna along the Gyantsé road, with a convoy of supplies, to establish this depôt with a small garrison

[1] Nine companies of native infantry, two 10- and two 7-pounders, Maxim guns and mounted infantry.

TIBETAN GENERALS ARRIVE TO PARLEY.

PARLEY WITH THE TIBETAN GENERALS BEFORE GURU.
Phari "General," Tashi General,
Gen. Macdonald, Col. Younghusband.

at Guru. A few inches of fresh snow had fallen, coating the plain with its white sheet, which, softening in the sun, clogged and balled under the soles of our boots and the horses' hoofs. On turning the end of the bare sandstone hill of Tuna into the great plain, the Tibetan block-wall at the Crystal Springs and the lines of fortifications on the heights above it, sprang into view, about 6 miles off. Our force, in four columns, advanced across the plain; the snow had now evaporated in the dry air and sunshine, and herds of *kyang* were quietly grazing in the offing or scampering to and fro.

About 3 miles from the Tibetan position, after about an hour's march, three majors of the Lhasa troops galloped up and asked us to withdraw to Tuna, or to halt there until the Tibetan General arrived. General Macdonald agreed to the latter alternative, and stopped about a mile from the wall at the springs. When the Lhasa General arrived, General Macdonald and Colonel Younghusband with their Staffs rode out to meet him and halted for a conference. This officer, the Leding Depön, was accompanied by the Namseling "General," the Phari "General" whom we had met at Yatung, one of the three truculent Lamas who had threatened Colonel Younghusband at the Guru interview, and some lesser officials. The Tibetans spread a rug on the ground for their dignitaries to sit upon, whilst a couple of overcoats served the same purpose for General Macdonald and Colonel Younghusband, who sat down with the Tibetan grandees, in a ring in the middle of the plain, to discuss the situation, our interpreter standing beside the two Englishmen, and the rest of the Staff from a short distance watching the proceedings. Amongst the quaint retinue of the Tibetans were three orderlies with Russian-made rifles bearing the Imperial stamp slung over their shoulders.

The Tibetan officials offered no fresh proposal, but merely with characteristic obstinacy reiterated their old demand: "Go back to Yatung." Colonel Younghusband again explained the position to them, and said: "We have been negotiating with Tibet for fifteen years. I myself have spent eight fruitless months in trying to meet responsible officials from Lhasa, and have been waiting here at Tuna for three months for this purpose in vain. We cannot now turn back, but are going on to Gyantsé. We don't want to fight, but should your troops remain there in front of us blocking our road, I shall ask General Macdonald to remove them. You therefore would be acting for the best if you ordered your soldiers to retire."

This reply evidently disconcerted the Lhasa General. He protested that he too did not want to fight, but that if we persisted in going on there would be "trouble." Saying this, with a fixed, determined look, he got up and excitedly galloped off with his companions to their troops at their entrenchments. Parties of Tibetans were then seen streaming along the heights to man their loopholed stone walls or *sangars*.

Thereupon General Macdonald, at the request of Colonel Younghusband, arranged to move the Tibetans out from their entrenchments without firing if possible. He sent the pioneers up the bare hills to sweep round the extreme left of the Tibetan position, which extended about a mile up the ridge overhanging their block-wall below on the plain, whilst our main body advanced onwards to this block-wall at the foot of the hills. The majority of the Tibetans, seeing their position thus outflanked on the hills, retired down to their block-wall, though many stuck to their *sangars* and had to be pushed and shouldered out thence by our Sepoys, when they retreated sullenly in small groups and tried to hide amongst the rocks until driven downhill to their wall on the plain by the extended line of our pioneers and Goorkhas which swept the hill-side. In this dislodging of the Tibetans from their fortified positions not a single shot was fired. The self-restraint shown by our men in advancing up to the armed Tibetans in their entrenchments and forcibly ejecting them without firing was most praiseworthy. It was like the dispersal of an armed mob after the ineffectual reading of the Riot Act. To some extent it recalled, as remarked by the *Times* correspondent, the field of Fontenoy, as on either side it was a case of "Gentlemen of the Enemy! Fire first!"

On our nearing the wall the Depön rode out and said that his men had orders not to fire, and that the General and the Mission could come up to the walls. Our men crept up to the wall quietly, taking what little cover there was by the way, and lined it. On our side of this loopholed, rude stone structure, recently built across the road, there now stood the line of our khaki-clad troops, and on its inner side behind the loopholes the wild Tibetans, clad in grey woollen homespun, a dense crowd of over 1000 of their soldiery clustering like bees along the barrier and amongst their tents. The members of the Mission and the General and his Staff rode up to the wall to see this strange sight and dismounted. Here the armed Tibetan warriors formed a dense packed mass, glaring with anger at the white-faced intruders only a few yards from them, and at our soldiers, who now enclosed them on three sides; whilst we stood by, alert but unsuspicious of the tragedy which was impending, some of us photographing or sketching whilst others were munching sandwiches.

As several of the Tibetans were seen fingering their loaded matchlocks menacingly General Macdonald deemed it necessary for the safety of the Mission to disarm them, and passed an order to that effect, and the reinforcements of more sepoys which he ordered up marched to the wall with fixed bayonets and commenced disarming the Tibetans inside. As the latter struggled to retain their weapons, and their leaders were inciting them to resist, whilst the fuses of their matchlocks were ready burning, matters began to look very threatening. Seeing this, from the inside of the wall whither I had strolled to look at their tents and equipment, I quickly stole back to our side of the defence. Just as I got there I heard a shot fired, and looking up saw the infuriated Lhasa Depön and some of his men scuffling with some Sikh sepoys on our side of the wall about 15 yards off. It appeared that when the Sikhs began to seize hold of the loaded muskets, and try to pull them out of the hands of the Tibetan soldiery, the latter struggled desperately, and, assisted by their fellows, hustled our sepoys and began to pelt them with stones. The Lhasa General then rushed forward and pulled the musket out of the hands of a Sikh and fired his revolver at him, blowing away his jaw. Immediately this shot was fired, as if it were a signal for attack, the Tibetans gave a wild war-shout and fired off their muskets point-blank at us, whilst a large number rushed out at us with their great swords already unsheathed. Then ensued a fierce hand-to-hand *mélée*. Our officers in self-defence, fighting for their lives, discharged their revolvers into the surging mass. Amongst the first of our party to fall were Major Wallace Dunlop, who had several fingers slashed off, and Mr Candler, Press Correspondent, who was fearfully hacked and slashed over the head and hands, and both of whom were saved from immediate death by the revolvers of the officers around shooting down their assailants.

The suddenness of this attack at such close quarters was startling; but within a few seconds our sepoys began to retaliate on their assailants. Under cover

TIBETAN BLOCK-WALL AT GURU, ONE MINUTE BEFORE THE FIGHT.

(Our sepoys are lining the wall on its outside; the building on the left afforded cover to many of our party from Tibetan bullets, and was a dressing-station during the fight.)

BATTLEFIELD OF GURU ON SHORE OF RHAM LAKE.
(14,800 feet above the sea-level.)

TIBETANS BEGGING TO BE SPARED.

of the wall, they poured a withering fire into the enemy which, with the quick-firing Maxims, mowed down the Tibetans in a few minutes with terrific slaughter. Those who had rushed out were soon all killed; and the remainder were so huddled together that they could neither use their swords nor guns. This mob in a few seconds, unable to stand against the concentrated hot fire of our men, surged to the rear, and throwing away their arms, broke and ran, as fast as they could, which in such an altitude was not swiftly. Most of them as they fled through this zone of fire sank quietly down, riddled by the hail of our bullets and shattered by the shrapnel of the mountain-batteries bursting over them, and perished almost to a man; whilst a throng of broken and disordered fugitives, consisting of those who had been further off, were pursued remorselessly by our mounted infantry, and their bodies strewed the road-side for several miles.

It was all over in about ten minutes, but in that time the flower of the Lhasa army had perished! When the rattle of our rifle-fire had ceased, it was found that half of the Tibetan warriors lay killed or wounded on the field of battle. Amongst the killed were the poor Lhasa General, who paid the penalty of his rashness, the Shigatse Depön, and that truculent mischief-making yellow-robed Lama. Our old acquaintance of Yatung, the Phari Depön, I was sorry to see amongst the wounded, and had him carried to a tent. Altogether the Tibetans lost about 300 killed, 200 wounded, and 200 prisoners. Our losses were only 13 wounded, as our people were protected by the wall.

This grim battlefield on the "roof of the world," 15,000 feet above the sea, deeply engraved itself on the memory of all who saw it—this blood-stained plain on the shores of the pure Rham lake (see photo here), under the shadow of the chaste Chumolhari and her train of dazzling snow peaks. It was a ghastly sight, and all the more so in such sublime surroundings; but all war is inevitably cruel and horrible, however necessary it may be at certain epochs of national life. Enemies as the Tibetans were, not only of ourselves, but in some sense, by reason of their savagery and superstition, of the human race, they nevertheless were entitled to the credit which belongs to brave men defending their homes against odds. And, it may be, they deemed it not a wholly unenviable fate to have died within the gateway of their country, this Tibetan Thermopylæ, where their beautiful hills, their protectors during life, can still keep guard around them in death.

Near the wall, and from 20 to 30 yards from it, the dead and dying lay in heaps one over the other amidst their weapons, while a long trail of piles of bodies marked the line of the retreat for half a mile or more; and cringing under every rock lay gory, wounded men, who had dragged themselves there to hide. The ground was strewn with swords and matchlocks, also several rifles, mostly of Lhasa manufacture, but a few Russian. At a distance many of the slain looked as though they were sleeping quietly by their arms.

It was especially pathetic to see the wounded Tibetans expecting us to kill them outright, as they frankly said they would have done to us, kowtowing with out-thrust tongues, holding up their thumbs in mute appeal for mercy, and grovelling in the dust to the humblest of our passing coolies. This attitude of the thumbs suggested a somewhat similar use of the thumb by the Romans in the case of the gladiators vanquished in the bloody encounters of the arena.

As soon as our own wounded had been attended

to, a party of our medical officers went over the battle-field, rendering assistance to the enemy's wounded and dying, and alleviating their pain and suffering. Many of the dying received water or brandy, or had their pain eased by morphia, or their bleeding stopped, or their wounds bound up with the field dressings of our men. I had several of the cleaner Tibetan tents torn up into bandages and dressings for these wounded, and the poles, scabbards and muskets served as splints. Afterwards these wounded Tibetans, to the number of about 200, were carried in our ambulance litters and on the backs of the prisoners into Tuna and Guru, where hospitals were improvised for their treatment. Many of the wounds were in the back, received in flight, yet many of the enemy stood their ground till the last, showing great personal bravery.

The springs which gave their name to the place are called by the natives "The Springs of the Crystal Eye."[1] They are those which were called hot springs by Turner, although at our visit they were not perceptibly hot, nor did we discover any traditions of their having been so; though all during the winter they never froze.

After about a quarter of an hour's halt at this fatal block-wall our force was formed up, and advanced through the piles of fallen dead to the village of Guru, 3 miles off, which was still held by the enemy. This position was shelled by our artillery, and the place captured at the point of the bayonet, about 100 being taken prisoners. Of these, one old man of seventy-three was a major, or *Rupön*, of the Lhasa army, who had just come from the capital with two companies of his retainers, his only son being too young to take command. The Rupön was slightly wounded. In this village vast stores of gunpowder were found; there were many tons of it in skin boxes

[1] *Shel-gô Chu-mik.*

in the houses, and it proved most unfortunate to some of our men. Many of the houses had been set on fire by our shells, and explosions were happening in various parts of the village. Being told that there were several Tibetan books in the house of the headman, I hurried in through a labyrinth of dark passages, crowded with boxes of gunpowder, and found some books, which I had brought out hastily as the adjoining house was afire, and I had to run the gauntlet of explosions, which were occurring all round, and the house in which I had been blew up a short time afterwards. In destroying a collection of boxes of the captured gunpowder, several of our sepoys were killed and others badly burned, so that, as was truly remarked at the time, the powder which the Tibetans abandoned proved more dangerous than that which they had fired through their matchlocks at us.

After establishing a small post at Guru (properly Gura) with a store of supplies, the rest of the flying column, after this long and trying day, bent its steps back over the freezing plain, eight more weary miles across the battlefield to Tuna, which we reached in the groping dark on Good Friday eve.

Next morning a reconnaissance to the Tibetan camp, which held the short-cut road to Lhasa on the other side of the plain, on the east, discovered that the Gyantsé soldiers, 2000 strong, who had held the stone block-house there, had abandoned it during the night on hearing the issue of the Guru fight.

Regrettable as it was that blood should have been shed in connection with this expedition, a collision could not possibly have been avoided. Sooner or later it was bound to come. The case seemed one in which a severe measure is the truest mercy; and where it was to be hoped that the sharp lesson might render further bloodshed unnecessary. Their foolish decision to offer forcible resistance to our advance was

MEDICAL AID TO THE WOUNDED TIBETANS.

doubtless inspired by their conceited ignorance and inability to realise the superiority of our modern firearms; and to this was also due their apparently fearless courage in continuing to advance in the face of our deadly rifle-fire, often with several bullets through their bodies. Their pitiful infatuation was also doubtless inspired to some extent by Dorjieff's promise of aid from Russia. There was some reason too to believe, in view of the inveterate treachery of the Tibetans and the circumstances under which the officers were induced to approach the wall at the Crystal Springs, that possibly there was a treacherous plot to get the leaders of the Mission inveigled there, and then by a sudden rush to overpower them. If this were so, the device happily miscarried.

The immediate practical result of this reluctant fight to clear our passage was that, as soon as the news of the Tibetan defeat reached Lhasa, a courier was despatched with a hurried note from the Chinese Amban, Yu Tai, to say that he was starting for Gyantsé forthwith, and would be there as soon as possible to welcome Colonel Younghusband; that he should have come before, but that the Dalai Lama had refused him transport; that he had now brought the Dalai to a more reasonable frame of mind, and that both the Grand Lama and the Tibetan people were deeply grateful for our "compassion" in rendering medical aid to the wounded Tibetans, as having "conferred incalculable blessings on Tibet," and he concludes his letter by saying, "I now bring the Tibetans before you with prayers of gratitude."

Neither the Amban nor the Tibetans seemed to have realised that under the soft glove of the peaceful commercial Mission they would find the strong hand of Britain's might.

CHAPTER IX.

THE TIBETAN ARMY AND ITS LEADERS.

"*The scabbard of my blue steel* [*spear*]
Is the liver of my enemy!
. . . .
No thought of death finds any corner in my mind!
I carry the red life on my finger-tip!
I have taken the vow of a hero!"

—TIBETAN WAR-SONG.

I OBTAINED a good deal of information about the Tibetan army from the wounded and prisoners taken at Guru, which supplemented the information previously collected by Mr Rockhill from Chinese sources, and which it is desirable to record here in explanation of the titles and rank of the various officials with whom we have to deal, the interior economy, etc., of the enemy's force, and for reference during our journey, as the Tibetan army had now so much interest for us.

The fierce martial spirit of the earlier barbarous Tibetans, expressed in the above popular song, still animates to some extent their present-day successors, notwithstanding the efforts of the Chinese to tame them by the teachings of Buddha and other means, and despite the grinding tyranny of their own priests, the Lamas. Tibetans, living in a country where they have to fight constantly against physical difficulties for a bare existence, still set much store by physical courage, and exhibit a contempt for hardships, from which more civilised men shrink. In the eastern

TABLE OF THE GOVERNMENT OF TIBET

Rank.[1]	Civil	Military
	DALAI LAMA.	
2nd Class or Coral Button	PRIME MINISTER, REGENT or "KING" (*Desri or Gyalpo*), and CHINESE AMBANS.	
3rd Class or Clear Blue Button	COUNCIL MINISTER (*Shapé or Kahlon*) 4, of whom 3 are lay and 1 a Lama.	
	CIVIL.	*MILITARY.*
4th Class or Opaque Blue Button	4 Chief Secretaries (*Tungyik Chenpo*). 4 Financial Secretaries (*Tsipön*). 4 Provincial Governors: 2 *Garpön* in Gartok; 1 *Teji* in Kham; 1 *Chigyapön* in Nyarong.	1 General (*Magpön Chenpo*). 6 Brigadiers (*Dahpön or Depön*).
5th Class or Crystal Button	2 Treasury Officers (*Chag-dzö-pa*). 2 Treasury Officers of Granaries (*Nyer-tsang-pa*). 2 Superintendents Road Police (*Lam Sang Shag*). 2 Lay Judges (*Shag-pön*). 2 Clerical Judges (*Shag-deba*). 54 Lay District Magistrates (*Jongpön*). 73 Clerical Magistrates and Lhasa Clerks (*Tsedung*).	12 Wing Commanders (*Rupön*). [54 Fort Commanders (*Jongpön*). Also collateral Civil].
6th Class or Opaque White Button	3 Lay Chief Clerks (*Drung-yik*). 3 Clerical Clerks (*Dron-yer*). 3 Master of Horse (*Ta-pön*).	24 Captains (*Gyapön*).
7th Class or Brass Button	2 Inspectors of Food (*Tsampo Deba*). 3 Inspectors of Medicines (*Man Deba*). 1 Inspector of Grass (*Tsa Deba*). 2 Inspectors of Wood (*Shing Deba*). 2 Inspectors of Wine (*Chong Deba*). 3 Inspectors of Cattle (*Chag Deba*). Village Headmen (*Tso-pön, Mipön*). District Treasurers and Accountants (*Nyer-pa*).	54 (?) Lieutenants (*Dingpön*). 120 (?) Sergeants (*Chu-pön*).

[1] Lama officials wear no button. The honour of riding in a palanquin is restricted to the two highest ranks, namely, the Dalai Lama, his Prime Minister, and the two Chinese Ambans.

province of Kham the people are still fierce savages, who notoriously indulge their predatory instincts as robbers; and their braves are the most dreaded warriors of the Tibetan army. The Tibetan possesses in a great degree that essential quality of manliness —fearlessness of death; although their Spartan disdain of death has not yet brought them the reward promised by the Western philosopher—"Despise your own life, and you are master of the lives of others," the truth of which has no doubt been exemplified by the masterful Japanese. The Tibetan, after all, it should be remembered, is a Tartar, and the courage of Tartars is proverbial.

Tibet possesses a regular army of some sort, and the head of it is the senior Chinese Amban at Lhasa, with the rank and title of "Military Deputy Lieutenant-Governor." He confers on the Tibetan officers under him the Chinese cap button of the several colours according to their rank (see Table, p. 165).

There are two Ambans, a senior and junior, who are appointed from Peking for a term of three years. They are Manchus, that is, members of the present reigning dynasty of China, who were undoubtedly a martial race at the time they conquered China, in 1651 A.D. Although no longer true soldiers who love fighting for its own sake, they still follow soldiering as a profession, and have a fairly good idea of the rudiments of the business of war. The Amban instructs the Tibetans in the best positions for defence, superintends the training of the army, and takes some steps to ensure efficiency by holding inspections and examination tests and sham-fights.

The troops are chiefly Tibetans, although there are in Lhasa, and in the Chumbi Valley and the larger towns, a considerable number of Chinese soldiers under Chinese officers, of whom the superior are called *Tungling* or Commanders, and the inferior *Ta-*

TIBETAN ARMY OFFICER AND INFANTRY SOLDIER.

CAVALRY SOLDIER IN MAIL ARMOUR.

Laoyeh or "Honourable Officers";[1] but they are more of a police than soldiers, and very poorly paid. Along the road from Lhasa to Peking, Mr Rockhill found that these Chinese soldiers "were never paid in cash but only receive brick-tea, the value of which is arbitrarily fixed by their paymaster, who cheats the poor devils most disgracefully."[2] At Chumbi and Gyantsé there are 50 under a "colonel" and a "lieutenant" respectively.

The Tibetan army consists nominally of 6000 regulars, with a militia and levies amounting theoretically to 60,000 infantry and 14,000 cavalry; their "cavalry," however, are in fact enormously under this figure. Of the regulars, 1000 are stationed at each of the three large towns, Lhasa, Shigatsé, and Gyantsé, and the remainder in fewer numbers at the smaller forts throughout the country and along the frontiers. The levies and milita (*yulmag*) are raised in feudal fashion, by each petty noble and each village headman having to provide 5 or 10 or more men or horses, according to the population. To call out these levies urgently, a flag formed by a white scarf tied to an arrow is sent through the glens, like the fiery cross of the Scottish Highland clans.

The leaders or officers, under the Amban, are six Brigadier-Generals or "Lords of the Arrows" (*Dah-pön*, also called De-pön, as they are collaterally Civil governors), and the senior is General-in-Chief (*Magpön chenpo*). Each of these commands 1000 regulars, and in addition cavalry and militia. Two of them are stationed at Lhasa, three in Western Tibet, namely, one each at Shigatsé, Gyantsé, and Dingri, and the sixth at the Tengri lake, to stop foreigners from the

[1] The Chinese titles of these officers are *Chen-tai*, or general; *Fu-chiang*, or colonel; *Yochi*, major; *Tu-su*, captain; *Shou-pei*, 2nd captain; *Chien-tsung*, lieutenant; *Patsung*, sergeant; *Wai-wei*, a corporal.

[2] See *Jour. Roy. As. Soc.* xxiii. pp. 276-278.

North. Under these *Dah-pön* are the commanders of 200 men, called "Masters of the Banners" (*Ru-pön*), who may be considered majors. Below these are centurions, or captains (*Gya-pön*), over each 100 men, with "Middle Masters" (*Ding-pön*), or lieutenants, over 50, and a sergeant (*Chu-pön*) over every 10 men.

The dress of the regulars scarcely looks uniform, as its basis is a grey homespun woollen suit provided by the men themselves, and of varying hues. The musketeers are supposed to wear a reddish waistcoat, the swordsmen one with a red border, and the bowmen white, and all wear a woollen wristlet. The dress of officers has already been described. Levies wear their own clothes and have no uniform. The uniforms of the Tibetan regulars at Guru were examined by Lieut. G. Davys, of the Indian Medical Service, who was in charge of the wounded Tibetans there, and he noted them to be as follows:—

1st Lhasa Regiment—Coat grey. Collar 5 inches deep, with red and blue squares and white triangles.

2nd Lhasa Regiment—Similar to above, but collar 2 inches deep.

3rd Regiment—Coat blue, collar as in 2nd.

4th Regiment—Coat blue, collar blue and red squares.

All the men wear their hair in a pigtail and shave the front of their head in Chinese fashion, and as a hat, the ordinary Tibetan felt turned up at the brim. A few still wear iron helmets and cuirasses of the type familiar to us in mediæval literature, consisting of small, narrow, willow-like leaves about 1½ inch long, threaded with leather thongs. A few also wear coats of chain-mail. The iron helmet of the cavalry was distinguished from that of the infantry, who have a cock's feather, by a red tassel or peacock's feather on the top. The high officers sometimes clothe their horse in armour, a new set of which was captured. The clothing of the horses and saddlery of the leaders was artistic and full of colour, with good carpet saddle-cloth, throat-tassels, and massive bits and stirrup-irons, silver or gold inlaid, mostly from Derge in Eastern Tibet. The horses of the men had often untidy, loose girths with bridles tied with string. The tents are mostly made of flimsy white Manchester cotton imported through Calcutta, occasionally showing the maker's name, and decorated with lucky diagrams in blue cloth.

The weapons of the Tibetan warrior are numerous and picturesque. On his back is slung a matchlock or a modern rifle; in his hand he clutches a long spear; from his belt hangs an ugly long sword, one-edged, with straight heavy blade. When guns are insufficient to go round, the remaining men carry bows and arrows, the latter of bamboo with barbed iron heads 3 inches long, also slings and heavy shields, wooden or wicker-work, or hide with iron bosses. Their flags or banners are triangular, with tufts of wool or yak's hair dyed crimson and blue, tied to the tip of the staff. The horsemen are armed with matchlocks only as a rule, though some have bows and arrows in addition. They are good shots at archery. The bow was the favourite weapon of the Tibetans; and their Generals, as I long ago pointed out, are still called the "Lords of the Arrows," and wear, together with their subordinate officers, a thick ivory or bone ring on their left thumb, to protect that member from injury from the bow-string. When the bow was replaced by the matchlock they still called the latter "the fire-*arrow*" (*mendah*), thus preserving in it the name of their old weapon. The matchlocks are long and heavy iron pieces, with two prongs hinged at their muzzle as a rest to steady the gun in firing. The larger ones have no prongs, but are supported on the shoulder of a second man, who stands in front with his back to the firer. Jingals are small long cannons made on the same principle. Refills of powder for the matchlocks are done up in small paper parcels or into small stoppered horn bottles, though often the musketeer pours the loose powder into his long-necked gun.

A large number of modern rifles of Lhasa manufacture were found at Guru. These are of the old Martini pattern, and are made at Lhasa by two Mohammedan artisans from India, who have been engaged for over ten years in the arsenal of the sacred city. They have, it seems, been making periodical visits to Calcutta and smuggling back the necessary materials. Some of these rifles they have made are fairly well finished with back-sights, and they throw bullets over three-quarters of a mile or more. Their cartridge-cases are formed by spirally twisted brass plate. Altogether, these weapons are of fairly modern pattern and are not to be despised.

Their gunpowder is manufactured chiefly at Chol-hak'ang in the Kongbu district, in the Lower Tsangpo Valley, where the article is turned out in enormous quantities. The saltpetre for this is said to be obtained to some extent artificially by nitrifying beds. The lead for the bullets comes mostly from China, from the Sze-chuan province, though some is said to be imported from Nepal. The bullets are sometimes moulded—we found several metal moulds of the British pattern—but many of the bullets in the pouches of the prisoners were evidently formed by pouring the melted lead into holes in the ground and then hammering the masses into a rounded shape. Many of the bullets also contained a small stone as a nucleus, which makes them expanding bullets of the Dum-Dum type.

For practice in the art of war, these soldiers are drilled in shooting and riding, and exercised in sham-fights under the direction of the Depöns; and they are regularly inspected by the Chinese Ambans to

RAW LEVIES.
From Kongbu.

TIBETAN INFANTRY IN MAIL ARMOUR

test their proficiency, especially in the first and second months of the year, when they receive rewards for proficiency, in money and presents, or punishment for want of skill, and in the fourth month many of them are sent to guard the passes, where they graze their cattle at the same time.

The official report of the Amban on his inspection of the Tibetan troops is interesting. In 1885, he wrote that he "held a review of the troops and has now to report that the three garrisons of Gyantsé, Shigatsé and Tingri, composed of Chinese and Tibetan troops, went through their various evolutions in good form, and their shooting, though not invariably excellent, was in fairly good style. Liberal rewards were bestowed upon those who displayed special proficiency, and their names were recorded for promotion on the occurrence of vacancies. Those who were less deserving were given presents of silk, satin, pouches, knives, tea, etc., and *the inefficient were publicly beaten upon the parade-ground.*"—*Peking Gazette*, 24th January 1886.

As expert military adviser, the Amban gives practical instruction on strategical points for the defence of the country.

As examples of the lessons given, the following are here cited :—

"It is 60 *li* (*i.e.* 20 miles) from Tashilunpo and is an excellent *location for an ambuscade* . . . at which last three places are *barriers*. . . . Four stages north of Phari is Gyantsé fort, and along the route thither are many strategical points. Thus from Gyantsé to Kangmar and its environs are a series of rugged mountains, and from Kangmar southwards (to Tuna) are defiles. . . . On the direct road between Lhasa and Shigatsé, the important points on this road if one is going from Lhasa, are Chushul, Patsé and Guidue (Chuntui), all north of Gyantsé. East of Gyantsé are Tsoma and Kung-po, which are passes, on the southern frontier of Western Tibet. . . . There is yet a northern road between Lhasa and Tashilunpo going north-east from the latter place, on the north side of the Tsangpo, and through the Yangpachen steppe, ten stages in all, to Lhasa. The important points along it are a defile to the east of Deching, the broad mountain of Pabulé, Marjyang and Latang, all of which are of strategic value."[1]

As to food, the Tibetan army needs little commissariat department. Each man can carry a fortnight's supply of the barley meal which forms his staple food, and if he is mounted, he can do this without any distress. On the march, like other Asiatics, he lives on the country he passes through. Levies have to bring with them a month's supply of food at their own expense. The simple fare of a Tibetan, when travelling, is a handful of parched barley meal (*tsampa*) kneaded with water into a doughy paste, to which a pinch of salt brackish with saltpetre is added, and the mass is then eaten uncooked. For the chief meal in the evening, flesh-meat is eaten when it can be got. It is always boiled—never roasted—and is eaten by itself, with butter-milk, the water in which it is boiled being usually thrown away, though sometimes a pinch of flour is added to thicken it, and this is eaten as soup. It is remarkable that the Tibetans never drink fresh milk or eat roasted meat, as they say that these impede the breathing. Their staple flesh-meat is dried mutton and to a less extent dried yak-beef, much of which is both semi-putrid and stringy, requiring a strong jaw and a good digestion.

The pay of the superior-officers, the Depöns, is obtained from villages which are assigned to them for this purpose, and for their civil duties they pay themselves out of the revenues and rents and taxes of their districts. The lesser officers, from the Rupöns down-

[1] Translated by W. W. Rockhill, *Jour. As. Soc.* xxiii. 18.

wards, receive small salaries of about £7 to £3 per annum; the Chinese officials receiving about six times the pay of the Tibetans. The soldier is usually starved and not paid. He receives so many bushels of barley twice a year, and, if on service, a ration of barley-meal and meat daily—he seldom gets any money whatever. The usual full ration for a month, per man, is 20 lbs. of barley-meal, 1 lb. of salt, and, if available, some yak or sheep's flesh-meat, a sheep's bladder of butter, and half a brick of tea.

Relying on the supposed strength of their army thus efficiently organised, as they fondly imagined, and on their Lhasa-made rifles and new drill, not only did the arrogant Lamas consider themselves of superior strength to us, but the common people were so impressed by their prowess, and the Lepchas and other smaller tribes so terror-struck by them, that numbers of our camp-followers deserted in the belief that we should be hopelessly annihilated by these invincible Tibetans. They certainly proved to be no cowards at Guru. Those of them who dared to come on when riddled by bullets, and the swordsmen who dashed out to certain death, showed a spirit as savage as any Afghan. The warlike courage is there, and under good training could doubtless be educated into forming a trustworthy frontier force for defensive purposes.

In working these poor deluded peasant soldiers up to fighting pitch, the Lamas played freely upon their superstitious faith in charms, and gave each of them bullet-charms,[1] with the promise that our bullets then

[1] These consist of a mystic letter written on paper with special enchanted materials, and surrounded by lotus leaves and concentric circles inscribed with texts from the Buddhist scriptures, outside which, amongst flames in the top corners, are a sword and thunder-bolt sceptre or *dorje*, and in the lower corners, the jewel symbol of the Grand Lama's spell, and the Divine lotus. The central mystic

could do them no harm. Thus every one of the warriors who opposed us at Guru had these new charms hung round their neck in amulet-boxes. But it all failed pitifully. Neither the Lamas' chorus of curses, nor their charms, had the slightest effect. On

CHARM—TALISMAN AGAINST BULLETS.

the contrary, as if in bitter irony of fate, many at Guru received their death-wounds through their charm-boxes. The Lamas afterwards excused them-

letter is marked, in a copy I possess, as being equivalent to "*dsam,*" which probably is intended to imitate the humming sound of a bullet, on the homœopathic system of the sympathetic magic of the ancients, selves on the plea that they had given only a charm against leaden bullets, whereas ours contained some silver in their composition, and hence the charms proved ineffectual on that occasion; but this defect would be rectified in the charms they would issue in future, which would be found infallible.

CHAPTER X.

DASH ON GYANTSÉ, PAST THE LAKES RHAM AND KALA, WITH FIGHT IN THE GORGE OF THE RED IDOL.

> "*The hornless yak gets the last line-rope;*
> *Helpless people the back of the door.*
>
> . . . .
>
> *If the heart be stout a mouse can lift an elephant.*"
>
> —TIBETAN PROVERBS.

LEAVING the ill-fated Guru, our force, with its way now cleared in front, continued its advance to the large market-town of Gyantsé, about 80 miles down the plain. Although the Mission had now assumed the character of a military expedition, its operations were not to be of a punitive kind, but confined to dispersing any forces blocking our road or attacking our camp; for there was absolutely no shadow of resentment on our part, and no quarrel with the people themselves.

It was a lovely spring morning, on the 5th of April, when we left, without regret, the inhospitable village of Guru, and marched northward under the low brown hills along the turfy western bank of the great Rham lake, an extensive sheet of blue water like a sea, about 15 miles long, by 4 or 5 broad, with its further bank of rolling uplands rising into bold snowy peaks and glaciers of the Chumolhari range. This is the lake on which Captain Turner skated in November 1783. Although its edges were still frozen, its shores and open pools already abounded

ALONG THE SHORES OF LAKE RHAM (14,900 FEET).

SHEEP OF NORTHERN TIBET, ON RHAM PLAIN.

DISMANTLING LOOP-HOLED WALL AT KANGMAR.

THE GOVERNOR (JÖNGPON) OF GYANTSÉ FORT.

with a great variety of water-fowl, wild ducks and geese, teal and crane, terns and waders, which breed on its shores. Across its sapphire waters were the black huts of the summer-grazing station of Rham, which gives its name to the lake, past which winds the short cut to Lhasa, seldom used, however, as it crosses two high passes, with no permanent villages on the way for shelter or food, and only inhabited by roaming shepherds and their flocks during a few months of summer. At the north end of the lake, shining as a white speck on the rocky hillside, is the small monastery of Lapchi, which curiously is a branch of the one on Mount Everest, about 150 miles off to the west, and quite invisible from here.

From this fine scenery our attention was repeatedly recalled to the painful circumstances of our march by the gruesome heaps of gory dead strewn along our path for several miles where our mounted infantry had crashed down upon the retreating enemy in their flight five days before.

As we went along, surveyors with their theodolites and plane tables were conspicuous mapping out the country, under Captain Ryder. About the sixth mile after passing some saline springs, with an incrustation used as soap, we came upon a refreshing green stretch of meadow-land at the hamlet of Do-chen (or Big Meadow) where a track led up the side valley over the hills to Khambajong. Here the coarse stiff pasture of the upper plain gave place to a tender green velvety grass, which our poor starving yaks[1] eagerly sucked up,

[1] Our transport yaks, which had to forage for their own food miserably, were of the usual three kinds, namely (*a*) the yaks proper, the large male beast, (*b*) the *dri-mo* or female, and (*c*) the *jo-bo* or cross-breed oxen between the yak and the Indian or Himalayan cow. Each carries a load of 160 lbs. about 6 miles, but owing to the length of our marches and the weakness of the animals, two or more yaks were detailed for each such load. The *jo-bos* were found to be more tractable and less subject to disease than the yaks proper.

as it was all too short as yet to bite. It was taken as a good sign here that none of the villagers had bolted. They were all here with their womenfolk, and stood kow-towing and gazing in astonishment at the procession of our carts passing by.

A Chinese mandarin under a red umbrella was here with his retinue, and represented that he was General Ma, and had been sent by the Amban to assist in the negotiations. Captain Parr of Yatung, the duly accredited representative of the Chinese who was accompanying us, ascertained that Ma was only a major who, according to an old Chinese custom, had been given this temporary brevet higher rank as a recompense for crossing the frontiers into the country of the barbarians. He was a fat, smiling, middle-aged man, and very anxious to made a good impression. He tried to dissuade the General and Colonel Younghusband from going on to Gyantsé, which he alleged was as bleak and inhospitable a place as Tuna, though he admitted that Lhasa was quite a fine place, with trees and many of the luxuries of China. He said he had just come from Gyantsé and had met many fugitives on the way. He went on in front of us, back to Gyantsé.

Meanwhile the sky clouded over and squalls of wind sprang up and lashed the waters of the lake into large waves, which broke up the ice fringing the shore and churned it with the half-frozen snow into white foam. Sleety snow began to fall as we reached the end of the lake where it pours down a defile to expand again into the smaller lake of Kala some miles below. At this point on the exposed shore, lonely, desolate and inhospitable, we encamped in the cold driving snow, and had much difficulty in lighting fires for cooking. Fuel was not, of course, obtainable here, but had to be carried along with us, enormously increasing our transport difficulties. This lake, I was told, begins to freeze in the middle of

October, and from November till the middle of February, when it begins to thaw, no water flows out. A track strikes off here from the Gyantsé road to join the Tuna-Lhasa road round the lake, thus making this camp of some strategical importance and liable to attack from two directions. A wounded Tibetan from Guru was found here and had his wounds dressed. When the snow ceased some of our more ardent spirits, undeterred by the bitter wind, went out and shot a few ducks for the pot. I got a tern and a gull as specimens, but had difficulty in retrieving them, as they fell in the water amongst floating masses of ice. When the storm passed the snow soon melted, and we had magnificent cloud-effects over the snowy ranges.

Next day (6th April) our route led us down through the defile where the lake, overflowing through a cleft in the rocky ridge which bars its lower end, pours down in a boisterous stream through a rather rocky valley into the lake of Kala, 4 miles below. Of this defile there is no trace whatever in the maps or itineraries of our native surveyors. Midway down we passed the village of Tsalu ("Chalu" of maps), standing amongst terraced barley-fields watered by elaborate irrigation channels from the stream. It was a pleasure to come again into the zone of cultivation, even though the hills were still so cheerless, bare and stony, without a single tree or shrub anywhere; and we could not but admire the daring of these hardy hillmen in forming a home for themselves so high up amongst those inhospitable mountains. Their houses were plastered over with charms against the devils of the storm and the evil eye. On the housetops, several pairs of ruddy sheldrakes or "Brahmany ducks" were sitting or strutting about, quite at home, like tame pigeons, and let you pass within a few yards of them. Even when some of our soldiers threw stones at them they still refused to leave. They breed in the rushy hummocks along the bank of the stream, and are not accustomed to be disturbed by the Tibetans, who esteem them especially sacred from wearing the yellow colour of a Buddhist monk's robe, the same garb which causes them to be called "Brahman's ducks" by the Hindus, on their winter visit to the plains of India.

I made special enquiries regarding the alleged visit here of the famous Chinese Buddhist pilgrim Hiuen Tsiang, who visited India in the 7th century A.D., and whose marvellously detailed and accurate record of his journeyings and exploration affords us the best, and indeed the only, accurate account we possess of the geography of Ancient India. He is alleged by a certain Chinese commentator[1] to have returned from India to China by way of Tibet, and "at *Ts'ai-li* on account of the farm of *Kao-lao* (or *Kao-lao chuang*), where it is believed that the Master of the Faith passed, they do good works." Rockhill, who translated the foregoing note, states that he was told by Tibetans that this "*Ts'ai-li* or *Tsa-li* is some three days' journey south-west of Tashilhumpo on the road to India." This, the chief road to India from Tashilhunpo, is south-east, and this village of Tsalu could be reached by courier in three days from Tashilhunpo. The reference to the farm of "Kao-lao" and "Kao-lao Chuang" seems intended for this Tsalu near Kala or Kala-tso, as the Chinese forms of place-names usually vary slightly from the Tibetan. But the people here retain no local tradition of such an incident. Nor do I think that there is any real foundation for it, as, according to his own records, Hiuen Tsiang seems never to have entered Tibet, but travelled both to and from China by way of Turkestan on the north.

[1] Rockhill in *Jour. Roy. As. Soc.* xxiii. 282. Klaproth says an alternative name of Ts'ai-li was "Begoni-thang," but no such name is known at Tsalu, nor at "Shalu," lower down in the Kungmar valley.

Further on we passed several hamlets all in ruins and deserted. These appear to be the identical ones seen by Bogle over a hundred years ago, which he was told were destroyed in border raids by the Bhotanese several years before his visit. About the fourth mile the defile opened out into the broad wind-swept valley of Kala, with its lake, which, though not so large as Rham, is a fine sheet of blue water 6 or 8 miles long and 2 or 3 miles broad.

Kala lake occupies a broad, shallow depression between bare sandstone hills rising 500 to 1000 feet above it, except at its eastern end where the valley is open, and the shore shelves gently upwards for about 100 feet or more to form a great plain about 10 miles long and 5 broad. The village, of about twenty families in two hamlets, is situated at the foot of the hills, about a mile from the present water-line, which has all the appearance of having receded in comparatively recent times, like that of the Rham lake from Tuna, and has left a low shelving bank, evidently the lake-bottom which extended up to the village in not very ancient times, although the villagers have no precise tradition regarding it, beyond the saying that the lake is receding. We see in these shallow, receding lakes the way in which the so-called "plains" of Tibet were formed. This lake, which is said to have no outlet, is subject to some change of level, rising in the rainy season for a quarter of a mile or so. Its shore is coated by a black muddy ooze full of small watershells and their débris, abounding in animalcule life, and overcharged with semi-putrid organic matter. The water, although clear, was slightly brackish, and the shore covered by a white saline crust, which supported the local report that the lake has no outlet—although in the maps of our native surveyors, and in Bogle's account, it is made to flow into the Gyantsé river on its east. It was full of fish, and swarmed with the waterfowl preying upon them—thousands of geese, ducks,[1] teal, all very wild, also sheldrakes, terns, gulls, lapwings, red-shanks, snippets, etc., all of which were mostly in pairs and evidently breeding here. We shot a few grey-barred geese, mallard, shovellers, and a fish-eagle.

Fish were extremely abundant everywhere and were good eating. Many were large, from one to three pounds or more. Most of them had very minute scales, and a moustache of a pair of bearded feelers. The Tibetans here catch fish by wading a long distance out into the lake and trawling with drag-nets, carried by four men, who catch huge fish in this way. Boats are also used, and some fish with a hook and line, baited with barley-flour dough. The fish are prepared for sale by slitting them open like kippered herrings, cleaning and drying them in the sun, and storing them, or sending them to Phari or elsewhere for sale or barter. Every house in the village having a large store of these in stock emitted a strong fishy odour. There was a good deal of cultivation along the bank of the river, the water of which irrigated the fields and grassy meadows (*panki*).

Large game were said to be found in the surrounding hills, the giant sheep or *nyan* (*Ovis ammon*), also antelope and gazelle; but the villagers had no skins or horns of the former to confirm this report, and we saw none of these animals except gazelle.

Only one able-bodied man was present in the village, the headman, who said that all the other men and youths had been drafted off to Gyantsé to fight against us.

I examined this lake in some detail with reference to the formation of the so-called "plains" of Tibet, which are clearly the broad flat bottoms of former great shallow lakes, like those of this one, of Kala, and

[1] Called "Mud-birds" (*Dam-cha*) by the Tibetans.

Rham. These lakes have all been formed by the damming up of the water-course of the central valley; but how this blocking has been caused is still a matter of dispute, on which question an examination of these lakes may help to throw some light. The cause of the damming up of the valley to form the lake, in the case of the Lingmo lake plain, is undoubtedly the detritus washed down from the hills at the lower end of the valley, or the landslips falling at the same place. In the case of both this Kala lake and the Rham the rocky barrier at the lower end forming the dam may have been there originally as the outer boundary of the depression which forms this lake, or it may have been lifted at a later period during the subsequent rising of the range. For the great mountain-chain of the Himalayas, originally thrown up by the contraction, cracking, and falling in of the earth's crust, with consequent upheaval of one of the edges of the cracked crust, continued in later ages to rise for a long period, through volcanic action or otherwise; and it rose unequally, certain portions of the surface rising higher than others, whilst other portions subsided. In this way, either by the lower end of an existing valley becoming raised, or by the upper end subsiding, a lake-depression would be formed above the point raised by this interruption and damming back of its drainage.

The bare sandstone and boulder-strewn hills surrounding Kala lake were very deeply furrowed and scored by water-courses, giving the appearance of suffering much erosion and denudation by heavy rainfall. At the western end of the lake a few dwarf juniper shrubs dotted the hillside for about 100 feet above the shore.

Next day (7th April) we went along the middle of the shingly plain, the old bed of the receded lake, towards the outlet of the valley, at its open east end. It was practically level for 8 miles; then it rose perceptibly about 200 feet or more over a fan-shaped slope of gravel and small boulders, washed down from a tributary valley on our right, which forming a dam here had cut off this lake-valley from the wide central valley in front of us, where a large rivulet, the Gyantsé river or Nyang Chu, rushed down from the glaciers of the northern spur sent off Chumolhari range, which here rose into a cluster of chaste snowy peaks called "The Nine Nuns" (*Ani-gumo*). The waters of the Kala lake clearly had their outlet here in former times, and their old deep-cut ravine still remains with almost vertical walls 50 feet deep and 200 yards across on the further side of this dam of gravel. Curiously, Bogle wrote that on his visit, one hundred and thirty years ago, the lake was actually outflowing here:

> "A stream runs from it (the Kala Lake) northwards. We kept close to this stream for several days; it falls into the Tsanpu at Shigatse."

That is to say, it was the Nyang river which is now separated from the Kala lake by the high bank of gravel on which we were standing. This observation, if true, would imply that during the past one hundred and thirty years this lake of Kala has fallen about 200 feet in level and has receded 15 miles or more. The shrinking of the glaciers, by allowing the temperature of the air to rise, doubtless contributes to the drying up of the lake, when once it falls below the level of its outlet. At present the lake appears to be lower in level than the river which flows outside the dam at its eastern end.

Such damming up of the central valleys by the fan-shaped slopes of gravel coming down from the tributary glens evidently played the chief part in forming those chains of confluent or semi-confluent shallow lochs, at frequent intervals, which fill up the bottoms of the valleys of Tibet, and the dried-up beds of which formed the so-called "plains." The absolutely level surface of the plains shows that these could not have been formed by running rivers, but only by the levelling action of lakes, and in Kala and Rham we have seen these plains in process of formation. The damming up of the rivers into these lakes was doubtless greater in the glacial period, when disintegration of the rocks by the moving ice as well as by the frost was greater than it is now, whilst running water was deficient to transport the débris for any considerable distance. The plains formed from these old lake-beds are thus relatively recent deposits, and the rivers in their course through them now cut deeply down 10 to 100 feet or more, tearing through this soft silt and gravel which it had deposited at the earlier period in its lakes.

The landscape here underwent one of those abrupt transformations to which we were getting accustomed. On reaching the top of the lake-dam we suddenly left the dismal, bleak stony plain, and with scarcely any descent emerged again into the tree zone, in a fine spacious green valley dotted with villages, through whose verdant meadows raced a boisterous river.

We camped upon the old bed of what formerly must have been the east end of a larger lake of the central valley, of which Kala lake was its western arm. The river of this central valley rushed noisily 100 feet below us in the broad channel cut through its old lake-bed, which now formed a high shelf on both sides of the river. This is the "River of Joy" (*Nyang*), which flows past Gyantsé; and we welcomed the sight of its pale bluish waters speeding through the refreshingly green sward below us as the first positive evidence yet seen that we had actually crossed the great water-parting of the Himalayas; for we now knew that these rushing waters we looked down on were hastening past Gyantsé and Shigatsé to meet the great central river of Tibet, the Tsangpo, and come out into Assam in India in the great Brahmaputra. Villagers from the hamlet of Shalu, with its dozen mean stone huts, soon came into camp, selling some fuel consisting mainly of top roots of dried thistles, which were rather abundant on the plain. In view of the name of this place, I enquired also about the great pilgrim Hiuen Tsiang without result.

Here, at an elevation of about 14,000 feet, we got again into the zone of shrubs. Dwarf red juniper trees 6 to 10 feet high dotted the hills thickly to their summits on the western side of the valley, and were evidently the vestiges of a natural forest growth which formerly covered all the hillside hereabouts, and had survived the attacks of man, for the present trees are in the most inaccessible spots where the villagers cannot easily remove them for firewood. The presence of a few shrubs also at the top of Kala lake suggests that the hills there may owe their deep erosion and present destitution of all soil and verdure to the removal of these protecting shrubs by man.

News arrived in the afternoon which showed that the Lhasa Lamas, notwithstanding the sharp sanguinary lesson given them at Guru, evidently meant to continue their opposition to our advance. Our mounted infantry picket found that the Tibetans were holding a strong wall 10 miles down the valley, and that the village of Samada, on the road a few miles down the valley, was fortified and held by some Tibetans and red-coated Lamas, who beckoned our men to approach. When the latter got within about 150 yards, the Tibetans opened a brisk fire on them, wounding one. For this treachery our party retreated to cover and then fired, killing and wounding several. The mounted infantry have already proved themselves invaluable to us as feelers to ascertain the presence and intentions of the enemy, and to follow them up when retreating. Although Tibet is too mountainous a country for cavalry, these little, wiry, rough-coated ponies, mostly of Tibetan breed, carry their sepoy riders, Pathans, Goorkhas and Sikhs, scampering over the plain and up and down the hillsides freely.

Next morning we descended the broad meadow of the Nyang river to Samada, whence we found the enemy had cleared out, leaving four dead. The village, too, was empty, the women and children having taken refuge in the monastery a short way off, under the hill, amidst fields. We now had come to willow bushes, amongst which hopped several great Tibetan magpies, black and white, with glossy dark green tails. As we descended the valley, villages became more numerous, and always near by was the parasitic monastery with its lazy priests. Most of these monasteries had texts in gigantic letters written on the hillsides above them by means of white quartz stones. Each letter was 15 or 20 feet long and could be seen several miles off. The next most common text after the "*Om mani*" I found was—"Hail to the Omniscient Grand Lama!" The increasing cheerfulness of the prospect was repeatedly marred by the innumerable ruined, old deserted villages which we passed, and which exceeded in number the occupied ones, and looked as if the valley had once supported a much larger population. The villagers alleged that most of these ruined villages had been destroyed by the Jungar Tartars nearly 200 years ago, whilst others sacked Lhasa,[1] whilst others had been deserted from time to time on account of the

[1] These are the tribe of Euleuth Mongols called the "Eastern" (or Jungar) which border the east of the Hindu Kush, who sacked Lhasa in 1710 (see p. 33, map, p. 40, and Appendix V.), and whose aggressive power the Manchu dynasty found it necessary to break.

devils of smallpox and other plagues which ravaged them.

The valley having narrowed into a gorge, through which the river descended rather rapidly to another old flat lake basin, opened out again and trees grew more numerous by forming, opposite a strongly fortified monastery like a mediæval castle, quite a thicket of birch, poplars, and willow, some of the trees being about 20 feet high. At a thriving-looking village here were the remains of the enemy's cooking fires of a few days before. The headman said that some 100 of the Gyantsé troops had gone up to oppose us in the gorge between the two lakes at Kala, but becoming alarmed had returned, and now were holding the wall across the road 4 miles farther down near Kangmar. This disagreeable news was presently confirmed by the mounted infantry, who sent back a message to say that they were in touch with the Tibetans holding the gorge ahead behind a loopholed wall which was continued up the hillside about 1000 feet above the river. We therefore halted 2 miles from this wall, at an old ruined castle—where we startled some woolly hares and Tibetan partridges, which fled up the hill—and our camp was surrounded by a fence of barbed wire as usual, in case of night attack.

Early the following morning the General advanced his forces cautiously, and after sighting the great wall sent a party up the heights to outflank it. When the position was scaled it was found that the enemy had fled, leaving a few dead from yesterday's skirmish with the mounted infantry. One prisoner who was caught said that they had lost six killed and three wounded. The wall, which had been built during the previous week, was a remarkably strong one, elaborately loopholed and cleverly built across the gorge where the Nyang river pierced through cliffs of red sandstone. As it might offer cover to the enemy for harassing our line of communications along this road, the General halted the force here to dismantle it.

The series of steep cliffy spurs of red sandstone which here project into the valley like giant toes gives, probably, the name to this place, namely, "The Red Foot" (Kangmar).[1]

The important village of Kangmar stood just behind the wall at the entrance of a grassy side valley, which turned up to the right, and along which branched off the trade route to Lhasa, saving, as compared with the road *via* Gyantsé, some four stages. Of such strategical importance is it considered to be by the Lhasa authorities that it is held directly by Lhasa officials, although it is within the western province, and this arrangement is mentioned by Bogle as existing even in his time. Some half-mile beyond this village is a hot spring, the water of which at Turner's visit in 1793 was 88° Fahr. when the temperature of the air was 44° Fahr. I find the water to be practically the same—87° Fahr., with an aerial temperature of 56° Fahr. The vapour had no smell of sulphuretted hydrogen, for the road for over a mile passed over a porous cindery-looking incrustation ("tufa") obviously lime, and freely powdered by a snowy efflorescence (see Appendix VIII. for analysis). As the mounted infantry scouts reported that the enemy had made a stand in the throat of the great gorge of the Red Idol at Zamdang about 3 miles ahead, and had erected cannon (*jingals*) there, we halted for the night near the mouth of that gorge, at a pretty little village surrounded by neat willow and birch trees like a cluster of suburban villas outside London. Before our tents were up sleet began to fall heavily.

We started off in battle array next morning (10th April) at eight o'clock, having as usual been up about

[1] Another spelling of the word, also by a resident, differed in giving it the name "Red House," although there is no red house in the village, nowadays, at any rate.

5 A.M. in the freezing air to snatch a bit of breakfast and pack up our tents, prepared for an engagement in forcing the passage, the baggage being left behind in camp, packed up ready to come on later when signalled for. On either side went the scouts along the heights on each side of the gorge; some mounted infantry and the advance column threaded along the deep bed of the river, followed by the General and his Staff; and then the batteries and main body and reserve companies.

We were now entering a great gloomy ravine, where the river pierced through a high mountain range, the Central Himalayan chain of Saunders, which rose steeply in cliffs on either side 2000 feet or more above us to a height of 16,000 to 17,000 feet, leaving a chasm with precipitous sides, along the narrow bottom of which ran our track. The whole country was as ill adapted as it was possible to conceive for a small invading force to push its way through against positions held by an enemy; and had this goıge been held by a small party of Afghans, it could not even have been attempted without a force six times the strength of ours.

The Tibetans were found to be lining a ridge on our left across the river, 1000 to 2000 feet above our road, where the gorge bent round almost at a right angle. As soon as we came in view, the enemy commenced a continuous fire from over a dozen *jingals*, or small cannon, which they had planted within entrenchments on the heights; but as we were still over a mile away their projectiles fell short of us. To dislodge them from this commanding position, General Macdonald sent up four companies of Goorkhas to scale the heights above them, whilst we all halted below with our field-glasses glued to our eyes watching them laboriously climbing up amongst the rocks to dizzy heights, and also observing the effects of the shrapnel thrown by our two 10-pounder guns from a knoll on our right, whence they were shelling the enemy along the cliffs on the sky-line about 2000 yards away. Meanwhile a snowstorm swept down and blotted out from view both the Goorkhas and enemy for over an hour; yet the Tibetans, although they could not see us nor any object 200 yards off, continued their bombardment all through the snow-storm, probably with the view to deter us from attempting to slip by unseen under cover of the falling snow. The cold was so intense that the men of our force below lit fires behind the rocks to warm themselves.

When the snow-clouds lifted, the Goorkhas were seen to have climbed about 2000 feet to an elevation of almost 16,000 feet in three hours, but were still about a mile off the enemy's entrenchments. As the enemy's *jingals* had so far proved harmless, the General sent the mounted infantry on to reconnoitre through the gorge, and they reported that a second position within the ravine and on our side of the river was held by the Tibetans. By this time the Goorkhas had begun a sharp fusilade on the ridge where most of the *jingals* had been silenced by our artillery; the Sikhs and the main body moved up the gorge to attack this second position. As we turned the corner in the defile, the Tibetans, ensconced behind the rocks, shouted their war-cry and fired furiously, and let loose an avalanche of stones from booby-traps; but the Sikhs got round behind them and drove them off, killing many and capturing others hidden amongst the rocks, whilst the mounted infantry were let loose in front to pursue those who had escaped down the valley, of whom they killed many and captured more.

This was the wildest part of the gorge. The valley here contracted into a narrow cleft between the great upstanding cliffs which towered almost perpendicularly overhead, and between rushed the river noisily, dashing and wriggling over the huge rocks fallen from the cliffs above. Here, where the crags rose sheer from the water's edge, amongst huge piled-up boulders, stood sentinel the great idol which gives its name to this gorge, amidst a fiery patch of crimson-leaved barberry bushes. It is a crude, repellent image of the wizard priest who founded the order of Lamas (see p. 115), and by his side is an equally large red-painted likeness of the Buddhist god who is supposed to be incarnate in the Grand Lama of Tashilhumpo.

Threading our way over the great fallen rocks and boulders for about half a mile, we emerged on a pretty meadow, where the valley opened out at the junction of the river with another large stream, and where in a thicket of birch-trees stood the country house of a Lhasa magnate. Here we halted for an hour, and found amongst the dead along the roadside a few wounded, who were then dressed by our medical officers and handed over to the villagers, consisting of women and a few decrepit old men who were forced to remain because they could not run away.

GOD INCARNATE IN TASHI LAMA.

The firing of our men on the heights ceased, and we could see them against the sky-line, descending towards us by springing down the rocks. They arrived, bringing about twenty prisoners and a few Lhasa rifles, and said that the effect of shrapnel on one of the *jingals* had been most fatal, having blown off part of the gun, around which were lying nine of the enemy's dead. The captured Tibetans were ordered to break up their matchlocks, and complied with evident delight, jumping on the splinters most cordially. They said that they were only peasantry who had been forced by the Lamas to fight under threat of having their homes burned down and their families taken from them. The enemy's losses this day were about 150 killed and wounded, and over 100 prisoners, amongst whom were several Lamas, and it was ascertained that 100 Lamas from the Gyantsé monastery had been present with our opponents. Our losses were only three wounded and none killed.

The Lamas seemed now to have fully committed themselves to hostilities, for this action was deliberately fought all through. The prisoners said that the troops opposing us numbered 1500, and came from Gyantsé and Shigatsé. They themselves, as they sat disarmed, huddled together under the eyes of our sentries, and clad in greasy skins and coarse blanketing, looked a truculent savage rabble, a

> "New-caught sullen people,
> Half devil and half child."

We resumed our march down the valley, which now bent round to the right, and widened out into flat alluvial meadows with some cultivation. Our path was strewed here and there with matchlocks, swords, boots, and bits of clothing thrown away by the retreating Tibetans, as we ascended to the "grassy ridge" (*Sao-gang*), where we halted for the night by the side of an old fort with some ruined *chortens*. The rocks near the river-bank were gaudily painted with Buddha's divinities over clumps of wild gooseberry.

Below this, next day, the valley opened out into a small land-locked meadow, where amongst some gnarled old willow trees stands the "Monastery of the Ancient Ear" (Na-nying—the "Naini" of the maps). This monastery is practically a fort with walls of enormous thickness. Both the monastery and its surrounding houses clustering under the hill are striped vertically by broad alternating bands of red, white, and blue, giving the appearance of a tent made of strips of coloured cloth.

Lower down we emerged from the rocky defiles on to a rich tract of alluvial flats with flourishing villages. At one of the larger of these, through which our road passed, at a Chinese staging-house (*tarjam*), the headman came out to pay his respects to the General. He wore a fluffy-topped, yellow woollen tam o' shanter, which all laymen should wear when visiting a Lama or high official, and, bowing with out-thrust tongue, he offered in his extended hands a silk ceremonial scarf (*Khatag*), which he placed around the General's neck like a priest's stole. This scarf is invariably offered by respectable Tibetans on all visits of ceremony, or when they wish to ask any favour. In addition, the headman brought as a peace-offering the skinned and dried carcass of a sheep, trussed up to sit on its hind legs like a cat—a ghastly arrangement of good-looking mutton. He gave the information that about 500 Tibetan soldiers had fled past this village on the night of the gorge fight, and were, he believed, in Gyantsé fort awaiting our arrival.

We were now in an open bay of the rich plain of the Gyantsé Valley, which we could see stretching up and down on either side about 2 miles ahead of us, although the town and its fort were yet invisible.

Our road had left the river-bank and ran between freshly-ploughed fields, below which it often sank several feet, evidently serving as a watercourse in the rainy season, when the hill torrents tear along here and rob the fields of much of their rich soil, leaving the useless pebbles and gravel.

On turning the corner of a spur on our left the broad plain-like expanse of the fertile valley of Gyantsé shot fully into view, dotted over with neat white-washed

THE GENERAL QUESTIONING VILLAGERS.
Note the headman carries a ceremonial scarf.

farmhouses and villas clustering in groves of trees amongst well-cultivated fields, and high over all near the middle of the plain the glistening white fort on its dark rock towered up boldly and apparently impregnable. Here our eyes rid us of the fallacy that Tibet is a vast treeless and barren country, peopled by roving pastoral tribes, whereas we saw a well-wooded plain with a settled peasantry engaged in agriculture.

As we drew nearer, the white houses of the town clustering around the foot of the rock came into view. There was no suitable open ground for camping on our side of the river, and the mounted infantry scouts having reported that the bridge over the river was within three-quarters of a mile from the fort, and therefore within range of the enemy's fire, the General forded the stream where we were, about 3 miles above the town, and we camped in the fields on the right bank, within 2 miles of the great fort or *Jong* of Gyantsé.

CHAPTER XI.

GYANTSÉ—ITS FORT AND TOWN.

"*A Jong on a suitable hill:*
A field on a suitable plain."
—TIBETAN PROVERB.

GYANTSÉ, or "The Dominating Peak," enjoys all the advantages of an ideal Tibetan town, as it possesses a commanding *jong* or fort on an upstanding rock to defend the town and its fertile fields in the well-watered valley which surrounds it. It was thus one of the earliest settlements of the Tibetans and the stronghold of petty kings, who had their castle on the rock, which thus gave the place its name; whilst its rich valley, extending all the way down to Shigatsé, was called "The Pleasant Province," or Nyang,[1] a name which the river still retains.

This flourishing large town, which is 213 miles from our base at Silliguri, and 140 miles from Lhasa, is of considerable commercial importance. Its central position at the junction of the roads from India and Bhotan, with those from Ladak and Central Asia, leading to Lhasa, well adapts it to be a distributing trade centre. Its extensive market is the third largest in Tibet, coming next after Lhasa and Shigatsé, and is especially celebrated for its woollen cloth and carpet manufactures. Several Nepalese and Chinese traders reside here.

[1] In a local inscription Gyantsé is called "The Upper Nyang, where all one's desires are spontaneously gratified."

GYANTSÉ FORT FROM THE NORTH.

SURRENDER OF GYANTSÉ FORT.

CHINESE GENERAL MA IS INTERESTED IN THE HELIOGRAPH.

The strikingly picturesque fort or *jong* crowns a bold precipitous rocky hill,[1] which rises with almost perpendicular cliffs from the river to a height of 500 feet above the plain. It recalls, to some extent, Edinburgh Castle, and, from one point of view, Mont St Michel, than which it is little less in size. Yet, strange to say, none of the three Englishmen who, prior to our arrival, passed by here—Bogle in 1774, and Turner in 1783, on their way to Shigatsé, and Manning in 1811, on his way to Lhasa—thought it worthy of detailed notice. The first attempts at description which we have are those of the exploring pundit, Nain Sing, in 1866, and of Lama Ugyen Gyatsho in 1883, whose account is reproduced by Babu Sarat Das, and fails to give any idea of what the place is like. It is the official residence of one of the two Depöns or governors of Western Tibet, assisted by two *Jongpöns* or district officers. Its garrison ordinarily consists of 50 Chinese soldiers under a lieutenant or *Chien-tsung*, and 500 Tibetan warriors under 2 majors or *Rupön* with their respective subordinates (see p. 165).

Its rock is connected by a saddle with another rocky spur of a hill behind it, about half a mile to the east, on the warm southern slopes of which, like an amphitheatre overlooking the town, stands the strongly fortified lamasery swarming with red-robed priests. Between these two rocky hills, on both sides of the saddle, lies the town of about a thousand well-built white houses, some of which also curve round to the south, underneath the walls of the fort (see map, p. 246).

General Macdonald, as soon as we arrived, on the 11th April, at the place fixed for our camp, in the fields about 2 miles from the fort, sent a note to the governor demanding the surrender of the *jong*.

[1] Its name is "Gyal-kar-tsé-mo" or "The Dominating Peak," from which the town gets its title abbreviated into Gyantsé.

Presently, as our camp was being pitched, a small crowd of officials, with a brilliant crimson umbrella, approached from the fort. They turned out to be our old acquaintance General Ma, and one of the *Jongpöns*, a fat, good-natured old man (photo, p. 177), with an opaque blue button in his cap, and wearing an especially long turquoise earring. They said that nearly all the Tibetan soldiery had left the fort that morning, but that they could not consent to our occupying it. General Macdonald replied that it was necessary that we should occupy it, and that if it were not handed over by 8 A.M. the next morning, it would be taken by force. They then went away, promising to send a reply.

No answer having been received next morning, General Macdonald advanced cautiously, with his force marshalled in battle array, to a mile from the fort, and our guns took up position to storm it. Just as we halted, a small party of officials rode out from the fort, led by General Ma under his crimson umbrella with the *Jongpön* and their minions. The Chinese General reported that all the Tibetan troops had been withdrawn. For fear of a plot, however, whilst a detachment of pioneers were sent up with fixed bayonets to occupy the fort, under cover of our guns, these Chinese and Tibetan officials were kept as hostages. Soon the khaki turbans of our men were seen streaming through the gateway and up the steep zigzag paths within the walls, and soon a message was signalled back that all was right, and over the castle flew the British flag from the topmost tower. So the fort was occupied without opposition, and the Chinese General, who had been interesting himself in the working of the heliograph (see photo, p. 198) was released.

Then General Macdonald, soon afterwards, with a few officers and a large escort, rode through the town, calling on the way at the monastery. Here he informed the Abbot, who came out with a crowd of his red-robed priests, of his displeasure at finding that a hundred of their number had taken part in the attack against us in the Red Gorge. The Abbot pleaded in excuse that they had been forced to do it against their will by the orders from Lhasa, and they now prayed to be forgiven. The General replied that the offence was most serious, that it was quite against Buddhist principles for anyone, least of all a monk, to fight, that in future they must confine themselves strictly to their religious duties, and if they did this they would not be interfered with; but if they were found in arms they would be treated like hostile laymen (see photo, p. 217).

As we rode on through the town, it was full of people; men, women and children, which was a good sign. Some of the former doubtless were unarmed soldiers with their arms hidden in the houses. There evidently had been little, if any, panic, though we were informed that several of the wealthy merchants had been sending off loads of their treasures during the previous five days to Shigatsé; whilst others, on the advice of their wizards, had hid theirs in the hills.

Next day our parties ransacked the fort for food-stores and ammunition. On nearer approach, its imposing piles of keeps, bastions and towers, all connected by walls and a network of stairways, were found to be generally in a very ruinous condition, and formed a rambling series of loopholed buildings with underground chambers suggestive of a giant's dungeons of dark torture.

Passing through a narrow lane of white houses in the Chinese quarter, skirting the south-eastern corner of the rocky hill—which we now saw to be a fine-grained sandstone banded by white quartz, accentuating the boldness of the cliffs—we ascended to the gateway of the fort by a rough stone pavement zigzagging up the face of an almost perpendicular rock, where our path was commanded by a tower on the battlements above. From the ceiling of the portico of the huge gateway—which is about 15 feet high, and supported by massive wooden beams in Tibetan fashion, the arch being here unknown—there hung the stuffed skins of four wild yaks, fearsome with great horns, protruding tongues, and glaring painted eyes. The wild yak, which stands nearly as high as a horse, is the most terrible beast known to the Tibetans, who, unable to secure living specimens, have placed here the stuffed skins of dead ones to protect the door, to scare away unwelcome visitors. The spirits of these dead beasts have also been invoked to drive away malignant devils from this gateway. The poor beasts were very much out of repair, they were deeply coated with dust, and the straw stuffing was projecting here and there through the gaping seams.

Entering the gateway now guarded by our sepoys, a longer zigzag led up about 100 feet under cover of a loopholed wall, past some ruinous houses to a large newly-built barrack, in which several tons of gunpowder were found, with about 100 miles of match-lock fuse-rope, and other munitions of war. From here there was a track across several chambers to the rear gateway, facing the town and monastery. Continuing our ascent, the path led through a small paved court to the yellow-walled chapel. Around this court a row of slate slabs with carved and painted Buddhas was let into the wall, and at one end was a finely inscribed stone[1] reciting the virtues of a chief who restored the

[1] This slate slab, carved in raised letters, I removed for the Calcutta museum, as a historical document as well as a specimen of fine carving. Its inscription begins "The religious King, the Sage, lived in the palace of "The Dominating Peak (Gyantsé), built of stone and beautiful as a vase of turquoise."

GATE OF GYANTSÉ FORT.

BLOWING UP OF GYANTSÉ FORT GATE.

fort and erected these carvings for the good fortune of his wife.

The chapel gate stood open, and entering it the attendant priest conducted us across a small courtyard, past some store-houses and dwelling-rooms of attendants, brightened by some flowers, stocks and asters in pots, to the door of the temple, which he unlocked and threw open. In the gloom of the small dark chamber, straight in front of us, only a few yards off above the low altar, was the usual colossal gilt image of the Buddha, seated placidly in the conventional cross-legged attitude, and in striking contrast to the bejewelled images around him, unadorned save for the white silk ceremonial scarf draping his shoulders, and the solitary turquoise marking the luck-spot between his eyebrows. His image, it was noticeable, was of the original Indian type, undisfigured by any "bump of wisdom," and thus very different from the sleek-limbed and oblique-eyed Japanese forms of the Great Teacher at Kamakura and elsewhere. On the altar (*chösam*) in front of this great idol were simple unchased brass bowls with perfumed water, the ever-burning, butter-fed lamp emitting a dim religious light, and a few artificial paper flowers, the offerings of votaries on a pilgrimage (*kyilkor*). Besides a massive white-metalled funereal *chorten* with ornate mouldings studded over with turquoises; a few books on shelves and some scrolls painted with figures of the saints, hanging like Kakemonos from the painted pillars and on the walls, there was little else remarkable.

Still higher up, beyond this temple, following the zigzagging path, we passed many more tall buildings on the edge of the precipitous cliffs, most of them mere shells with their roofs fallen in and their high walls seamed with gaping cracks, and in such a tottering state that we involuntarily hurried past lest they should overwhelm us. Climbing still higher near the crest, where the British flag flapped noisily in the wind, were more chambers and dark cellars crammed full of grain.

From the topmost rampart of the castle a magnificent bird's-eye view is obtained of the wide valley and its surrounding hills for many miles around. Far beneath you lies the town, with its people like crawling black ants; rising beyond it is the great red-walled monastery (p. 216), like a rival fort, enclosing the glittering golden-domed pagoda, and across the green plain, in the middle distance, some 5 miles off, rises the dark hill of Tse-chen, dotted with the white cells of its monks, a town in itself (see sketch, p. 266). From this high-perched eyrie the old warrior king must often have looked down with pride on his prosperous town and the far-reaching fields, studded over with the trim white farms and dark garden groves of the nobles and rich merchants of the town. Our own outspread camp was within easy rifle range from here, and each individual tent stood sharply exposed to view.

Enormous stores of gunpowder were found, as a result of our search, amounting to several tons, in addition to other military munitions, which showed that the Tibetans had prepared for and expected war. This gunpowder was destroyed by us by throwing it into the river. Very few guns were found, most of these having been removed. As we were so short of food, what was of much more importance to us than this country-made gunpowder, was the huge stock of grain, about 100 tons, of barley, flour, and peas. This had evidently been accumulated for years to enable the garrison to withstand a siege. As this food was all in good condition, strings of mules and coolies were soon removing it to our camp. Large stores also of dried sheep and yak meat were found, which our Nepalese and Tibetan coolies carried off with avidity, being gluttonous flesh-eaters.

As we were searching for grain, a horrible chamber was discovered full of decapitated human heads of men, women and children. One of the men's heads seemed almost European in countenance. The gory necks of several showed that the heads had been struck off during life, which disposes of the idea that the Buddhism of the Lamas stops short of the atrocious crime of murder.

As the fortress was of too large area to be held by the small escort available to remain with the Mission at Gyantsé, and no good water-supply was near at hand, the General decided to dismantle the fort; and he selected as a suitable residence for the Mission and its escort the country house of a grandee, at the bridge over the river, thus commanding the bridge and securing an inexhaustible water-supply. This old summer-seat and farm of the Changlo family was at the time the property of the governor of Gyantsé, the "Duke" Tapshi, one of the five in Tibet who bear this Chinese title, which is mostly reserved for the brothers of the present and past Dalai Lamas and of their successors. Our large camp was accordingly moved to this place, which was about 1100 yards south of the fort (see plan, p. 246), and opposite the similar country-seat of the Phala family, the unfortunate friends of Sarat C. Das, which being commanded by an adjoining hill, was unsuitable. Under the shelter of the Changlo woods, we were screened to some extent from the whirlwinds of dust which tore every afternoon through our camp, and were largely due to our having had to turn off the irrigation channels from the surrounding freshly-ploughed fields, which in the dry air quickly dried up and deluged us with their dust when the wind blew. The wind now was not cold, but in January we were told its intensity and cold were such that it kept the people indoors for the greater part of the day.

We had an interesting visitor in the person of the elder son of the Raja of Sikhim, who should have been heir-apparent to his father; but under the Tibetan intrigues in Sikhim sixteen years ago was carried off by the Lamas, as a child, to Tibet, and as he refused to return was deposed by our Government from the succession, his younger brother being appointed in his stead. Meanwhile he has married a Tibetan lady of rank, and has a country house and small estate presented to him by the Lhasa Government about 10 miles up the valley above Gyantsé. He is a sturdy, sensible-looking and well-mannered young man of about twenty-seven years of age. He was really brought in as a captive by the mounted infantry, but on his identity being discovered was set free, after having stayed to lunch in our camp.

After making arrangements for the defence of this post at Changlo, and establishing the Mission comfortably there with 600 rifles, two machine Maxims and two 7-pounders, under Lieutenant-Colonel Brander, with over three weeks' supply of provisions and ammunition, and after dismantling the fort by blowing up its two gateways, General Macdonald left Gyantsé on the 19th April with the rest of his force for Chumbi. This was done in order to push up more food supplies and ammunition and reinforcements from India, and to arrange fortified posts on the road for the safety of the convoys which had to pass up and down this difficult and dangerous line of communications, carrying the supplies necessary for the existence of the advanced posts ahead,[1] while exposed to attack in the numerous defiles and gorges, thus causing General Macdonald great anxiety for their safety.

[1] As an instance of the rate at which food supplies dwindled on the way up the line by being eaten up on the road by the posts and the coolie porters, of 360 loads from Silliguri only 45 would reach Gyantsé.

Changlo Manor, with its farm and out-buildings on the river-bank, was soon converted into a fortified defensive post, by a little loopholed wall enclosing its 300 yards or so of circuit, and by removal of all out-buildings beyond. The space within accommodated, in tents or in buildings, both the Mission and the whole of our garrison. The Mission occupied the best block of buildings within the weakest corner of the walls; the hospital and commissariat stores got most of the other buildings. The troops were encamped in the courtyards, whilst the regimental officers turned the private chapel into a messroom, not before the Tibetan books in the library, to the number of about 450 volumes, had been secured by me for the British Museum. I got a nice room in the Mission block, the special room of the "Duke" himself. Its walls were lavishly adorned with rich coloured frescoes of Lamaist saints, the wooden pillars were finely carved and painted, the windows were papered in Chinese fashion, and its floor was a tesselated pavement of pebbles and mortar worked to a high polish like marble. One gallant officer secured a neat, comfortable room inside the shrine of the great water-driven praying-wheel. When the water was switched off, this great painted barrel of prayers, 5 feet high, which turned on its pivot at the slightest touch, was made a useful dumb-waiter by fixing on it a few nails and a bracket or two.

An enormous stock of fire-wood was found in cellars and outhouses; there must have been at least thirty tons of great logs. Wood, however, was very plentiful outside, as a dense coppice, about half a mile long, of great willow and other trees, ran along the river-bank up to our very walls. This, indeed, was one of the most obvious strategical defects of our position, as it would clearly afford cover to the enemy should they attack us.

This objectionable thicket was therefore slightly thinned near our post whenever building wood was required, though it was no easy matter to fell such large trees; and all straggling walls and outhouses were removed to give as clear a front as possible. Inside our wall a small unoccupied plot, under the great trees, was fenced off and planted out as a vegetable garden, for as it was known that the Mission must inevitably be some months at Gyantsé, and General Macdonald could not possibly return with the provisions and reinforcements to go on to Lhasa, should that advance be necessary, for over two months, one member of the Mission, with admirable forethought had brought up a box of Sutton's seeds.

As gardeners, a buxom Tibetan dame and one of her husbands—as these polyandrous ladies are endowed with several — were engaged. They brought in rich, loamy soil from the woods and formed it into beds, with gravelly paths in between, and after the seeds were sown, watered them tenderly with pails of water which they brought in from the river. Under this assiduous care we soon had croppings of young cress salad, with which and with our mutton and a dairy of half-bred yak cows, abundant eggs, fowls, potatoes, turnips, dried apricots, and other fresh supplies from the town, we were able to live in luxury after our meagre fare and hardships of the long winter and the march.

The almighty rupee began to work wonders amongst the people. Within a few days the people of the town and the adjacent villages—men, women and children—came flocking in scores to our camp, bringing in all kinds of things for sale, laden on their own backs or on strings of yaks and donkeys. The Lamas, too, having partaken of the largess of the British army, came trudging in under bags of grain or sheaves of fodder, so that quite a large bazaar or market was formed immediately outside the gate of our post.

Here thrifty housewives, bedecked with barbaric jewellery, their broad smiling faces smeared repulsively over with patches of brown pigment, spread their wares on the ground or on stalls, and assisted by their pig-tailed menfolk in long coats of cherry-red homespun, blue girdled at the waist, and shod in brilliant parti-coloured long cloth boots, drove a thriving trade. Their customers were not only the Commissariat department buying grain and fodder, but crowds of our soldiers and followers, bargaining for eggs, fowls, butter, etc., all of which were ridiculously cheap. Officers, too, in quest of curios, wandered in and out amongst the stalls. There was nothing the people were not willing to sell in exchange for rupees. They would take off their turquoise earrings and other ornaments, also their treasured amulet charm-boxes, and press you to buy them. Even the sleek Lamas brought out their sacred scrolls and books and images and bargained them for cash, and everybody seemed supremely pleased, never having had so much money in their lives before. A free hospital was opened for their sick, in which Captain Walton of the Indian Medical Service began mending hare-lips, removing the blindness of cataract, and treating other ailments, for which the people seemed most grateful. Several of them offered their service as labourers or carpenters or otherwise. In the fields everywhere around the peasantry were ploughing and sowing peaceably. Even the big Lamas of the monastery, who had paid up the small fine of grain inflicted on them for fighting against us at the Red Gorge—part of which had been remitted on an appeal from the Tashi Grand Lama to forgive them—made a display of proffering their friendship.

In this seemingly amicable state of affairs many

of us began to go about sight-seeing to the town and the monasteries and hermitages in the neighbourhood, and wandered up and down the valley and up the hillsides for miles, after game or fishing, or collecting birds or butterflies, whilst survey parties with small escorts went long distances over the mountains without mishap. The people everywhere were elaborately civil, though most of the Lamas looked askance at us.

It was always a pleasure to get out of our walled post to ramble in the spring mornings along the shady river-bank, where the birds with joyous notes were busy building, and out into the open reaches where wild bar-headed geese and mallards, still unmolested, strutted about unconcernedly in the shallows, and to wend our way towards the town and the temples or hillsides. From these were obtained ever-changing views of the upstanding fort as we passed through the well-cultivated valley dotted over with trim white-washed little farmhouses, nestling in copses of large trees with fluttering prayer-flags stretched from tree to tree by the pious hands of the cottagers. Along the footpaths by the brooks, lined by hedges of pollarded willows, with here and there a tall poplar, parti-coloured rags inscribed with prayers to the water-spirits drooped from the bushes overhanging the stream. Every house seemed crammed full of sacks of meal and other food, while cattle and hundreds of sheep grazed on the hillsides above the plain. It was much more like the scenery in a prosperous bit of continental Europe than the bleak conventional pictures of treeless Tibet which figure in the accounts of previous travellers.

The bazaar or market-place had a special attraction for many of us, as the centre of business and commerce, in view of the object of the Mission in coming here being to remove the barriers raised by the hostile

CHORTENS AND WAYSIDE TEXTS AT GYANTSÉ.

NUN AND ATTENDANTS.

TIBETANS OF GYANTSÉ.
The women are wearing the fashionable Lhasa tiara.

Lamas against the trade of this town passing to India, and to divert it again to India from its present eastern outlet to the manufacturing districts of China, many hundred miles further off by road than India is.

The road to the market led us round under the cliff of the high-perched *jong*, past some deep, old wells, dug for use in a siege, and past a cluster of *chortens* and shrines erected to the protecting divinities of this rock (see photo here). Most of these little shrines were in a rather dilapidated state, giving the impression that religion was somewhat neglected here. Above all the other gods, and above the countless repetitions of the Grand Lama's spell, the "*Om! mani padme Hung!*"—that universal panacea for all ills, which in crudely carved letters covered the face of the stones everywhere—the highest place of all was given to the Lady of Mercy, a sort of Virgin Mary, who is the especial saviouress of those who are in distress on rocks as well as of sailors on the sea. She is one of the most popular of the Buddhist divinities, and is the especial patron of women, amongst whom her name Dölma (the Indian "Tara") is as common a personal name in Tibet as Mary is with Christians. The next highest place is given to the four-armed picture of the white Grand Lama (see frontispiece), and slightly below is the most popular saint of the Lamas, St Padma, with his two wives (see p. 115). All the shrines are open in front, where a screen is hung to protect the frescoes from the rain (see photo here). Beside these are several niches with inserted stone tablets and plastered posters bearing pious sentences and texts in ornamental Tibetan letters, to improve the minds of passing readers, the gifts of devout laymen—not Lamas, as the latter are not ecclesiastics, and do not preach or teach the people, but keep their learning to themselves. They are mostly maxims of a moral kind,[1] and some of them contain beautiful similes :—

MAXIMS BY THE WAYSIDE.

"The great King Srongtsan Gampo has said: 'Speech should float forth freely like a bird in the sky, and be clothed in charming dress like a goddess. At the outset, the object of the speech should be made clear as the unclouded sky, the speech should then proceed like the excavation of treasure, the arguments should be agile like deer chased by fresh hounds without hesitation or pause, lastly, it should be suitably ended, otherwise its effect will be lost.'

"*The Five Qualities of Speech.*—Speech must be bold as a lion, soft as a gentle hare, impressive as a serpent, pointed as an arrow and evenly balanced like a sceptre (*dorje*) held in the middle.

. . . .

"*The Ten Faults.*—Want of faith in religious books, disrespect for teachers, unpleasant conduct, covetousness, talking too much, laughing at another's misfortune, using abusive language, getting angry with old people, robbing and pilfering.

"*The Eight Acts of Low-born Men.*—Improvidence, using coarse language, disrespect, boasting, 'making big eyes' or staring, loose conduct, coarse manners and stealing.

"*The Nine Follies.*—Praising oneself, coveting another's wife, having no wife, conferring power on one's wife, cursing a well-wisher, borrowing things which one cannot return, not cherishing one's brothers, ignorance of right and wrong, coveting the things of others.

. . . .

"Talk regarding Religion and the cause and effect of deeds should only be spoken into the ears of clever

[1] Some of these are extracts from the manual of trite sayings called *The Jewelled Rosary of Deep Subjects*.

monks; tales of worldly misery and joys should only be spoken into the ears of relatives and friends.

. . . .

"*The Roots of Quarrels* are three, namely: Yes! (assertion) What! (doubting sarcasm) and You! (abuse). The kite quarrels and fights with other birds, the horse with the yak, the weasel with the snake, the crow with the owl, as these are enemies through their actions in former existences."

Nearing the town, we passed a few suburban houses of the better class, with their walls painted with long broad stripes of alternating red, white and blue, giving the appearance at a distance of a palisade of coloured beams, or a wall hung round with Tibetan floorcloths of these favourite stripes. The small gardens and courts of these houses are enclosed by low mud-walls similarly striped, or built of sun-dried bricks in ornamental fashion, leaving spaces in the form of squares, diamonds, or crosses, and containing pots of carefully tended stocks and hollyhocks, which already so early in spring glowed brilliantly in the mid-day sun.

On the outskirts of the town, which is not walled as was alleged in some native reports, we were always met by swarms of sturdy beggars of all ages, roguish, ragged men, women and children, who prowled about on the outlook especially for newcomers and strangers. They were not easily shaken off. When failing to extract alms by whining, they hummed a song and capered about trying the opposite tactics.

In the narrow streets we met people going to or from the market, men in flowing cherry-coloured coats riding lean ponies, which they flicked with their dog-whips; lines of donkeys plodding in single file with loads of grain or fodder; chattering women, slatternly dressed, carrying baskets or children slung on their backs. The dogs here were very cowardly, slinking away on our approach, and seldom growling unless when tied up. It is a compact town of stone-built houses, mostly two-storeyed, with wooden balconies facing the tortuous main street, whence narrow lanes strike off into uninviting slums. The better houses have papered Chinese windows, and have printed texts and charms pasted over the doors and walls. All are white-washed and have their doors and window-frames picked out in dull red, giving the exterior an artistic appearance; but the open doors reveal the squalor inside. The air everywhere is heavily laden with "the odours of the East," as Tibetan notions of sanitation are most rudimentary.

As there are no regular shops in which things are displayed for sale, excepting some eating-houses in the Chinese quarter, everybody having things to sell brings them to the bazaar, which is a largish square at the entrance to the great pagoda of the monastery, a celebrated place of pilgrimage. The bazaar thus intercepts the pilgrims, most of whom come prepared to combine a little business with their round of devotion. Indeed, the market-place belongs to the monastery, which derives a large revenue from it, and from a tax on the houses surrounding it.

The trade season is in the winter months from the end of November, when the rains are over, the crops harvested, and provisions everywhere obtainable; when the streams are all fordable or frozen over for passage, and caravans come from Ladak, Nepal, and upper Tibet, bringing gold, borax, salt, wool, musk and furs, to exchange for tea, tobacco, sugar, cotton goods, broadcloth, and hardware in large quantities (see p. 476). Still, even now in April, when it is not the regular trade season, as we approached the bazaar it was humming with the noise of a motley throng driving a petty trade. The traders displayed their wares in booths or on the pavement by the roadside, where they sat behind their piles of goods, waiting to sell or barter their commodities, which consisted, amongst other things, of tea, tobacco, sugar, cotton cloth, brown and yellow broadcloth, and dark corduroy, cotton thread — red and white — matches, pipes, enamelled iron tumblers, kerosene oil—bearing the Russian mark, but which came by way of Darjeeling—and a host of Tibetan nicknacks, drugs, fresh vegetables, meat, including pork, and the barley beer of the country. The most attractive exhibits for us were the carpets and saddle-rugs of local manufacture, for which this town is famous. Although these are full of delicate art tints of faded rose and blue and gold, showing that the colour sense is well developed, the weavers have no specific names for any but the more elementary colours. In this way the Tibetans will say, "Saddle me the *red* horse," meaning a chestnut-coloured one. Thus, these people afford another piece of evidence against Gladstone's assumption that the ancient Greeks of the Homeric age were either colour-blind or deficient in colour perception, because they did not record names for secondary and tertiary shades, whereas, like the Tibetans, they may merely have been deficient in the terminology.

The pedlars and traders were mostly Tibetans. The lanky men, oblique eyed, with fairly formed nose, have their weather-beaten broad unwashed face brightened by turquoise earrings, their pigtailed locks are capped by a fur-lined winter hat with upturned ear-lappets, or the ordinary soft Chinese felt with turned-up brim. Shod in the universal, bright cloth boots, their greasy garnet-coloured coat is girdled at the waist like a dressing-gown, and hitched up to form a capacious breast-pocket, from which they produce all sorts of things for sale with one hand, while they devoutly finger the beads of their rosary with the other. The women generally resemble their sisters at Phari, though somewhat less unclean, and wear the same head-dress, except a few perceptibly more addicted to washing, who come from Lhasa, who wear as a head-dress over their smoothly-brushed black locks, parted in the middle, a red cloth fillet like a tiara (*patuk*) studded with coral, turquoise, and amber. All wear a big apron of striped home-spun, and the married women usually a massive bracelet of white conch shell on the right wrist. Most of them, down to the wrinkled old dame sitting behind her outspread pile of trifles, twirl a prayer-wheel in hand (see p. 66) and incessantly drone the mystic spell, "*Om mani!*"

Nepalese, or more properly Newaris, from Nepal are here to the number of six or seven. They are all Buddhists and have married Tibetan wives. One of them informed me that the Tibetans threatened to kill them when they heard that Goorkhas were assisting us in our army. They wear small turbans like a pork-pie cap, the head-dress of their native country, and a longer and tighter coat than the Tibetans.

A very few of the Chinese are traders, most of them are officials, living in their own quarter of the town to the south of the *jong*. They lord it over the Tibetans; even the lowest of them never salute the Tibetan grandees. There were a good many half-breeds, called "Koko," the descendants of Chinese who had married Tibetan wives.

Some shaven Lamas were always loafing in the bazaar, fingering various things and evidently helping themselves without payment. Lounging about were a few criminals with their necks in a great square wooden stock (*Tse-go*), the Chinese "cangue," a mode of punishment by which the Tibetan Government saves the cost of feeding and housing the criminal, letting him provide for himself. It was amusing to see how some of our Tibetan coolies who had been enlisted at Darjeeling as hospital ambulance-bearers, and who had been so terrified on the way lest we should be defeated by their countrymen, now strutted about the bazaar and town giving themselves great airs as part of the victorious army of the conquerors.

So many of these people in the bazaar were pitted by smallpox; some of them only just recovering from this disease, which is well known to ravage this country very frequently like a plague, that we took the precaution to get re-vaccinated, and all remained entirely free from this pest.

As the weather rapidly grew milder and more springlike, we ventured farther into the country to see the carpet factory at Gobshi down the valley, and some celebrated temples and hermitages among the mountains.

CHAPTER XII.

TEMPLES, PRIESTS, AND CONVENTS OF GYANTSÉ AND NEIGHBOURHOOD WITH VISIT TO THE CAVES OF THE ENTOMBED HERMITS.

"*Without a Lama in front there is no* [*approach to*] *God.*"
—LAMA PROVERB.

MUCH finer and very much more numerous than any we had yet seen were the temples of Gyantsé and neighbourhood. Here in this fat valley swarms of sleek Lama-priests, who live idly on the labour of the laity, have congregated in and around this flourishing town and its castle, and thrust down the throats of the peasantry that Buddhism consists in sacrifice to idols. They have thus induced the people to lavish all their wealth upon building and beautifying scores of temples, and filling them with idols; and through their power over the latter, the priests, as the sole mediators between God and man, are supposed to be able to drive away the hordes of evil spirits that are ever on the outlook to inflict on the poor Tibetan and his family disease, accident, or other misfortune; and the malign influence pursues him through every detail, not merely of his daily life in his present existence, but in the life beyond the grave.

From these vexatious imposts by the Lamas, paid with abject and pitiful subservience, it has resulted that some of the more luxurious temples possess features of considerable architectural interest, and occasionally

FORTIFIED MONASTERY OF GYANTSÉ.
(Note white specks of Hermitages on the hill above.)

GREAT TEMPLE AND PAGODA OF GYANTSÉ.

INSIDE GYANTSÉ MONASTERY.

art treasures of value, the votive offerings of wealthy devotees.

The temples of the large fortified monastery of Gyantsé were particularly fine. This monastery, with its quarters for 600 monks, and numerous shrines, is a little town in itself. It covers the whole crescent-shaped southern slope of a rugged hill which rises some 250 feet above the plain and town, about a third of a mile to the north of the precipitous crag crowned by the *jong*. Its clusters of buildings rise up in several tiers like a huge amphitheatre, and encircle at their base a great pagoda standing on the edge of the plain below a celebrated place of pilgrimage whose minaret-like top, of massive plates of burnished gold, towers up nearly 100 feet high, a glittering landmark for all the country round. The whole is surrounded by a great fortified and loopholed wall about 20 feet high, which curves round the sky-line on the hill-top, like a gigantic horse-shoe of battlements and turrets, a mighty rampart. On asking why a monastery was so strongly fortified, I was told that the wall was meant to protect it from its rival, the *jong*, at a time when a former abbot of the monastery disputed the temporal power with the reigning chief, whose castle was the *jong*. This, if true, is curious, as the building of this monastery is ascribed to the same princelet, Rabtan the Religious King, who built the *jong* about six hundred years ago. In any case it shows the militant character of the Lamas.

This monastery is named "The Illustrious Circle [of pilgrimage]" or *Pal-k'or*, with reference to its enclosed pagoda, and as it so closely adjoins the town, the busy haunts of men, it is known not as a hermitage or *Gompa*, but as "The Religious Ward or Residence" (*Cho'i-de*).

As we rode up, clattering over the paved street from the market-place, we were beset outside the great doorway by a crowd of clamorous beggars, who lounged beside the prayer-barrels, and amongst whom I noticed a leper. Satisfying these with a few coins, we entered a wooden portico under a balcony supported by beams, modelled, as is the whole doorway, after the fashion of the entrances to the Buddhist cave-temples of mediæval India, as figured by Fergusson, and like those and all the stone buildings of Tibet displaying entire ignorance of the arch.

In this porch, on either side of the door, are ranged as janitors the colossal leering figures of the four mythological guardian kings of the quarters. These are clad in mail armour of Chinese pattern, each bearing a special emblem and having a different colour: the complexion of the guardian of the East, the quarter of the rising sun, is white like the dawn; that of the guardians of the West is a glowing red, testifying the setting sun; the southern guardian, as king of the Genii of Riches, is a golden colour, and the northern as presiding over the realms of ice is a cold green. Flanking these giants are two sturdy, dark blue, ferocious devils (see photos, p. 223 and for others of this class), the same which we find at the entrance to Japanese Buddhist temples, who are supposed to scare away all harmful intruders, human or of the spirit world. Like Milton's embodiment of Death;

> "Black" each stood "as night,
> Fierce as ten furies, terrible as hell,
> And shook a dreadful dart."

Riding through the gateway, whose massive wooden doors, nearly 10 feet high, embellished by iron bosses and ornate hinge-bars, stand always open in the daytime, we entered an inner porch bearing some notices in Tibetan and Chinese and a poster with the rules of conduct for the monks. Beyond this, in the paved courtyard which runs up to the great pagoda and the chief temple, we were met by the abbot and some of the monks to show us over the buildings, and here we dismounted. The abbot was a middle-aged man of dignified mien and fair intelligence, but as he had only recently come here, and was not familiar with the place and its history, he referred me to one of the local monks as a guide. The bevy of shaven monks, in their dark ruby-coloured robes, who now surrounded us were anything but ascetic or intellectual in looks. All were visibly unfamiliar with ablution, as if purity of soul was not compatible with cleanness of body. Only the abbot has the right, strictly speaking, to the title of "Lama," equivalent to "superior one." The other monks are called "*Tāpa*," or "learners or students," though honoured in the popular language with the higher title.

This monastery is peculiar in being of a catholic kind, tenanted by both yellow- and red-cap sects. It formerly was a stronghold of the red-cap Sakya sect, when the latter possessed the temporal sovereignty over Tibet; and this sect, as well as the unreformed red-caps (the Nyingma), were allowed to retain portions of the monastery when the yellow caps overthrew the Sakya rule. This concession was doubtless made for political reasons, as this monastery and its surrounding valleys were the home of the "discoverers" of the popular apocalyptic "revelations" (fig. p. 220), which prescribe a large amount of profitable devil-worship that is openly admitted and practised now by the yellow-caps, although unorthodox. These diverse sects thus housed together live side by side as in different colleges within one wall. Each has its own separate cluster of temples and residential buildings, dormitories, store-rooms, etc., where each lives according to its own customs and rites, not mixing with the others except at "High Mass" in the general assembly hall of the great temple. On this occasion all must don the yellow cap for the time being, in acknowledgment of the pre-eminence of the dominant yellow caps. It contains nominally 500 monks, but not half of that number were present.

A DISCOVERER OF "REVELATION-GOSPELS."
(*Lha-tsun chempo.*)
Holds a trumpet of human thighbone in right hand, and a skull-bowl in left.

Proceeding across the courtyard—here bounded by buildings faced by rows of slabs of stone bearing gaudily-painted, engraved images of Buddhas and the saints, below which are rows of prayer-barrels to be turned by the passing hands of the faithful — we approach the great temple with the pagoda towering beyond it.

The great temple, or "House of the Gods" (*Lha-k'ang*), is Egyptian in its massiveness, and in the tapering style of its walls. Its three-storeyed façade, a fine specimen of wooden architecture, repeats the features and figures of the outer doorway, but on a larger scale, brilliant in crimson and green and gold. Heavy brown woollen curtains hang as a sunshade over the porch of the two lower storeys, and on the deep, terra-cotta turf wall of the upper storey is emblazoned on either side of the central window a huge gilt monogram of the mystic "*Om mani*" like a heraldic shield of arms. From each of the four corners of the roof projects a small turret of black yak-hair cloth banded by a white cross of calico, supported on a framework of loops about 6 feet high, the so-called "banners of victory" (*gyal-tshan*). These circular lucky banners are also planted on the roofs of palaces and the houses of the nobility and headmen, and some of them are surmounted by a trident on a short pole with silken streamers (*chab-dar*), symbolic of the Buddhist trinity (see also photo, p. 9). Near the centre of the roof, over the great altar with the chief image, rises a gilded roofed pavilion of Chinese pattern, topped by the great gilded vase, the finial ornament of so many Indian Buddhist monuments.

Ascending the broad flight of steps, as we passed between the crimson pillars of the verandah, it was noteworthy that amongst the images behind the grating the yellow king of the Genii of Riches, who is usually attended by Caliban-like genii resembling the slave of Aladdin's lamp, carries in his hand a weasel like the rat in the hand of Vulcan in Memphis. From here we entered the sacred portals of the great door which faces the west, and passed into an inner vestibule covered with gaudy frescoes. On either hand a stairway leads off to the upper storey, while in front is the door of the great temple or "assembly hall" (*Du-k'ang*), on each side of which hang the mouldering stuffed skins of two black watch-dogs, recalling the old Roman gateway inscription, "*cave canem.*"

As I entered, two monks were looking at that picture on the right of the door (photo, p. 222), which I called "The Wheel of Life" when I first discovered it in a fresco in the ancient cave-temples of Ajanta in India, and brought it to the notice of Western readers. It has since been popularised by Kipling in his *Kim*, as the quest of his old Lama. It looks like a large painted spoked plate held in the clutches of a monster, and depicts in concrete symbolic form round the rim the chain of abstract conceptions upon which Buddha hung his doctrine of delivery from the circle of rebirths and all their entailed misery. Between the spokes are portrayed the miseries of the soul, or its Buddhist equivalent, in all the various forms of transmigration, from the heavens of the gods where Zeus is depicted with his thunderbolts nodding on the golden hill of his Olympus, to the tortures of hell (for many old western superstitions have place in the Tibetan mythology), which are pictured in a horrible way, somewhat as in Dante's *Inferno*, as a warning to evildoers. But the ethical value of this doctrine of retribution, or *Karma*, is heavily discounted by the pious fraud which assigned such superior influence to the services of the Lama-priests, who are here credited with the power of ameliorating the destiny of sinners, even if already in hell, should their earthly relatives offer the Lamas gifts and employ them to do costly rites and sacrifice for this purpose. Thus in all the various worlds through which souls transmigrate in the Buddhist metaphysics, Lamas are pictured as going about like Anchises acting as the guide of Æneas in the infernal regions. In the hells they are plying their

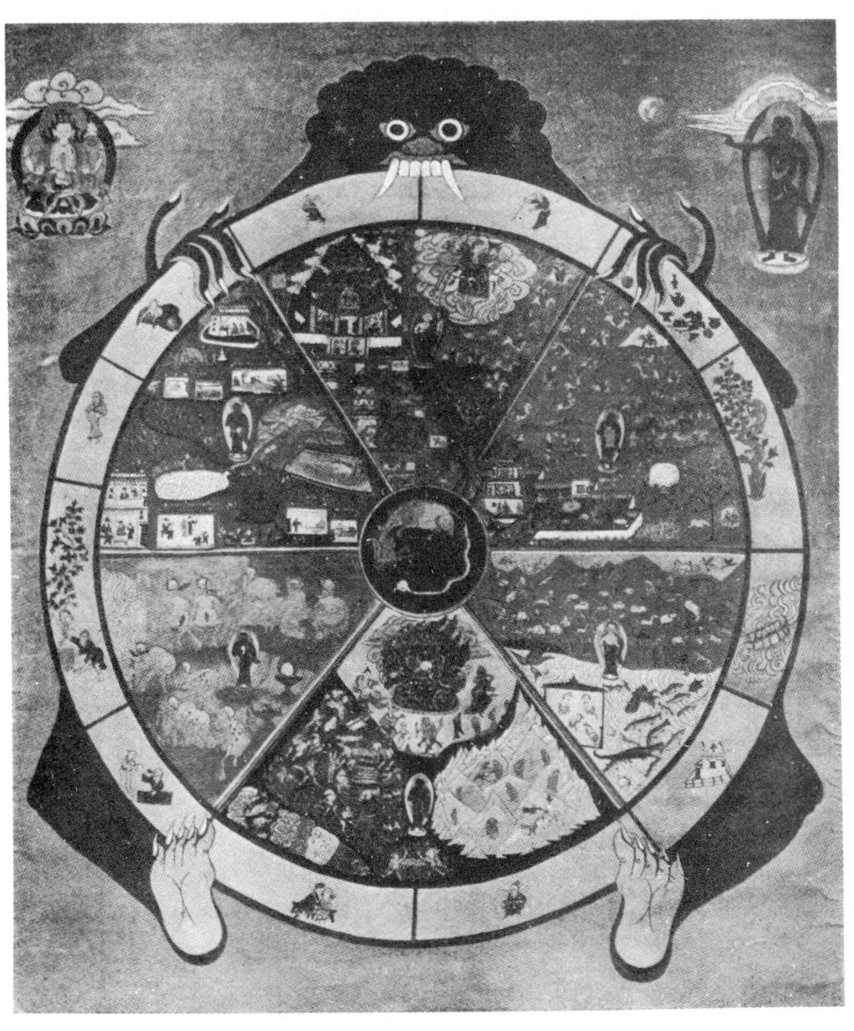

THE BUDDHIST WHEEL OF LIFE.
From a Tibetan painting.

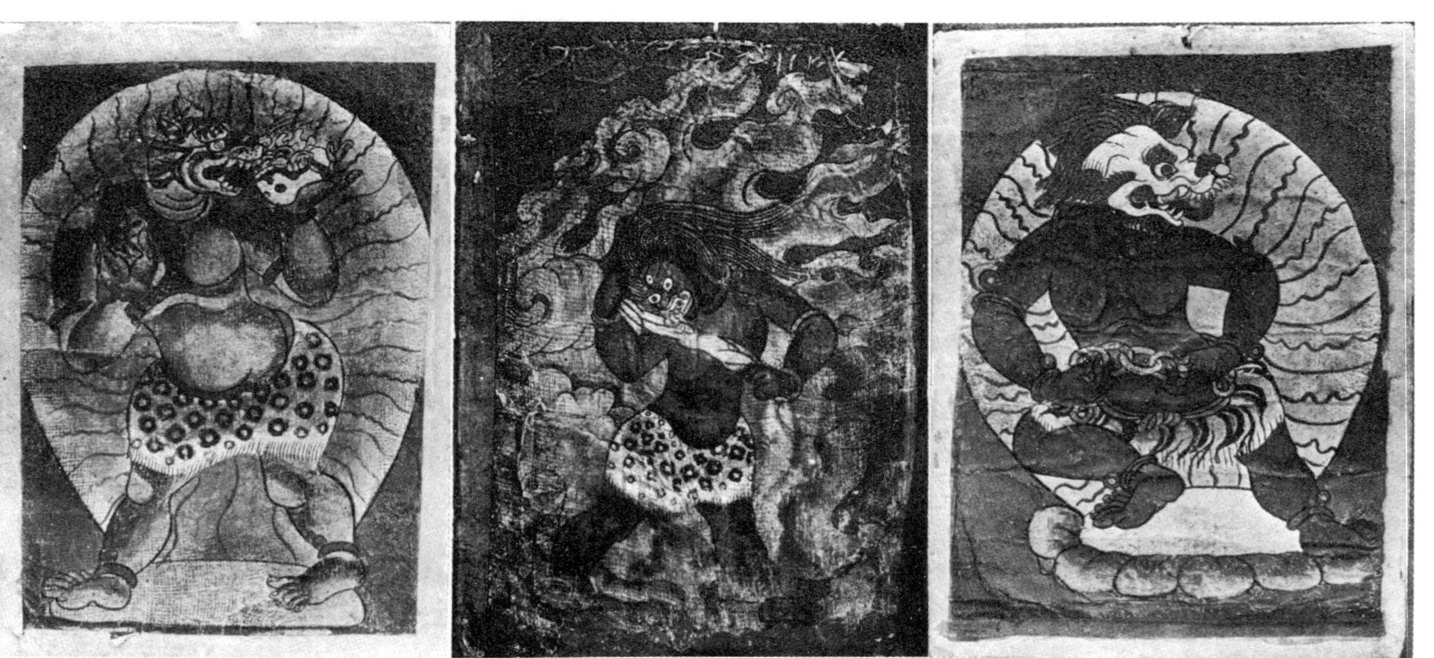

MAN-EATING DEVILS.

These are aboriginal *Bon* demons and are exorcised by the Lamas with texts from the Buddhist Scriptures.

prayer-wheels and muttering spells for the benefit of tormented souls whose relatives make it worth their while. More than once have I been told by a sad-looking Tibetan that the reason for his distress was that his Lama had told him that he had got the poor man's deceased wife or child half-way through such and such a hell, but unless he paid much more money to do such and such rites not only would the soul of the deceased suffer more terrible torture, but there was a risk of its becoming a malignant ghost to come back and haunt its living relatives, one of the most dreaded inflictions. This particular "Wheel" at Gyantsé was about five and a half feet in diameter, but was not so elaborate nor so well painted as the specimen which I published some years ago. In the centre of hell is the merciless King of the Dead judging the deceased by the ordeal of scales, weighing the souls against the good deeds, represented by black and white pebbles respectively. In the "celestial" mansions is depicted the Wishing Tree of Paradise, which produces on its branches any object desired by the Just, a widely diffused old world myth, and the prototype of our Christmas Tree.

The assembly hall or church (*Du-k'ang*) in which the Lamas congregate for High Mass was as usual on the ground floor, and at its far end opposite the door, through a vista of pillared nave and aisles (see p. 401), was a small chapel with the high altar on which great butter-lamps burn everlastingly sacred fire before the chief idol. So much butter is consumed in feeding this and the other lamps of the temple, that the abbot pleaded the necessity of keeping alive these sacred fires as an excuse to be forgiven the fine of butter levied on the monks for taking part in the fight against us in the Red Gorge. The hall itself was a large dark room about 20 yards each way and 15 feet high, faintly lit by the entrance door, and small windows on the roof, through which filtered a "dim religious light." When our eyes grew accustomed to the gloom we could see that the walls were covered by brilliantly painted and gilded frescoes of Buddhas, canonised saints, and State-gods and grotesque devils, above which, and also on the scarlet pillars, were hung pictures of the same kind painted on cloth and framed in brocade like Japanese Kakemono scrolls (see p. 401).

On the high altar, where a colossal gilt Buddha sits looking down serenely amidst a multitude of satellites, were many offerings of the pious. Silk scarves hung several deep round the necks of the favourite idols.

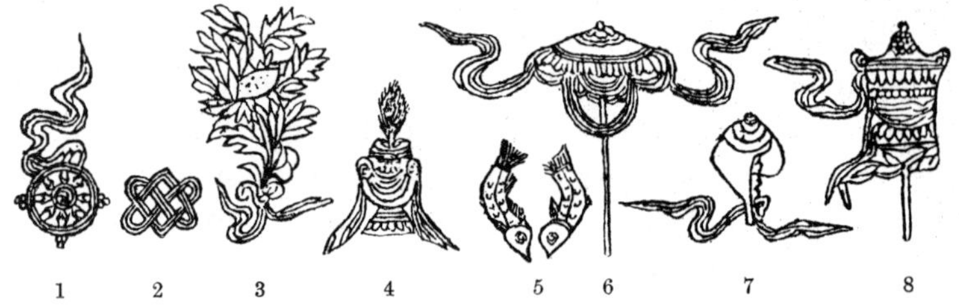

THE EIGHT LUCKY SIGNS OR GLORIOUS EMBLEMS.
Described in footnote.

Behind the grimy row of cake-offerings (*torma*) ornamented with flowery patterns moulded in coloured butter like a confectioner's fancy sugar-cakes for children, which are only renewed once a year, I noticed a few bowls of old Ming *cloisonné*, and at one side was an offering of flowers stuck into an English beer-bottle still bearing its label. Here also, decorated with ribbons, were "The Eight Glorious Emblems"[1]

[1] *Ashta mangala*, in Tibetan *Tashi tagyé*. They are (1) The Victorious Wheel of an empire on which the sun never sets; (2) The Lucky Diagram called by the Tibetans "Buddha's entrails," but really a symbol of endless rebirths in worldly misery; (3) The Lotus Flower of heavenly birth; (4) The Vase of divine ambrosia of immortal life; (5) The two Golden Fish of good fortune, the mascots of Yamdok Lake; (6) The White Umbrella of Sovereignty; (7) The Conch-shell trumpet of Victory; (8) The Victorious Banner. See above illustration.

or Lucky Signs, which are figured on Buddha's footprints, and embroidered and painted on innumerable articles and furniture, lay and clerical, for good luck (see sketch on opposite page). This altar with its intrinsically sacred objects is placed in the middle of its small chapel to allow of pilgrims making a circuit around it as a devotional exercise.

In pigeon-holes on either side of the entrance to the chapel of the high altar were ranged the sacred books, the Buddhist scriptures (the *Kahgyur*), translated from the Indian Sanskrit about a thousand years ago, and their commentaries (the *Tängyur*), the former in one hundred volumes and the latter in two hundred and fifty. Each volume forms a cumbrous, unwieldy, heavy package about 2½ feet long and 8 inches broad, weighing 10 to 30 or more pounds, and containing several hundred loose leaves wrapped in cloth and strapped between heavy wooden boards with the label at one end. Most of them are written by hand, and some of the more favourite volumes—such as the fictitious gospel on Transcendental Wisdom, the *Prajña paramita*—are written in golden or gilt letters and illuminated in a way which would have delighted the heart of William Morris. Although the writing of most of these books must have taken several laborious years, but few of them are ever read afterwards; they are simply kept near or on the altar, tied up in their wooden covers, which are often elaborately carved with figures of Buddhas. Those which are mostly read are a few volumes containing more or less unintelligible spells prescribed by the Lamas for the cure of disease and for good luck. Yet these musty volumes in their faded wrappings are believed by the Lamas to contain all knowledge, everything worth knowing, as were once the voluminous works of scholastic philosophy which still encumber the libraries of Europe. The volumes are deemed to be intrinsically sacred. They are always placed reverently on the head when taken out and when replaced. They are carried round the fields in procession in spring to charm away evil spirits, and round the house and bed of sick people, and are used like our own Bible to swear by. The so-called "Tibetan" letters (see p. 22) consist of the Indian alphabet (in its turn derived from the West—the Phœnician) as it was current in the seventh century A.D., at the time when Tibet received its Buddhism from India and had its language reduced to writing by the Indian monks; the language itself, however, is akin to the Chinese and Burmese. The books are usually written on a paper made from the bark of the Himalayan laurel or the root-fibre of a native lint-like plant. Many of the leaves, I noticed, bore two circular marks in imitation of the holes by which the Indian palm-leaf and ancient birch-bark manuscripts were threaded together. The paper is preserved against mould and insects by a wash of arsenic.

A special service was about to be begun on account of some one who was sick, for "saints will aid if men will call," *through a Lama.* A crowd of nearly a hundred claret-robed monks came trooping in and took their seats on a line of cushions in rows along either side of the nave, the head priest, who alone wore a yellow cap, the others being capless, occupying a higher cushion at the top of the left-hand row near the altar, whilst sacristans lit several hundred additional small lamps like candles and burned incense. When all was ready they began a chant, which distinctly recalled that of a High-Church service at home. The deep, organ-like bass of the singers, the swell and fall, the intoning, the silvery-toned bells, accentuated at times by the muffled roll of the drums in the second row, gave altogether a majestic and sacred character to the service, whilst the flickering lights and the figures of the priests, looming out of the darkness and through the thin clouds of incense fumes, like shadows, vivid yet veiled, made up a most impressive spectacle (see photo, p. 401). The early Catholic missionaries, as well as Huc, have all remarked upon the striking resemblance of much of the ritual of the Lamas to that of the Roman Church, so much so that Huc exclaimed that the devil in his hostility to Christianity had anticipated his coming.

The massive wooden pillars of the hall have a fluted, moulded appearance which, on closer inspection, was found to be due to their each consisting of clusters of beams bound together by iron clamps. On a pillar at the door, where the proctor sits, were hung up a whip and an iron-shod rod for corporal punishment of young offending Lamas when it is necessary to enforce the discipline of the Church.

Another library of some hundreds of volumes, stacked in pigeon-holes in a large side chapel on the left, was of more interest to me than the fairly well-known scriptures and cyclopædia of commentaries in the main building, as being more likely than the latter to contain works hitherto unknown to students. The monks, however, denied having any catalogue of them, and even the oldest and most intelligent professed ignorance of what they were, which may have been in part true as the books were loaded with the dust of ages. Only a few were labelled, and those which I was able to glance over were of an historical kind, the chronicles of monasteries and biographies of kings and abbots of different sects. I specially looked for traces of Indian manuscripts, without finding any. The abbot promised to have a catalogue of all the books in the monastery made out for me, but he never did so. It was surprising to find in this "grand temple of learning," as the worthy Babu calls it, how very illiterate the monks were. Not one in twenty or more could even write, and only two or three out of a hundred had ordinary intelligence. Even the abbot knew very little about the history of his own religion and country. As the result of several visits and interviews with its Lamas, I consider it absurd to call this a very learned monastery, which confers degrees in divinity that are prized throughout Tibet. On the contrary, it trains chiefly in incantations and silly mystical gestures and puerilities, and has little that is intellectual about it.[1] The monks generally are of a low type of intelligence, lower than the laity—probably owing to their self-indulgent life—and their discipline is rather lax; for during the intervals in the service they gabbled away and joked amongst themselves indecorously, and several refused to obey the orders of their superior when he asked them to come out to be photographed by me, though he himself came willingly.

Upstairs the flat roof is plastered over to make a spacious open-air court, bordered all round by numerous small chapels dedicated to various saints, as well as by reception-rooms, including the throne-room of the Grand Tashi Lama, and a few cloisters for the sacristans. The chief chapel here contained the shrine of the wizard priest, Saint Padma, the founder of Lamaism (see figure, p. 115), whom the generality of Lamas place higher than Buddha himself.

Here, in these better lighted apartments, one saw more of the wealth and luxury of the establishment, in the delicacy of the frescoes and painted scrolls, the elaborate ornamentation and richness of the images, censers, furniture, and hangings. Much of the latter was Chinese brocade embroidered with the squirming five-clawed imperial dragon, evidently a present from Peking.

One of the rooms was the Devils' Chamber of Horrors (*Gon-k'ang*), a sort of satanic Aladdin's cave in

[1] He who masters the antics for the black hat dance is called "The Chief of the Wizards" (*Ngak-ram-pa*).

the dark, designed to awe and impress the superstitious pilgrims. Here are collected the hideous colossal images of all the demons which infest the world and prey upon the poor Tibetans. They have the forms of men, but the heads of ogres and monstrous beasts, the hideous creations of a nightmare, and all are eating human bodies and surrounded by a variety of weapons. They mostly belong to the pre-Buddhist indigenous pantheon, the Bon. They are worshipped with offerings of blood and spirits, as well as of all the grains eaten by man. Poisons and tobacco are also offered to them. Here, too, are hung the ogres' masks which are used in the devil-dances. Gyantsé is celebrated for its devil-dances, in which the central figure is the black-hatted priest, a survival of the pre-Buddhist Bon religion. He bears the title of "Chief of the Wizards," and wears a conical black hat somewhat of the shape of the old Welsh dame's hat. Around its brim is tied a deep broad band of coarse black velvet, on its apex a geometrical arrangement of coloured threads surmounted by a death's-head tied with black ribbons topped by the trifid jewel, whilst as lateral wings between the brim and crown rise up two reddish serpents or dragons to sting the round skull. He dances frantically to quick music in clouds of incense burned from large swinging censers, and an offering of pastry cakes (*torma*) or the effigy of a human body on a tripod concludes the ceremony.

The great pagoda by the side of this temple (photo, p. 216) is locally known as the "*Gandhola*," the old Indian title of the great pagoda of Gaya in India erected on the hub of the Buddhist universe, the spot where the sage Sakya obtained his supreme enlightenment and became a Buddha, and the attendants of this Gyantsé pagoda had a tradition that their building was a model of the Indian one transplanted to Tibet. Were this really so, it would be of immense interest as helping us to ascertain what the original, or at least the mediæval, form of the Buddh Gaya temple was before its ruins were "restored" by the Bengal Government about a quarter of a century ago, when the great liberties taken with its structural features excited severe adverse criticism. As I knew the Buddh Gaya pagoda well, I was in a position to form an opinion as to the truth or falsity of the tradition regarding this one.

At first sight there is little resemblance between the two present-day buildings, except that both are semi-solid, tapering, domed buildings about the same height, and each encloses a large shrine with an image of Buddha in the centre of its basement, the so-called *Vihara-chaitya* of the Indians. In both the entrance door and the chief image face the west, and in this one a small tree grows on the eastern face in the position of the great Bodhi tree at Gaya. Making due allowance for the plastered facing of the Gyantsé one and the sculptured stone of its reputed original as permitting of some alterations creeping into the former in the course of years of repeated renovations, I am of opinion that the resemblance is undoubted, and that this one was really modelled after the Indian one, and so affords us indications for the restoration of some details of the latter.

This pagoda is nearly 100 feet high, with a circumference at its base of about 200 yards, and has the general form of the "*chorten*" or relic-tomb that we have already seen so frequently, and which is considered to symbolise the five elements into which bodies are resolved on death (see diagram opposite). It has stepped terraces of plinths below, surmounted by a drum-shaped body which is crowned by the spire of great gilt rings and an umbrella canopy. It is eight storeys high, the lower five forming the steps of the plinth, the sixth the great drum, and the seventh the gilt spire and its basement. Each of these terraced storeys has an outer balustrade, reached by the inner stair, for the pilgrims to perambulate around and enter the shrines on each flat. It may be considered an octagonal building with the alternate faces notched into a double recess, an arrangement that gives a many-cornered star shape of twelve faces to each storey, and a vertical ribbing to the sides of the building (see photo, p. 216). In each of the twelve faces is a small chapel dedicated to a different Buddhist divinity, whose effigies are many-armed and identical with those at Buddh Gaya in the house of the Hindu caretaker there, the Mohant. Entrance is gained to the upper storeys by inside stairs, which go off to the right and left of the central chapel facing the entrance. On the topmost storey, under the gilt dome, are the large "magic circles," the exact counterparts of those two large circular black stones now lying at Gaya engraved with figures within a ring of thunderbolts, which I showed some years ago to be "magic circles" for exorcising evil spirits. Here also is a fresco of the local chief Rabtan, whose reputed sword is kept here to touch the heads of pilgrims. The thirteen rings forming the spire above the drum are heavily gilded copper, and represent the heavens of the Indian Buddhists. They are capped by a wide projecting gilt umbrella of royalty, from the margin of which depends a deep fringe of bells with wide leafy tongues, which chime in the breeze as in the pagodas of Burma. Foreshortened from below as we look up to it, it seems a cluster of terraced corners capped by

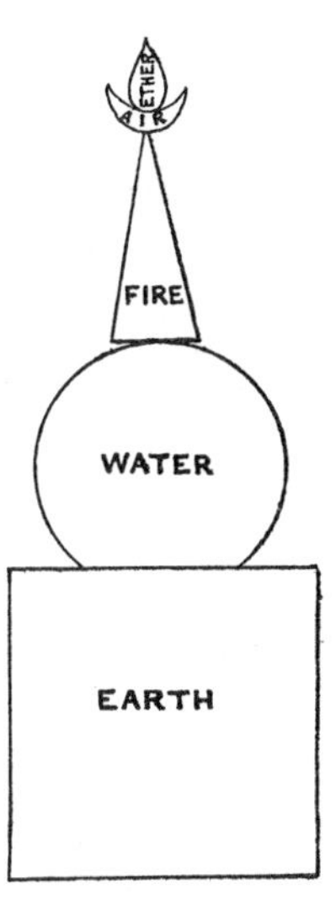

CHORTEN, SYMBOLISING THE ELEMENTS.

the mushroom top of the drum and its umbrella. It is noticeable that this Gyantsé pagoda wants the four corner towers on the roof of the first storey which are such a striking feature of the restored Indian building. These, if present in the original, may have disappeared from the ruin at the time it was taken as a model for this one. There is an oral tradition that the pagoda is much older than the temple itself.

The walls and upper cornices are faced by images and ornamentation painted on the plaster. Only a few sculptured stone slabs exist, and are of rude local workmanship. Neither in this building nor in any other of those I visited did I see any ancient stone or brazen images from India, nor could I hear of any.[1]

I visited several other of the smaller temples, all of which were on the identical plan of the larger one, also some of the dormitories, and the residence of the abbot himself. He excused himself for the dismantled appearance of his rooms by saying that he was packing up various rugs and things to furnish a tent for the Amban, on his coming to meet our Mission. At the entrance to the dismal chamber of horrors attached to the abbot's quarters was the usual collection of "guardians," stuffed watch-dog skins hanging from the ceiling.

On the hill above the monastery, some 3 miles higher up (see photo, p. 216), was a hermitage (*ri-tö*) consisting of some twenty white-washed cells, where the monks of the convent retire for certain periods for "meditation." In the next valley to this, about 2 miles distant, was a convent of thirty nuns of the yellow-cap sect. They were all shaven, some wore ordinary monks' conical yellow caps, but a few had huge fluffy wigs of curly wool, giving the appearance

[1] In one chapel was the footprint of the Indian monk Sras Guru Chö-wang. It was in black basalt containing a well-carved impression of a natural-sized foot.

of the great frizzy, shaggy shock-head of a South Sea Islander. These nuns, who are very plain in looks, dirty and illiterate, go begging about the town and villages. There were two more nunneries in the neighbourhood (see photo, p. 208). In one of these I saw their teacher, a miserable-looking, middle-aged monk, who visited the place daily to instruct them in ritual. Only one of the establishment could write. Their few books were all manuals of worship and charms for sacrificial rites. Doubtless the prevalence of polyandry, combined with celibate monasticism, by which so large a number of the women remain unmarried, drives many of them into convents.

On a hill-top below the above hermitage was the local Golgotha, the place where the dead bodies are thrown to be devoured by dogs, vultures, crows and other carrion feeders. This revolting mode of disposing of the dead is doubtless owing in part, as Bogle says, to the scarcity of wood for cremation, and to the difficulty of digging the frozen soil for graves. Only the bodies of Lamas and of those dying from small-pox and other infectious disease are burned. Near by is the Chinese cemetery at the foot of a bare hill, where a collection of a few hundred closely-set tombs, like an encampment of tents, marks the spot where these expatriated Celestials sleep in a strange land.

The still larger monastery of Tse-chen, with quarters for 2000 yellow-cap monks, covered the side of a hill 5 miles across the valley (see sketch, p. 266). It is said to have been founded over 800 years ago, and to have been visited by the founder of the yellow caps, Tsong-khapa. It possessed, however, no features of special interest, beyond some mysterious underground passages, and at one side, near the adjoining carpet manufactory of Gobshi, was the eerie red house of the wizard magician, one of the oracles.

Everybody now appearing to be so friendly, and our scouts reporting that all was quiet up and down the Gyantsé valley for over a day's journey on either side, we thought it safe for us to venture out for a little sight-seeing farther off. One of the first places we decided to visit was a curious hermitage we had heard of amongst the mountains, about 14 miles down the valley on the road to Shigatsé, where it was reported that the hermits were sealed up in dark caves like burial vaults and kept imprisoned there until they died, never seeing the light or any human being, "ruined in body and shattered in soul."

On the 30th April (1904) four of us made up a party to go and see this strange community of anchorites in their living tombs. We started off, after an early breakfast, mounted on shaggy little Tibetan ponies, accompanied by a guide and four of the Sikh mounted infantry, the latter to hold our ponies and assist in our defence in the event, apparently improbable, of our being attacked.

Our road at first led out from our little fortified post, past the town of Gyantsé, dominated by its towering castle, which from afar glittered in the early morning light like a jewel on the bosom of the plain. Thence we cantered through thriving suburbs on to the open plain beyond, where the many-armed Nyang river wound in curving links through the meadow-land 3 or 4 miles wide, and dotted freely over with the neat cottages of the farmers, nestling in clumps of poplar and willow trees. Here we reined up and rode along at a walk to enjoy the scenery and drink in the piquant fresh air. From the meadow hemmed in by bare purple hills, the glistening white monasteries which studded the hillsides of this priest-ridden land led the eye up to the rugged peaks softened with freshly-fallen snow, piercing the sapphire sky.

It was a perfect spring morning! All Nature was

PLOUGH YAK-OXEN BEDECKED WITH TASSELS.

TIBETAN LADY AND HER MAIDS.

vibrating with the joy of new-found life. The frost-bitten land had thawed under the few weeks' genial sun, and through the soft soil by the roadside and on the borders of the fields, fresh green shoots were pushing themselves up alongside deep olive-beds of exquisite pale-blue iris lilies, and pink clumps of dwarf primulas and gay saxifrage which already begemmed the ground amongst the golden gorse bushes. From every hamlet the cottagers had swarmed out into their fields and were busily ploughing and sowing in the glorious sunshine, forming pleasing bits of bright colour. The men were ploughing with oxen gaudily bedecked with plumes of wool dyed glowing scarlet and blue, with long throat-tassels of dyed yak's-tails, and harness of jingling bells, whilst close behind the ploughers came the gaily dressed women as the sowers, scattering broad-cast the seed from their baskets. Most of them, men and women, were humming snatches of song in light-heartedness, or in pleasing vision of the new season's crops. Amongst the tall poplar trees embedding the homesteads neatly picked out with red ochre and white-wash, and among the pollarded willow-bushes fringing the irrigation canals, flitted rose-finches, fieldfares, hoopooes, pert tits, cinnamon sparrows, shy doves, warblers and thrushes, all blithely pairing and nest-building; and beyond in the fields real English larks were singing skyward above the chirpy red-legged crows and foraging ravens. Occasionally flocks of sand-grouse sped swiftly past us, and a few wild duck and geese, scaring the partridge and hares from their cover, or the terns from their trout-fishing, whirred noisily down amongst the reedy hummocks fringing the turquoise pools on the river where they breed.

From this genial valley, pulsating with life, our guide turned us abruptly about the thirteenth mile up into a small sequestered glen, and at once the scene was changed. A bare, stone-strewn valley stretched away up to savage grim hills, and in its throat where it narrowed into a rocky ravine we could discern, about a mile away, the hermitage we were in search of. The small streamlet of this valley was hushed and silent, choked by the stones fallen from the hillside and from what seemed the moraine of a dead glacier above. The rocky cliff on the left was dotted over irregularly with the sombre cells of the buried anchorites, and the smoke from the cooking fires of their attendants hung ghost-like in gauzy drift over all. Below, in a grove of wild rose-bushes—blasted-looking, as their dead foliage of last year had not yet dropped—some peach-trees, as if in mockery, had burst into luxuriant pink blossom, whilst above, a hoary old willow-tree watched solitary over the living graves.

Disturbed by our clatter over the stones, some of the attendants came out and met us. They had not the appearance of ordinary Tibetan monks. They were thickly clad, and not in the monkish robe, but more like ordinary laymen. Their hair was not cropped or tonsured; it hung down in long matted locks over their shoulders, giving them a shaggy, wild look, or it was loosely knotted up on the crown in the style of Indian ascetics, the *jogis* and *fakīrs;* but was not plaited into a pigtail as with laymen. Altogether, their mode of doing up their hair gave them the look of Indian devotees rather than Tibetans, and this was the impression they wished to convey. They told us that they also were hermits of the order, which was founded by ancient Indian ascetics. They, however, had only undergone, so far, entombment for the first or second stage of holiness, namely, for six months, or for the period of three years, three months, and three days; and they had not yet taken the vow for the third or final stage, the plunge for life. Meanwhile they attended upon their holier brothers, carrying food for those who were entombed for life. I got one of them to write down in my note-book the name of their hermitage, and I then found that they gave it the euphemistic title of "The Cave of Happy Musings on Misery" (*Nyang tö-ki-p'u*).

We were then led up a narrow winding path and across a stone-flagged court to their small chapel. From the roof of the porch, above the door, hung two

THE HERMIT ST. MILA.

stuffed bear-skins, which they explained to me were their symbols or coat-of-arms as cave-dwellers in the mountains. Inside the chapel, which was of the usual form, the chief place in a large fresco-painting of semi-nude, Indian-looking ascetics on the wall above the altar, was given to the patron saint of their order, the Tibetan hermit St Mila. This hermit was a sort of wizard-poet, the author of many popular songs, who lived in the eleventh century A.D., and, adopting the style of an Indian ascetic, had his chief hermitage on the flanks of Mount Everest, about 150 miles west from here. The next place in the fresco was given to an Indian wizard named Saraha, who, they said, founded this particular hermitage about six hundred years ago.

From this chapel we were led, at our special request, to the "caves." These, to the number of over twenty, are perched irregularly on the rocky hill-side, and have their entrance built up solidly with stones and mortar, leaving a stout, padlocked door for entry. The only other opening besides this and a small dark sewer is a tiny aperture like the door of a rabbit-hutch, about 6 inches square, and only just sufficiently large for the hermit to pass out a hand for his daily dole of food of parched grain and water. The former is tied in a napkin which is deposited on a narrow sill outside the small window-hole, and the water is poured into a perforated saucer-shaped depression in the same place whence it flows inside.

Immured in this dark cell, from the moment the door closes on him the hermit remains in total darkness throughout his voluntary imprisonment — for the first or second stages, or for life. He has no means of distinguishing day or night or the passage of time. His only communication with the world is when his daily food is left on his sill, and then by his vows he is bound to let in no light and not to peep out. He can see or talk to no living person throughout this confinement.

In the first cell to which we were led was confined an old hermit, who had not seen the light, nor had been seen or spoken to by anyone, for over twenty-one years! Whilst we were standing outside and pitying the poor man who voluntarily pent himself up in this prison, one of us asked to be shown evidence of the hermit's presence inside. Thereupon the attendant gave the signal which they use when they deposit the food. He tapped very gently thrice on the sill, so softly that it was almost inaudible to us, and then, after ten or twelve seconds, whilst we held our breath expectantly, in a silence like that of the tomb, the tiny rabbit-hutch door in front of us trembled, then began to move and was jerkily pushed ajar about 3 inches or so, and from the deep gloom came slowly faltering forth A GLOVED HAND! This was all. Only a gloved hand! It protruded about 4 inches on to the stone-slabbed sill and slowly fumbled there for two or three seconds, and finding nothing, it returned slowly, trembling as in a palsy, and the door closed up like a snail retreating into its shell, and nothing broke the agonizing silence save, as I fancied, a suppressed moan. The whole action was muffled like a dream, so slow, so stealthy, so silent and creepy. In the daylight it was unearthly and horrible to a degree. Only a gloved hand! So the stimulus of light even was denied to the poor wretch's hand, another drop in the cup of his misery. It was difficult to realise that a human being could be so confined voluntarily; it was only fit for a caged wild beast.

HERMIT WITH SKULL-CUP.

From this cave we were conducted to four or five others, and it was all the same sickening sight; and it was remarkable that the gloved hand of the younger men trembled almost as much as that of the older.

The last cell at which we stopped was that of a very old man of about sixty, who had been in this cave for over twenty-two years and had just died the previous day. He had not removed his food for several days, and when the senior attendant elicited no response to his enquiring taps and knocks he unlocked the door this morning and found that the poor inmate was dead. Our request to be allowed to see the body was not acceded to, as it was alleged that no one, not even the other hermit attendants except the senior one, was permitted to look upon the sacred corpse. A funeral banner stood outside the door, and lamps were being lighted for the soul of the deceased.

Several of the young hermits who had accompanied us on this round, boys of twelve to eighteen years of age, had already undergone the first or the first and second stages of the imprisonment. Most of them aspired to become eventually like this wretched old man whose jaded spirit had just passed away, and whose conduct was being held up as a model for imitation to these poor boys, of whom one seemed almost an idiot, and no wonder. Indeed, the wonder is that any one can remain sane after undergoing so terrible an ordeal even for six months.

A still more famous hermitage of the same order as this one, we were told, was to be found several miles down the valley, at Shalu, which has a great repute for black magic. In it there is an underground cave, in which a man is shut up for twelve years, during which time he tries to acquire magical powers by chanting Indian spells and incantations, and silly stories are seriously related of the miracles which happen. At the end of the twelve years he notifies his desire to return to the upper world by blowing upon his human thigh-bone trumpet. On the first blast all his belongings are blown to the surface in a miraculous way through a small orifice like a keyhole. With the second blast he emerges himself by an equally small hole, in the well-known cross-legged attitude of Buddha. He is then examined to ascertain if he has acquired the recognised magical powers of casting no shadow, ability to sit on the top of a pyramid of barley grain without displacing a single seed, flying in the air, etc. But, added our informants dolefully, very few ever succeed in passing these tests, although there are many who try.

Now what does all this ghastly self-imprisonment mean? Why do these poor men, illiterate peasants all of them, voluntarily give up their liberty, their home, and all that enriches life, and sacrifice themselves in this horrible way?

The evolution of so repulsive a form of religious observance offers, it seems to me, another instance of the mistaken and mechanical way in which the semi-savage Tibetans, sunk in the depths of ignorance, try to imitate the rites and practices of Indian Buddhism, which is their great model of orthodoxy, but which the great majority of their priests so imperfectly understand.

The average Tibetan, and especially the priest or "Lama," is extraordinarily low in intelligence, and almost incapable of conceiving any new abstract idea or the rationale for a particular practice, if it demands much mental effort. Thus the Lamas, in copying Buddhist practices, often seize upon externals and merely accidental features, and, interpreting them in a grossly materialistic way, make them an end and object in themselves. This superficial mimicry has led them into absurd perversions of the original and to "derangement of epitaphs," as I have shown in my *Buddhism of Tibet*. So I think it has been with these poor hermits.

Temporary retirement has, of course, been recommended as a moral and religious discipline by many besides Buddha. Its design is partly to enable the anchorite to escape from the attractions of the world and the busy society of his fellow-man, but chiefly, and in a special degree in the Buddhist system, to secure leisure for self-examination and constructive thought for the devotee's personal benefit, and also to some extent for the teaching of others.

In this way, by resorting to hermitage for a short time, Buddha himself evolved his doctrine of "The True Way" of salvation, and formulated the metaphysical basis on which it rests. So, too, the patron saint of this particular hermitage, St Mila, composed in his mountain cave his rough religious hymns which are still sung by the people all over Western Tibet.

"HAPPY MUSING ON MISERY."

But these miserable men with whom we are here concerned, being gifted with neither intellectual nor moral assets to start with, are capable of the physical part only of the life of monastic seclusion, and in this respect their zeal must be allowed to exceed that of the greatest saints and philosophers, seeing that they remain in retreat not for a short time, but for life. It would be humorous were it not so pathetic. This meaningless confinement, so far from elevating, must inevitably cramp and deteriorate them in mind and morals; and in fact it was noticeable that most of the men who had passed through the first and second stages were even below the low general level of intelligence. One was of the type of a congenital criminal, and one decidedly imbecile. But all of them were not fools; the fat old senior attendant, when asked when he was going in for his final plunge, replied that it was over twenty years since he had done the second stage, and it was uncertain, he added with a smirk and a shrug of his shoulders, whether he would ever go in for the final stage at all. Sensible man!

The reason why votaries are "voluntarily" forthcoming for such a revolting form of hermitage as this seems to be that the members are enlisted as children, between the ages of ten and twelve, at a time when they cannot be supposed to realise what it is their parents are apprenticing them to; and once in the grip of the order they are unable to escape from its obligations. There is thus nothing of a religious mania about it.

Whilst interred in his living tomb, the hermit is given ghoul-like implements for his work and food—a rosary of bits of human bone, a trumpet of human thigh-bone, a goblet made out of the top of a human skull to hold his food (see p. 239). The tasks set him consist chiefly in the mummery of repeating millions of times a spell in meaningless Sanskrit jargon accompanied by certain gestures and attitudes of the fingers and limbs for the purpose of expelling devils. At various stages of the repetition he must conjure up in fancy the most malignant of the devils, one of those hideous monsters which disfigure the walls of all the Lama temples, whom he must then vanquish by his spells. This ability to conjure up a vision of devils should not be difficult to the credulous Tibetan who has not yet passed the stage of mental development when men see visions and dream day-dreams, who believes that he lives in a world full of demons, all scheming to do him harm, and the wholesale exorcising of which is a profitable source of income to all the village priests—though we must remember the day-mare of Martin Luther when he threw his ink-pot at the Devil. The benefit to the hermit in his cave in thus exorcising these devils is that he imagines himself by this means to be earning good marks towards raising him nearer to Paradise in his next birth.

How pitiful it is to see such a wicked abuse and waste of life as this monstrous theory entails on its victims! These poor devotees, with perverse and misdirected zeal and a mistaken sense of duty, leave the sphere of human pleasure and duty to become the ghostly tenants of a subterranean world, in whose dank unwholesome atmosphere their feeble intellect, still more enfeebled and benumbed, sinks miserably into a lethargy of drivelling imbecility.

Glad was I to get away from this "Cave of Happy Musing on Misery," with its melancholy captives entombed and inarticulate, and to emerge again into the priceless freedom of the air and sunshine of God's splendid earth, and get back through the pleasant Gyantsé valley safely to our camp. We were indeed fortunate to get back *safely*, for within the next three days the whole valley down which we had been was up in arms against us, and swarming with some thousands of Tibetan soldiery from Shigatsé, who were hurrying up to attack our little camp at Gyantsé, which they did with very un-Buddhistic ferocity on the fourth night after our return.

CHAPTER XIII.

BESIEGED AT GYANTSÉ.

"*There is no sin so great as killing.*"—LAMA PROVERB.

THE alarming events which now happened to us revealed the Lamas as past masters in the art of diplomatic dissimulation. Whilst they were making an ostentatious display of friendship, and bringing in supplies under the joint stimulus of money and menaces, they really never meant to negotiate at all, but were all the time secretly maturing their plans to massacre us, notwithstanding that their own religious law expressly forbids them to kill any living thing, not only human beings but even animals. Their demeanour so deluded our political officers, that Colonel Younghusband declared in his published despatches that "on the 12th April all resistance in this part of Tibet is ended," and added, "neither General, nor soldiers nor people have wished to fight."

This sanguine confidence soon received a rude awakening. Hitherto the Lamas had simply opposed our passage; now they decided to assume the offensive and attack us in overwhelming numbers. They thought the favourable time had come to put their plans into execution, when they heard that our small post at Changlo was immensely weakened on the 3rd May by two-thirds of our small escort having marched off to attack a position held by the Tibetans on the Kharo

Pass, four days' journey distant, on the road to Lhasa.

The intelligence department of the Lamas must have been excellently worked, for no sooner had the detachment started for the Kharo Pass than mounted couriers flew with the news of our weakened condition to Shigatsé, 50 miles down the valley, and from that place the same evening a force of 1600 warriors hurried up to attack us, travelling all night and all next day to take swift advantage of our hopelessly defenceless position, as they considered it.

Fortunately some inkling of this impending attack reached us the previous day, when nearly all the Tibetan patients from the hospital, which had been opened by Dr Walton outside our post, deserted, along with the locally engaged servants, who, before going, confided to our other Tibetan servants that they were running away to escape being massacred along with us on the morrow. This news seemed to Colonel Younghusband sufficiently authentic to warrant his sending for the governor of the town (the *Jongpön*, see photo, p. 177) and keeping him in our camp as a hostage. Personally I remember that evening, in looking at our depleted post from the outside, to have remarked how very deserted it appeared, and how it seemed almost to invite attack. Before retiring for the night I told the sentry of our building of the report we had heard, although scarcely any one of our party took the rumour seriously.

Sure enough, we were attacked that night, or rather in the early morning. Just before daybreak, about half-past four A.M. on the 5th May, we were suddenly awakened by the weird war-whoop of the Tibetans,[1] the shrill barking yell of "*kī-hu-hu-u-u! kī-hu-hu-u-u!*" which burst forth from several hundred hoarse Tibetan

[1] This is the favourite cry also of Tibetan robbers as they rush on caravans brandishing their knives.

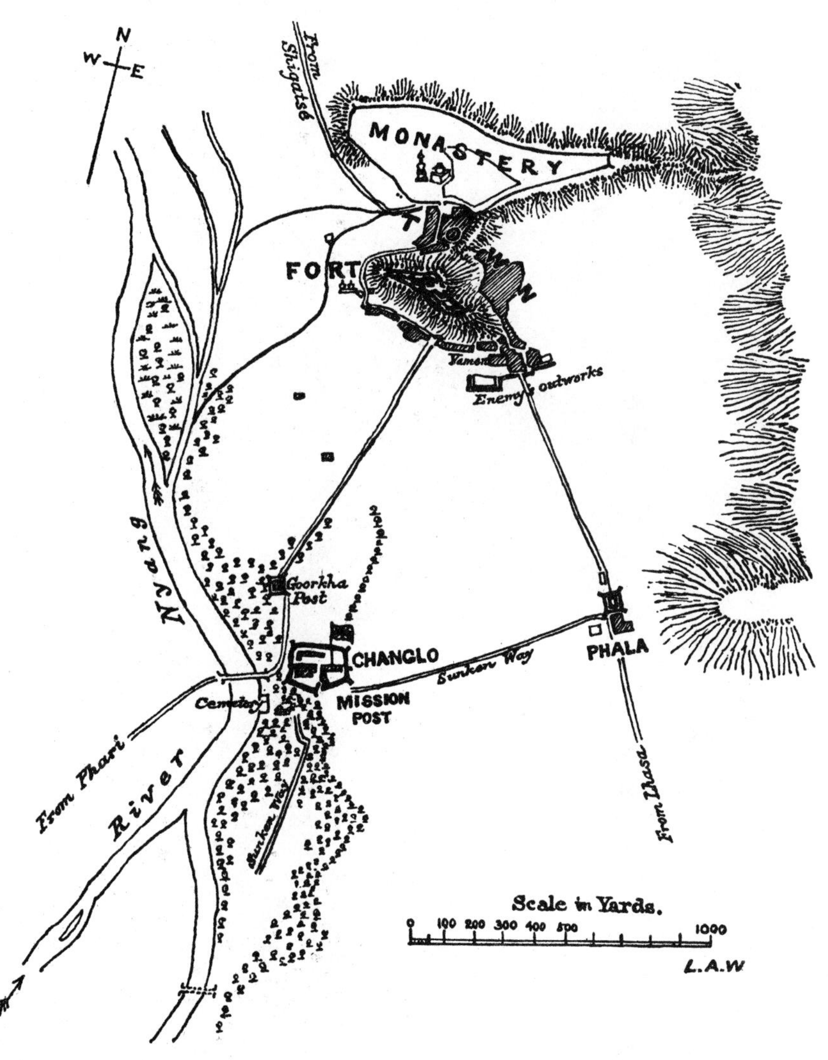

MAP OF MISSION POST AND FORT OF GYANTSÉ.

FORTIFIED MISSION POST AT GYANTSÉ.

This view shows the interior, to the lee of the fire from the Jong. Ramparts of bags of earth are seen on the roof. Colonel Younghusband's tent is the one in front of which a sentry is standing below the British flag on the roof.

throats a few yards off, outside our low wall, followed almost immediately by the crack of hundreds of muskets and the whizz of their bullets from every side, and the long belching flash of their gun fire.

So complete was the surprise, that it seemed several minutes before our sentries got into position and began to reply. Meanwhile it was a struggle to jump up speedily, and before I could get my loaded revolver from under my pillow, and grab my rifle and bag of cartridges, with a haversack of surgical dressings, several bullets had shot through the paper panes of my window upstairs. When I reached the outer passage I was met by a crowd of unarmed servants, who rushed up terror-struck, and jostling each other, huddled into a corner, gasping out that the Tibetans had got over the wall and were following them up. Just then a Sikh sepoy ran up to me, followed by Captain Ryder, shoeless and coatless, as indeed we all were; and there we three, in a long narrow room at the top of the stairway, and with small windows commanding the court below, prepared to make a stand, as we were cut off from the rest of our party, and knew that capture meant for all of us death by cruel torture. By this time daylight had nearly set in, and although the fire had not slackened we could see no Tibetan inside our inclosure, along the stretch of some 30 yards, which separated us from the large central house in which was our main body, and which the General had called the "citadel." Remembering his parting advice—"In case of attack make for the citadel," I suggested our making an effort to get there. Captain Ryder then rushed across the intervening open space, swept by the enemy's fire, without being hit. I afterwards followed suit across the zone of fire, and also luckily escaped being shot, and was glad to find Colonel Younghusband and the rest all safely in the "citadel," as they had hurried across immediately they heard the first shot fired.

It was now broad daylight, and we saw several hundreds of armed Tibetans firing along the outside of the wall, and blazing from behind all the trees in the neighbourhood. Several of them stubbornly seized hold of the muzzles of our soldiers' rifles projecting through the loopholes and tried to wrench them away. Our sharp-shooters, from the roof of our "citadel," soon laid most of these low; and after about twenty minutes the remainder broke and ran off to the town and fort, whereupon Major Murray and some of his Goorkhas, having thus flung back our assailants, rushed out and pursued the fugitives for about half a mile, in a slight snowstorm, killing many of them, until forced to return by a brisk rifle-fire from the fort, which the enemy now held in force.

We counted about 120 dead Tibetans outside our wall and a few inside it, and 40 wounded, who were carried to a hut in the neighbourhood for treatment, and 12 who were taken prisoners. Each of these Tibetan soldiers, dead and wounded and prisoners, had a net bag to carry off the rich loot which their leaders had promised them they would get from the camp of the "foreigners," so confident were they of overpowering us; whilst the prisoners said that they had received instructions to massacre every one of us from the Commissioner down to the meanest follower, and expressed their thankful surprise that we did not torture and kill them now that they were in our hands.

They also told us that there were 1600 of them, the regular soldiers of the Shigatsé and Gyantsé garrisons, eked out by militia, and that 800 had come on in front and marched night and day from Shigatsé, led by a Lhasa Lama, doing the journey of 50 miles in two nights and one day, and arriving outside our post about midnight, whereupon they crept up under our wall and lay there undetected by our sentries till near dawn, when they received the signal for attack. Had they had any good determined leaders among them to have "rushed" our camp, every one of us would have been cut up and not one could have escaped, as they could have got over our low wall easily and quietly. Their war-shout before attack assisted us greatly by effectually waking everybody. Their attack was chiefly delivered at the outer enclosure, the least defensible part of our position, which the Mission had selected for its residence, and where the Union Jack flew, for the Tibetans doubtless hoped to secure here the person of the Commissioner. The losses of our small garrison of 125 rifles were only one killed and three wounded, two mortally, in addition to the three servants of Captain Parr of the Chinese Commission, who were all killed in his house in the town, Captain Parr himself escaping a similar fate by being absent with the Kharo Pass party. As showing the temper of the Chinese and their hostile attitude, it was noticeable that General Ma deliberately concealed from us the Tibetan plot to attack us. That our losses were so few was owing to the Tibetans thrusting their muskets and rifles through our loopholes and firing recklessly through without being able to take aim. Several of the men were armed with Lhasa-made Martini rifles, which were effective at a distance of over 1200 yards, one of our men being mortally wounded a little later in the day by a bullet from these modern rifles fired from the fort, which was now bristling with the black-headed Tibetan soldiery, who began to bombard us with missiles weighing 3 ozs. to 1 lb., fired from small cannon, the so-called "*jingals*" of the Indians, which were now set in position against us.

As it was necessary to send news to Lieut.-Colonel Brander of our being attacked and beleaguered, and no one could be spared from our already dangerously small garrison, and no native volunteer was forthcoming, the imprisoned *Jongpön* was ordered to send his servant with the message, under penalty of losing his own life if it were not promptly delivered; and it is but right to say that under this threat the letter was not only duly carried the 50 miles or so, but the answer that our party was quickly returning was brought back *all within thirty-six hours!* The poor *Jongpön* himself was, however, demented with fear, and sat cringing comically in a corner with his head inside a large iron cooking-pot for protection, and would not be persuaded to lay aside this ridiculous head-piece for days.

All day long the fort was alive with the Tibetan soldiery, now evidently reinforced. They swarmed busily as thick as bees, and looked, through our glasses, no larger. Under cover of a dropping fire they were to be seen actively building fresh defences and repairing the old broken ones. The monastery, too, was filled with their troops, and the disaffection of the monks was no longer a matter of doubt. In the firing in the morning from the fort, when our pursuing sepoys were forced to return, the red-robed Lamas stood by in clusters to see the effect of the Tibetan shots, and they could be seen inciting their men to further bloodshed. At that time these groups of militant Lamas and the thick lines of the teeming builders would have made excellent targets for our Maxims and mountain-guns, but these had all been carried off by the Kharo party.

Meanwhile our own defences were strengthened by Captain Ryder, who improvised breast-works and shelters for sentries on the roof by bags of earth, stones, and bales of rope, raised turrets for enfilading the outside of the walls against lurking assassins, deepened the surrounding ditch, and cut down some of the nearer trees in the copses which gave cover to the enemy. All this had to be done in the face of a constant bombardment from the *jong*, which, however, caused remarkably few casualties. The perimeter of our post was reduced by more than half, as our small force of about 120 rifles could not man more. In this reduction of our limits we vacated, needless to say, that dangerous corner in which we had been caught in the morning, and all removed to the citadel.

In the afternoon the wife of our hostage, the *Jongpön*, came in under a flag of truce, bringing some food for her husband. She was a rather refined and well-featured woman of middle age, and brought the news that the reinforcements with 300 Lamas had arrived from Shigatsé, bringing up the number to about 2000, and that more were daily expected. The Tibetan commander, who with twelve of his officers was accommodated in the monastery, was, she told us, "the Honourable Teling," so-called after his estate near Khambajong. He is a son of the old mad minister of Sikhim who for long intrigued against us, and the same who seized and imprisoned Dr Hooker. This Teling was a frequent visitor at the Mission camp at Khambajong eight or nine months ago, and he was there shown, amongst other things, our rifles and the working of the Maxim guns. He was then a stoutish young man of about thirty years of age, with a pleasant face and manners, and very talkative. He professed to be very much annoyed at the obstinacy of the Lhasa Government, and pleased to meet the English in his country, and he expressed a hope that Tibet would now be opened up freely to trade, for the benefit of everybody. Whether he was sincere in these declarations must be doubted, seeing that he is now after so short an interval pitted against us.

The *Jongpön's* wife also informed us that Captain Parr's house in the town was gutted, all his papers destroyed, and his servants hacked to pieces alive in the same brutal manner as was one of our Goorkha followers, who was mutilated and cut in pieces this morning outside our wall. The Tibetans have hitherto been credited by many with being so deeply imbued by Buddhist principles as not to take life, much less inflict pain; but we now know that they are sheer barbarians at heart—like the Burmese, who are also professing Buddhists of a purer type, but who also proved to be inhuman monsters of cruelty to their prisoners and political opponents in Thebaw's time, not many years ago.

At sunset, when our evening bugle sounded the "last post," the Tibetans from the fort replied almost immediately by a blast from their large conch-shell trumpets, as if in defiance, and it sounded as if they were mustering to resume their attack under cover of the night.

There was no sleep for any of us all that night. In the darkness our handful of men, outnumbered by about twenty to one, stood or lay alert and watchful, each at his post awaiting attack by the Tibetans. In our vigil the hours crawled with a slowness that was maddening. Several times during the night I climbed to the roof, and from behind a parapet scanned with straining eyes, in the starlight, the fields strewn with the dead of yesterday's battle and the black clumps of trees, and out towards the *jong*, or fort, which stood up dark and gaunt in tragic silence. At last, about 2 A.M., the rising of the waning moon brought some relief to our anxiety, as then we could peer a little further into the darkness, although in the thick gloom of the wood below might be lurking concealed, for all we could see, some thousand men only a few yards off.

As the ruddy glow in the east shot up the first streaks of dawn, we stood by, listening still more expectantly, knowing that the Tibetans consider that time, "the third cock-crow,"[1] especially lucky for attack; but the dark outlines of the hills loomed into distinct-

[1] *Gha-po-sum.*

OFFICERS OF BELEAGUERED GARRISON AT GYANTSÉ.

Front Row.—Mr Hayden, Captain Cowie, Major Rowe, Major Murray, Lieut. Hodson, Captain Cullen.
2nd ,, Lieut.-Col. Brander, Colonel Younghusband, Lieut.-Col. Waddell, Captain Minogue, Captain Shepherd, Mr Wilton, Major Wimberley.
3rd ,, Mr Mitter, Captain Walton, Lieut. Haddow, Captain O'Connor, Major Peterson, Mr Landon, Captain Ottley, Captain Ryder, Mr Tulloch.
4th ,, Lieut. Lynch, Lieut. Gurdon, Lieut. ...., Lieut. Mitchell, Capt. Coleridge, Lieut. Franklin, Capt. Easton, Capt. Luke, Mr Newman.

ness, and the soft light of day stole over the land and penetrated the gloom of the woods without a disturbing war-yell or shot. Then in the broad light a solitary gun flashed out, and every one sprang to action, till it was realised that it was from the distant fort, and was merely the beginning of the day's bombardment; and when our picket reported that the wood was free from the enemy, many of us thought of snatching a short sleep with some feeling of security.

Evidently the loss inflicted on our assailants the previous morning had deterred them from venturing on another attack so soon after. Either they had some unlucky portent, or they considered they were better employed in entrenching themselves; for an inspection of the fort showed that during the night they had been busy building high loop-holed stone walls which screened them and their *jingals* almost entirely from our view. It was now obvious how cleverly their commander was taking advantage of the absence of our men and guns with the Kharo column. Had the full garrison and guns left by General Macdonald for our defence been here, the Tibetans could easily have been driven out of the fort, and would not have been given time to entrench themselves. Even now they could be dislodged with the aid of the 7-pounders and Maxims, but these had been taken off to the Kharo. Our small garrison, however, armed with rifles only, was too weak to venture out to attack them; besides, the energies of our men had to be saved up for the trying business of watching by night for our bare defence. So there was nothing for it now, but for us to remain on the defensive, and to go on strengthening our defences. In this latter work Captain Ryder was busy from morning till night, raising the wall, building hornworks and bastions, deepening and spiking the surrounding ditches, erecting entanglements, etc. It was satisfactory to find how this summer-seat of

Changlo, in common with other country-houses of the nobles and the rich merchants, readily lent itself to fortification, for originally they were nearly all built with strong walls like little forts, as a protection in stormy times or against robbers.

A rumour reached us during the day from a few wounded Tibetans in the hospital outbuilding, who had been visited by their friends from the town during the night, that the astrologers had fixed midnight that incoming night as a lucky hour to attack us. As this meant again darkness—the moon not rising till after 2 A.M.—it was not a pleasant prospect to look forward to. To add to our troubles, our citadel caught fire in the early part of the night, owing to a stupid cook having kindled his fire over some beams; and had we been deprived of this shelter, with a fire within, and our deadly enemy's firing and prowling forces outside, our position would indeed have been pretty hopeless. The fire, however, was got under by tearing down the burning part of the building, and stamping and hammering out the flames.

We spent another anxious, wakeful night on the battlements, but midnight passed without attack, and the apparently interminable night emerged into day without any assault by the enemy. After two more busy days at our fortifications, and two more stirring long nights of watching—curiously, still without any further attack—we were relieved by the return of the Kharo party on the 9th May, which, bringing up our rifles to 500 with the guns, made us feel that we could now hold our own safely—although perhaps not strong enough to act on the offensive—as our defences were very efficient, and we had in store three months' food supplies of kinds and unlimited water.

We now received particulars of the fight at the Kharo Pass. This high pass, about 16,500 feet, is on the road to Lhasa, 45 miles from our post at Gyantsé.

When it was discovered that it was held by a large force of Tibetans, Lieut.-Colonel Brander, who was left in command at Gyantsé, resolved to attack it, although it was off our line of communications and its force had not directly threatened these. His column of 400 rifles with guns and mounted infantry was assured by the villagers on the way that there was no gathering, but on reaching the spot they discovered 3000 Tibetans in a strongly loopholed position, bounded by precipices beyond the pass (see photo, p. 286), and 500 more were coming up to reinforce them. They were chiefly stalwart, fierce warriors from Kham or Eastern Tibet, and fought stubbornly for six hours, most of them being armed with Lhasa rifles and 6-feet spears. During the greater part of this grim battle in these terrible icy altitudes, bordered by glaciers, it was snowing. Eventually the enemy were driven out by the Goorkhas, under Major Rowe, and by the Sikhs, who climbed a precipice and turned the position, when the enemy fled down the other side with a loss of over 100 men. Our casualties were Captain Bethune and 4 men killed and 14 wounded.

Several Lamas were amongst the leaders. In the enemy's camp a curious document was found which shows how some of the men are sworn in to the levies, and the determined character of their opposition to us. It reads :—

"AGREEMENT OF THE THREE BRAVES.

"The English, acting in an insolent and rapacious manner, have entered our country. We are unable to sit silent under this infliction. Soldiers must be sent to fight, and the Government has given orders that the noble Kyme is to proceed as head of the army in place of the deceased [Lhasa General] Lheding Depön. With him are we three responsible Braves. We have consulted together and made this agreement, taking no account of our lives, fighting for honour only. We have bound ourselves not to quarrel with other servants, to drink no wine, not to gamble, not to lie, not to steal: if we should do any of these things we are prepared to suffer any punishment inflicted by the Master. If we do well the Master will reward us well. Each man of us will receive a yearly gratuity of 30 ounces of silver. Should we depart in the least degree from what we have bound ourselves to do, we must pay a fine of three ounces of gold."

Then follow the names and seals. Some of the captured warriors who came from Eastern Tibet (Kham), 20 marches distant, stated that each had to bring one month's food at his own cost, carrying it on his own back, also to provide his own gun, sword and spear.

Although we were now reinforced by the welcome return of the rest of our garrison, it was decided that it would be folly to attempt to retake the *jong* for the present, strengthened as it was, and considering the large number of the enemy in and around Gyantsé. The latest information at this time from prisoners gave the numbers of these at 8500, distributed as follows:—

Gyantsé, 2500.
Rong Valley, 1500 (reported to have gone to Gyantsé).
Nagartsé, 2500 (beaten back from the Kharo Pass).
Ralung, 1000.
Shigatsé, 1500.

In addition to these it was reported that reinforcements were marching from Lhasa, and that the whole country was up in arms against us, as the Lamas had been going from valley to valley preaching a "Holy War," like the fanatical Mullahs and Madhis of Mohammedanism, and inciting the people against us. We also heard of swarming horsemen from the steppes of Mongolia hurrying on to save the sacred city. As it was now evident that the Grand Lama was obstinately bent upon opposing us tooth and nail, it had at last to be acknowledged that we were "at war" with Tibet, and that the peaceful "Mission" had become transformed into a military expedition, involving still larger operations. The storming of Gyantsé *jong*, and the clearing out of the large hostile force now investing us, was imperative, and an advance to Lhasa was considered to be absolutely necessary.

General Macdonald therefore made arrangements for the speedy despatch of sufficient additional troops from India. Meanwhile he sent us up as immediate reinforcements 200 more rifles, with two 10-pounder guns and a Sapper company, and instructed Lieut.-Colonel Brander to keep the attention of the enemy at Gyantsé busily occupied, whilst he, the General, pushed up supplies to store the posts[1] along the line for the general advance, when a vigorous attack could be made with a fair prospect of success.

In compliance with these orders, Colonel Brander, in addition to posting numerous sharpshooters to keep down the enemy's galling bombardment and rifle-fire, began a series of sorties out to villages suspected of harbouring the enemy, and had a few skirmishes with the Tibetans driving them from a building in the neighbourhood, which they had been bold enough to seize, with the view to cannonading us at closer quarters. When the small reinforcement with the guns and Sappers arrived on the 24th May, he was able to undertake the larger operation of driving the enemy out of the adjoining villa of Phala (see plan, p. 246), which they had occupied with the intention of starting a deadly cross-fire into the exposed south-eastern side of our camp.

This fine country-house and farm belonged to the ill-fated Phala family, who were ruined for befriending Sarat Chandra Das, as we have already seen, and by

[1] For this was required 11,000 maunds (or 7856 cwts.) of rations, 6900 maunds of grain, and 9500 maunds of fodder.

a curious irony of fate, their house, which had thus special claims on our protection, was doomed to destruction at our hands, as it became essential for the safety of our post at Gyantsé that it should be dismantled. It was early used to harbour the enemy. On the eve of the attack on our camp, on the 4th of May, I went thither with one unarmed attendant to see some fine frescoes of which I had heard, and was surprised to see a number of men peeping stealthily out of windows in the inner courtyard; and on my asking the resident steward who these men were, he denied that there were any, and beat a maid standing by who was beginning an explanation. I thought this circumstance very suspicious at the time, and remembered it next day when we were attacked. There is no doubt that at my visit the previous evening there were many armed men hiding in the house, an advance party of the Shigatsé ones, and doubtless they did not attack me because their main body had not yet arrived. I believe, however, that they may have forced themselves into the house against the steward's wish and protest, as he alleged in self-defence when taken prisoner by us some days later.

This strongly-built residence, almost a little fort, stood 900 yards to the right or east of our entrenched Changlo camp at the foot of the hills (see plan), and 900 from their *jong* or fort. The enemy had occupied it about the 20th May with the view to outflanking our position, but were driven out and part of the building was destroyed by our party. The Tibetans again occupied it and built loopholed walls on the roof, and commenced connecting it with the fort by a long high wall along a sunken way. On the morning of the 26th May, before dawn, our force attacked it, and after a desperate fight, lasting eleven hours, expelled the enemy, killing about 150 and taking 37 prisoners.

Captain Shepherd, R.E., and Major Peterson were in charge of the mining parties, wrecking and blowing up the village from end to end, as house after house was held and had to be breached. Our losses were Lieut. Garstin, R.E., and three men killed, three officers and nine men wounded in desperate hand-to-hand fights in dark chambers. The determination, resource, and bravery shown by the Tibetans in this fight was no surprise to those who had seen them at the attack on our post, and should dissipate, once for all, the absurd delusion that the Tibetans cannot fight. Their daring is superb. Although generally clumsily armed with antiquated weapons, they have some modern firearms and know how to use them. They have little to learn in the matter of fighting behind defences and taking advantage of cover, and they know how to charge. No finer feat of personal bravery could be conceived than the charge made by a party of 15 warriors, mounted on black mules with a party of 40 infantry, who burst out from the fort in a storm of bullets which slew them almost to a man, to carry aid to their comrades at Phala, whom they thought too hardly pressed.

It was a sad funeral of poor young Garstin, who had arrived from Chumbi only two days before he was killed here. A grave was dug in the shade of a willow-tree on the bank of the river outside our post, and in view of the *jong* (see photo, p. 441). Here at dusk next day, when the *jong* had ceased firing, his body, to the trumpet-call of the "Last Post," was lowered into a grave amidst a bed of wild blue iris lilies, a few of which some of us plucked and laid upon his coffin.

As Phala was a point of much importance to us, one of its buildings was strongly fortified and a detachment of 50 men under a native officer posted in it, and a sunken way dug at night across to our post as a safe mode of communication across this zone of fire. A few men still were hit in this crossing, some of them mortally, although the track was about 6 feet below the surface of the fields; but by care and ducking at places one could get over without much danger. Finding out this, the enemy sent a party one night and flooded it up by turning a stream into it, which made it impassable for a few days. After this, pickets had to patrol it, as well as the stream at nights to prevent a repetition of such inconvenient tactics, whilst our commander retaliated by cutting off the water-supply of the fort and town.

The strategy displayed by the Tibetan General was considerable. In addition to the unremitting bombardment, he tried repeatedly to close round us and invest us more narrowly by seizing several houses near us and in our rear. Then finding this did not work out well for him, he concentrated his warriors in the *jong* and sent bands of them out at night to prowl round our camp and try to find out the weak spots in our defences. Latterly, as they lost heavily by these tactics, they used to yell in the darkness and fire off their guns from a distance, while our men stood quietly at their posts, not wasting ammunition by reply until the enemy came near enough to rush out on them. They tried to imitate the havoc wrought by our sappers' dynamite by bravely placing bags of gunpowder, their only explosive, against our walls, and setting fire to them in the face of our sentries, not evidently aware of the impotency of gunpowder as compared with dynamite.

Curiously they never thought of attacking the communications, our weakest point, until nearly a fortnight later, and even then they did not do it in a sustained way, so as to besiege us completely, but only intermittently, so that we continued to push through and receive letters under a large escort of mounted infantry every few days for most of the time. Although these parties had frequently to fight their way through on the road, they were only once completely over-mastered by falling into an ambuscade, losing letters and their lives. In this case the firing attracted assistance from our post, but not before the Tibetans had commenced to mutilate our dead sepoys, inflicting curiously the mutilation for robbers, namely, cutting off the right hand and plucking out the right eye.

As the monastery of Nanying ("Naini" of map) was the chief harbourer of these parties which interrupted our line of communications, a party was sent out to wreck it. On the 7th June a still more daring attempt was made to cut our communications by an attack on the post of Kangmar by 700 Kham warriors, which was, however, repulsed with a loss of some 116 killed and about the same number wounded, for as Kangmar was situated at the important strategic point where the short road to Lhasa branches off General Macdonald had it especially strongly fortified.

An attempt was again made by Colonel Younghusband to open negotiations without any result. On the 1st June he sent a letter by the hands of a prisoner to the Tibetan general in the fort, asking him to forward it to Lhasa. The letter mentioned the 26th June as the latest date at which he was prepared to meet at Gyantsé the Amban and Tibetan delegates. This letter, however, was returned next morning by two Tibetan warriors, under a white flag of truce, with an oral message from the Tibetan general that he could not forward the letter, but that we might send it by the Chinese. This was the old pretext of Chinese suzerainty which directly conflicted with the object of the Mission, though the Chinese had, to some extent, recognised the independence of Tibet in a notice which they had lately placarded over the suburbs of

Gyantsé and the villages along our communications, stating that, "*Tibet and England are at War! China is a friend of both!*" It was quite in keeping with Mongolian arrogance to place Tibet before England in this way, and the Chinese were asked to alter it accordingly.

All through these long weeks during which we were beleaguered, the fort kept up its incessant shooting, and pelted us all and every day with cannon-balls persistently. The enemy's marksmen found the range of every building in camp with marvellous accuracy, and fired whenever any one showed himself above cover. The result was that as none cared to make a target of himself we all soon became adepts in the art of ducking our heads as soon as a puff of smoke was seen from the fort, or we heard the warning shout of our sentries, until this ingrained habit of ducking became an instinctive impulse. It was comical to see a little knot of officers on the roof discussing some piece of news or other, or pointing out some new development of the enemy's entrenchments, suddenly scatter and crouch for dear life till the shot whistled by and then laughingly resume their conversation to be similarly interrupted again a few minutes later. The whole of our camp became a network of covered ways like a rabbit warren, in all directions were sunken ways and covered passages and traverse walls. There were only a very few paths left unprotected, along which we had to run the gauntlet of the bullets which now wreaked their vengeance chiefly in breaking branches of the trees overhead, though every day or so, one or two of our people were hit and a few ponies or mules killed.

The guns which they mounted against us went on increasing in size and number every few days, until over twenty were counted, and on the 13th June they mounted a fresh arrival from Lhasa, throwing shots weighing 4 pounds and acting as shells, as most of them had a stone or wooden core with lead or copper envelope outside, this resulting in a jagged missile immediately it struck any object. Their small cannons were at first contemptuously called "silly billy," and their larger ones "big billy," but this latest large one was so serious an addition, that it received the respectful epithet of "William," the title of "Kaiser" being reserved for a still larger, should it be forthcoming. Its advent was announced by great shouting and blowing of trumpets and beating of drums in the fort. One of its first shots made a huge hole in the stone wall of my room, the shot, as large as a cricket ball, burying itself 1½ feet down and nearly passing through. Several of our best sharpshooters were put on to its port-hole, which was protected by a closing door, like a disappearing gun, and with binoculars riveted on to this spot a steady watch was kept up. At the words "William's open" every one dipped behind a shelter, while the sharpshooters plugged at the opening and immediately ducked down till the thundering boom and the missile itself had passed or it had smashed a bit of building or a tree near by. The Tibetan name for this gun we afterwards ascertained was "Putty [mouth]" (or *pag*), and a still larger one at Lhasa is called "stupid" (*phuk-pa*).[1]

Our servants latterly grew so accustomed to the swishing and buzz of these bullets, that they used as they dodged the missiles to jeeringly imitate the singing notes of the more musical ones which screamed a shrill treble or hummed a deep bass. When some of the shots ploughed up bits of our strip of vegetable garden our honorary gardener would venture out to ascertain casualties and return with a gruesome face with the news, "Three more radishes killed!"

[1] The one captured at the Jelep in 1888, and now at Gangtok, was called *Ladaki*, as it had been taken from the Sikhs in Ladak.

After enduring this monotonous life of a blockaded post for nearly two months, and the indignity of being pelted at with shot and cannon-balls all day long, suffering considerable privations in the way of food, all of us looked forward anxiously for relief from our long and tiresome imprisonment.

CHAPTER XIV.

RELIEF OF GYANTSÉ AND STORMING OF THE JONG.

"*It is no use trying to tug the* [*irresistible*] *glacier backwards.*"
—TIBETAN PROVERB.

THE time had now come when steps could be taken for the relief of the beleagured camp at Gyantsé and for the further prosecution of the Mission. General Macdonald, therefore, threw forward a chain of supports as rapidly as possible, and arrived himself on the 26th June with sufficiently large reinforcements to storm the *jong* and clear the country of the armed Tibetan force which was facing him, as well as for the eventual advance to Lhasa, a movement that had become imperative in view of the open uncompromising manner in which the Mission was being opposed. It was obvious that the Dalai Lama rejected the Mission altogether and would listen to no proposal for a peaceful settlement. The terrible punishments inflicted on his troops at Guru, at the attack on our post, at the Kharo Pass and Phala, had made no impression whatever; and our occupation of Gyantsé had only stimulated the people to increased resistance, whilst our threat to go on to the capital, coming as it did from a beleaguered camp, was received with derision. They were raising levies in all parts of the country, and were collecting most of them at and around Gyantsé, where they were evidently making their great stand attracted by the smallness of our post there. Their strength was now judged, from the most authentic sources obtainable, to be about 16,000 men, distributed as follows :—

Place	Men	Remarks
At Gyantsé Fort . .	8000	Composed of 600 regulars from Lhasa, 1500 from Gyantsé and Shigatsé, and 1500 from Kham, and remainder peasant militia and levies. (applies to these three entries)
At Tsechen monastery.	1200	
At Naini monastery .	800	
At Gobzhi . . .	1200	
At Nyeru . . .	800	
At Dongtsé . . .	2500	(of which only 100 are regulars).
At Kharo La . .	1500	(mostly from Kham).

Our reinforcements for the front consisted of over 2000 fighting men,[1] which, added to the garrison already at the Gyantsé camp, brought up our strength to nearly 3000 rifles.

On the way up, the Nyeru and Naini forces of the enemy were dispersed, the former on the Lhasa road near Kangmar, and the latter at the monastery near Gyantsé which had been persistently menacing our communications, firing upon convoys and was latterly garrisoned by Kham warriors who repaired the breaches in the wall which had been made by our troops as a punishment. It was held in force against the General's advance on the 26th June, and captured after four hours' hard fighting, the Gyantsé garrison co-operating by cutting off retreat to the north. Our losses were one officer and six men wounded and five men killed. The enemy lost heavily and several Lhasa-made rifles were found.

The relieving force encamped about a mile from our post so as to be about 2 miles from the *jong* and beyond reach of *jingals*. The General immediately paid a

[1] Royal Fusiliers, 1 wing.
40th Pathans, 2 wings
2 Sections British Mountain Battery.
1 Section 7-pounders.
1 Company Mounted Infantry.

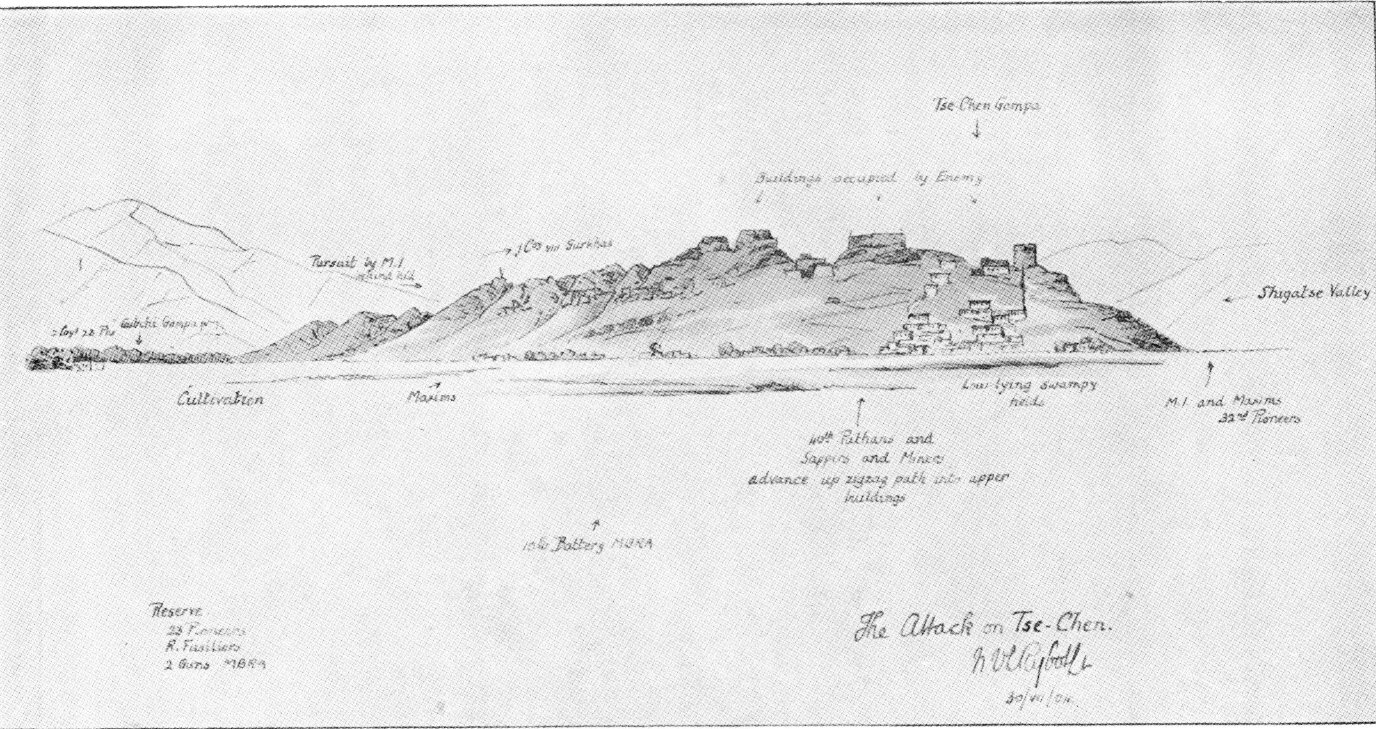

ATTACK ON TSECHEN MONASTERY.

THE CHIEF OF BHOTAN, OFFEN WANG CHUG, K.C.I.E., THE *Penlop* OF TONGSA.
Standing beside him are four *Jongpöns* or commanders of forts, with embroidered caps.

welcome visit to our post along the sunken way, and made a minute inspection, through the telescope, of the new fortifications of the *jong*, from the breastworks of our roof, in order to complete his plans of assault.

After one day's much-needed rest for the troops, on the morning of the 28th June the General began to prepare the way for the capture of the *jong* by a wide movement down the valley, clearing out the twelve villages, including the carpet factory at Gobshi held by the enemy on the plain to the left of the river, to the north and west of the *jong*, and the large monastery of Tsechen beyond them on the end of a strongly fortified spur running out into the middle of the valley, 5 miles down the Shigatsé road, which it commanded. Although the operations were impeded by heavy rain which flooded the marshy fields and their network of irrigation channels, rendering them a morass intersected by deep streams very difficult to traverse, the villages were cleared without much opposition; but the monastery, in a position of great natural strength, was held by 1200 armed men, who offered a desperate resistance by a furious fusilade and hurling down heavy volleys of stones and rocks. After a fight lasting the whole day the Tibetans were dislodged, and eventually driven headlong from their positions, by the gallant assault of the Pathans below; by Goorkhas scaling the sharp crest along the sky-line, and by the other movements, as shown in the accompanying sketch. The enemy, who included several armed Lamas, suffered heavy loss. We had one officer killed (Captain Craster) and two wounded, also five men wounded. The small number of our casualties was largely due to the rain which prevented the fuses of the enemy's matchlocks from igniting their powder, and to the angle at which they fired being so steep downwards that their bullets often fell out before firing. Those who were captured informed us that the Lamas on finding that their spells up to date had not prevented any of those wearing these charms from being hit or killed, had this time issued new ones and had gilded them, with the promise that even if the new charms failed to stay the fatal bullet, the wearers would certainly be resuscitated within four days. These poor men implicitly believed the consoling promise, and thus only had been prevailed on to face our bullets. The Lamas, doubtless, on their own part, with their transmigration theory, would point to the newly-born babes of the locality and allege that these were the reincarnated, fallen warriors. The prisoners also informed us that none of those who had once been exposed to our fires could be prevailed on to face it again until stiffened by impetuous fresh arrivals who were ignorant of the terrific effects of our breech-loaders at close-quarters.

The net result then was that General Macdonald drew a cordon round three sides of the fort, held both the Lhasa and Shigatsé roads, and fully cut off the water-supply of the fort and town. Pressed thus hardly it was scarcely surprising that next morning a Lama accompanied by a Tibetan warrior came into camp from the fort under a white flag of truce asking for an armistice. The reason alleged was that two high officials were about to arrive from Lhasa who were prepared to negotiate. An armistice was therefore granted for one day, for which everybody was thankful, as the last week had been especially trying with hard work and fighting. It was a great pleasure to be able to wander once more outside the camp and within range of the *jong* without being shot at. The Tibetans also enjoyed it, as they could be seen in hundreds, clad in their grey, homespun woollen coats which matched the grey rocks, sitting on the walls in the fort and town basking in the sun.

The armistice was to expire at midnight on the 30th June, and if the peace delegates had not arrived by that time General Macdonald held himself free to resume operations against the *jong*, as military considerations were paramount. As they had not arrived by mid-day on the 1st July, a few shots were fired to notify that the armistice was at an end. These were not replied to and in the evening a message came under a truce flag to say that the delegates had arrived and desired that a time be fixed for them to come in the morning. This was an important advance, as it was the first time that high representatives of the Tibetan Government had communicated directly with the Mission.

The peace delegates were duly received with full military honours next day within the post, in the presence of all the officers. The General sat on one side of Colonel Younghusband, and the ruling Minister of Bhotan, the Tongsa Penlop[1] on the other.

The latter official had come to act as a mediator between the Dalai Lama and the British Commissioner. He is the prince of eastern Bhotan, but holds at present supreme temporal power over the whole of Bhotan as Regent there, during the minority of the hereditary ruler, the Deb Raja. He is a shrewd, middle-aged man of strong character. The appearance of our military force in the Chumbi Valley and the occupation of Phari fort had naturally alarmed him, and while conceding our outstanding demand for a road and railway through the strip of Bhotan separating the Bengal plains from the Chumbi Valley, he held aloof for a time, doubtless out of fear that Bhotan as well as Tibet might be subjected to our permanent intervention. But as the months went by he felt reassured and visited the camp, when General Macdonald asked

[1] The Tongsa Penlop, or "Minister of Tongsa District in Bhotan," bears also the spiritual epithet of "Lord Teacher." His official title is "The All-embracing Protector of Bhotan" (*Duk spyi-kyab*); the first part of this title is applied to governors, and to our Commissioner, Colonel Younghusband, who is called "The Great, All-embracing Protector" (*Spyi-kyab Chembo*).

him to use his influence with the Dalai Lama to try to effect a peaceful settlement. He at once agreed to do all he could for this object, and being a frequent visitor to Lhasa as a pilgrim, and on terms of personal intimacy with his spiritual lord, the Grand Lama, he sent the latter a statement of our case against him. In reply the Dalai Lama wrote to him a letter containing the Tibetan version of matters, and stating that he would be glad if the Tongsa Penlop could assist in bringing about a settlement, and in it he mentioned the names of the two peace-delegates, who were two of the four chief Ministers of State composing the Lhasa Council. One of these was then in the fort here, namely, the great Lama Minister of the Lhasa Council, known by the Chinese title of "Ta" Lama. The other, the new Prime Minister, the Yutok Shapé, was reported to be still at Nagartsé, about five days' march up the Lhasa road beyond the Kharo Pass. This letter was shown to Colonel Younghusband by the Tongsa Penlop, whose assistance was welcomed, and his jaunty figure, and white European felt hat, had been a familiar sight in our camp for the past two days.

RULING CHIEF OF BHOTAN.
TONGSA PENLOP.

The peace delegates came clad in brilliant yellow silks, amber and old gold, headed by the Ta Lama, a good-natured old man, with prominent teeth, and more like a farmer than a priest (see sketch, p. 416). They included the Grand Lama's chief secretary or *Tung-yik Chembo*, named Lopu Tsang, a crafty and masterful monk, and also the representatives of the three chief yellow-cap monastries of Lhasa, which play an important part in the government of the country, "the Triad *Sen-dä-gä*," a contraction for *Se*ra, *Dä*pung and *Gä*lhdan. They were received in the finely-painted reception hall of the Changlo mansion, and made a picturesque group with their numerous attendants.

When discussion began, after a short speech by Colonel Younghusband, it was discovered that the delegates had no credentials or authority to make any arrangements, and did not clearly know what their orders were. These informalities and deficiencies were nevertheless waived by Colonel Younghusband, who insisted, as a pledge of their sincerity and good faith, that the *jong* should be evacuated by a given hour, as General Macdonald had demanded as a first condition. The Tibetan envoy neither granted nor refused this, but explained that if he gave such an order the Dalai Lama would decapitate him. During the discussion that astute and conceited prelate, the chief secretary, was always interrupting the speakers, both Colonel Younghusband, the Ta Lama, and the Tongsa Penlop, with some remark, usually interjected in scorn or in reproach of our action. He is the same who visited the Mission at Khambajong, and he knows something of the outer world, having been to Calcutta, Shanghai, and Peking. He manifestly exercised great influence over the others of his party, and was bitterly hostile to us. The envoys had been informed privately by the Tongsa Penlop of the exact terms of our conditions of peace, and now they had a written note of these handed to them. They went away rather sadly, and returned next day considerably later than the appointed hour. They were again informed of the final conditions, and were given forty-three hours to evacuate the *jong*, but left again without any results beyond much vague talking, evidently in the belief that good round assertions and accusations, and reiteration of these, were quite as likely to produce conviction as facts. One of their expressions was that we would break "the ass's back" of the Grand Lama if we attempted to impose such heavy conditions on him. Next day they visited the Tongsa Penlop, who advised them to accept the peace conditions at once, and to remember their defeat at Tsechen when they talked of defending the *jong*. Altogether these negotiations gave the impression that they were a pretence, and merely a fresh prevaricating device of the Lamas to gain time, with a view to allowing the Grand Lama's agent to see for himself and reckon up accurately the invading forces, and then act according to circumstances; whereupon the envoy, finding our army smaller than he had expected, and hoping the *jong* could hold out, seemed to have decided to decline to negotiate. Be their motive what it may, the Tibetans gave no signs of evacuating the *jong*, but on the contrary employed this interval of the armistice in strengthening its defences there and building new ones, despite their promise not to take advantage of the armistice to do so.

Hostilities, therefore, were resumed on the 5th July at noon by a gun fired from our camp to indicate that the armistice was over, and an hour later some shells were thrown into the *jong* to which the Tibetans did not reply. Next morning the *jong* was attacked by General Macdonald and carried successfully the same day by a daring assault of great bravery.

The capture by a comparative handful of British

STORMING OF GYANTSÉ JONG FROM PHALA.

DONGTSÉ MONASTERY.
Country residence of the late Sengchen Prelate.

and Indian soldiers of this almost impregnable fortress, held by 7000 of the enemy, must rank as one of the most heroic achievements in the annals of frontier warfare.

The attack was directed by General Macdonald from the roof of one of the ruined buildings at Phala. Storming parties crept up before daybreak, under cover of the darkness, to the fortified houses of the town, fringing the base of the cliff on which the fort stood, to gain an entry by blowing up the walls. The enemy were on the alert on the houses and the fort, and promptly poured a heavy fire through every chink of the buildings, and the great guns of the *jong* woke up and shot forth their missiles into the darkness, streaking it with long flashes of flame. The fighting went on all morning to the roar of musketry and cannon. The *jong* was almost hid at times in the clouds of thick smoke from its cannon and thousands of puffs from its ragged blazes of gunfire, whilst our smokeless powder scarcely revealed the position of our men. The Tibetans were driven from house to house till by noon the whole of the fringe of the town up to the great gate of the fort had fallen into our hands; but the gate itself could not be carried on account of its approaches being so fully guarded by defences and swept by a deadly fire. Several Lamas were seen, stick in hand, urging on their soldiers and beating them back to their posts as at the Kharo Pass. In the afternoon, after our wearied troops had rested for a short time, the 10-pounders set fire to the enemy's powder-magazine and made a breach, to the right of the gate, in a screen of wall, through which our troops entered by a splendid rush, led by Lieutenant Grant (who was wounded at Phari, the first to be injured in the expedition) and his Goorkhas, who scaled the heights in brilliant style in the face of a furious fire. The Tibetans soon fled precipitately, and our soldiers' hats, turbans and helmets were seen swarming up the topmost battlements, and the Union Jack was soon flying from the citadel once more. The interior was found thickly strewn with the enemy's dead, including several of the militant Lamas. Our losses were one officer (Lieutenant Gurdon) and three men killed, and seven officers and thirty men wounded. This was a surprisingly small number of casualties, considering the perilous and daring character of the assault upon a fortress of such natural strength in the face of such resolute opponents, for our men no longer advanced on Tibetan positions with light hearts. The smallness of our losses was mainly due to the extremely careful and able way in which General Macdonald had planned and personally supervised the attack. The Tibetan wounded were as usual treated by our surgeons.

The bravery of the Tibetans was now beyond dispute. Here they courageously stood their ground when our shrapnels were bursting over them, and pluckily returned shot after shot to our guns for hours, notwithstanding that few of their shots carried far, whilst our shells were seen to be inflicting on them much loss. They have a good eye to positions, and are almost perfect at fighting behind defences, and would make excellent soldiers if trained and led by competent officers.

Next day I went over the *jong* and saw the havoc wrought by our rifle-fire, shells, and dynamite. The sappers were busy demolishing the remaining walls to make it untenable. The monastery and nearly all the town was deserted. Looting was strictly forbidden by the General. In the houses most articles of value seemed to have been carried off by the people, except the bulky family "bibles," which were left behind as in the Boer War.

To disperse the enemy, who were reported in the neighbourhood, flying columns were sent off on the

9th July up and down the valley. I accompanied the one down the valley, which had also the double purpose of bringing in fodder and other supplies. I was thus enabled to see the castle of the ill-fated abbot, the Sengchen, and the country-house of the Phala family at Dongtsé, 13 miles down the Shigatsé road, and 45 from that western capital.

This monastic castle with its cluster of *chortens* is perched picturesquely upon the rocky end of a bold, hilly spur overlooking the richly cultivated plains, here about 4 miles wide, and below it is the confiscated manor of the Phalas. Both of these buildings had a painfully blighted look. The caretaker of the monastery led me up to the private apartments of the Sengchen which have remained unoccupied since that abbot was killed nearly twenty years ago, under the sad circumstances we have already seen. In one room—where the previous incarnations of this saintly Lama and his predecessors are painted on the wall in the conventional form of Buddhas, with scenes from their lives, all duly labelled after the manner of the frescoes of the great saints—our attention was specially called to a "miraculous" picture in the fresco allotted to the late Sengchen which was painted shortly before his deposition and death. In it is shown a fort of a peculiar form on a cliff overlooking a river in which are the bodies of some bathers, and it is alleged that the Sengchen had this picture painted as the closing incident of his earthly career, and after he was dead it was discovered that this was an exact portrait of the fort of Shoka in Kongbu, in which he was imprisoned, and of the river into which his body was ignominiously thrown, and that he thus prophetically foretold his own fate. Here also is figured the favourite dog of the Lama, and his drinking-cup, which give the room an even more grimly deserted appearance. In the temple below were some fine images and scrolls, and a set of the scriptures and commentaries. The immense private library of miscellaneous books of this learned monk was carried off to Tashilhumpo on the confiscation of his property—so our attendant, who was visibly affected with deep emotion at those unpleasant memories, nformed us.

The Phala manor is a fine four-storeyed house (see photo, p. 9), with a courtyard enclosed by stables and granaries. The latter were used as Government stores, and contained an enormous quantity of provisions for military purposes, the accumulation of years, in walled-up chambers, the doors of which were all sealed and stamped with the words, "*Depa Zhung*," which means, "The Government" (see p. 396). In these were found no less than 300 tons of grain and other food-stuff, about 100 tons of which were carried back to our camp at Gyantsé, to which place we now returned to take part in the advance to Lhasa; for no Tibetan representatives had even now, after the capture of the *jong*, come forward to sue for peace, or to give any indication that they were convinced of the futility of further resistance.

CHAPTER XV.

GYANTSÉ TO LHASA, PAST THE YAMDOK SEA, AND ACROSS THE TSANGPO VALLEY.

THE dispersal of the Tibetan forces, which for nearly two months had menaced the Mission camp, cleared the air of the war-clouds which had been hanging over Gyantsé, but was not followed by any sign whatever that the Lamas were anxious to seek a settlement or cease from further hostilities. His Majesty's Government were therefore forced to decide that the Mission, with its large military escort, should proceed to Lhasa; that the negotiations with the Tibetan authorities must take place at that city itself; and that the expedition should be withdrawn as soon as possible thereafter. This indeed was obviously the only course possible to effect a speedy solution of the question without prolonging the operations into another winter season, with its many disadvantages and expenditure of life and money, and to prevent the expedition developing into a campaign of conquest and annexation, which was never contemplated.

Whether the advance to Lhasa was to be by peaceful marches, or whether we should have to fight our way thither, was still a doubtful question; for even so late as seven days after the capture of the *jong*, the Bhotanese mediator, the Tongsa Penlop, received a letter from the nominal peace delegate, Yutok, the Tibetan Councillor in charge of the troops at the Kharo Pass, stating that he had no orders to negotiate; and reports were received that the Kharo Pass was held by 2000 men. It was therefore necessary that the advance to Lhasa should have the character of a military operation prepared to break down any organised resistance that the Dalai Lama might offer on the way. It was also desirable to push on to the capital without more delay, before the Tibetan troops recovered from their recent defeat sufficiently to make any further serious stand, at the several high fortified passes and numerous defiles which had to be traversed before the Holy City is reached. It was calculated that the Lhasa authorities could still raise about 15,000 more men for the defence of Lhasa and its approaches; and most of these men were from the eastern province of Kham, and more or less accustomed to the use of modern firearms.

The movement upon Lhasa was therefore an operation calling for the greatest military care and forethought in planning out its details, and in providing for all contingencies, as a false step might bring more serious consequences than a mere check. General Macdonald chose out of two or three alternative routes that by the Kharo Pass, about 150 miles in length, leaving a strong advanced base at Gyantsé, so as to prevent any danger to his line of communications. His force of more than 2000 rifles,[1] and over 2000 followers; carrying Berthon boats manned by Indus boatmen from Attock for crossing the great Tsangpo river, and food and fuel for the journey across the uninhabited tracts, left Gyantsé on the 14th of July.

[1] The Lhasa column comprised:—

No. 7 Mountain Battery.
1 Section No. 30 Do.
½ Coy. Sappers.
2 Coys. Mounted Infantry.
Norfolk Maxim detachments.
Coys. Royal Fusiliers and Maxims.
4 Coys. 32nd Pioneers and Maxims.
6 Coys. 40th Pathans.
6 Coys. 8th Goorkhas.
4 Sections Field Hospitals.
Supply and other Departments.

The new world into which we now plunged had never been seen by any previous Britishers except Manning, nearly a century ago. The weather was as unpleasant as it could be. It had rained heavily all night until early morning, soaking through our tents and almost doubling their weight, and flooding the sodden fields and irrigation ditches across which lay our route for several miles. The mules, refusing to ford the latter, leapt across them like goats, their loads falling off into the mud and needing reloading and readjustment causing long delays. It began to drizzle and continued till the afternoon, when every one was wet through; then the sun shone out scorchingly, and when our baggage came up an hour or so afterwards, and was opened out to dry, the steaming camp looked like a huge laundry.

Our track led eastwards up the valley to the source of the river, in the glaciers of the Kharo Pass. The valley narrowed as we proceeded, the hills drawing closer together, till about the seventh mile, beyond the neat country-house of the Sikhim Raja's exiled son, where the fields were overlaid by shingly slopes of *débris* from the hills, and the cultivation was mostly confined to the alluvial banks of the river, which itself flowed about 40 feet below the now undulating plain. We had by this time reached the upper end of the old lake-bed forming Gyantsé plain, and were passing into the higher terrace of a chain of smaller ones above it, formed by the dams of *débris* from the flanking mountains which now became larger and more rugged. Trees were mostly confined to the bank of the river, but a tract of green-terraced fields stretched up the bottom of the larger side-valleys in sweeping curves for a mile or more to the rocky uplands, giving the appearance of emerald glaciers. The "tableland" now ceased, and once more we were traversing the stony defiles of bare wild mountains, our track following more or less closely the bank of the river, which was now a torrent brawling over boulders. Or we curved round the bays of the affluent side-valleys, under and amongst rocks banded with wavy streaks of vivid yellow, and crimson, and pale green, and dark blue from their crumpled strata of serpentine, and lime, and green slatestone, the former especially bare, supporting only scanty tufts of grass, whilst the latter had more luxuriant vegetation and bushes.

The rocky defiles we were entering were as ill-adapted for campaigning as could be conceived, for they could be held by a few determined well-armed men against a host of enemies. As a precautionary measure pickets were sent out in front, and to crown the ridges commanding our immediate line of march. We encamped in a broad bay where the hills receded some distance at the junction of a side-valley; and across the river was the large, somewhat ruinous, walled camp of the Grand Lama for use when he moves in state along this road from Lhasa to Tashilhumpo. Its chief paths were conspicuously marked out with white quartz, and in the centre at one end was an elevated platform for the throne of that dignitary. The following day we continued up these defiles to the junction of the two headwaters of the river at Gobzhi, or "The Four Doors," for here converge three important trade-tracks to Lhasa and a fourth smaller one. It stands at the apex of the triangle where the direct Indian route to Lhasa through Kangmar meets the Gyantsé one. At this important strategical point the Tibetans had built a strong fort on a bold rock commanding the entrance to the precipitous gorge pierced by the Lhasa road, which now leaves the Nyeru river and threads its way up the branch which passes Ralung. At Gobzhi there is a considerable village with several cultivated fields, a Chinese staging-house, and two other hamlets across the river. All the people

GOBZHI CASTLE.
On Nyeru River, 14,100 feet elevation.

ENTRANCE TO RALUNG (14,500 ft.)
(Mt. Nöjin on left.)

ENTRANCE TO KHARO PASS ABOVE RALUNG.
(Mt. Nöjin on left.)

had fled except an old man who declared that he had lost his family through the war, and was now left quite alone, and did not care what happened to him; his two sons were both killed at Guru over three months ago, and his daughter had deserted him out of fear. He had a large room in the village ready cleaned up to accommodate the Ta Lama and the Yutok minister, who, according to the orders they had sent him, were coming here that day to meet the Mission; this reminded us that we had met earlier in the day the Tibetan, with a white flag, carrying a letter to the Tongsa Penlop stating that these two personages were at Nagartsé and wished to negotiate there, so that matters again began to look more peaceful. A flattish ridge here with eight peaks is worshipped as "The Tent God."[1]

Beyond the gorge the valley of the Ralung river opened out considerably, and at the larger alluvial flats were several small hamlets, on both banks of the stream, with a good deal of cultivation, mostly mixed barley and peas, with bright yellow patches of mustard. Nearly all the houses in this valley had their walls striped vertically with broad red white and blue bands; one of the small monasteries here, a red-capped one named Gyabrag, was the most remarkably striped one we had yet seen (see photo, p. 431). The roadsides were luxuriant with a wealth of wild alpine flowers, among which the Ranunculus family was well represented, there being two kinds of buttercups, a profusion of trailing clematis both yellow and purple flowered, and an immense quantity of larkspur and the deadly aconite.

This aconite, which is called by the natives "poison-grass" (*San-duk*), was chiefly *A. ferox*, like the monkshood of gardens at home, with several large stalks, though some of the plants with single stalks and already ripe seed capsules seemed to be *A. heterophyllum*, the "Atees"

[1] Gur-lha.

of druggists. The people gather the roots in November for sale or barter as an export to India, and as a medicine, first of all baking them slightly to reduce their virulence. Notwithstanding the widespread distribution of aconite there has been no single case of poisoning by it amongst the men, but many fatal cases have occurred amongst the ponies, mules, and sheep—the usual physiological antidote, namely belladonna, or its alkaloid atropine, was not found to be of much service, probably owing to there not having been a sufficiently large quantity available.

The rain again this day in "rainless Tibet" was terrible. It had poured the greater part of the night, and we awoke in the morning to find its horrible and ceaseless patter continuing; but it cleared up by 8 A.M. to allow our wet tents to be struck and packed. Before we reached, however, the place selected for the camp—the terraces of fields at the village of Taklung, the crops of which afforded fodder to the animals—the rain visited us again in torrents, delaying the arrival of our baggage till dusk, as the long line of several thousands of mules and the donkey and yak corps had to thread their way along the narrow bridle-path by which we had come, in single file over 6 miles in length, and there the falling of any load delayed the whole of the column behind it. Meanwhile we had to wait in the chill rain and sleet which soaked through our waterproofs, and when the tents did come up they had to be pitched in this downpour on the sopping slimy mud; and as fuel was only available for cooking a little food, and none for the luxury of drying clothes, the discomfort of the whole bedraggled force that night can well be imagined. Next morning, however, nearly everyone felt as well as ever, despite his cheerless sleep in damp blankets, for the rain had stopped at daybreak and had let us enjoy a few stray gleams of sunshine before we started off again up the valley. The village gets its name of "The

Tiger's Valley" (*Taklung*) from the great horizontal bands of black limestone which streak the light yellow sand-stone of the bare hillside, suggesting the stripes of a tiger. On this hill, about 2 miles above the camp, were seen a few of the rare gigantic wild sheep, the *Ovis ammon.*

At the village of Ralung (14,500 feet), 8 miles farther up the valley, there shot into view another great snowy range which blocked our way to Lhasa. Its dominating peak of Nöjin Kangsang, or "The Noble Glacier of the Genius," rose up, 10 miles off, a majestic mass of snow and glacier ice, over 24,000 feet high, and on its western flank could be seen the cleft of the Kharo Pass which we had to cross. As this bleak hamlet of a dozen shepherds' stone huts is the last habitation in the valley, we encamped beside it on a high shelving meadow overlooking the river, whilst the mounted infantry rode on to reconnoitre the pass to which we had to march on the morrow. They reported that it was held by a large force, and an armed Tibetan and some shepherds were captured, who stated that the enemy numbered 2000, and that the Yutok minister had left Ralung the previous day for the other side of the pass, presumably to resume his command of the troops there. Ralung being such an important site, a post was formed here to keep our communications open with Gyantsé.

We were now quite above the limit of cultivation, and apparently also of trees and shrubs, for none were visible on the bare rounded slopes under the snow-line; but as if to compensate for this want, the hills were much greener with verdant turf than those in the less inhospitable regions below. The large monastery of Ralung is situated in a side-glen under the snows, 2 miles from the village. It is a celebrated one, and is of interest as being the original headquarters of the red-hat sect of Lamas, the *Duk-pa*, which monopolises all the monasteries and temples in Bhotan, and of which the priest-king of that country, the Dharma Raja, is now the spiritual head. This being so, the Tongsa Penlop, as the temporal representative of the latter, put up at this monastery for the night. By its side is a convent of some thirty nuns, who, as well as the monks, were profuse in their welcome of the officers who visited the building. They call the place, after their sect, "*Duk* Ralung," or the "Dragon," and point to the hog-backed ridges of the surrounding hills as the backs of the squirming dragons, who are their spiritual protectors. "Ralung" means the "Valley of Horns," a title which aptly designates the icy horns which encircle its site. This snowy range is a continuation of that spur from Chumolhari which we saw ran off to the north along the Rham lake at Tuna.

The road to the pass, next morning, led over a fine open moor, bounded by rolling downs and grassy uplands, stretching to the dark red sandstone rocks which, covered in part with verdure of deepest emerald, under the white snow-line gave wonderful bits of vivid colouring; whilst underfoot the springy turf was begemmed with pink primulas, striped blue gentians, yellow potentillas, cobalt poppies, and the air was scented by the fragrant wormwood. Some snow-pheasants were flushed here, and on the hills several wild blue sheep (*burhal*), as well as gazelles, were to be seen. About the eighth mile our track left the central valley, which runs up to the great western glaciers of Nöjin Kang, and, turning sharply to the right, struck into a narrow, rocky gorge coming down from the eastern flank of that mountain (see photo, p. 281). The relative warmth of this gorge was at once evident, not only in its scorching temperature in the sun, but in the thick growth of shrubs and trees which we met here again, after having apparently passed above the tree limit lower down at a height of about 14,000 feet. The water of the streamlet, too, was clear as crystal, and

OUR CAMP UNDER NÖJIN GLACIER.
In Kharo Pass, 16,200 ft.

KHARO PASS LOOKING NORTH (16,400 feet).

Shows first phase of the action. The Tibetan wall blocked the valley one mile lower down and ran up the ridge on the right to the heights, 19,000 feet. In the photograph the line of Goorkhas can be seen climbing these heights on the right.

not of the muddy glacier type of the icy river of the main valley which contributed so much to the cooling of the latter. It was particularly noticeable that several trees, of a prickly sort like buckthorn and with the contour of dwarf pines, about 20 feet high, shot out of crevices in the rocks and tossed their heads in the breeze, nearly 16,000 feet above the sea-level, which is by far the highest elevation for trees that I have seen recorded. The shrubs were juniper, willow, barberry, and a few copper birches—which are called "Stripes," with reference to the bark peeling off transversely, leaving tiger-like markings—with a rank herbaceous undergrowth of hemlock, dock, rhubarb, arnica (smoked as tobacco), aconite, and nettles, pungent leek, cottony everlastings, speedwells, saxifrages, and a profusion of other wild-flowers, mostly yellow and blue.

Ascending more steeply over a rough rocky track, and crossing the bed of the streamlet, black with shaly shingle, and skirting a shallow lake about a mile long with numerous marshy islets, we encamped at its upper end on an old moraine under the icefall of an almost dead glacier, half a mile below the Kharo or "Wide-Mouthed"[1] Pass.

From our camp we could see on the higher ridge, 2 miles beyond and facing the pass, even with the naked eye, swarms of Tibetans moving against the sky-line in their strongly-fortified position, which was a loop-holed wall running across and barring the valley in a narrow gorge flanked by almost impassable precipices and snowy mountains. The General, on riding up to the pass with an escort to get a better view of the position and arrange for storming it next morning, was met by a menacing fire from the enemy's *jingals*, which were, however, fortunately beyond range. The mounted infantry scouts reported that they had actually seen about 700 armed men hold-

[1] Spelt "Kharol La."

ing the line of wall, and doubtless there were many more behind. It looked, therefore, as if a desperate resistance was prepared for the morrow; and the possibility of an attempt to rush our camp at night was accordingly provided against.

Under the cold shadow of the icefalls of this glacier—on the foot of whose lateral moraine we were encamped at an elevation of over 16,000 feet above the sea-level—the air became piercingly chill at 3 P.M., and a freezing blast blew down on us all night. Although the glacier had receded up to the massive granite of its rocks, leaving its later terminal moraine as a great isolated mound nearly a quarter of a mile below its present extremity, there was still a considerable fall of ice and snow from its tumbled snowfields terraced and seamed by blue crevasses; and the roar of its avalanches was heard repeatedly during the afternoon and night. The temperature fell to 12° Fahr. below freezing.

A desperate battle was believed to be impending when we started up the pass next morning (19th July) in warlike array. Immediately our troops showed themselves on the pass (16,600 feet) the enemy opened a harmless fire from the precipitous ridge of jagged crests and cliffs on the right, which rose over 2000 feet above us (see photo here). The Goorkhas were sent up these heights to outflank the Tibetans, whilst the Fusiliers were moved down the middle of the valley towards the main block-wall. On a knoll below the pass, where the artillery had its position, we pulled out our glasses and telescopes, and could see all the movements distinctly, the Goorkhas climbing up the sky-piercing crags, and clambering across the steep slopes and loose rocks of the stone-shoots to the snow-line, whilst the Fusiliers boldly advanced to the main wall below. As the latter crept along under cover of the river-banks, and got nearer and nearer to the wall, and still no fire was opened, the excitement became intense, as it seemed that the enemy were withholding their fire for the actual rush. When the Fusiliers climbed the glacis and dashed across to the strongest part of the wall—at the same place where poor Bethune was killed here three months previously—and then emerged on the other side, we realised that this part of their defences had been abandoned by the enemy and was now in our possession without a single shot having been fired. It was very different with the Goorkhas on the heights. After scaling these to an elevation of nearly 19,000 feet, they were assailed by a heavy fusillade from the Tibetans. We heard the sharp rattle of our rifles in reply; and under cover of the shells thrown by our 10-pounders, the Goorkhas were seen to advance steadily on. The Tibetans, after a dogged resistance, and hiding amongst the rocks, whence they kept up their fire, retired slowly and then broke and fled. Some of them threw themselves down the precipices, while many of them escaped up to the snow-fields, where they could be seen, like a string of ants, threading their way into the eternal solitudes of ice, at an elevation of about 23,000 feet, where venturous man never trod before, where it was impossible to follow them, and where doubtless most, if not all of them, must have perished miserably by the intense cold or by falling into the numerous crevasses and ice-clefts. Some who had hid in the lower rocks and attempted to make a stand below the wall were pursued by the Pathans and dispersed with great loss. Amongst those killed was an important chief dressed in blue silk. When the Tibetan prisoners passed his body they all turned and saluted with prostrations the earthly remains of their fallen lord. These captives gave the information that 1500 men held the wall on the 18th, but, alarmed at our arrival, half of them retired during the night down the valley to Nagartsé fort, leaving the remaining 700 or so, who were levies from Kham, to occupy the heights under the snows from whence they were driven by our soldiers. Thirteen hundred additional Kham men, they added, were expected at Nagartsé fort that day. In this battlefield amidst those icy solitudes, nearly 19,000 feet high, on the Roof of the World, the enemy lost about 300 men, whilst our loss was only one man killed and two wounded.

A halt was made to demolish the wall where it crossed the road. This place was called Zara, or "The Slaty Defile," the rock here being chiefly a bluish slate underlying the honeycombed cliffs of reddish sandstone. The wall across the rivulet ran up the lateral moraine of the great glacier, on whose snow-fields the escaping Tibetans were still to be seen struggling —the snowy peak above this glacier was called the "Black-headed God's Bird" (Lhaja-gonak). Taking advantage of this halt I climbed to the foot of the glacier, which ends in a wild lake hemmed in by a wall of rock, through a cleft in which its green waters rush out to meet the main stream. This wild gorge is notoriously infested by brigands, so below the wall we found a guard-house, to shelter wayfarers, and a Chinese staging-house, both of which were temporarily deserted.

For the night we pushed down the valley a few miles farther to the shrub-zone, for the sake of fuel, crossing the turbid white waters of a glacier torrent which gave the name of "The Milky Plain" to the meadow. There was no cultivation, however, and only a very scanty grazing, rendered dangerous by abundant aconite; so the poor mules, deprived of their customary grass, spent the night, which was miserably cold, in squealing out their discontent. The Mounted Infantry who reconnoitred the road down to Nagartsé found that place occupied and several ravines on the way held by armed Tibetans, of whom a few were brought in as prisoners.

FINAL PHASE OF KHARO PASS ACTION.

At wall (16,100 feet elevation) which is seen being demolished by our soldiers, below the Glaciers of Mount Lhaja-gonak. (*The wall ran up to crags on right* [19,000 *feet elevation*] *and Tibetans fled up over the snow-fields on the left.*)

AN ARM OF YAMDOK INLAND SEA.

(14,900 feet above the sea-level.)

These stated that some of their number who had bolted from the Zara wall two days ago were pursued by Tibetan cavalry and killed by these their own people. So it seemed as if we should have to fight our way on to Lhasa.

The descent to Nagartsé, in the basin of the great Yamdok Lake, was easy and gradual along the bank of the river, which gathered up fresh feeders from every side valley where glacier-clad snow-peaks shot into view. Some of the ice-cornices were exquisitely beautiful in form and in their delicate shades of cobalt and pale green, and several old ruined keeps, perched boldly on the jagged crests and silhouetted darkly against the sky, like the familiar ancient castles on the Rhine, added a romantic suggestiveness of the blood-feuds of warlike chiefs and freebooting lords, to the picturesqueness of this wild valley.

Where the valley broadened out into a small meadow, called "The Horses' Plain" (*Ta-t'ang*), the river cut through an old bank of conglomerated boulders, exposing a cluster of caves made by prehistoric men. They numbered about forty. Some of the largest were examined by two of us, and found to burrow 10 yards or more within the cliff of boulders. Their floor was deeply overlaid by the débris of ages fallen from the roof, and was too consolidated to be scraped away during our hurried visit. Excavation here would doubtless reveal deposits of much interest regarding the earlier physical character of the Mongolian race, which curiously in its present-day features approximates to the large Asiatic ape, the orang-outang — just as the negro approximates in physical traits to the great ape of the African continent, the gorilla. The position of these caves, too, near the former shore of that old sea whose bottom, uplifted by the rising of the Himalayas, forms the plateau of Tibet, are thus all the more likely to contain traces of primitive man.[1] The prisoners said that these were the abodes of wild men who lived here before the Tibetans arrived. In this regard it is interesting to recall the widespread tradition amongst the people of Tibet that their country was formerly covered by water (? the Deluge), and was only comparatively lately inhabited, about two thousand years ago.[2] Some of these caves are used by robbers, for which this gorge is notorious, and a bend of the ravine below is named "The Robbers' Nook."[3]

The valley expanded more and more as we descended, till, turning a corner, the bold outline of Nagartsé Fort shot into view at the end of a spur on our left, and beyond it the light silvery streak of the great Yamdok Lake gleamed amongst dark-blue hills, whilst the tall poles of the prayer-flags, projecting over the house-roofs of the village, looked like the masts of fishing-boats at anchor on the lake—the famous "ring lake" of the older maps of Central Asia, a vast inland sea without an outlet.

The mounted infantry rode up to the fort, and were met by a messenger under a white flag, who brought the news that the Tibetan troops had all left, and the place was only occupied by the "peace delegates" from Lhasa. These turned out to be our old friend the Ta Lama, and that truculent secretary who had fled from Gyantsé, and the new Prime Minister, the Yutok Shapé, and they asked for an interview with the Mission. This was at once granted,

[1] A large number of neolithic stone implements has lately been found on the outer hills at Kalimpong, in British Bhotan, by Mr C. A. Bell, C.S.

[2] For geological evidence that the elevation of the Himalayas commenced only in middle Tertiary times, see Oldham's *Geology of India*, p. 477.

[3] Chūr.

and they rode into camp in procession, dressed in gorgeous yellow silks as at Gyantsé. The new Minister, Yutok, was a stout, stolid little man, with nothing of the courtier or soldier in his appearance, wearing a blue silk robe over his yellow tunic. They informed Colonel Younghusband that they had come in finally to make peace, as a result of a council meeting at Lhasa, and they demanded that we should return to Gyantsé—(it was not Yatung this time!) to discuss the terms. Colonel Younghusband enquired whether they had received a written statement of his terms from the Tongsa Penlop. They admitted having received this, but stated that negotiations could only begin when we retired, and that a treaty made at Lhasa could not be lasting, as the latter was a purely religious city, and did not concern itself with political affairs, whilst our presence there would profane it. Our Commissioner retorted that there were many non-Buddhists, Mahomedans, Nepalese, and others always in Lhasa, and that we had decided to go there only after giving them an extensive time to treat at the various places along the road in vain, and that they had attacked the Mission instead. The treaty must now be signed at Lhasa, but he was willing to discuss the terms during the journey, and it depended on the Tibetans whether there was to be further fighting, for we wished to travel as peacefully as possible; and if there was no resistance we would treat them as friends, pay for our supplies, and would not stay long at Lhasa; meanwhile their men were to evacuate the fort. This latter request the delegates absolutely refused to comply with. At this point in the discussion news arrived that a large body of armed Tibetans had come out of the fort, and as they were making off towards Lhasa, they fired on our mounted infantry when the latter approached to ascertain who they were. Several of them were taken prisoners. They were all armed with breech-loading rifles. After this episode the fort was occupied by a garrison of our troops; for there is no doubt that our vain-glorious enemy, like all Asiatics, are more amenable to the logic of facts and personal experiences than to reason. The fort was of small size and in a crumbling condition, overgrown with weeds and nettles. In it was found a large stock of the food supplies of the Tibetan army, also suits of clothes and blankets. The building is about a mile from the shore of the lake, with a few poor huts of the villagers, and a Chinese staging-house nestling under its walls facing the lake.

The delegates came again next day, but after three hours' abortive talk, left without repeating the demand that the Mission must return to Gyantsé, and making it clear that they had not come prepared to negotiate at all. They also declined to promise that we should not be opposed farther on and their bearing altogether was rather insolent and overbearing. Some Chinese couriers proceeding to Chumbi brought in the news that serious riots had occurred in Lhasa, owing to some of the Kham levies, who had escaped from the Kharo Pass, having mutinied, and had been joined by fresh ones who had refused to fight us, and had begun pillaging the Chinese quarter of the town. The Amban had attacked them with his guard, and had several of his men killed.

Taking advantage of our halt and that day's armistice, I rode over with a few others to see the sanctuary of the tutelary genius of this great sacred lake, the famous sorceress called the incarnated Pig-faced Goddess, a Tibetan Circe, who in holiness ranks almost next to the Grand Lama himself, and whose shrine does not appear to have been visited by Europeans before.

It was a pleasure to leave our warlike surroundings

and enter again the world of dreams and magic which may be said to be ever with us in the mystic Land of the Lamas. Passing the fort of Nagartsé, brilliant in reds, blues and whites, rising boldly from the old shore of the lake, at the foot of a rocky promontory, above the fields bestarred with myriad pink primulas and pale mauve daisies, and cobalt sheets of forget-me-not, a ride of 4 miles took us across the marshy isthmus of the blue "ring lake" to the purple hills of the central island. Amongst these hills, in a bare, shallow glen, our guide pointed out a white speck 4 miles away as the abode of the divinity we were in search of; it is called "The Soaring Meditation" (*Sam-ding*). Our road along the foot of the hills was fringed with wild roses, barberry and trailing clematis, and skirted for some distance a fine wood of tall juniper trees within the grounds of a small monastery (*Sam-jo*), showing that trees if protected can grow freely at the great elevation of this lake, which is about 15,000 feet above the sea-level (and not 13,800 feet as recorded by the Survey *pundits*). A considerable grove also of willow trees, laid out with gravelled walks as a pleasure-garden, lay below the convent of Sam-ding, which is built near the foot of a smoothly rounded and non-precipitous spur of bare hill, about 300 feet above the plain and lake and near a small village. As we approached it dense snow-clouds suddenly descended and shut it out of view, and then as suddenly disappeared, transforming and retransforming the landscape as if by magic from summer to winter, and from winter to summer, in the course of a few minutes; curiously, the white mantle was confined to the hill on which the convent stood and did not extend to the plain over which we rode or to the hill above us.

We dismounted at the foot of the convent hill at the prayer-flags on the large *Chorten*, and walked in the slushy snow up the long zigzagging dilapidated pathway of small loose stones, probably the remains of roughly-built steps, and bordered by a breast-high wall with a stepped coping. The building itself also, we now could see, had a rather decayed and neglected look and a small and altogether mean appearance, which was disappointing in one of the most reputed shrines of Tibet. We saw no signs of inmates, and on entering the main court of the building found that the pig-headed divinity and all her sisterhood had fled. The latter had evidently decamped that morning, as our guide had found them present the previous evening. It was unfortunate that they had been so panic-struck as to have deserted their hermitage, for they of all others were sure of friendly treatment at our hands, because the incarnation of this vestal priestess in the days of Bogle visited the Indian Mission at Tashilhumpo, and was on the friendliest of terms with its members, and because the last one befriended Sarat Chandra Das in an attack of illness here. The present representative is a child of only six years of age,[1] who we were told had left for Lhasa with her mother nearly a year previous to our visit.

This august, if youthful, lady is alleged by the Lamas to be the human incarnation of one of those monstrous creations of the later Indian Buddhists who followed the Brahmans in admitting female energies into their grotesque pantheon. The deity in question is depicted as a Fury with a pig's face, called "The Thunderbolt Sow" (*Vajra varahi*, in Tibetan *Dorje Pa'gmo*),[2] and owes her origin to the ancient Eastern myth of that primeval source of energy, the productive pig, which was made the consort of a demoniacal sort of centaur, "The Horse-necked Tamdin," and was given with

[1] She was born at Tö-lung.

[2] She is worshipped by Nepalese merchants as the Hindu goddess Bhawani, a form of the dreaded Kali.

him the joint task of defending Buddhism against its enemies. In this connection a legend tells how, when Tibet was invaded by the Jungar Tartars in 1717, on the approach of the soldiery to sack this place, their General sent a mocking message asking the abbess to come out and show her pig's head, and when she meekly begged that she and her nuns might be left alone, the infidel warriors burst into the place, only to find eighty pigs headed by a large sow grunting in the assembly hall, the abbess having converted all her retainers as well as herself into swine. As the hog is the most "unclean" of all animals in the eyes of a Mahomedan, the Tartars beat a hasty retreat, and this religious place was thus saved by its presiding sorceress. She receives divine honours from the Lamas of all sects—although strictly speaking she belongs to the red-capped Nyingma sect—and she shares with the Dalai Lama, the King Regent, and the two Ambans the royal privilege of riding in a sedan-chair when she travels. Mr Bogle described her appearance in her mature form when she visited Tashilhumpo, at the time of Warren Hastings' mission, when Dr Hamilton cured her of an illness.

"The mother went with me into the apartment of Durjay Paumo, who was attired in a *Gylong's* [monk's] dress, her arms bare from the shoulders, and sitting cross-legged upon a low cushion. . . . She is about seven-and-twenty, with small Chinese features, delicate though not regular, fine eyes and teeth; her complexion fair, but wan and sickly; and an expression of languor and melancholy in her countenance, which, I believe, is occasioned by the joyless life that she leads. She wears her hair, a privilege granted to no other vestal I have seen; it is combed back without any ornaments and falls in tresses upon her shoulders. Her *chanca* [hand-benediction] like the [Grand] Lama's, is supposed to convey a blessing, and I did not fail to receive it.

After making presents and obeisances I kneeled down, and stretching out her arm, which is equal to 'the finest lady in the land,' she laid her hand upon my head."[1]

At our visit we saw neither nuns, monks, nor pigs. The convent buildings, three storeys high, are ranged round a roughly-paved courtyard some 20 yards square, the whole recalling somewhat the appearance of an old country inn or hostelry in Normandy. On the right, above the stables and cook-houses, are the dormitories of the abbess and her nuns, whilst the monks — for, curiously, half of the 160 inmates of the establishment presided over by the virgin abbess are monks—live on the left, beyond the *Chortens*, which enshrine the bodily relics of the founder and successive abbesses before the present one, and in front is the chief temple. As the apartments of the nuns were deserted, we peeped into a few and found them very neat and tidily arranged as by a woman's hand. They each contained a small altar with butter candles, images, and a few books; the walls were hung with paintings of deities, and the windows screened with white muslin curtains. The temple, as well as the block of shrines on the left of it, is entered by a flight of wooden stairs up to a verandah, protected from the weather by the usual large curtain. The frescoes were of the common kind and of coarse execution, with the pig goddess frequently figured therein. The images were of gilt brass, and adorned with precious stones. Amongst articles on the altar I noticed a large *cloisonné* jar of the Ming period. The only books I could see were the ordinary scriptural text and commentary, and there was no library of special works. The relic shrines were cased in gilt copper studded over with poor glass imitations of jewels.

[1] Markham's *Mission*, etc., pp. 244, 245.

CONVENT OF THE PIG-FACED ABBESS AT SAMDING.

PALTÉ FORT ON LAKE YAMDOK.

The promenade on the flat roof commanded magnificent wide views of the surrounding country and part of the Yamdok Lake in its encircling hills to the west. To the south and east rose the grand snowy range of the Kharo Pass, from which ran down steep, bare ridges to the deep blue waters of the "Devil's Lake" (*Dum-Tso*) about 6 miles long, immediately below us. This latter was reported by Sarat to be of terrible appearance, with black, frowning cliffs and stupendous crags, and 500 feet above the level of the Yamdok. It is, however, on practically the same level as the Yamdok, not more than 1 or 2 feet higher, and is merely a portion of the latter which has become detached and isolated by the drying up of the waters of the great lake, and its investing hills cannot be said to be steep except for a short distance on the southern and eastern shores. In the recesses of the central mountains of the "island" of the "Inside Rocks" above Samding is said to be a cave which was inhabited by the founder of Lamaism.

Our march to Lhasa was resumed next day (21st July) and continued for the next four days, winding along the western shore of the great lake; the Tibetan delegates had left during the night post-haste in the same direction.

The lake gets its name from the elevated district in which it lies, namely "The Upper Pastures" (*Yam-dok*).[1] It is frequently known as "The Turquoise Lake"[2] on account of its colour, and was called by the early Capuchin monks, who nearly all passed this way to Lhasa, "Palté Lake," after the name of the chief village on its shores. Its circuit is about 150 miles, and takes over two weeks to traverse. Its elevation is raised by Captain Ryder over 1000 feet above that recorded by the pundits, to about

[1] Spelt *Ya-brog*.

[2] *Gyum-mts'o*, pronounced "Yum Ts'o."

14,850 feet above the sea-level, though the frequent thunderstorms affect the barometer and boiling-point thermometer so much as to render its precise estimation difficult.

The shape of this vast inland sea was one of the most striking features in the old maps of Tartary. It was figured as a symmetrical ring of water completely enclosing a circle of land in its centre. This error, derived from the old Lama survey of the Emperor Kangshi, was repeated by the Capuchin monks. The idea of a complete ring was exploded by Pundit Nain Sing in 1866, who showed that the mountainous "island" in its centre, over 25 miles long, was connected to the mainland by the narrow isthmus which leads to the Samding monastery. Its true shape was mapped out for the first time by the Lama surveyor, Ugyen Gyatsho, in 1882-83, who travelled round it and found that the ring was broken in two places, the mountains in the centre forming a bulbous peninsula (see large map), called the "Inside Rocks" (*Donang*) lying within the lake and connected with the mainland on the west by a neck within which lay the Devil's Lake. When its outline was projected on paper, it had somewhat the shape of a scorpion with recurved tail, a resemblance, however, which was unnoticed by the Tibetans themselves.

Although this magnificent curve of land-locked water winding among the hills is not now a complete ring, it probably was so originally in its glacial period, when its waters overflowed the stony promontory of the Tag or "Rocky" Pass.[1] It certainly must have been almost a complete ring in comparatively recent historical times, when it was continuous with the Devil's Lake, across that narrow isthmus now so consolidated that we cantered over it all the way on our visit to

[1] This pass has not yet been visited by any European, but it seemed to me to be not more than 1000 feet above the Dum Lake.

Samding. Its two ends are only separated by the Tag ridge. The people say, and indeed there is ample evidence, that the larger lake is drying up and receding. As we passed along its shore we could see the old tracks on the hillside 20 to 30 feet above the present road, and in the side valleys were well-marked shallow terraces, for 100 feet or more, marking evidently former levels of the beach. Its waters undoubtedly extended in former times up the side valley down which we came to near the Kharo Pass, as the shelving shingly plain, spotted with white saline incrustation forming the bed of that valley, was clearly continuous with the floor of the lake. The level of the water nowadays fluctuates within narrow limits from year to year, and with the season according to variations in the local snow and rainfall. The desiccation of this lake is doubtless due in part to the increased evaporation consequent on the disappearance of its glaciers and glacial feeders permitting the air to become warmer, whilst the rising of the Himalayas, which has continued up to recent times, must have cut off a considerable amount of its former rain-supply.

The water of the lake tasted slightly saline, as was to be expected in a lake which had no outlet, and which was fed by rain and snow from the hillsides, dissolving portions of the lime and other rocks, and on evaporation leaving the salt behind; but although slightly brackish it was quite drinkable and made good tea. I collected a sample of the water for analysis, also some of the white efflorescent salt on the old lake-bottom forming the plain.[1] The shore in places was strewn with small shells and masses of feathery water-weed which gave off a smell like that of the sea-shore.

Our road struck the lake-side at a little village of wretchedly poor stone huts, malodorous with the heaps of putrid fish inside, small dried fish about the size

[1] See Appendix VIII., p. 472.

of a herring and less; but no boats or fishing-tackle were anywhere visible, and the people, too, had all deserted. From here we wound along the shore, under the gently rounded grassy hills, keeping generally close to the water's edge where the beach was sandy or rocky, and making slight detours where stretches of rushy peat-bogs filled in the bays. The lake, here about 3 to 5 miles broad, in its setting amongst softly-swelling hills with purple patches of the pea-like *pedicularis*, had so much the appearance of a wild Scottish loch, that, even despite the entire absence of trees, I involuntarily scanned the headlands for a steamer coming round the corner. Its climate, too, was suggestive of the Highlands in its misty moods and fickleness. The fleecy clouds flecking the deep sapphire sky and mirrored in the sparkling pale bluey-green waters of the lake, would bank up at times into great masses of grey thunder-clouds which rested on the hill-tops and threw dark purple shadows over the glens, or resolved into a passing mist which drizzled over us in the dancing sunlight, or became a steady downpour drenching us through, until the sun in pity burst out again and dried us from its sportive mists.

We encamped at the head of a fine sandy bay at the foot of the wide valley of Yarsig, up which runs the direct road to Shigatsé by way of the Rong Valley beyond the head of this one. We crossed the stream dry-shod by a small perforated causeway called "The Blessed Bridge," an artificial structure and not a natural bridge, which shortens the shore-road by over a mile. Fish were so abundant in this stream below the bridge that they seemed literally to jostle one another, so that some of the Indian followers, wading in, scooped them out on to the bank, and in a short time caught in this way over 300 lbs. weight. Several officers who had brought fishing-rods hooked, with a small "spoon" or flies, an incredible number in a few minutes; one officer, Major Iggulden, landed in less than half an hour 48 lbs. weight, many of the fish lusty fellows scaling 4 to 6 lbs. and giving good play. They were all like carp in general appearance, and almost scaleless; though some of them differed in the size and arrangement of their spots (see photo, p. 306), all were excellent eating. As they were likely to be new species, seeing that the lake has been isolated for so long from all outlets, I collected a few for identification. They doubtless came from the Tsangpo Valley over the Yarsig Pass, which is now over 1000 feet above the lake, and 16,000 feet above the sea; but in those earlier times, before the later rising of the Himalayas, it must have been much lower. The meadows here as well as the shore along which we had come were tenanted by numerous Pika mouse-hares, who scampered timidly in and out of their shallow burrows. On the lake swarmed countless ducks and geese with their newly-fledged broods, and a few gulls and terns hovering overhead screamed disapproval at our intrusion on their favourite fishing-ground.

We were again victimised here by the weather. A refreshing stretch of restful green velvety turf, besprinkled with springy white gravel of bleached shells covered with a small sweet-scented golden buttercup and a glowing amber potentilla redolent of new-mown hay, had been chosen for our camp on the shelving beach. But before our tents and baggage arrived, the sky suddenly became overcast, and rain began to descend in torrents till sunset, when it turned to sleet and snow, which lasted all night, and did not leave off till eight o'clock next morning. When the sun shone brightly out again, the lake smiled once more alluringly, and everyone, refreshed by the night's rest, struck tents, and marched off in lovely, bright weather with spirits undamped by the discomforts of the night.

As we wound out of this valley across a rocky promontory, we passed the shrine to the local genius. It was at an eerie wild spot where the crumbling rocks from above shot down into the lake, and here the peasantry had smeared the stones over with daubs of bright red paint, and tied coloured rags and prayer-flags to the large barberry and juniper bushes as a propitiatory offering to the malignant *Ts'än* spirit of the place, who is figured as an ogre of a bloody crimson colour. The local legend says that here a troop of the invading army of the Tartars who tried to desecrate the temple of the Pig-faced Abbess at Samding were engulfed in the lake when making for Palté. At this weird spot, too, the villagers consign the bodies of their dead to the transparent turquoise depths of the lake, and one of these gruesome objects could be seen entangled in the water-weeds below, under the wild blue poppies, dog-roses, and a deep blue myrtle which fringed the rim of the lake here. Amongst the grey lichen-covered rocks grew also some bushes of a kind of hawthorn in bloom — May-flower blossoming in July — and several ragged heads of a golden rod, as well as wormwood, violet larkspur, and rank nettles, and a delicate harebell, and many pink saxifrages, "breaking up the stones." Several heavy showers now came down, but by this time we all had got into the frame of mind that it did not much matter to us whether it rained or not as we pushed on all the same.

Palté[1] fort was discovered when we rounded the bluff, standing picturesquely on the water's edge on the further side of another bay, and reflected in the lake with its village under its shadow. Our mounted infantry had found it abandoned the previous day, so we moved on and encamped on the turfy meadow beyond it, whilst a detachment of the

[1] This name is spelt by the Tibetans *d* Pal-*s*de ; also *d* Pal-di.

mounted infantry reconnoitred the Kamba Pass into the Tsangpo Valley, and found that its fortifications also were evacuated; thus the effects of the storming of Gyantsé had been so far-reaching as to enable the Kharo Pass and the forts of Nagartsé and Palté, and the Kamba, the last of all the passes on the road to Lhasa, to be gained with little or no loss. The villagers of the dozen houses of Palté had nearly all fled to the hills with their valuables. The few who remained said that the Tibetan delegates had left the previous morning for Lhasa, and that Tibetan troops, mostly Kham levies, had collected on the other bank of the Tsangpo to defend the crossing of that river. This fort is not a government one, but belongs to the local baron of these rigorous upland pastures. Owing to the elevation there is scarcely any cultivation, all we saw being one or two poor fields of barley near the villages. The inhabitants of this and the other villages on the shore live largely on fish, but do not seem to export much. They had hidden their boats, only one of which was found. It was made of untanned yak-hides stretched on a wooden framework and of a tub-like shape. They are so light that a man can carry one inverted, and are very apt to capsize and founder. The fish are caught by drag-nets in summer, or by spearing through holes in the ice in winter. Our collapsible Berthon boats, for use in crossing the Tsangpo, were opened out to-day, and several officers passed the summer afternoon in being paddled about the lake by the Indian boatmen from the Indus.

Another hideously wet night made our tents heavy again for the pack animals; but the weather improved as we started along the curving beach of a sunlit sea in the bright, fresh morning air. Beyond another bay in which stood the crumbling ruins of an old fort with bastions called "arrow towers," a newly-built loopholed block wall was found in a very strong position about the sixth mile, where a rocky spur ran down from the Dok Pass (16,800 feet) somewhat steeply into the lake. It was continued upwards for over 7 miles along the crest of the spur, and reminded one of the great wall of China, and must have taken some thousands of Tibetans to build it; and showed their intention to defend the road to Lhasa. After a halt here to demolish the portion near the road where there were some rock-caves, we continued for 8 miles to near the hamlet of Toma-lung, or "The Valley of Peas," at the foot of the Kamba Pass. This was the most fertile and cultivated part we had seen in the lake basin. There were several fields of barley, peas and turnips; and flocks of sheep and yaks were grazing on the hillside as well as on the hills across the lake, here some 4 miles wide, where there was also a small hamlet of some half-dozen houses whence the bay of the mastiffs could be heard distinctly. There is here, as at Palté, a ferry to the central peninsula.

Our camp (see photo, p. 289) filled the whole meadow, and in the evening, as the purple haze crept over the hills, made a pretty picture on the grassy bank of this hill-girt lake, with its marvellous colours and the glorious cloud-effects of light and shade on the mountains. The pale turquoise colour of the lake was shaded away into the deepest sea-blue towards its furthest shore, where rose the purple hills, and on the right the white-topped, glacier-clad Nöjin Kang and the Kharo snows towered so high as to be mirrored in the restful, placid waters. Suddenly, without any warning, its mood altered. A gloom overshadowed the land and blotted out its colour; and instantly a blast sprang up and blurred the reflections in the lake, and broke its surface into ripples and then into waves which lashed each other into foam till white-crested "sea-horses" chased each other over the surface and sent breakers up the shore, whilst a dark thunder-cloud swept over the grey sky, and sent down pelting hail and sheets of rain. The squall disappeared as quickly as it came; a gleam of sunshine broke the spell of the storm, which slunk away with a low, vexed moan, and the water and hills regained their colouring and repose. The natives, of course, attribute these storms to supernatural agency, and say that they are caused by a great green dragon which lives in the depths of this enchanted lake, and lashes the water in its fits of anger. This idea is doubtless suggested by the serpentine form of the green lake winding in and out amongst the mountains. They also believe that a golden fish of good luck has its abode in this sea, and they jealously treasure it as their mascot.

Next day gave us the long-looked-for sight of the Tsangpo, the great central river of Tibet, which is believed to be the upper course of the Brahmaputra river, and took us down to its banks, across the Kamba Pass. There was a good-natured but gasping race for the first view. On the way up to the pass I looked out for the hollow echo of travellers' footsteps observed by the Capuchin fathers, and attributed by them to some great volcanic caverns which they supposed must underlie the surface here. A hollow sound was indeed noticeable, but it obviously was caused by the tread over the semi-separated flags of shale and stratified limestone which here underlie the gravelly soil, and whose strata run parallel to the slope of the hillside. There is no trace of coal anywhere in this area, as has been alleged; the blackish slates and veins of serpentine have evidently been mistaken for it; nor is the use of coal known to any of the Tibetans I have met. Looking back from near the top of the pass (16,500 feet), which is a rounded saddle, we got a magnificent bird's-eye view of the great lake, imposing in its dreary vastness, as it fills the bottom of a great network of valleys. Its want of ruggedness and of bold cliffs along the shore, and the severe bareness of its hills, were still more accentuated by the distance. Nevertheless, it impressed itself indelibly on the memory as a vast curving sea of unruffled azure framed in a chain of bleak, round grassy hills.

The first view of the Tsangpo river and its valley from the cairn (*labtse*), decorated with wild sheep's horns and prayer-flags, at the top of the pass was rather stern and inhospitable. We looked down over the arid, rounded slopes of the hillside beneath us into the deep trough of a barren-looking valley 4000 feet below, nearly the whole bottom of which seemed to be taken up by the stony bed of a sluggish river, whose arms wound through it like silver threads. The only cultivation noticeable was a fringe of fields along the foot of the bare stony mountains forming the opposite side of the valley, which rose up steeply to a greater height than the ridge on which we were standing. The peaks of the northern ranges across the river, many of them snow-clad, were sharply pointed, more so even than those in the south, which was quite contrary to the current theories of the Himalayan ridges, ascribing rounded and flat tops to the northern ranges. No trees were anywhere visible except a slight sprinkling near the bottom of the valley. There was no glimpse of Lhasa as had been alleged.

When we left the pass behind us we entered Central Tibet, as this ridge which divides the Yamdok basin from the Tsangpo Valley also divides the Central province from Western Tibet, or Tsang. Our track zigzagged down a stony path so steep that we descended over 4000 feet in 4 miles. In these bleak uplands the most conspicuous plants were dwarf wild rhubarb, arnica, blue gentian, and, lower down, the prickly-stemmed blue poppy and edelweiss; and here

TSANGPO VALLEY FROM KAMPA PASS (16,500 feet).

NEW CARP FROM YAMDOK LAKE.

Gymnocypris waddelli. (Reduced to ⅛th natural size.)

VALLEY OF THE TSANGPO IN CENTRAL TIBET.
(12,100 feet above sea-level).
Above Chaksam Ferry.

we flushed a covey of snow-pheasants. About half-way down we entered the upper part of a rocky ravine wherein, in the sheltered moister and less stubborn soil, grew numerous shrubs of juniper, barberry, wild white roses with scarlet hips, and yellow furze bushes in bloom. Near the bottom several irrigation channels led the water of the ravine off to fields below, and presently the gorge opened out into some terraced fields at a prosperous-looking hamlet, nearly half a mile above the bank of the river, and about 200 feet above its level. The houses were surrounded by a few walnut, peach and willow trees, and the crops of wheat and barley were already yellow and ripe for harvesting. We encamped partly in the fields and partly in a grove of woolly alder-trees near the river-bank underneath the adjoining village of Partsi with its Chinese staging-house.

The valley here is called "The North Kamba Plain," after the name of the pass; and the central river, which runs east and west, is known as "The Upper River," or *Yaru Tsangpo*. The bed was about a mile wide, a boulder-strewn depression, in which wound in great curves the placid river as a majestic stream, never fordable at any season, and about 300 feet across. The banks showed a recent flood-water rise of over 10 feet above the present level. The running water had a temperature of about 40° Fahr., and, though turbid with glacier and flood-silt, was usable for drinking purposes. I washed a little of its mud for gold dust and got a "show" of colour in the sediment.

The climate, at this elevation of 12,000 feet above the sea, seemed almost tropical compared with the inclement regions of the Yamdok from which we had suddenly descended. The sun felt oppressively hot and was so sultry that many of the Indians soon stripped and were bathing in the Tsangpo river; and the vegetation and insect life were almost rank in the damper spots. Gaudy butterflies and brilliantly iridescent dragon-flies hovered over the forget-me-nots, buttercups, mauve daisies, ruby and violet *pedicularis*, and a pale-belled lint clustered along the road-side and the streamlets of the irrigation ditches, which teemed with small fish, frogs, and brilliant insects; and stealthy lizards basked on the warm stones or scampered after the "lady-birds" amongst the trailing masses of yellow-flowered clematis which clambered over the dykes, taking the place of the purple-flowered variety of the uplands. Rank plants of Indian hemp, 6 feet high, and thorn-apple, grew luxuriantly amongst the tall docks and nettles in neglected corners. Flocks of snow-pigeons and red-legged choughs settled on the fields and trees, and doves flitted about with magpies, rose-finches, tits, and chattering laughing-thrushes. In the alder-grove myriads of cockchafers were dropping moribund from the branches, an unpleasant reminder that summer had passed. It was particularly noticeable that there were no rhododendrons, fir-trees, or brambles anywhere in this valley. At our side was the camping-ground of the Grand Lama, marked out with quartz boulders, and the usual high platform for the throne occupying the centre; it was remarkable how frequently these encampments coincided with those selected by our General for military considerations.

We had wide views of the valley from our camp. The narrow shelving plain, from a half to 2 or 3 miles on either side of the river-bank, was covered with terraced fields for the most part, and dotted over sparsely with the white houses of small farms and hamlets, usually encircled by large trees, and had altogether a prosperous agricultural appearance. Up-stream the straight stretch of valley was closed by a bold, snow-capped rocky mass which rose some 15 miles away into two prominent peaks, and by its precipitous sides thrust the river northwards, where the Tsangpo had to make its way through a rocky chasm so narrow as to leave no room for any mule-track, hence the reason why there was no road to Shigatsé along the river-bank above this point, as the track had to climb over the Yamdok basin and rejoin the river in the Rong Valley above our former camp at Yarsig on the great lake. These bold peaks dominating this valley are interesting as being the northern terminus of the spur sent off by Chumolhari at Tuna, past the Rham Lake and the Kharo Pass, and seem to form a part of the Central Himalayan chain of Saunders (see p. 190).

Down the valley the view was blocked by a rocky spur which ran out into its middle. At this point there is a ferry beside the ruins of the old iron suspension bridge—Chak-sam. To seize the passage the General had sent on a mounted party under Major Iggulden, who made a dash there, and heliographed back the news that he had captured both ferry-boats, and had commenced, according to instructions, to pass over the mounted infantry. It afterwards was ascertained that our mounted troops on approaching the ferry found that the large boats were still plying, and that the last boat-load of Kham warriors was just being landed on the opposite bank, where over 200 of them were bivouacked; these at once made off into the woods along the foot of the hills. Our party seized the ferry-boat and its oarsmen on the south bank, and under cover of rifles sent over a Berthon boat which captured the ferry-boat on the other shore. The passage was thus secured without firing a shot. Had these boats been allowed to escape down the river, bridges would have had to be built, delaying our advance for some weeks, as the four Berthon boats were quite inadequate to transport the large force and the heavy loads of guns, stores, and transport animals. To hold the passage, a battalion of infantry and guns was hurried on to the ferry, where we were now only 45 miles from

Lhasa, and only one-half day from the telegraph at Gyantsé and London; for the General had left at each of the fortified posts along our communications at Ralung, Nagartsé, and Palté, in addition to a company of infantry, twenty mounted men, who galloped between these places with His Majesty's mail-bags.

The ferry soon became a busy scene, bristling on both banks with khaki-clad officers and men, all energetically working like clockwork in pushing over the greatest number of troops and amount of loads in the quickest time. The local ferry-boats are huge barges made of walnut planks, flat-bottomed and square cornered like boxes, and bear on their prow a beam carved with a great horse's head, suggesting the vehicle of Neptune in Western myth, as the Tibetans call their boat "the wooden horse," just as we call our railway engine "the iron horse." Each boat carries over in a single journey about twenty ponies, as well as a dozen men and a ton of loads. They are poled along by the boatmen up-stream in the backwater under the great cliff of the promontory, assisted by men on the shore dragging by a rope and pushing in the shallows. Immediately the nose of the boat heads into the stream beyond the point it is caught in the swirls of the river, whose waters, striking on the cliff and sunken rocks, become here a series of violent whirlpools and boiling eddies, which seize the boats and carry them swiftly down-stream, whilst the boatmen excitedly strain every nerve to paddle the boat diagonally across the current, when a yak-hair rope is thrown shorewards, and if secured there the boatload is towed to land. This primitive mode of crossing was found to be very tedious, and caused long delays, through the boat missing the hawsers on the further shore and being carried half a mile or more down-stream before they could be secured. A system of hawsers was rigged up by Captain Shepherd running them on pulleys over

FERRY OVER THE TSANGPO RIVER AT CHAKSAM IN CENTRAL TIBET.
(12,100 feet elevation).

IRON SUSPENSION BRIDGE OVER TSANGPO RIVER AT CHAKSAM MONASTERY.

a wire rope thrown across the stream, and on either bank were relays of some hundred sepoys and coolies to seize the guiding ropes and haul the boats ashore. In this way one of them would be loaded up and sent across and return again within half an hour, each making over thirty trips daily. It was interesting to recall that the Capuchin monks crossed here a century and a half ago by a "pulley on a cable" in a similar way. Some skin boats obtained from the village were also used, reminding one of the coracles employed for a similar purpose by Cæsar. The four Berthon boats were also utilised, two of them being formed into a raft by a framework of planks laid across them. The other two were plied about, with the Attock boatmen to give a helping hand with the hawsers and otherwise. A lamentable accident occurred on the 25th July by a raft made of these Berthon boats capsizing in the whirlpools, by which Major Bretherton, the Chief Supply and Transport Officer of the force, was drowned, along with two Goorkhas and two Indian followers. The hide boats were also rather dangerous; during the crossing of one of these a sheep, which was one of the passengers with a party of officers, in stamping its foot made a hole in the bottom, through which a spout of water rushed in, but the Attock boatman nonchalantly placed his bare flat foot over the leak, and went on rowing to the other shore as if nothing had happened.

An attempt to swim over the mules at the ferry resulted in several of them being carried down in the eddies and drowned; but afterwards about 2000 of them were swum over at a part of the stream some miles higher up where the current was less violent.

The rocky promontory of blue granite cliffs at the ferry, jutting far out into the stream, had dammed up the river above it into a wide bay, in whose still backwaters a vast amount of the sand of the turbid water had become deposited, which on the falling of the floods had been blown by the wind over the surrounding country for several miles, deluging the fields with its tawny billows, and converting them into a desert. These destructive sand-waves are still advancing, and along the foot of the rocks they form high rolling dunes of shifting hillocks over 20 feet high, and have sent off yellow arms fingering away up the mountain sides for a mile or more.

The old iron chain suspension-bridge spans picturesquely the main stream of the river about 200 yards below the ferry, under the monastery which bears its name, "The holy hill of the Iron Bridge" (*Chak-sam ch'ö-ri*). It is of the kind met with in Western China, and, according to the local tradition, was built in the early part of the fifteenth century A.D. by the sage T'angtong-the-King,[1] now a canonised saint, whose image is worshipped not merely in the adjoining monastery, which he is also said to have built, but in the chief temples throughout the country as well. This pontifex is figured of a dark complexion, with long white hair and beard, and seated holding a thunderbolt in his left hand and an iron chain in his right. He is credited with having built eight such bridges over the Tsangpo. His monumental handiwork here of itself certainly entitles him to the respect of the inhabitants; for although it is not used at present, owing apparently to the river having burst for nearly half its waters a fresh channel to the north, and so having left the northern end of the bridge stranded amidstream, the structure itself still stands firmly after all these centuries, a magnificent piece of engineering work in the wilds of Tibet. It is about 150 yards in length and 15 feet above flood-level, and stretches between two tall masonry piers which are characteristically given the shape of the sacred *chorten*. The northern

[1] Born in 1385 A.D.

pier stands on a large mound, doubtless founded on a rock, on what is now a wooded islet in the middle of the river, and the other stands on the rocky southern shore below the monastery (see photo, p. 314). The two double chain-cables, made of 1-inch thick iron links of a foot long, are fastened at each end to great beams built into the piers and into the rocks beyond them. Between and connecting these two tightly-stretched cables were suspended, throughout their length, at intervals of about a yard, loops of yak-hair

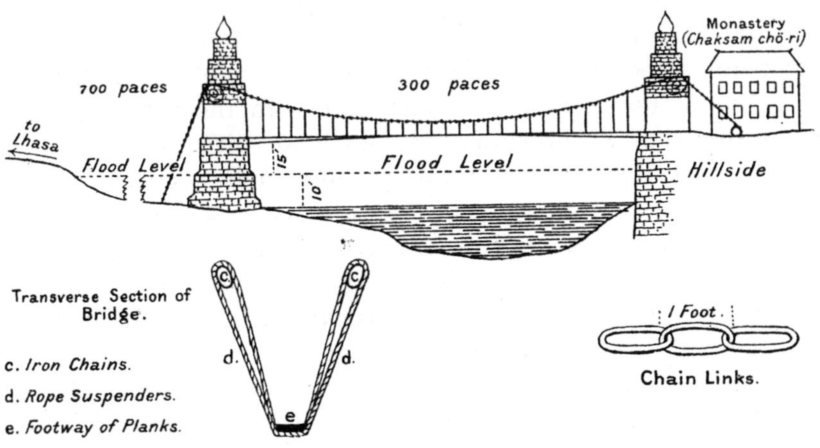

IRON SUSPENSION BRIDGE OVER TSANGPO.

rope, carrying, in their apex below, a footway of planks 1 foot broad and lashed end to end. The bridge was still in use in 1878, when visited by one of our Survey spies, whose diagram of it, here reproduced, shows the whole river as running under the viaduct, and this is still said to occur at low water in the dry season. At present, being out of use, the timber footway and its suspensory ropes have been removed. The chief defects of the structure are its want of lateral stays to prevent the alarming swinging, and its open sides with narrow footway prevent it being used for cattle—only for human passengers, and not more than one of those could pass at a time. No toll was said to be levied for transit over it, as it was kept in free repair by the villagers for the Government; whilst for the ferry the fee of about twopence per passenger, and fourpence a pony, went to the local monastery.

The monastery is prettily perched on the rocky ridge overlooking the bridge. It nominally contains eighty monks, though only two or three were present at the time of our visit. It was of the usual kind, but had a larger display of bright flowers than any we had yet seen, in pots two deep around the courts and balconies, the hollyhocks, asters, and nasturtiums being especially luxuriant. The surface of the granite cliffs at the ferry rocks, dark-blue with their large proportion of hornblende, was covered with carved and painted images of divinities and their spells. Most of these were images of the tutelary guardian of this dangerous spot, "The Wielder of the Thunderbolt," and his spell, and copies of the latter on paper were profusely placarded over the rocky cliffs near the river-bank. Fish were freely caught at the ferry during the enforced wait for transport; they were chiefly spotted carp and mud-fish with two long moustache-like feelers. On the monastery hill were many wild blue sheep with their lambs, and numerous woolly hares; a badger and otter were also seen, but as all shooting had been forbidden by the General, for political reasons, nothing was shot at this time.

The delegates again paid the Mission a visit at the ferry. They were headed by the Ta Lama, who was accompanied by the Grand Chamberlain, and the abbot of the largest monastery in Lhasa, Däpung, both of them dignified and distinguished-looking priests (see photo, p. 430). They represented that they had been sent back from Lhasa by the National Council, with the old request that the Mission should not

IRON SUSPENSION BRIDGE OVER TSANGPO RIVER.
At Chaksam monastery, 12,100 feet above sea-level.

FIRST VIEW OF LHASA.

proceed to that forbidden city; for, urged they, if we did go there, the Grand Lama might die from the shock to his religious feelings. They also gave the unsatisfactory news that this dignitary had left his capital, and had retired to a monastery several days' journey beyond. In the suite of the envoys came an English-speaking Chinaman, who, with a keen eye to business, interviewed the chief commissariat officer on the quiet, and told him that he would contract at Lhasa to supply him with as many stores of grain and common provisions as he wanted, which looked as if we were really nearing a metropolis at last.

The crossing of the river was accomplished in six days, the whole of the force having been ferried over by the 30th of July.

The left, or northern, bank was delightfully fertile and well wooded, and it was satisfactory to find that the people had not bolted from the villages, a sure sign of returning confidence. The villages were pictures of agricultural peace, and the prosperous-looking inhabitants were busy harvesting, reaping, threshing the corn, and building stacks. So populous was this part, that I counted over a dozen hamlets within 2 square miles. The fertility of the fields here was amazing; the wheat, barley, peas, and beans were breast-high, and quite equal to the best English crops, as were also the vegetables, so that many of our people, after their long privations, revelled in the peas and radishes.

We encamped at the village of Chagla, in a grove of alders and poplars, alongside an orchard of apricot and walnut trees with the fruit almost ripe. Some of the alders and willows were fine old trees 40 feet high; and the dense rank growth of wildflowers and weeds along the borders of the fields was such as to make this part of the Tsangpo oasis a quite suitable habitat for the rhinoceros and to bring the discovery of the fossil remains of that animal by Sir R. Strachey near the source of this river into harmony with present-day facts.

Leaving the ferry without any regrets, we once more turned our faces Lhasa-wards, and, proceeding 4 miles down-stream, entered on the 31st July the tributary valley which led directly up to the holy city, now under 40 miles distant, and with no more intervening passes to bar our way. The cultivated valley, with its rich crops of oats (*yogo*), peas, mustard, rape and coriander, ended abruptly about 2 miles below the ferry. Here a bold, jagged spur of granite, destitute of all verdure, ran down abruptly into the middle of the river, whose deep main stream swept the foot of the cliffs, and seemed to leave us no passage whatever.

Our track—the great trade route to Lhasa!—now narrowed into a stony trail along which we had to pass in single file, over masses of rocks fallen from above, threading in and out amongst giant rusty boulders, and climbing giddy staircases hewn across the face of the granite cliffs overhanging the rushing, swirling tide of the muddy Tsangpo, a few yards below. At these dangerous spots, where many travellers must have lost their lives, the cliffs and boulders were profusely covered with rock-cut sculptures of various divinities and their mystic spells, all brilliantly besmeared with their conventional colours. The image most frequently figured was appropriately the "Saviour-Goddess of the Sea and Rocks," Tara (in Tibetan *Dölma*), a form of the "Goddess of Mercy," the benefactress who guards the traveller from the dangers of the falling rocks, and of the seething waters below his path. The next most frequent image was that of the wizard founder of Lamaism, one of whose shrines was perched on a small rocky islet with an old gnarled weeping willow drooping over it, whilst the founder of Buddhism was scarcely represented at all. This defile was nearly 2 miles long, and about the most formidable natural barrier we had yet encountered. The strongest part of all was at its lower end, where it joined at right angles the valley leading up to Lhasa. Here the rocks rose up in almost sheer cliffs into colossal columns and aiguilles, owing to the massive crystalline granite splitting sharply along its lines of cleavage, and on the topmost pinnacle, nearly half a thousand feet above us, outlined against the sky, stood looking down upon us the old castle of Chu'sul and its lower fort on a knife-edge ridge much nearer. These two forts, although now more or less ruinous, had evidently been of enormous strength, and this marvellously strong natural position, commanding so effectually the trade-routes from India, Nepal, Bhotan and Shigatsé to Lhasa, and also the approaches to that city against a hostile force, tends to corroborate the tales told of the prominent place this stronghold took in bygone feudal wars and invasions. Luckily it was not held against us, although an immense heap of newly collected stones at its lower end showed that the Lamas had intended to hold it; so our long column laboriously emerged, winding in single file into the open valley of the Lhasa river, the Kyi or "River of Happiness," at the village of Chu'sul.

The Lhasa Valley, here at its mouth about 3 miles broad, seemed less fertile and cultivated, and with fewer trees than the central valley we had left, being blocked by a broad belt of sand from the Tsangpo, which river, now deflected from its westerly course by the Chu'sul cliffs, turns sharply down southwards, looking like a continuation of the Kyi river; and on its opposite or right bank, about 6 miles below, stood the large red-walled fort of Gongkar and its monastery, surrounded by trees and considerable cultivation.

Turning up the valley of the Kyi, we passed through

the village of Chu'sul, consisting of some forty dirty, stone-built houses arranged in a narrow lane, along which scurried several black pigs as we rode past. Beyond the village we came out on to an arm of the Kyi river watering some rich fields, and I gazed intently on its crystal waters, possessed by the thought that, only a few hours before, that very water doubtless had passed the Forbidden City, now so near to us. This river was surprisingly large in volume, seemingly almost as large as the great Tsangpo itself. It seldom flowed in one stream, but spread out into many arms, which curved through the bed of the valley in a wide network of ramifying channels, joining here and separating there to enclose sandbanks or fertile fields or swamps. As several swamps lay in the direct dry-weather track, up the middle of the valley, we skirted the shingly hillside on our left for several miles; thence undulating across the sandy foot of several spurs with a sparse growth of yellow gorse bushes and pink pedicularis, we encamped on a sandy plain by the river-bank at the almost shadeless hamlet of "Inside the Heat" (*Tsäpa-nang*), where the grilling heat was almost overpowering until we got into the shelter of our tents.

The valley here looked like a part of the dismal Egyptian desert, so barren and hot-looking were the rocky hills, and so deeply engulfed was it in sand. The drifting sand blown from the Tsangpo banks, as well as from the Kyi and its tributaries, and from the crumbling granite peaks, had not only covered the bottom of the valley deeply with its sterile waves, but had overwhelmed all the mountains to their very summits, 2000 feet and more above the river-bed, filling up their hollows and crevices with its broad glistening sweeps of yellow sand like tawny snow-wreaths, through which the tips of the rugged granite crests and pinnacles peeped darkly. Every side-ravine which we could see, up and down, as well as those in the Tsangpo Valley beyond, presented the same extraordinary weird appearance through being enveloped in the devastating sand, and gave some idea of the terrific force of the whirlwinds which blow here in the months of January and February. It also showed that we were now getting near the physical conditions of Central Asia and Baluchistan with their moving deserts of sand. The yellow drifts and hillocks have their surface rippled by wavy markings like driven snow, and lie chiefly at right angles to the prevailing winds up the valley, their long slope to windward, and a steeper slope to lee. It was difficult to believe that these barren wind-swept wastes, more severe and forbidding than any we had yet seen, were the gateway to the fertile plains and benign skies of the Lhasa Vale.

All this, however, was only another of Nature's devices to mislead the traveller seeking to penetrate her paradise in this remote tramontane land, in her *ultima Thule*. For, a few miles above this desert we entered next day (Bank Holiday, the 1st of August) a series of rocky defiles, between which, as we proceeded, the sand-drifts grew less and less, and the valley opened out into wide, more or less cultivated, meadows, 4 to 5 miles broad, with many villages and groves of trees on both banks. In the defiles, the crystal waters of the Kyi, united for a time into one stream, swept swiftly along under the narrow pathway built as a ledge over bluffs, or chiselled with infinite labour across the hard rock of beetling granite cliffs, and curving past the edge of giant boulders, along which we had to pick our way circumspectly in single file as in the Chu'sul defile.

At the entrance to one of the strongest of these formidable clefts, where the granite cliffs towered almost vertically above us, we came on a fresh barrier, a newly-built, strong, loopholed wall barring the road, which had to be dismantled. The granite rock here was so remarkably coarse in its grain that it looked almost like a conglomerate of pebbles, and it was largely mixed with great stretches of stratified black shale and limestone, through which it had obviously burst in a molten state, as large angular pieces of this shale and limestone were embedded within the crystalline structure of the intrusive granite. We halted at the village of Nam, a fief[1] of the great Sera monastery of Lhasa, and found it deserted by everybody except two cripples who could not run away, and who now flourished a white flag, having evidently been informed of its magical sheltering powers by the Ta Lama or others.

In the intervening meadows were numerous monasteries with their priests fattening on the people, also a few shrines. Two of these latter were especially interesting, one an imposing stone-built and unwhitened structure with four striking *chortens*, across the river on the left bank, and ascribed to the King Ralpachan, one of the most popular of the Tibetan sovereigns, who lived in the latter half of the ninth century A.D. The other was the tomb of the Indian monk Atisha,[2] who came to Tibet in 1038 A.D., and finding that Lamaism was much tainted by admixture with devil-worship, founded a reformed order upon a purer Buddhist model, which afterwards became the Yellow-cap sect, and now as the State Church holds the entire secular government of the country. I was surprised, therefore, to find the tomb of this saintly reformer in semi-ruinous condition, neglected by the ungrateful and now wealthy sect, who profess indebtedness to him for their own superior purity; but who in their turn have again degenerated by incorporating once again so much of the degrading devil-worship which he condemned and

[1] A religious endowment-fief is *chö-zhi*, whilst a lay one is *zhi-ga*.

[2] His proper name was Dipankara Srijnana.

eliminated. Atisha died at this place, Ne-t'ang,[1] in 1052 A.D., on his way from Lhasa to other monasteries down the Tsangpo. The tomb[2] enshrining his relics is within a ruinous, barn-like room, painted yellow outside, standing in a clump of old willow-trees, and is in the form of a large *chorten* about 15 feet high, and the same in diameter at its base. Its surface is plastered over, and is covered by poorly executed frescoes of Buddhas and the conventional image of the saint himself seated cross-legged, Buddha-wise. On the basement plinth are painted the white elephant, the white umbrella, and the other seven symbols of an emperor of Ancient India which are usually ascribed to Sakya Muni, and which the modern Buddhist kings and chiefs of Siam and Burma still appropriate in their titles as Lord of the White Elephant, etc. It is in the charge of six illiterate monks, who reside in a small convent at the foot of the bare stony hillside about 200 yards off. I spent half an hour here, enquiring especially for Indian manuscripts, and could find no trace of any, not even a single leaf, beyond the local tradition that a few sheets were buried with the saint's body. The only one amongst the attendant monks who could read and write did not know the Indian written characters of Atisha's time, and I believe he was sincere in his protestations that none of them had ever heard of Indian manuscripts having been seen here in recent times.

The rock-sculptures hereabouts bore abundant evidence that Atisha and Indian monks of his class had been in this locality. For the carvings covering the rounded shoulders and cliffs along the roadside were more in the old Indian style, whilst the contour and general appearance of these dark be-lichened, rounded granite hills reminded one forcibly of similar hills in the Buddhist Holy Land around Buddha Gaya, whence

[1] Or "The Smooth Meadow" (Mnye-t'ang).

[2] This building is called Sgro-ma temple.

Atisha came. The subjects carved, when they were not the simple form of Sakya Muni himself, were often those ancient forms of Buddhist divinities that are to be seen engraved on the rocks in Mid-India. These older forms, however, evidently did not find much favour here with the latter-day Lamas, and have not received votive smears of brilliant red and yellow and blue paint at the hands of the priests, but remain in unbedaubed obscurity alongside the gaudily coloured popular favourites, chief amongst which was the four-handed form of the Grand Lama and his mystic spell. This spell, which opens heaven and closes hell, is repeated endlessly over the rocks; and where the spell is repeated many times in succession below each other, it bands the rock with vertical stripes of brilliant colours, as each of its syllables is given a different hue. The tints are the distinctive mythological colours of the six regions of Buddhist rebirth, namely—

Om	*ma*	*ni*	*pad*	*me*	*Hūng*
white,	green,	yellow,	blue,	red,	black, or dark blue.

Another of the most common inscriptions here was "The Lama is omniscient," obviously to instil belief in the divinity of the priests. If Atisha could now revisit these scenes of his former labours he would be shocked at the introduction of so much false indigenous paganism into his teaching, and would be altogether unable to recognise many of these later Tibetan innovations which are as degenerate as those which he took such pains to overthrow by his great reformation. Some of us also visited a thriving monastery, 2 miles up a side valley, called "The Academy of Ra-töd." This was one of the ancient monasteries which the despotic first Dalai Lama forcibly converted into a Yellow-cap one. His image here is given the high place of honour immediately next to Buddha, behind which in a dark corner is the effigy of its founder, the Lama Longdol, who is believed to be permanently reincarnated as the ruler of the fabulous Utopian continent Sambhala, which the Lamas place in the neighbourhood of Afghanistan.

As showing the ignorance of Lamas, even so near to Lhasa, I should mention that on entering another monastery near here, on the roadside higher up the main valley,[1] I noticed that they had figured the lucky fly-footed cross, the *swastika*, in the reverse way, that is, with the feet going not in the diurnal course of the sun or the hands of a clock, but in the opposite direction, which the merest tyro should know is not only wrong, but is the form of this symbol used by the non-Buddhists, the indigenous Black-caps, the Bon, and the use of which is regarded by the Lamas as wicked. When I pointed this out to the chief Lama of the convent of thirty monks he did not realise the mistake he had made.

We caught our first glimpse of the Lhasa suburbs on zig-zagging over a stairway hewn across the shoulder of a sheer bluff, which rose over 100 feet above the clear green waters of the Kyi river, and dammed the latter above it into a great shallow lake filling the whole valley here about 2 miles broad. From this bluff we sighted the glittering golden roof of the temple of the Oracle Royal, about 4 miles below Lhasa, showing some 12 miles off over a low rocky spur running out from the hills on our left. When we pierced through the neck of this spur we found a colossal figure of the seated Buddha carved on the rock in low relief, facing Lhasa; but no view of the latter nor of any of its surrounding buildings, nor even the dominating hill of the Dalai Lama's palace, could be seen from hereabouts. Across the valley an incense-kiln sent forth a dense column of

[1] This institution curiously belonged to the Red-cap Sakya sect, although they also gave the tyrant Dalai Lama Lobzang (p. 30) the place of honour next to Buddha on their chief altar.

smoke up the mountain side as a sacrifice to the spirits of the locality, as this promontory acts as a barrier to the river here and is said to cause disastrous floods, so that every passer-by deposits in front of the great idol a pebble as a propitiatory offering: these contributions now form a little hillock in front of the image.

Our first view of any part of Lhasa was not obtained until about 4 miles above this colossal Buddha, at a long cairn or *mandong*, faced with slabs carved with the "*Om mani*" legend. At this place suddenly burst into view up the valley, now a broad sea of fields and groves, the red palace of the Grand Lama, like a small glittering speck crowning the conical-looking hill of Potala, 10 miles away, and, moving on a few paces further, the still sharper "Iron Hill" of the Medical College disclosed itself. We could see nothing whatever of the town of Lhasa, which was hidden behind these two hills; but most of us strained our eyes in trying to see through our glasses some glimpse of the city, and all felt a thrill of excitement in being actually within sight of our goal.

Another sudden transformation now pleasingly changed the face of the valley into fertile cultivation, which stretched several miles broad and with numerous groves on towards Lhasa on our right, and up the Ti Valley on our left, as we went forward through rich fields of oats, wheat, peas, and potatoes, and past water mills where flour was being ground, to encamp at the junction of these two valleys, by the side of the bridge over the Ti river and near the village of Tilung (or Toilung). The Ti river was swift flowing and of surprisingly large volume, seemingly as large as the Kyi, although the latter appeared in its turn to be unreduced in size. Its bridge was an exceptionally fine one about 100 yards long, with masonry piers and substantial stone embankments and protecting outworks between the five waterways through which sped the somewhat turbid green flood. From our camp Potala was in sight 7 miles off, and in the stream large "trout" leaped, and were so abundant that many weighing from one to three pounds were caught in a short time with a ground bait of barley dough. Nearly all of them were infested by parasites which sowed their bodies with sooty black spots.

In the afternoon the delegates reappeared, this time with a larger following than before of abbots and other Lamas and lay officials in a great variety of brilliantly coloured costumes and peculiarly shaped hats. The headgear was amusing in its fantastic variety. There were fluffy yellow Tam o'Shanters, large deep-fringed circular bonnets, like pink silk lamp-shades, flat crowns of claret-coloured velvet with long bushy crimson tassels, and the Chinese brimmed hat of the Lama Councillors with yellow satin peaked crown. Those worn by the cup-bearers to the abbots were the most remarkable, being in the form of a large water-jug or ewer, as indicating the office of their wearers. The procession was headed as before by the Ta Lama, who brought with him again the Abbot of Däpung, and the Chamberlain of the Grand Lama, both wearing gold-lacquered flat hats with a button-like knob on the top and tied under the chin. They were much more conciliatory in demeanour than they had been before, and shook hands most affably all round, and brought ostentatiously forward a pompous train of servants carrying a large number of poor but bulky presents of bundles of country worsted cloth. They again asked that we should not enter Lhasa, and stated that at a mass meeting of the citizens some 10,000 strong held that day a large band of desperadoes had offered to fight to the death to prevent the British defiling the holy city with their presence. Nevertheless, added the delegates, the Government, although sympathising with the populace in the matter, refused the offer in order to avoid further bloodshed, and had sent round criers to announce by beat of drum that no armed resistance or violence must be offered to the English, otherwise these invaders would make both the place and people "as the dust beneath their feet." This showed that the Tibetans had at length learned to respect the prowess of our troops. The delegates now contented themselves with stipulating that none of the soldiers be allowed to enter the town, which was agreed to as a temporary measure on condition that the Lamas allowed the city traders to open a bazaar outside the British camp for the supply of goods to the men.

Some Chinese officials also arrived with a letter from the Amban to say that he would come out to meet the Mission in camp on the following day on its arrival outside the gate of Lhasa. This seemed a concession on his part, for as he was a plenipotentiary minister with the rank of a viceroy, he might, as the Chinese are such sticklers for etiquette, have demanded that he should be called on first, or it may have been intended to postpone even by one day our entry into the city itself; in any case, it was satisfactory to find that the Amban seemed at last to be bestirring himself to obtain an interview with the Mission.

The last stage of our long and toilsome journey was reached on the 3rd August 1904, when we arrived at our final destination, the mysterious city which had preserved its isolation for so many centuries, and which was now for the first time in its history entered by a European force. Fired with a kindling enthusiasm, our feelings of eager anticipation as we started off that morning, when every step we took brought us nearer to our goal, and every turn of the road might reveal the sacred city, can be imagined and must have been akin to the emotions felt by the Crusaders of old on arriving within sight of Jerusalem, after their long march through Europe; or to those of the unsentimental

OLD CASTLE AT DONGKAR ON THE LHASA RIVER.

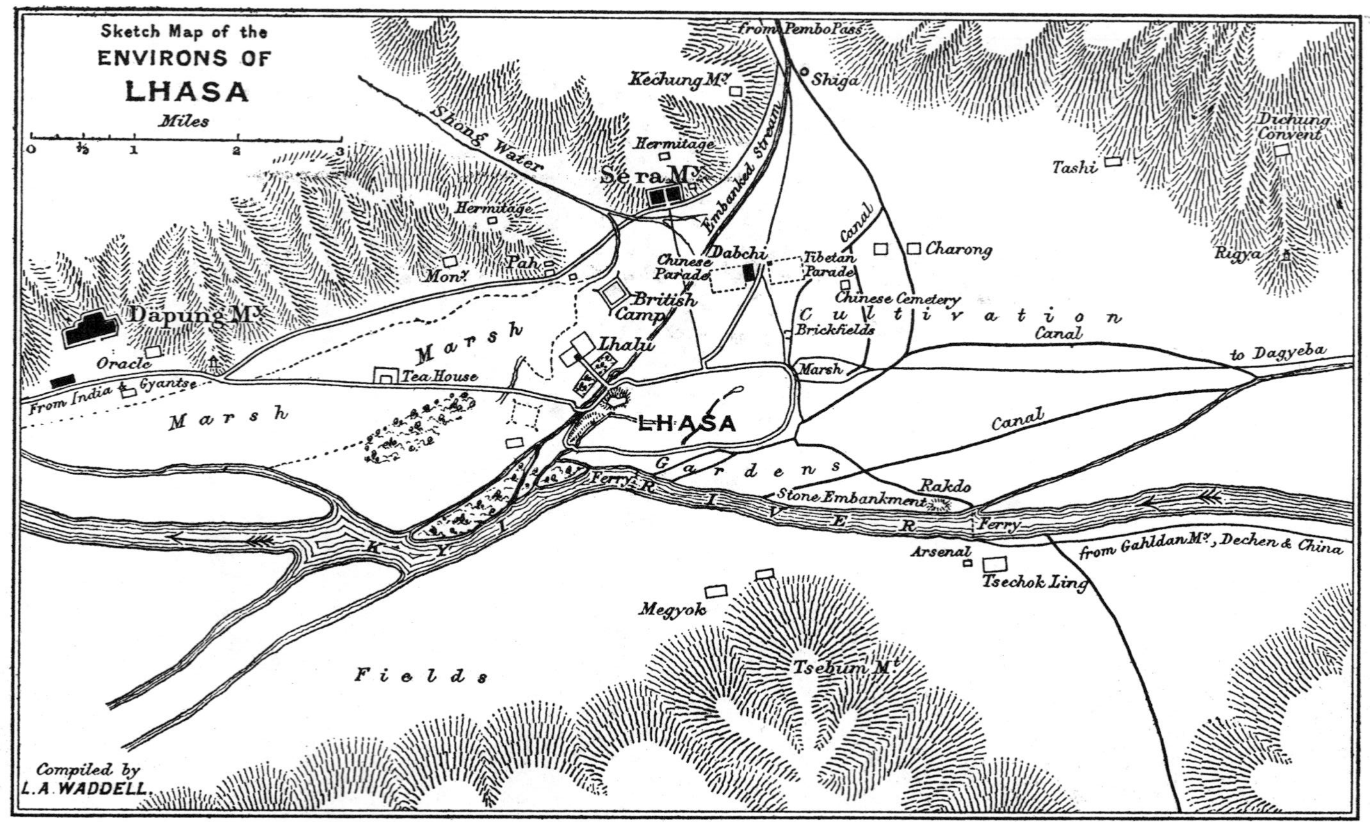
Sketch Map of the
ENVIRONS OF
LHASA
Miles
0 ½ 1 2 3
from Pembo Pass
Kechung Mʸ
Shiga
Shong Water
Hermitage
Sera Mʸ
Embanked Stream
Hermitage
Tashi
Dichung Convent
Rigya
Canal
Charong
Dabchi
Chinese Parade
Tibetan Parade
Chinese Cemetery
Mony
Pah
British Camp
Dapung Mʸ
Cultivation
Brickfields
Canal
Marsh
Lhalu
Oracle
Marsh
Tea House
to Dagyeba
From India & Gyantse
Marsh
LHASA
Canal
Gardens
Ferry
Rakdo
Stone Embankment
KYI RIVER
Ferry
Arsenal
from Gahldan Mʸ, Dechen & China
Tsechok Ling
Megyok
Tsebum Mᵗ
Fields
Compiled by
L. A. WADDELL

Gibbon, when he first trod "with lofty steps the ruins of the Eternal City," and listened with strange uplifting of spirit to the singing of the "barefooted friars in the temple of Jupiter." The scenery also was the most romantic we had yet seen, the sides of the valley rising boldly into rugged pinnacles of fantastic shapes, such as Doré fancifully pictured for his errant-knights, with castellated monasteries crowning the heights and clinging to the cliffs. The weather, too, which had continued showery for the greater part of every day, cleared up and became bright and sunny. So fertile and picturesque was the valley—"This country is certainly worth fighting for," was the common remark of the soldiers as we ascended this beautiful valley. Many trees, chiefly walnut, apricot, willow, elm, birch, and alder, diversified the landscape.

The old fort with its ruined battlements on the sharp limestone peaks above the village of "The White Alder Tree" (*Shing dongkar*) was especially striking, and here on the rocks a Lama pointed out to me the footprints of the mythological guardians of this place: the hoof-prints of a magic horse, a buffalo, a monkey and a bear; but as I listened confidingly to his tale the marks clearly showed themselves to be the holes in the rock from which nodules of limestone had weathered out. Further on, a loop of the river swirled by the hillside, and we passed the village of Cheri containing a large slaughter-house, where dozens of sheep and yak-oxen are slaughtered daily for the consumption chiefly of the 9000 monks of Däpung and neighbourhood, who, whilst professing to be Buddhists, nevertheless participate in this way in the taking of life, and so contravene the first of all Buddhist commands. Not far off was a village of butchers and beggars by the roadside, in which the walls of the huts were built of the horns and skulls of the slaughtered sheep and oxen,

The great monastery of Däpung, the largest in the world, with several gilded roofs, stood up proudly above this, under the foot of the hills. Its huge piles of clustered buildings in their mountain setting looked at this distance like a grand hotel in the Riviera. Crowds of its Lamas were coming and going to Lhasa, some riding on ponies and all of them looking askance at us and bewildered at our intrusion in such force. Below the great monastery and nearer to the road in a fine grove of large trees peeped the golden pagoda roofs of the residence of the State Oracle, the Magician Royal, and his hundred monks, the tip of which building was the first vestige of these suburbs we had seen from far down the valley. From here the road to Lhasa led by an enbankment across a morass of bulrushes whose shallows glowed with the marigold blossoms of a pedicularis; also pink water-lilies like lotuses, marshmallows, marestails, watercress, forget-me-nots, while a host of ordinary European wild flowers, including harebell and shepherd's purse, covered the roadsides, and in the water amongst shoals of small fish of the size of minnows I noticed a newt, as well as frogs, and in the deeper pools swarms of ducks.

During a halt in the fields beyond the marsh until a suitable site for the camp could be found, the Nepalese Consul of Lhasa (see photo, p. 358) rode up with a following, and saluting the General, warned him to be careful of the Lamas, who had still several thousand armed men in the immediate neighbourhood. A sufficiently dry site having been found, the force moved up and pitched camp on a fine open turfy heath ("The Wild Asses' Meadow") outside the city gate (see plan, p. 330), by the side of the summer palace of the Dalai Lama, "The Jewel Continent," and in full view of the Grand Lama's castle on Potala, which, with the Medical College hill by its side, towered up grandly about a mile away.

LHASA VALLEY AT DONGKAR.

DÄPUNG MONASTERY.

The monastery is at the foot of the hill, on the right is the grove of the State Oracle (Nächung), and in the foreground are Lamas coming in under a flag of truce.

It was a moment of mute but heartfelt exultation to every member of the expedition, most of all perhaps to General Macdonald, who by flawless arrangements had led his little band of 650 British and 4000 Indian troops and followers across the backbone of the world, and foot by foot pushing his way, opposed at every point by the hostile climate and the Lamas, had encamped them beneath the windows of the Dalai Lama's palace, at the gate of the long-closed capital.

To catch a glimpse of the sacred city, several of us hurried on, riding up to the gateway in the cleft through a ridge that screened the town from sight. On climbing the ridge alongside the gate, which was crowded with several hundred inquisitive monks and townspeople thronging out to see the white-faced foreigners, the vast panorama of the holy city in its beautiful mountain setting burst upon our view, and we gazed with awe upon the temples and palaces of the long-sealed Forbidden City, the shrines of the mystery which had so long haunted our dreams, and which lay revealed before our eyes at last.

CHAPTER XVI.

LHASA, "THE SEAT OF THE GODS."

"*All roads lead to Lhasa.*"—TIBETAN PROVERB.

HERE at last was the object of our dreams!—the long-sought, mysterious Hermit City, the Rome of Central Asia, with the residence of its famous priest-god—and it did not disappoint us! The natural beauty of its site, in a temperate climate and fertile mountain-girt plain, with the roofs of its palatial monasteries, temples, and mansions peeping above groves of great trees, to some extent explains why the Lamas were so jealous of intruders, and fits Lhasa, when once its natural and artificial difficulties of approach have been removed, to be one of the most delightful residential places in the world.

The most superb feature of all, undoubtedly, was the majestic castle of Buddha's vice-regent on earth, which far exceeded the highest expectations we had formed of it. From first to last, from far and near, this imposing pile on Potala hill dominates the landscape and catches and holds the eye. Wherever else we might direct our gaze for a time, we invariably found our eyes involuntarily returning to this towering mass and resting on its fascinating outlines (see photo, p. 1). As we neared this palace of the Buddhist Pope, encircled by hills rising above the marshes[1] of the

[1] *Dam-ts'o* or "Mud-lake."

BRITISH MISSION ENTERING THE GATE OF LHASA.

INSIDE THE GATE, PASSING UNDER POTALA PALACE.

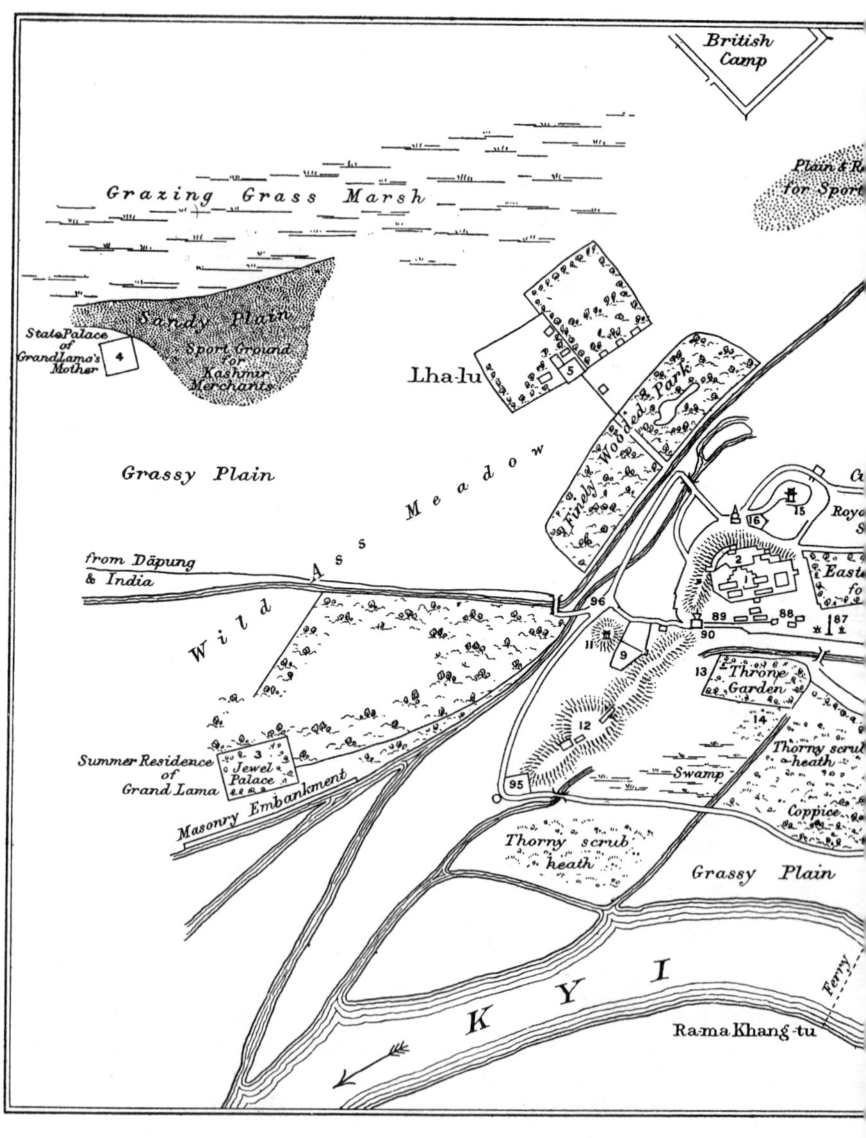
British Camp
Grazing Grass Marsh
Sandy Plain
Sport Ground for Kashmir Merchants
State Palace of Grand Lama's Mother
4
Lha-lu
5
Finely Wooded Park
Grassy Plain
Wild Ass Meadow
from Däpung & India
96
11
9
2
1
16
15
89
90
88
87
13
Throne Garden
14
12
Summer Residence of Grand Lama
3
Jewel Palace
Masonry Embankment
95
Swamp
Thorny scrub heath
Coppice
Grassy Plain
K Y I
Ferry
Ra-ma Khang-tu

Villas & Fields
to Parade Ground of Tibetan Troops
Brickfield
to Se-ra Monastery
Shong Chu
to Chinese Parade Ground
from Brag-yal-ba & Pon-po
Phen-tsa marsh
Circular Road
Min-tol Bridge
Ra-mo-che Jo-wo temple
School
Ford
Pha-la marsh
Cho-mo-Ling Palace
Fields
Stone Bridge
mud
Circular Road
Re-ting
Ten-gye Ling Palace
Slaughter House
Horse & Grass Market
Flower Garden
ex Minister's House
Garden
Mud Wall
Town Latrine
Butchers
Mosque (Kashmiri)
from Gah-den & Kong-bu
Yutok Bridge
Chinese Theatre
Chinese Vegetable Garden
Pig Styes
Barracks of Chinese Troops
Butchers Qrs
Pha-la Pleasure Garden
Irrigation Canal
Cemetery infested by dogs
Circular Road
Circular Road
Ke-salig Bridge
Garden of Dalai's Brother
Chak-dso Pleasure Garden
Lamas' Gardens
Lay Officers' Gardens
V E R
Plan of
LHASA
by
L.A.WADDELL, Lt COLONEL, I.M.S.
Scale of Miles
0 1/8 1/4 1/2 1

REFERENCES TO

LIEUT.-COLONEL L. A. WADDELL'S

PLAN OF LHASA.

1. The Great Cathedral, the true "*Lhasa*" or "Place of the Gods."
2. Grand Lama's Palace on Potala Hill.
3. Do. Summer Palace (*Norbu Ling*).
4. Do. Mother's Palace, for Receptions.
5. Do. Parents' Palace, or Paradise (*Lha-lu*).
6. Ex-Prime Minister Yutok's House.
7. Residence of the deposed King-Regent (*gyal-po*).
8. Do. Ex-Regent of *Tso-mo-ling*.
9. Do. Do. of *Kun-de-ling*.
10. Chinese Residency of the Ambans.
11. Ba-mo (*Bong-ba*) Hill, surmounted by Chinese temple to Kesar.
12. Chag-ga or Chag-pa Hill, surmounted by Temple of Medicine.
13. Throne Garden, with a stone or brick seat for Grand Lama.
14. A heath, called the "Centre Snake-waiting," alleged to have been visited by Buddha Sakya Muni.
15. A Snake-Dragon Temple, surrounded by a moat, and connected by a lock with marsh to the east.
16. Elephant stable of Dalai Lama.
17. Camping Ground for troops going to the Race-course and Sports in first month of year.
18. Ra-mo-che Temple, alleged to be erected by the Chinese Princess Konjo or Tara (*Dol-tang*) in seventh century A.D.
19. Upper School of Mysticism.
20. Temple of the Buddha of Boundless Life.
21. *Kang-da Khang Sar*, Palace of former lay "Kings."
22. Residence of the late deposed Regent Re-ting, a Lama of Se-ra, who died in banishment to China, about 1860. Now used as an Academy.
23. Assembly Hall of Turki merchants.
24. "Nam-de-le" cross-roads.
25. Residence of Dowager Mother of (previous) Grand Lama.
26. Chang lo-chen.
27. Chinese Restaurant.
28. Tibetan Restaurant.
29. Jail.
30. Chinese torture-chamber.
31. Pottery Market.
32. Chinese *Gya-bum-kang chorten*, and by its side a temple erected 1891.
33. Lower School of Mysticism and Printing-house.
34. Muru Monastery.
35. Residence of the General (*Dah-pon*) who visited Darjeeling in 1892 (Nga- pö-sa).
36. Guard-house
37. Tannery.
38. *Phun-kang chorten*.
39. Oracle of Darboling.
40. Saddlery and Harness Bazaar from Eastern Tibet.
41. Salutation Point (as here the Pilgrims by the Circular Road catch a glimpse of the Grand Lama's Palace of Pota-la, which they salute).
42. Chinese "Valley" (*Gya-mo-rong*).
43. Grass Market.
44. Nuns' Restaurant.
45. Chinese Drug Shop.
46. Eating House.
47. Inner Chinese Meat Market with double row of stalls entered through Chinese arch.
48. Shops of Newars from Nepal.
49. Rice Market and large Prayer Flag.
50. Mohamedan Chinese Eating House.
51. Bhotanese and Chumbi Shops.
52. Summary Magistrates' Court for Disputes.
53. *Su-khang*.
54. *Sur-gyar-khang*.
55. Large Prayer Flag, "the Eastern Mountain."
56. Chinese Eating House.
57. Bankye-Shag (*Phala*) Palace.
58. Karmashar Oracle.
59. Horse Market.
60. Chinese Military Paymaster.
61. Slaughter House.
62. Gye-ton Jong-pön.
63. House of Kashmiri Magistrate for Mahomedan Disputes.
64. *Rab-sal*.
65. *Kun-sang-tse*.
66. Shata Palace.
67. The Lama-Defender of Religion.
68. Shata-ling.
69. Nepalese Consul's Summer House.
70. *Sam-dub* Palace.
71. Old Palace.
72. *Kah-shag*.
73. *Gah-ru shar*.
74. Square of *Song-cho ra* where Thanksgiving is held in first month and where Whipping is inflicted for thieving, etc.
75. Meat and Leather Market.
76. Rag-ga-Shag.
77. Edict Pillar.
78. White Tara's Shrine.
79. Dancing Hall.
80. Lodging House for Tashilhumpo people.
81. Mi-sad Bridge and Chinese Arch.
82. Fairy spring of Chinese princess.
83. Triad Chaitya, *chorten*.
84. Turquoise-tiled bridge (*Yutok sampa*).
85. Summer Garden for Ministers and Civil Officers.
86. Do. for Lamas.
87. Edict pillar.
88. Bazaar and Foundry.
89. Grand Lama's Stable.
90. Gateway of *Pargo-kaling*.
91. Temple of the three Lords.
92. Council Chamber.
93. Nepalese Consulate.
94. Four-doored *chorten*.
95. Gallery of Rock Paintings on Medical College Hill.
96. Beggar's Horn Huts.

"River of Joy," a circular bastion gave it a remarkable resemblance to the Vatican of Rome, the city of the seven hills (see photo, p. 388).

The first glimpse of the sacred metropolis is dramatic in its suddenness. As if to screen the holy capital from view until the last moment, Nature has interposed a long curtain of rock which stretches across between the two bold guardian hills of Potala and the Iron Mountain, entirely shutting out all view of the town from the side of our approach on the south-west. This rocky curtain is pierced in its middle by the western gate of the city, called "The Middle Door - Barrier" (*Pargo-Ka'ling*),[1] whose top is given the form of the religious *Chorten* monument, and it is not until this gateway is passed, or until the ridge above it is scaled, that any view whatever of the town is obtained.

The vista which then flashes up before the eyes is a vast and entrancing panorama. On the left is the front view of the Dalai Lama's palace, which faces the east, and is now seen to be a mass of lofty buildings covering the hillside—here about 300 feet high—from top to bottom with its terraces of many-storeyed and many-windowed houses and buttressed masonry battlements and retaining walls, many of them 60 feet high, and forming a gigantic building of stately architectural proportions on the most picturesque of craggy sites. The central cluster of buildings, crowning the summit and resplendent with its five golden pavilions on its roof, was of a dull crimson, that gives it the name of the "Red Palace," whilst those on the other flank were of dazzling white; and the great stairway on each side, leading down to the chief entrance and gardens below, zig-zagging outwards to enclose a diamond-shaped design, recalled a similar one at the summer palace of Peking. A mysterious effect was given to the central

[1] Spelt Bar-*s*go-*b*kag-*g*ling. The prefaced consonants in italics are as usual, silent.

portion of the building by long curtains of dark purple yak-hair cloth which draped the verandahs, to protect the frescoes from the rain and sun, but which seemed to muffle the rooms in secrecy.

On our extreme right, and connected with the Potala hill by the knife-edged ridge, towered the still higher Iron Hill, topped by its medical college, and foreshortened from here into a tall pinnacle. Between these two hills stretches out in front the well-wooded, fertile plain of the winding Kyi river, like a fine European landscape, 4 or 5 miles broad, and 7 or 8 up the valley to where a side spur from the mountains blocks the view. In the foreground are numerous orchards, gardens, and parks up to the river bank and between its many channels, and about a mile off, the town shows up as a thin white line amongst the trees, in the centre of which shines out the glittering roof of the great "cathedral," with the smaller burnished roof of Ramoché temple; to the left and further off, at the foot of the hills, Sera, the greatest monastery in Tibet after Däpung, and, as a background, beyond the green plain, studded over with the white villas of the nobles and little farmsteads, rise on all four sides, lofty mountains 3000 to 6000 feet above the plain, penetrated by the white tracks threading straight ahead to China, and to the Tengri Lake and Mongolia, passing by Sera on our left.

The town was entered for the first time on the 4th August, the day after our arrival, when the British Mission, escorted by a considerable force of our troops, marched in state through the streets of Lhasa, on the way to the Chinese Residency, to return the ceremonial visit paid by the Amban the previous evening. On this historical occasion, when foreign civilized troops first paraded the streets of the Forbidden City, the Mission and its escort formed a picturesque procession headed by a contingent of the Amban's bodyguard and

PANORAMA OF LHASA (from the west).

Potala castle is on the left, the circular road and river on the right, and the city in the middle distance.

CHIEF GATE OF LHASA—(*Pargo Ka'ling*).

pikemen, in quaint costumes and arms (see photo, p. 359).

The details of this parade, as duly chronicled at the time, were as follows :—

"The uniforms of the Chinese retainers of the Amban, whom he sent to escort the Mission, set off the khaki of the escort to great effect. We are all immensely struck with the handsome uniforms and smart appearance of the Amban's entourage. His own bodyguard were dressed in short loose coats of French grey colour, embroidered in black, with various emblems in black both in front and behind. Then came the pike-men, dressed in similar coats of bright red, similarly embroidered in black, with black pugarees. They carried all sorts of weapons, pikes, scythes, and three-pronged spears, on all of which hung red banners with devices embroidered in black. Then there were ordinary soldiers in blue, embroidered with red, and with Chinese symbols in white, both in the front and in the back of the coat. These were followed by the Commissioner's escort of No. 2 Company Mounted Infantry, under Captain Peterson. Behind the Union Jack rode Colonel Younghusband and Mr White in Political Officer's uniform, together with Messrs O'Connor and Wilton in uniform. Then came Colonel Waddell, and the rest of the Mission, and the Press correspondents, consisting of Captains Ryder, Cowie, and Walton, and Messrs Hayden, Magniac, Landon, Candler, Newman, and Bayley. Two companies of the Royal Fusiliers followed, headed by Colonel Cooper, and with the following officers; Captains Legge and Johnston, Lieutenants Gardner, Chichester, Daniel, and Currie. Half a company of mounted infantry, two guns, a detachment of sappers, and four companies of infantry were held ready to support this escort if necessary."

At 10 A.M. the cavalcade and escort left camp on the heath and headed for the gateway through the ridge. Outside the gate the sacred Circular Road — which is piously threaded all day long by strings of pilgrims twirling their prayer-wheels—was crossed at the sandhills by the corner of the alder coppice of the monastery of Kündeling, one of the four "royal" convents of Lhasa from which the Regents used to be chosen during the minorities of the Dalai Lamas (see plan, p. 330) Here also on a hillock was a Chinese temple to the deified Mongolian Emperor of Siberia, Kesar, and the ancient white cocks, offered to it as native gifts, to the number of nearly a hundred, crowded the roadside in front of it; while on the sandhills outside the holy road, so that their abode would not defile the city, was a loathsome encampment of beggars and outcasts, huddled in dirty huts built of the horns of yaks and sheep and other offal, and roofed over with ragged blankets.

The gateway itself was besieged by swarms of these sturdy beggars who grovelled by the puddles of the flooded roadsides. Passing through the gateway we were met by the magnificent front view of Potala and its palace, towering up majestically only 100 yards or so from our roadway past the houses of the subordinate officials, retainers and store-rooms and shops at its base; several of the shops here, it was noticeable, were butchers' stalls kept by women, who were cutting up the carcasses of yaks and exposing the flesh on sale for consumption by Lamas and others, right under the windows of Buddha's Vice-Regent. Looking up at the hundreds of windows of that massive palace, seemingly deserted, one wondered whether the report were true that its saintly master had really fled on the day that we crossed the Tsangpo, or was he still in hiding here with an army of his warriors behind these strong walls, lying in wait for a favourable opportunity to pounce on us unawares. We also wondered when, if ever, any of us might be privileged to explore the mazes of its hidden interior.

Beyond this, at the tall edict pillar, a monolith in dark granite, about 18 feet high (see plan, p. 330) and photo, p. 336), and flanked by two Chinese temples, the path branched off into four, passing amongst gardens, groves, and a large park. Our road to the Chinese Residency was the inner one, which led between the woods of two pleasure-gardens, where the track for nearly a quarter of a mile was a slushy quagmire, through which our infantry marched unflinchingly, or skirted the deeper parts in single file. This brought us to the house of one of the old nobility, that delegate Councillor or Minister of State whom we met at Nagartsé, and who takes his popular title from the Yutok or "Turquoise Crowned" bridge (see photo, p. 341), that here bestrides an old channel of the Kyi river, which now, even in flood season, is silted up into dry fields. This bridge is walled up and roofed over like a corridor, and gets its name from the coloured tiles of its Chinese pavilion roof, in imitation of the bluey-green turquoise-hued tiles of the old imperial palaces in the Celestial Empire. This seems to be the only coloured tiled roof in Lhasa, except a small one on the Dragon temple, and its dingy green hue would never suggest "turquoise" were it not for its name.

The town of Lhasa was entered about 200 yards further on, when, alongside heaps of putrid refuse, we passed under a small Chinese archway into the large square between the Chinese quarter and the great "cathedral." Crowds of people, chiefly Chinese and their Tibetan wives, stood on every doorstep and thronged out into the streets, staring stolidly at our party, while women peered in timid curiosity from every window of the two- and three-storeyed houses. As we turned to the right toward the Amban's quarters, past a Chinese theatre and restaurants, the houses were nearly all one-storeyed, as in the Flowery Land, with neat turf-walls in front enclosing little flower-gardens with pots of blooming asters, marigolds, stocks and holly-hocks, and nasturtiums within and on the window-sills; but the streets were in a revoltingly filthy condition, dirtier even than Peking, and littered over with all sorts of refuse and miry sewage in which scores of unwholesome pigs wallowed repulsively. The Amban's residence (see plan, p. 330) was of the usual pattern of *Yamen*, or Chinese Government office. Before the doorway, with its painted dragons and its blue-robed, pig-tailed warders, stood an incense-burner, flanked by tall poles for banners, and two great masts bearing a dovecot-like framework for lanterns; and inside were the usual tablets and succession of paved courtyards, with their reception-rooms, separated from each other by a gateway bordered by sign-boards bearing Chinese inscriptions and seals.

The Amban[1] received the Mission with elaborate ceremony. A salute from bombs heralded our approach, and shrill pipes struck up a weird blast as our party entered the gateway and rode over the paved causeway between the double row of Chinese soldiers, in bright yellow and blue, edged by scarlet, who stood shoulder to shoulder armed with breechloading rifles which they held at the "present." His Excellency, who is a middle-aged man of pleasing manners (see photo, p. 337), advanced into the third court to receive Colonel Younghusband, and here everyone dismounted and shook hands with this Celestial dignitary, those who had not seen him at his visit to camp the previous day being now introduced and receiving his cordial greeting.

He led the way into an inner court, evidently the inmost of all, in the small reception-hall of which there was a semicircle of red-cushioned chairs with a tiny table in the middle of the curve, in front of a plain red cotton curtain. Here he invited Colonel Younghusband and his Staff to be seated on the left-hand chairs, with the Colonel next to the table,

[1] This is a Manchu word meaning "Minister of State."—Rockhill in *Jour. Roy. As. Soc.*, xxii. p. 7.

ROYAL LONDON FUSILIERS MARCHING THROUGH LHASA.

EDICT PILLAR AND CHINESE TEMPLES BELOW POTALA.

ENTRANCE TO CHINESE EMBASSY, LHASA.

THE CHINESE AMBAN AND GENERAL MACDONALD.
(The Amban is standing next to the General, and the third beyond him is the French-speaking "Second Amban.")

and he himself sat down on the other side of the table, with his tail of eight assistants ranging round the curve on the right side of the entrance door. All these Celestials, separated by the table from the British officers, were dressed in almost identical fashion—in dark blue silk jackets with lighter blue collar and frock-skirt, black velvet boots and black upturned rimmed hat, with the button of rank and peacock's feathers on the crown. The button worn by the Amban was a coral one, that of the highest class of mandarin next to the Emperor (see p. 165); and his chief assistant—who, by the way, spoke French, having been at Paris for some years—wore a clear blue button, the others ranging down to colourless glass. They all sat round demurely, bolt upright, and most of them with their palms resting on their knees. After the interchange of a few compliments refreshments were brought in, unsweetened tea and English biscuits, and a tasty sweetmeat of shredded kernels of nuts, followed by cheroots and cigarettes. In the general conversation that followed, the Amban apologised for the poor tawdry furniture of his room, which had been evidently improvised on a few days' notice, consisting mostly of a deal framework covered over with red cotton cloth. He asked eagerly for the latest telegraphic news of the Russo-Japanese War, as his information was several months old.

This Amban, Yu Tai, is a brother of the envoy Sheng Tai who signed the Sikhim Convention in 1893. He is a Manchu of noble birth, a scion of the royal house, and was specially deputed from Peking by the Empress-Dowager to settle the Anglo-Tibetan dispute, under a threat of punishment should he fail. His evasive and dilatory tactics will be remembered—how he was appointed in September 1903, but did not reach Lhasa till the 12th of February 1904, and despite repeated assurances that he was hurrying on to Guru, and afterwards to Gyantsé, and giving dates for his starting, under various pretexts never left this capital at all. Indeed, there was every reason to believe that notwithstanding their plausible professions of friendship the Chinese have been all along hostile, playing their old game of making a cat's-paw of the Tibetans against us. They certainly gave false information several times during this expedition, minimising the strength of the Tibetan forces, and they concealed from the Mission the plot to attack it at Gyantsé, while in the Chumbi Valley they are believed to have acted as spies, giving information to the Tibetans of our strength and movements, and are alleged by the Tibetans to have opposed the sending of delegates. On the other hand, they offered some support to our advance, probably with a view to weaken the Tibetans by inducing them to fight against us and so enable China to recover her vanishing power over them with greater ease.

Be this as it may, the Amban's excuses for his non-appearance were now accepted by Colonel Younghusband, and his promises to assist in reaching a settlement were cordially welcomed. He was handed a note disclosing the terms, which he promised to communicate to the Tibetans without delay. It was quite possible that he was sincere in his desire to effect a settlement, as long experience of China has proved that local pressure, such as has now been applied by the military strength of the escort, is always much more efficacious than mere diplomatic action. He contemptuously referred to the Tibetans as ignorant, blustering savages, and deplored their dark cunning, duplicity and dilatoriness, which, he naïvely remarked to the Commissioner, "You and I" would never think of practising. Colonel Younghusband asked him to get the Tibetans to appoint three or four delegates with due authority to negotiate, as he could no longer submit to interview a succession of irresponsible persons; and perhaps the Tibetans would not delay matters longer when they learnt that one of the conditions of the treaty was an indemnity which would increase daily so long as we remained in the country. Referring to the reported conflict between the mutineer Kham troops and his Chinese guard in the previous week, the Amban tried to minimise its importance, as it reflected on his authority. He said that it was only a small matter, some robber bands who had been enlisted by the Tibetans to fight us were encamped near the Chinese quarter and commenced to practise their profession there; but the Nepalese Consul gave a more serious account of this affair.

On leaving-taking, His Excellency again conducted the Commissioner to the third courtyard, and after a hand-shaking all round, our own escort having lined up inside, the procession re-formed and made a detour through the city.

Near the door of the Yamen stands an old city gate with remains of the wall which formerly surrounded the city, and which was destroyed during one of the wars, over a century ago. Amongst the crowd here stood a criminal with his neck in a huge padlocked *cangue*, or wooden collar, looking not a bit ashamed of his uncomfortable manacle, and carrying us back to the days of the stocks in Europe. As the capital penalty is inflicted on small provocation, the minor punishments of the *cangue*, manacling by iron chains, and barbarous lopping off a hand or leg, are administered in retribution for as trival offences as in the days of our Queen Bess,[1] and

[1] By the Draconian English law—8th Elizabeth—the exporter of sheep, lambs or rams was for the *first* offence to forfeit all his goods for ever, to suffer a year's imprisonment, *and then to have his hand cut off* in a market town upon a market day to be there nailed up; and for the second offence he was to be adjudged a felon and suffer death accordingly. It is interesting to see that only a few months ago (in the latter part of 1904), the barbarous practice of mutilating

the prisoner is then set free to find his own food and lodging by begging or as he may. In this way Tibet saves the cost of keeping prisoners in jails.

The procession now streamed through the heart of the city, followed everywhere by the eyes of a rather sullen crowd of Lamas and laity, which filled the side streets and the doors, windows, and roofs of the houses along the line of march, many of them being seen to bolt across to get a second look at a point further along.

The city generally was smaller than had been anticipated. The compact town is barely half a mile square. Its streets are rather narrow and neither drained, nor paved, nor metalled, but the main ones are laid out on a fairly good plan. The houses are substantially built of stone walls two to three storeys high, with flat roofs (none sloping) and carefully white-washed, the beams of the eaves being often elaborately picked out in red, brown and blue. The streets, although cleaner than in the fœtid suburbs, are as dirty as one expects in an Eastern, and especially Chinese town, where all attempts at even the elements of sanitation are utterly neglected. Indeed, the chief market-place in the great square surrounding the "cathedral" was uncommonly clean considering the circumstances. The articles displayed on the stalls in the streets outside the shops were chiefly native eatables, trinkets, drugs, books, clothes, and broadcloth. A few European stores were also offered for sale, amongst which I noticed two quart bottles of Bulldog stout at six shillings a bottle; it was in good frothy condition, and I was told that it was drunk by the wealthier people as a liqueur. Many of the shops, especially those of the Chinese and Nepalese merchants, looked tidy inside, but the open doors and windows of most of the Tibetan

thieves in Afghanistan by lopping off the hand has been abolished by the Amir since he experienced the pain of a gunshot injury in his own hand.

SMALLPOX EDICT AT LHASA.
(Note the "cup-markings.")

THE "TURQUOISE" TILED BRIDGE (*Yutok*).

THE GRAND SQUARE AT LHASA.
The building with curtain is the Council Chamber.

houses revealed disgustingly dirty and disorderly interiors, although their dazzling whitewashed exteriors were brightened by caged singing birds, larks, rose-finches, and doves, and on the window-sills pots of flowers.

The temples were all lavishly decorated with their verandahs painted in bright colours. The great temple, however—the chief temple, and shrine in Tibet, "The House of the Master" (*Jo-Kang*), to which pilgrims flock from the remotest part of China and Mongolia, and which, from the flattering accounts of the Lamas, I had called "The Cathedral"—was especially disappointing, from the outside at least, as it was a squat and rather mean-looking building, buried amongst narrow streets from which its gilt roof could scarcely be seen at all. At its entrance, the façade of which is emblazoned with two great purple and gilt monograms of the mystic *Om mani* legend like a coat of arms (see photo, p. 363), stood a crowd of red-robed monks whose anxious looks betrayed their fear lest we should push our way into their most sacred temple, which, however, we passed by, to their evident relief.

In the market-place, facing the door of this temple, under the shade of a fine old willow-tree, is a curious stone tablet bearing a bilingual inscription in Chinese and Tibetan, containing quarantine directions for small-pox, which is the great plague of Lhasa and Central Asia. Its base is defaced by numerous cup-like depressions, said to be caused by children playing round it, and these have obliterated a good deal of the inscription, especially on the Chinese side. It was erected under Chinese supervision, and is remarkable in being framed in an arch of brickwork, the only example of the arch I have seen in Tibet. Near this monument is the tall edict monolith, containing an inscription in Tibetan (see plan, p. 365) recording a treaty of peace between the Chinese and Tibetans. It is surrounded by a high wall of stone, and on one side it is overshadowed by a huge willow-tree whose twisted roots writhe like dragons —one evidently of the famous pair which bordered its sides over a century ago.

On leaving the town we passed by two more of the four "royal" monasteries or *lings*, namely, Chomo-ling and Tengye-ling. At the last, the Tongsa Penlop has taken up his residence with his crowd of retainers. From here, past the Royal Dancing Grove on our left, we skirted the "Pasturage" swamp, where the elephant of the Grand Lama was feeding on the rank reeds,[1] and proceeded along an avenue of twisted old willows squirming like snakes, to the "Dragon Temple" with its green and gold roof and deep pool, where we again struck the sacred Circular Road, which we invariably traversed in the "wrong" or unlucky direction, that is, against the course of the sun, which no Tibetan ever dares to do. It was very gratifying to me to find that the provisional map of Lhasa, which I had compiled from native information, and a copy of which had been issued to each officer by Government, proved to be very accurate, and indicated the various streets and buildings with remarkable precision.

FASCIMILE OF POSTAL STAMP WITH DATE OF ARRIVAL.

Back in camp, we hurried with the news of our visit to catch the outgoing post, which now brought Lhasa into close touch with the outer world; for relays of mounted infantry galloped with His Majesty's Mails from the sacred city to the telegraph terminus at Gyantsé in three days, whilst special messages were flashed to London within fifty

[1] This young tusker, about 8 feet high, was presented some years ago by the Raja of Bhotan; others had been sent from time to time by the Sikhim Raja, but seldom survived long. It is housed behind the Dragon Temple at this marsh, and is considered a mascot, especially as the old Indian word for elephant—namely, *naga*—means also "dragon," which is the mythical guardian of treasure.

hours from Lhasa, but curiously the postal authorities made the odd mistake of spelling the name as "Lahssa" in the stamp which imprinted our first missives from the holy city.

A market was speedily established outside the camp, at which merchants and hawkers, to the number of about 400, mostly women decorated with turquoise jewellery, drove a brisk trade in fruits, vegetables, sugar, and sweetmeats; candles also with wooden wicks were in demand.

When negotiations began in earnest, which they did within the next few days, the orders against entering the city were relaxed so that we could visit it fairly freely, though the temples and monasteries were closed to all but a few official visits.

The bazaar was always attractive with its human kaleidoscope of changing form and colour. For this holy city being the pivot of the Buddhist world of High Asia,[1] the Mecca, which all good Lamaists must visit, "all roads lead to Lhasa" as the Tibetan saying goes; and pilgrims from all parts of Central Asia throng to its market-place as well as to its shrines, combining a little worldly business with their devotions in the sacred metropolis.

Here, therefore, you could see nearly every day coming in from the North, a caravan of travel-stained nomads from Mongolia and the Russian steppes of Siberia. The ruddy-cheeked stalwart men in dingy yellow[2] woollen and felt suits, or greasy sheepskins ride unkempt ponies, and are armed with spears and matchlocks by which they have fought their way past

[1] The spiritual authority of the Grand Lama is not recognised by any of the Chinese or Japanese Buddhists—only by the Tibetans and Mongols.

[2] This yellow colour gives the Tibetan name for the Russians and northern Mongols who are known as "The Vast Yellow-clad" (*Gya-ser*), whilst the other two adjoining empires of China and India are similarly called "The Vast Black-clad" (*Gya-nak*), and "The Vast White-clad" (*Gya-Gar*) respectively.

the bands of brigands in their tediously long journey of four or five months across the upland deserts. Their fair complexioned women, also mounted, are covered with bright silver and brass trinkets stuck over their dress, and tied to the long plaits of their hair, and help their spouses to escort their valuables laden on shaggy double-humped Bactrian dromedaries and a string of ponies, whose tinkling collar-bells give timely warning of their approach to other wayfarers at the sharp corners and cliffy bits of the track in the narrow defiles and gorges, as well as in the confined and crowded thoroughfares of the town.

In the cosmopolitan crowd, you see shiny-pated ruby-robed monks moving about amongst the drab and purple-clad populace, or mingling picturesquely with the blue and yellow-coated richer classes and bejewelled townswomen in all their silks and finery. You see indigo-gowned pallid Chinese in their self-complacent pride, the half-bred "Kokos,"[1] white-turbanned Mahomedan merchants and Turks from Ladak, Kashmir, and Tartary, like swarthy Jews; the still swarthier bare-headed crop-haired and kilted Bhotanese; the fairer Nepalese with pork-pie caps; and the quaintly garbed country-folk from the distant provinces—the upstanding athletic Khams from the east with the fine physique and free carriage of mountaineers, wearing a thick fringe of hair over their brows, the diversely-clad men and women from Tsang and the west, and the squat begrimed people of the Lower Tsangpo, many of whom are utter barbarians of a very low type, and entirely in the skins of wild beasts. But nearly all of these, Tibetans, Nepalese and Mongols, however wild, reflect the religious atmosphere of the city by twirling their

[1] Most of the Chinese marry Tibetan wives as a celestial edict prohibits the taking of any Chinese women beyond their frontier. A few Chinese women, however, have been smuggled into Lhasa by way of Darjeeling, coming by sea to Calcutta.

prayer-wheels or counting their rosary-beads even when chatting and trading.

Their beardless faces, though coarse-featured and small and restless-eyed, had a contented cheery expression, since they had lost their fears, having seen the futility of further resistance, and experienced our forbearance. Their friendly demeanour did not bear out Marco Polo's wholesale denunciation, that "The people of Tebet are an ill-conditioned race."[1] It was almost always a good-humoured grinning crowd that gathered round us in our shopping or photographing excursions, and smiled in childish pleasure at our lavishness, or stared with open-eyed curiosity at our strange ways, invariably respectful, though never cringing. Seldom was a sullen face seen, except amongst the Lamas, but many of these too would occasionally relax so as to let a good-natured smile lighten up their broad faces. Their worst defect, perhaps, was their too infrequent acquaintance with water, but even in this respect they were not so very much worse than many other hill people, who have for it the excuse of the cold and the scarcity of fuel, indeed, we ourselves could not boast of being over-fastidious in this particular after all the rough and tumble life we had been leading in the cold.

The inhabitants of Lhasa have been pithily summarised as consisting of "monks, women, and dogs"; there is much truth in the description, for out of a permanent resident populace of about 30,000 persons, nearly a fiftieth of the total population of Tibet,[2] the monks of the city and suburbs number about 20,000, and in the remainder the women vastly outnumber the men. This preponderance is due to the enormous numbers of men who join the Church as celibates, as well as to the prevalence of polyandry, which tends to drive the surplus women from their homes into the

[1] Yule's Second Edition, ii. 40.

[2] Estimated at 1,500,000. See Appendix VI., p. 469.

town, where they contract promiscuous marriages as both marriage and divorce are easy in Tibet.

No census has been taken for several decades,[1] and the exact figures are unknown even to the government itself; the Nepalese Consul, however, gave me the following approximate estimate of the residents:

Tibetans . .	7000	of whom 5500 are women.
Chinese and Kokos	2000	traders, military and police.
Nepalese . .	800	mostly Newar merchants and artisans.
Mahomedans . .	200	traders from Ladak and Western China.
Mongols . .	50	traders.
Bhotanese . .	50	traders.

The paucity of the Tibetan laymen in their own capital is thus remarkable. The floating population numbers, it is said, a thousand or two, and during the winter time and great festivals many more, chiefly pilgrims and traders.

The physical type of the Tibetans I find here as elsewhere from Gyantsé onwards, is of two well-marked and almost equally prevalent kinds, the one round-headed, flat-faced, and oblique-eyed, approximating to the pure Mongol from the Steppes (*Sok*), the other longer-headed with nearly regular features, a fairly shapely long nose with a good bridge and little of the "Kalmuk" eye, approximating to the Tartars of Turkestan and the nomads of the great Northern Plateau (*Hor*). It was noticeable that a large number of the nobility and higher officials, the *Jong-pöns* and others, belonged to this longer-headed and longer-nosed group, which seemed also to comprise many of the Mahomedan Balti coolies who had come with us to Lhasa, by way of India, from their country bordering

[1] According to one in 1854 there were 27,000 Lamas and 15,000 laity, of whom 9000 were women. Since then the population has decreased enormously, falling from 24,000 to about 10,000.

the Pamirs. The latter are indeed scarcely distinguishable in features from the long-headed Tibetans. They are called by the Chinese "Black Tibetans" (*Kara tü-pet*), and by Mr Shaw, who has described them in their own country, "Mahomedan Tibetans." Several recent migrations of these nomad Hor Tartars, have taken place, I am told, far into South-Western Tibet, to the east of the Yamdok Lake, near the borders of Bhotan.

The stature of the Tibetans of Lhasa is even less than that of the Chinese, and considerably below the European average; whilst the men from the eastern province of Kham are quite up to that standard.

In complexion the people are generally of a light chocolate colour, though many of the better class, and a large proportion of the women, are almost as fair as a South Italian. Many, especially the children, have rosy cheeks, and showed an acquaintance with soap, a commodity which was evidently much in demand, as it appeared for sale on most of the stalls, and has for years been one of the chief imports.[1] Even the men can have no inveterate dislike to this toilet article, for in the attack on our post at Gyantsé nearly every one of the killed and wounded had a cake of soap in his haversack. The surprising cleanliness of the Lhasa townspeople, however, may have been exceptional and involuntary. It may have been due in part to the excessive downpour of rain at the time, and in part to the circumstance that our visit also coincided with the great ceremonial bathing festival, when every one is supposed to indulge in this luxury for once, at least, during the year.

Silks and jewels are worn here to a much greater extent than at Gyantsé. The love of jewellery is indeed one of the leading traits of a Lhasaite. He is a poor man who does not sport a long earring with a pearl and turquoise pendant, massive silver bangles,

[1] See Appendix X. p. 476.

a huge bone thumb-ring and amulet box in addition to a turquoise inlaid prayer-wheel. It is, however, his women-folk who lavishly indulge this taste. They are literally loaded from top to toe with massive trinkets, tiaras of red cloth encrusted over with great pieces of coral, amber and turquoise as big as marbles, encircle the smoothly polished locks of their plaited hair; huge gold or silver earrings studded with turquoise sweep their shoulders; large filagree gold or silver amulet boxes like breastplates picked out with turquoises hang round their necks, waistbelts with enormous silver buckles gird their loose wrapper-like gown and suspend a chatelaine with a bunch of keys, silver toilet implements and chop sticks, all of which articles were in great demand by our people as curios. The rosary of the women is generally of white shell or coloured glass beads, whilst those of the men are commonly yellow willow wood, and the prayer-wheel which they piously twirl usually contains a few inlaid turquoises.

The partiality of the Tibetans for turquoise and coral is remarkable. For the larger pieces of the latter they pay about £4 an ounce, equal to their weight in gold. Nor is this taste of recent growth; writing so long ago as the twelfth century Marco, the Venetian, says regarding his visit to this land: "Coral is in great demand in this country (Tebet) and fetches a high price, for they delight to hang it round the necks of their women and of their idols."[1]

Still greater do they esteem the turquoise, as they attribute mystic talismanic virtue to it. They believe that it guards against the Evil Eye, and brings good luck and health. Like the Ancient Egyptians[2] and Persians,[3] they suppose that it wards off contagion, and

[1] *Marco Polo*, Yule's Edition, chap. xlvi.

[2] Emanuel's *Diamonds*, p. 182.

[3] Fraser's *Khorasan*, p. 469, and Campbell, *Ind. Antiquary*, 1896, 137. It was specially valued in the Middle Ages in Europe for

LHASA WOMEN.

NEPALESE CONSULATE IN LHASA.

MAHOMEDAN CONSUL OF LHASA AND LADAKI MERCHANTS.

that when it changes colour and blanches, it betokens mischief or sickness, and then they promptly get rid of it for a full-coloured one. An immense number of these diseased gems were doctored up with a wash of blue dye and brought for sale to our confiding soldiers at Lhasa, who, however, soon discovered the imposition, and became experts in testing the genuineness of the colour before purchasing. In addition to personal wear, turquoises are also inserted as lucky spots into the forehead of Buddha and other images, in which case if large enough they are sometimes engraved with a mystic spell or dragon. Perhaps their brilliancy also conduces to their popularity as setting off the dark skins and darker dress of their wearers.

The only persons who were not extravagant in dress were the poorer children, many of whom dispensed with garments altogether and ran about flying kites and playing in the streets naked, notwithstanding the severity of the climate, with snow lying in August on the hills about 800 feet above the plain. Few very old people were noticed. The rough exposed life which the people lead causes them to age rapidly; even the men are wrinkled at thirty, and the number of children is remarkably small.

The houses of the citizens are substantially built of stone or sun-baked bricks, the walls neatly whitewashed, and the woodwork picked out in colours, with charms against the Evil Eye pasted over the doorway, give a general look of comfort from the street. But, a glance within dispels the illusion, and shows the interior to be quite as squalid and dirty as those of the wretched hovels in the country, and reflects the general poverty of the place. The more well-to-do also live in a curious mixture of squalor and dirt. Their

protecting horsemen, as no one using a turquoise could be thrown by his horse or tire out the latter. In the gem language of modern Europe the turquoise means prosperity.

larger houses have similar mean and untidy interiors, although some of the more wealthy, imitating the Chinese, have sufficient taste to ornament their interiors with paintings, frescoes, and better furniture, and a very few may have one or two glazed windows, a great rarity in Lhasa.

The houses of the poorer class have usually two rooms, one to sleep in and another to eat in, each of which, especially the latter, has a firehearth usually in the middle and without a chimney, so that its smoke japans darkly the whole interior. The floor is littered with all sorts of malodorous refuse that is seldom swept away, and forms rotting heaps in the corners. The removal of such trifling things as the remains of food and washings of kitchen utensils is considered superfluous. They are thrown down anywhere until the pile becomes inconveniently high, when some of it is cast into the street in front, or on the nearest reeking dunghill. Amongst this dirt near the fire or a stove-pot, lies the bundle of unclean wraps which forms the bedding, as the Tibetans never undress when they retire for the night, and do not indulge in a couch or bedstead nor in bedclothes as we understand them, but cover themselves over with skins and extra wraps. For furniture a rudely-hewn low bench serves as a table and some logs of wood or boxes as chairs, in one of these boxes are treasured the valuables of the family, a few fine clothes, trinkets and a spare rosary or prayer-wheel, and the horoscopes. From pegs in the wall hang bladders of butter, which may have been kept for years, strings of cheese, bits of meat, yak-hair rope, cooking ladles, and other implements, and in a niche in the wall, or on the top of a box, is a little shrine for the image of the household gods, beside a small religious picture and a few charms. Some clay and iron cooking vessels and utensils strewn between tubs containing water and evil smelling stores of grain and other provisions, complete the furnishings of the room in which the average Tibetan lives in miserable poverty.

His food, even in the town, consists of the few simple staple dishes with which the nomadic class all over Tibet must perforce be content. As a beverage he drinks all day long cupfuls of hot "buttered tea," which is really a soup or broth, made by boiling tea-leaves with rancid butter and balls of dough, and adding a little salt, and straining—a decoction which was invariably nasty to our taste, though no doubt it is wholesome; for it is not merely a stimulating hot drink in the cold, but overcomes the danger of drinking unboiled water in a country where the water supply is dangerously polluted. Instead of bread he eats unleavened scones of wheat or barley meal (*jimpa*) eked out with the meal of roasted grains of barley (*tsampa*)[1] dry or made into a brose. The chief dish is a stew of meat and potatoes, turnips, cabbage, and other vegetables, with, as a relish, some dried cheese (*chura*), and on festive occasions a nibble at brown sugar, which is never used for tea. His strong drink is the beer of the country made from fermented barley, it is not strong in alcohol, and has a vinegary taste and smell, but when newly made it is cool and refreshing in summer. A coarse, fiery brandy is distilled from it, but is not extensively drunk. Although a good deal of beer is consumed, drunkenness does not seem to be a common vice amongst the people. Altogether one is glad to escape from these low-ceilinged wretched interiors into the street.

The streets are lined by two to three storeyed houses, generally with shops in the lower flat in the main thoroughfares, which are about 25 feet broad, and without pavements, as there is no wheeled traffic whatever. The lanes are much narrower. None of the streets are paved, and as they act also as drains, they become

[1] Like the "Sattu" which the Indians make by parching rice and maize.

in the rainy season a chain of slimy puddles through which you have to pick your way. A religious look is given to all the streets by the tall prayer-flags at the chief corners, and the numerous little incense kilns beside the door of most houses; though the countless mangy dogs and pigs which infest the thoroughfares, gnawing bones and foraging in the refuse heaps, recall the revolting dirt of a Chinese city. Order is maintained, and maintained very well, by the native police (*Korchak*).

The shops were thoroughly ransacked by our people hunting for curios; but were found to contain little of the kind of things we wanted. The Tibetans having no arrangements to display their wares inside, exhibit them on stalls in the street. The Chinese have proper shops with a counter, behind which are silks, porcelain, brick-tea and other goods. The Nepalese had on view chiefly cloth and drugs, brass bowls and lamps, etc.; and the Mahomedans, spices and dried fruits. Thus nothing in the way of curiosities worth purchasing was to be had in the bazaar; but on learning what was wanted the shopmen would enquire further amongst the private householders and bring the things to our camp. In this way were obtained some pieces of old Chinese cloisonné (*kugushā*), old China and other articles, but of local Tibetan manufacture there was practically nothing of artistic value.

The stalls and booths in the streets on which most of the merchandise[1] was displayed by the jewelled shopwomen, contained, amongst other things of interest to us, a great variety of furs brought in from the neighbouring hills, chiefly of the civet and weasel tribe, and including some Tibetan sable, for which about eighteen shillings per skin was asked. Larger skins of the silver lynx, tiger cat, clouded leopard cat, otter,

[1] See Appendix X., p. 476.

woolly tiger and bear were also brought in. Amongst the fruits were excellent persimmons, cooking peaches, crab-apples, mulberries, gooseberries and red currants. The eggs here were so old that many of them were black with age, as the Tibetans imitate the Chinese in esteeming them a great delicacy when putrid, and boast of these ancient relics as much as any squire of the port in his cellars.[1] Even when our eggs had been carefully selected by our cooks, we came by unpleasant experience to know that it was unsafe to hazard an attack on a boiled egg, the only way being to have them poached so that their condition could be seen from afar. The "bricks" of Chinese tea were interesting in view of the possible openings for Indian tea in these regions, where tea is deemed a necessity of life. They consist of cakes, about four pounds in weight, of compressed leaves and twigs, rolled in yellow paper wrappers and stamped with the quality.[2] Twelve of these bricks are sewed up in hide to make a load, a pair of which are carried by yaks, asses, and ponies, from the great tea centre of Dartsendo (Ta-chien-lu) in Western China, many hundreds of miles over the mountains to Central and Western Tibet. Sheep are not used here to carry loads as they are in the rocky tracks of the North-Western Himalayas; this is not from any religious scruples, but merely because the roads are sufficiently good for the employment of the larger animals. The tea caravans seldom go more in a day than a stage of 5 miles (*pag-ts'ad*).

As trade in Tibet is chiefly by exchange or barter, and comparatively few articles are paid for in cash, bricks of tea are often used as a convenient currency instead of money, being in such universal demand, whilst, at the same time, they are limited in production, fairly portable, and of nearly uniform size. Money is,

[1] Eggs are eaten by Lamas except the few who have taken the highest vows.

[2] Appendix X., p. 476.

however, also current, and coined by the Tibetans at their mint in Lhasa.[1] It is in the form of crudely fashioned silver pieces about the size of a halfpenny, but thin as a sixpence, and modelled after the Nepalese "Tangka," which Indian name it also bears. Tibet used to import these coins from Nepal, but has for several years been minting its own, and retaining on it the eight lucky symbols.[2] It is of its silver value, being equivalent to fivepence, and like its Nepalese prototype is clipped into half, a third, or a quarter to form coins of smaller denomination. The almighty Indian rupee is, however, in great demand, and the image of the late Queen-

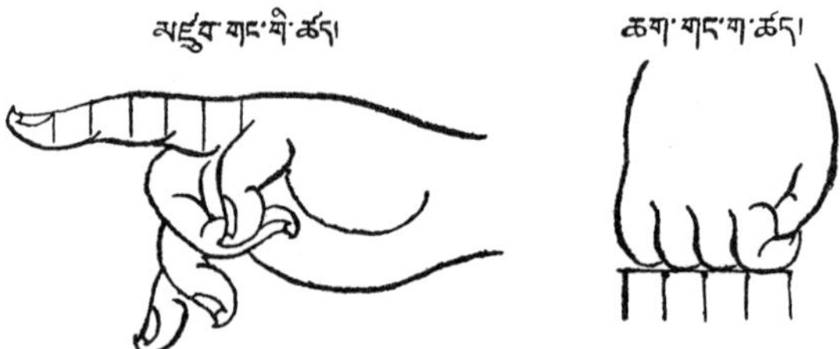

BAZAAR FINGER MEASUREMENTS.

Empress upon it was regarded with reverential awe as being the effigy of the mild form of the dread Buddhist Goddess, who is called "The Great Queen." As our money consisted mainly of the new rupees bearing the head of the King-Emperor most of the Tibetans at first refused to receive these unaccustomed coins which they called "The Lama's head." Russian roubles were found, also a Chinese coin bearing a Turkish legend on the reverse; and some pure bullion in the form of Chinese ingots of silver or "shoes" (Tibetan Dotsa), in value about Rs. 150. The small measure of length in the bazaar was by the finger breadth and joints of the forefinger.[3] The Chinese quarter in the north-

[1] The mint is called Gahldan p'odang, "The Happy Palace," a title of Potala.

[2] See p. 224, footnote. [3] Chak-kangi-t'säd. See above figure.

east of the City was entered at either end through wooden arches of the kind seen near temples in the Celestial Empire.

As our camping ground outside the city gate was becoming dangerously flooded by the drenching rainfall and the overflow of the river and its branches, the troops moved to a drier site on the plain near Sera monastery, where as a precautionary measure against attack, General Macdonald fortified the camp into a strong defensive post with loopholed turf walls 5 feet high, and a moat and ditches bristling with wooden spikes. At the same time the Mission moved into the adjoining palace of Lhalu (No. 5 on plan, p. 330), a fine, exceptionally clean, newly-painted mansion standing in a large grove, the residence of the family of the previous Dalai Lama's father, the heir of whom, a pleasant young man of about twenty, bears the Chinese title of "Duke" or "Kung." The childish objections offered by the Tibetans to the moving of our camp were amusing. The Lamas urged that the sodden plain on which we had first camped was a very good place, and that "no common people were ever allowed to camp on it before!" and that no building could be occupied as they were all temples and sacred.

On the way to the new camp, in crossing the plain, which, as I pointed out some years ago, was known as the "Meadow of Wild Asses," we came upon several of these animals. They were so tame as to allow me to go near and photograph them. They had been caught, I was told, when quite young, and brought as a present to the Dalai Lama, who had them fed and stalled at Lhalu and let them run about here as they liked. They at once made friends with our mules, and two of them were soon afterwards captured and brought into camp, to be sent as a present[1] to the

[1] Both of these *Kyang* were mares; one of them was unfortunately drowned in crossing the Tsangpo.

King, and although not permitting any one to ride them, they received quietly the usual pony's blanket, and did not attempt to discard it during the cold nights.

Whilst negotiations were slowly progressing we were able to pay visits to some of the Tibetan officials, to the Nepalese Consul and the Tongsa Penlop, the chief of Bhotan.

The Nepalese Resident or Consul who has lived in Lhasa for over twenty years had been most friendly and obliging; so that I gladly availed myself of his invitation to visit him at his house. The Consulate stands in a crowded part of the town to the south of the great temple square, and as the Nepalese lieutenant, who had come to guide me to the place, led me past the mansion of my friend the Prime Minister (see photo, p. 8), now deposed by the Dalai Lama because he had failed to keep the Mission out of the Chumbi Valley, I was tempted to dismount and look through the gateway. The Shata mansion has the general form of that of a Tibetan noble, like that of Phala (see photo, p. 9), a large central paved courtyard surrounded by two to three storeyed buildings, and on the ground floor the stables. A large stone wall as a screen stood outside the gateway as in Chinese houses, and on one side of the door was a large fresco of the guardian Mongol giant leading a tiger (see photo, p. 358), like the warning inscription on the portals of old Roman houses.

At the Nepalese Residency the Consul came out and gave me a cordial reception, shaking hands heartily. He is a pleasant-looking man of medium height and middle age, with regular features and robed in silks, with an aigrette spray in his head-dress. He is a captain in the Nepalese army,[1] and has a guard of some dozen Goorkhas, who were drawn up at the

[1] He is called by the Nepalese in Lhasa by the Indian title of *Vakil* or "Deputy."

door and presented arms to the English words of command, and gave the English bugle call as I entered. In his reception-room upstairs, which was neatly furnished, there hung on the walls several coloured prints, including one of the Raja of Nepal, and a Chinese one of the Rulers of the World, containing good likenesses of the late Queen Empress, the Emperor William, the Tsar, the Presidents of the French Republic and the United States, and the Emperor of China. There were also two large maps of the world. My host was quite an enlightened man, and we talked on many subjects. After some refreshments, including English biscuits and tasty shredded nuts, and before speaking about the Lamas, he shrewdly looked round the room and ordered all his attendants away, and when we were alone he leaned forward and spoke almost in a whisper, his eyes snapping with intelligence. He said that the people of Tibet were well pleased that we had come, and that it was only the officials and the Lamas who were discomfited, but they were like fresh bullocks put under a yoke for the first time, and did not quite know what was expected of them, but in a short time they would pull all right. The people who a few days before were preparing to run away, and had been furbishing up old muskets for their defence, had remarked to him what extraordinary people the British were, for although they carry invincible guns on their shoulders, yet they pay for all the food they take, whereas our own Tibetan soldiers forcibly take from us as much food and clothing as they want without any payment. He said that Dorjieff had gone off with the Grand Lama towards Mongolia, and they were now at Nagchuka beyond the Tengri Lake (see map, p. 40), which subsequent information showed to be correct, notwithstanding the Amban's story that Dorjieff had left Lhasa three months previously, and that the

Dalai Lama was still only about two days' journey off. He told me that the deposed Minister Shata was very popular, and it was really on this account that the Dalai Lama, jealous of his growing influence, had made use of the pretext of our entry into the Chumbi Valley to turn him out of power. Shata was not only friendly towards the British but also to the Russians, a party of whom he had met near the Tengri Lake. The Dalai took a very active part in politics, and had such a violent temper that most people were afraid of him, but he was quite in the hands of Dorjieff. The Amban had very little power over the Tibetans, and latterly had been almost a prisoner and unable to venture out for weeks until our force arrived. Both the Lamas and people on the extreme east in Litang and Dartsendo (see map, p. 40), on the borders of China are friendly to Europeans. The Tibetan chief of Dartsendo (Tachienlu), the King of "Chala," is especially well-disposed towards Europeans, and when the Dalai Lama threatened to punish him on this account he is reported to have become "sworn brothers" with the Protestant Christian Tibetans, of whom there is a flourishing colony at Dartsendo, and the latest reports stated that he was building forts in his country, and could put 10,000 fighting men in the field.

I enquired whether there were any Europeans resident in Lhasa, and especially whether there was a Roumanian, M. Chevron, for whom, curiously, a post-card had come in our mail bag from India; but he knew of no such person, only Asiatics. Before I left we were joined by his good lady, and they were kind enough to allow me to take the accompanying photograph of them. As a present he sent a dozen wild goose's eggs from the Tengri Lake, and they were excellent eating, with none of the coarse flavour of the tame goose's egg at home.

The Mahomedan community has a Consul of its

NEPALESE CONSUL AND HIS WIFE AT LHASA.

AMBAN'S PALANQUIN AND PIKEMEN.

own in the person of the Chief of the Ladak merchants. He is an amiable old gentleman (see photo, p. 349), and is practically a native of Lhasa, having spent the greater part of his life here. He lives in the chief market street (see plan, No. 342), and has the powers of an honorary magistrate to settle all crimes and misdemeanours occurring amongst his co-religionist. Many of these latter who posed as natives of Ladak and Kashmir looked more like Persians, Turks, and Armenians, and when asked for particulars of the road from Ladak, most of them said that they entered Tibet by way of the Nepal passes, and not by Leh and Ladak.

The Amban paid the General a few visits in camp after conferences with the Mission. He travelled always in great state, his sedan chair, which is like a brougham without its wheels, being preceded by a long string of men in scarlet and black bearing banners, followed by the pikemen, and these by horsemen and his mounted staff. The chair was always carried at a swinging pace up to within 10 yards of the reception tent, and then set down, when His Excellency would briskly step out, and with an exchange of bows and smiles shake hands all round, whilst the pikemen during the halt stuck their battleaxes and other insignia of the Lord High Executioner in the ground, forming an avenue of these antediluvian weapons (see photo, here). The Amban was always very pleasant and charming in manner. Speaking of the eastern limits of Tibet he said that Jyade is practically independent, and neither under Lhasa nor China. The eastern districts of Dergé and "Chan-we" (? Jyade) or Chiamdo (see map, p. 40) were forcibly annexed by the Sze-chuan Viceroy a few years ago, about 1896, but on a deputation of Tibetans proceeding to Peking with a protest, the Viceroy was ordered to restore them. The chief thing that the Chinese got good in Lhasa was musk, the furs were all of poor quality, and the hairs too stiff at their roots to make up into pleasant garments. On his way across from China he saw little evidence of game, but travelling in his chair, and not being interested in the matter, could give no information about it. He was impressed, however, by the great extent of mountain gorges which had to be traversed before China was reached. During his first visit to our camp he was much alarmed by the great chorus of braying which suddenly burst from the throats of the 4000 mules when the bugle blew at their feeding time. He started from his seat, as if it were some war cry, but resumed his usual composure, with a smile, when the incident was explained to him.

With the Amban's aid it was arranged that small parties of officers might visit the "Cathedral" and the chief monasteries in the neighbourhood, and see the sacred shrines of the holy city.

CHAPTER XVII.

TEMPLES AND MONKS IN THE HERMIT CITY: THE LAMAS' HOLY OF HOLIES.

"*What! Been in Lhasa and never seen 'The House of The Master,' the Jo-k'ang!*"—TIBETAN PROVERB.

THE first temple we visited was, naturally, the famous shrine of Buddha, "The Master," the largest and holiest in all Tibet, and the one from which the city that has grown up around its idol house receives its name of Lhasa, or "The Place of the Gods."[1] These local divinities one might have thought must have been the "rain gods," judging from the steady downpour which had deluged us every day for hours together, since our arrival outside the Hermit City, where :—

"The hooded clouds, like friars,
 Tell their beads in drops of rain."

The local genius of the place is appropriately a water-dragon which lives in a sacred pool inside the great temple.

It was still raining as we made our way to this celebrated sanctuary in the heart of the city, where it stands so closely hemmed in amongst the houses that its dimensions cannot be seen to advantage (see photo over page), and you have little evidence that you

[1] The great temple of Lhasa stands at an elevation of 12,290 feet above the sea-level in N. lat. 29° 39′ and E. long. 90° 57′ (or 91° 55′). The new observation has not yet been worked out.

are approaching it until you actually reach its gateway in a narrow street facing the smallpox tablet (M in plan) in the market-place standing under the luxuriant shade of the old writhing, weeping willow of the ancient treaty pillar (p. 365) or *Doring*, which fortunately had escaped much defacement by cup-markings that mutilate the former. Here we dismounted, and I took a photograph of this tablet (see p. 340), and examined it in some detail. It was erected by the Chinese[1] to combat the scourge of smallpox which ravages Tibet, Lhasa in particular; and, placed here at the entrance door of the chief shrine so that all pilgrims may see, it prescribes the procedure to be adopted on the occurrence of an outbreak. The Tibetans are great sticklers for such proclamations, for, as they say :—"Unless words are spoken a son even will not understand his own father: Unless a proclamation order is hoisted in the market-place every man will do as he listeth." It has, however, been unavailing, and only four years ago, in 1900, over 6000 people died of the plague in this very city.[2]

A loud clanging of cymbals and bells, and the muffled swell of the priests' chant in the "cathedral," caused us to turn to that sanctuary, the St Peter's of Lamadom. It is very ancient, having been erected in 652 A.D., about the time when Christianity was being introduced into barbarian England, when Mahomet had just died, and when the fanatical Saracens, having

[1] It was probably erected in 1794 when the Chinese records (Rockhill, *loc. cit.* 235) state that in that year "the Talé Lama, under orders from the Emperor, erected special hospitals for smallpox patients, in which they were supplied with food and every necessity, and which were in care of a special officer." This was shortly after the death of the Tashi Lama from that pest at Peking (see p. 15). The Tibetan heading to it is written vertically like in the Chinese, and not horizontally as usual.

[2] This number was estimated by the Japanese monk, Kawaguchi, who was a resident in Lhasa at the time.

CATHEDRAL OF LHASA (from roof of adjoining building).

ENTRANCE TO LHASA CATHEDRAL.

conquered Palestine, were preparing to overrun Europe, before the Middle Ages. It was originally built to enshrine the images brought in that year by King Srongtsan's Buddhist wives, the Chinese Imperial princess and the daughter of the King of Nepal (see p. 24); and around this central shrine, now the "Holy of Holies," the building grew to its present size by additions, up till two and a half centuries ago, when it attained its present dimensions.

Its entrance, which faces the west, is neither grand nor imposing. From the street you can see only its rather mean two-storeyed façade, with no swelling mass of any dome or stately building behind it, and above, only the tip of a gilded Chinese pagoda roof, of no great height, from the burnished surface of which, as the rain had now ceased, some tongues of fiery light leapt into the sky. From the hearsay accounts of Lhasa Lamas ten years previously, when publishing a translation of the pilgrims' guide-book to its chapels and altars, with a native drawing of the place itself, I had remarked[1] that:—

> "The chapels and other buildings which compose the temple do not appear to form a pile of grand architectural proportions, but rather a cluster of squat buildings with glittering gilded roofs."

Its appearance now quite bore out this estimate, and also recalled to mind that many a true word is spoken in jest, for a newspaper[2] at that time, in noticing my translation of this handbook, said, "Perhaps the day is not far distant when this English version of the guide-book will be used in the great temple itself;" and now I was approaching the gateway with the book in my hands.

[1] *Jour. Bengal As. Soc.*, pp. 259, etc., 1895.

[2] Calcutta *Englishman*, 1895.

The countless feet of thronging pilgrims passing continuously for ages have worn deep ruts in the hard stone flags which lead up to the gateway, grooves as deep as those in the great doorway of St Mark's or in Milan Cathedral. The ruts have also been in some measure made by the heads and hands of kowtowing devotees, a row of whom were at this time performing endless obeisances in front of the closed door, prostrating themselves full length on the pavement, and rising, and throwing themselves down again, and so on incessantly for hours together to earn good marks for Paradise; to protect their palms, which bear much of the strain and friction in raising the body, these men wear on their hands padded wooden clogs, the soles of which are studded over with hob-nails and a small horseshoe, all of which made a great clattering as the zealots threw themselves down and slid back on their hands to lift themselves erect again. They sometimes make a thousand protestations in one day.

The gateway was besieged by a crowd of importuning beggars, repulsively dirty, young, as well as toothless old, whining with outstretched hands for alms which they freely received, for nowhere else does the gift of a coin or other charity confer such benefit to the giver as on this threshold to the Holy of Holies.

The verandah (A in plan) with its pillars and beams was dirtier than any we had yet seen. It was lined with large slabs of dark limestone engraved with Chinese and Mongolian characters, giving a laudatory account of the Potala hill at Lhasa as "the best of all the three Potalas,"[1] and a translation into Tibetan on smaller slabs ranged around the great prayer-

[1] The other two are the original Potala at Cape Komorin on the southern extremity of India, and the one on the eastern coast of China.

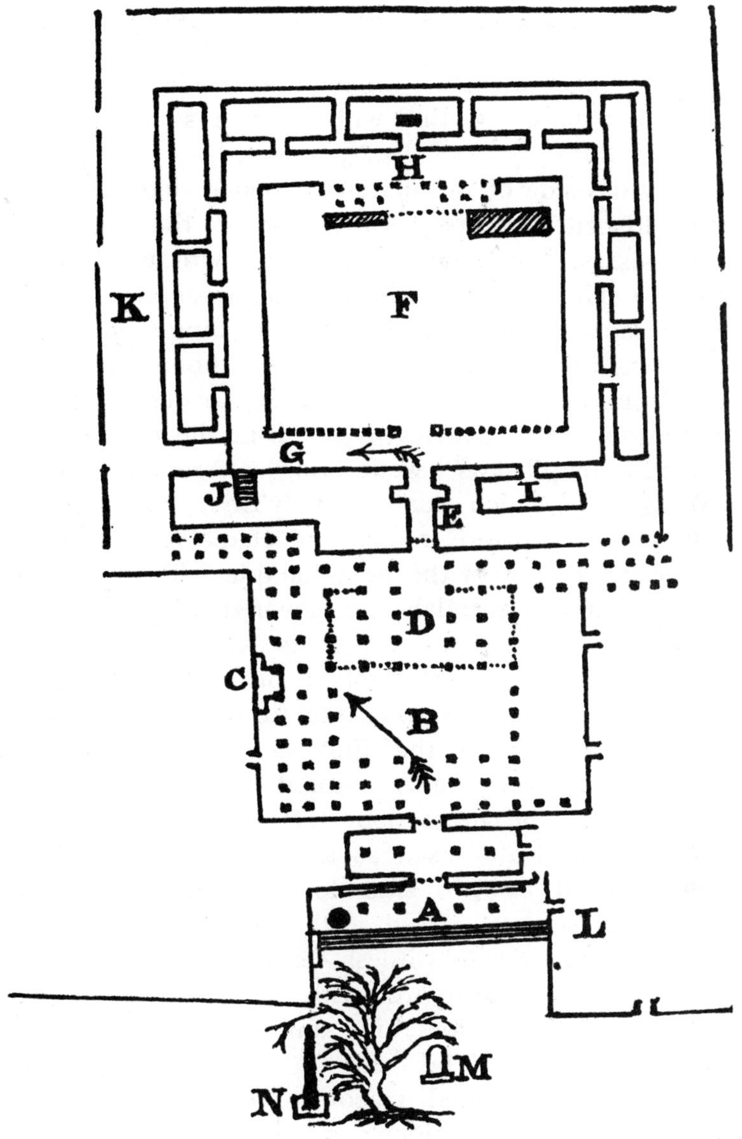

Scale—1 inch = 13 yards.

GROUND PLAN OF LHASA CATHEDRAL.

References.

A Entrance.
B Inner Court.
C Throne of Dalai Lama.
D Outer Chapel with offering altars.
E Dragon Shrine.
F Inner Court with two large images of the Coming Buddha.
G Inner Circle.
H Holy of Holies (the letter is in front of door).
I King Srongtsan's Shrine.
J Stair to Upper Storeys.
K Middle Circle.
L Room with Chenlung's edict.
M Smallpox edict.
N Old treaty edict pillar.

barrel on the left, which was being constantly turned round by the willing hands of relays of the faithful.

By the side of the massive wooden door which was embellished with iron scrollwork on the hinges and nail-bosses, stood the janitor-priest with his bunch of keys. He sullenly unlocked the door and threw it open, and as we passed within its dingy portals, the veil was lifted from this long-sealed home of mystery.

A short passage, barred by a similar door at the end, led into a central courtyard (see B in the attached plan, which I compiled as I went along). Around either side of this court, which was also very dirty, runs a pillared verandah with store-rooms and chapels; and in front is the inner door of the great temple. The three walls of this inner verandah are covered with dilapidated frescoes, the chief of which is about 8 feet high, and represents the Mongolian prince,[1] Gushi Khan, (see p. 27), offering presents to the Regent Grand Lama,[2] who, with the first Dalai about two and a half centuries ago, restored this temple. The vestibule of the inner door (D) is screened off from this courtyard and used as a chapel, so that entry is gained to it by two side doors. Proceeding to the left of these, we passed a throne (C) on which the Grand Lama sits to witness certain religious performances in the courtyard with plastered benches of different heights for his staff, according to their several ranks. The throne is merely a dirty platform of plastered masonry 3½ feet high, carrying five grimy cushions; on its front are painted the two lions as on the pedestal of Buddha's images

[1] Go-sri bstan-'dsin cho'-gyal. This seems to be the picture which the Chinese officials at Lhasa have mistaken for Hiuen Tsiang (Conf. Rockhill, *Jour. Roy. Asiatic Soc.*, xxiii. p. 263). There was no fresco of any group on the outside of this outer wall.

[2] Sangyä Gyamts'o, see pp. 377 and 388.

and as a fresco behind is a picture of that saint, Sakya Muni. The whole structure as well as this entire courtyard was in a disgustingly unclean condition, and had not been swept of late nor painted for years.

Groping along a dark corner amongst the pillars, we pass an alley going off to the left, "the inner circle" (K), by which pilgrims circumambulate the main building, and keeping on to our right passed through the vestibule to the inner door. On the altars (D) in this vestibule were burning 1000 candles, and about fifty monks were chanting a mass for the benefit of the soul of some one deceased. The boyish voices of the younger monks and the deep bass of the older, rising and falling sounded like sacred music on an organ in a cathedral, although at times the trumpet-blowers tried to make up by strength and volume for the lack of harmony.

Another dark passage of nine paces, guarded by a gate at each end, gave entry to the temple proper (F). On the right-hand side of this passage is a small shrine (E) to the Water-Dragon of the lake on which Lhasa now stands. For current tradition alleges that previous to 640 A.D. the whole of Lhasa was a lake, such as we have seen it must have been within historic times. The legend goes on to relate that in that year King Srongtsan, persuaded by his Nepalese wife to build a Buddhist temple, went with her and threw up a ring to find a lucky site. It fell into the middle of this lake, upon which a *chorten* sprang up. Then the king and his people filled up the lake with stones, and on this lacustrine site Lhasa was built. In the dark passage by the side of the Dragon's shrine is pointed out a large stone flag about 3 feet long and 2 broad, and here we received with deferential incredulity the terrifying information that the flag is the barrier which shuts in the springs of the lake. This stone is removed with mysterious rites every year in the second month, when the noise of a great wind is heard; precious offerings are then thrown down to the Dragon who, were this not done, would cause the waters to rise and engulf the city.[1]

The main temple (F) had its chief shrine at the remote end (H) facing the door but screened off by open lattice-work, on each side of which was a fine gilded image of the seated Coming Buddha, that on the right being of colossal size. In the centre of the floor was a mass of brilliant variegated blossom from clusters of potted hollyhocks, stocks, and asters. In niches in the wall were small gilt images of the thousand Buddhas. It had no roof, but was open to the sky overhead, and the chapels were ranged round it like boxes in a theatre, separated from the court by carved wooden pillars of the top-heavy kind as pictured in the cave-temples of India in the eighth and ninth century. As a cornice round the top ran a row of sphinx-like, couchant lions, ten on each side. It was utterly unlike the plan given of it by Giorgi.[2]

To visit the chief shrine our guide lit a torch and led us to the left around the outside of this central court-temple along a dark covered passage (G) lined by a closely-set row of images of saints[3] and divinities, life size; between each group of four or five a passage led off to cryptic side-chapels full of idols and relics (each of which is duly named and described in the guide-book). In front of these idols burned butter-candles in their massive egg-cup-shaped candlesticks of solid gold, to protect which valuables heavy iron chain curtains hung padlocked down in front. Nearly all of these images had been "self-created," or miraculously transported.

[1] See also Rockhill, *loc. cit.*

[2] Reproduced in my *Lamaism*, p. 302, which compare with plan on p. 365 here; and there is no history of its being rebuilt since then.

[3] One of these was the canonised builder of the Iron Bridge over the Tsangpo.

GOLDEN ROOF OF LHASA CATHEDRAL.

THE HOLY OF HOLIES.

Note the flame of lamps on the altar shining through the chain curtain.

LHAMO, THE SHE-DEVIL.

The "Holy of Holies" (H in plan) looked the most unholy of all (see photo here). Before it a knot of close-shaven priests keep jealous guard perpetually. Here the central image is supposed to represent the "Master" Sakya when a youthful prince of sixteen in his home at Kapilavastu,[1] and to have been brought from Peking by the princess who married King Srongtsan, the founder of this temple. It is, however, a repellent image, about a man's size, seated with goggle eyes and coarse, sensual face, and is of very rude workmanship. So inferior is it to anything that I have seen in China, and so unlike in feature any type of Buddha's image there, that I doubt the story of its foreign origin.[2] Nor does it resemble any Indian ones, nor have I seen anything so uncouth in Buddha's images in Burma, Ceylon, or Japan. It is thickly encrusted with jewels, the accumulated pious offerings of the faithful throughout Central Asia for centuries; its diadem, crown, canopy and throne are covered with great chunks of rough uncut precious stones. All its ornaments, with the exception of two golden dragon standards presented from Peking (similar to those in photo, p. 400, where the image in the gloom on the left resembles that of "The Master"), are of the crudest barbaric kind, unredeemed by any artistic qualities. Even the massive candle- or lamp-stands of solid gold on its altar are as coarsely worked as common brass. Two of the smaller candlesticks were the offerings of the monks and people of Bhotan, and placed here by Ugyen Kazi (see photo, p. 84) two years previously when he brought that letter from the Indian Government to the Dalai Lama.[3] Altogether as seen through the iron-ringed netting (see photo),

1 The lost site of which was discovered by me in the Nepal jungles.

2 It is said by the Chinese to have been cast by a Chinaman from Tsolang (Rockhill, *loc. cit.*, p. 263); but the first Dalai Lama ascribed to it an Indian origin, in his guide-book.

3 See p. 50.

in the lurid light and suffocating atmosphere of the smoky rancid-butter lamps, it seemed more like a foul felon in his prison, or a glaring demon in a web of chains, than an effigy of the pure and simple Buddha. It only wanted the orgies of some bloody sacrifices to complete the likeness to the she-devil Kali, and her image, too, was found upstairs presently.

From this revolting and bizarre spectacle of barbaric idolatry we hurried on through the rest of the dark passages, and, completing the circle, ascended the staircase to see the almost equally famous shrine of Kali, called the "Great Queen,"[1] and so dreaded that her name is seldom spoken, and then only with bated breath. In one room she is depicted as a fury in even more repulsive form than her Indian sister. She is made to be a hideous black monster clad in the skins of dead men and riding on a fawn-coloured mule, eating brains from a human skull, and dangling from her dress is the mystic domino of fate containing the full six black points; and as the goddess of disease, battle and death, she is surrounded by hideous masks with great tusks and by all sorts of weapons—antediluvian battle-axes, spears, bows and arrows, chain armour, swords of every shape, and muskets, a collection which gives her shrine the character of an armoury. Libations of barley beer under the euphemistic title of "golden beverage" (*Ser kyem*) are offered to her in human skulls set upon a tripod of miniature skulls. Her black colour is held not only to symbolise death, but profundity and black magic, like the black Egyptian Isis and the Black Virgin of Middle Age Europe.

In the adjoining chapel is a pleasing golden effigy of her in her mild mood in the form of a handsome queen, about life size, richly inlaid with turquoise and pearls, and clothed in silks and adorned with necklaces. In this chapel, as well as in the adjoining

[1] Lhamo Mag-jor Gyăl-mo.

one of the she-devil, tame mice ran unmolested over the floor, feeding on the cake and grain offerings, under the altar and amongst the dress of the image, and up and down the bodies of the monks who were chanting her litany, and were said to be transmigrated nuns and monks; these attendants, however, of this disease-giving goddess, it seems to me, may represent the mouse which is constantly figured with Smintheus Apollo when he showered the darts of pestilence amongst the Greeks, and which has been regarded by some as symbolic of the rat as a diffusive agent of the plague.

The roof, to which we now ascended, is only some 25 feet above the ground—flat, like the rest of the houses in the town. It has no cupola or dome, but from three of its borders rise the three so-called "golden" pavilions of Chinese pagoda shape. This nearer inspection showed that they were only copper gilt, however, and that the eaves were richly ornamented with embossed plates (see photo, p. 368).

On the way down to the door, the same by which we entered, we had to run the gauntlet of a whole galaxy of ugly gods, and realised as never before what a debased, thorough-paced idolatry Lamaism has become.

In the large market square round to the south were the great copper tea-cauldrons (see photo, p. 377),[1] for infusing the tea for the 20,000 monks at the great New Year's festival when the Dalai Lama proceeds to this temple in state with a procession of all his staff. The tea is part of the subsidy of several hundred tons supplied every year to the Lamas by the Emperor of China. On this side of the temple in the centre of

[1] They measure about 9 feet in diameter and 3 feet in depth. They are lifted on to a masonry fire-place, and planks are laid across so that the cooks can stir up the contents and ladle out the tea, soup, or rice, which is boiled therein.

the city are also the great council chamber (see photo, p. 341), the magistrates' court, and treasury said to contain vast stores of gold and precious stones.

The great yellow-cap monasteries of Sera and Däpung were visited by some of us. They are the two largest in Tibet, and were founded about 500 years ago, and their abbot, as we have seen, takes a leading part in the government of the country.

Sera, which receives its name from a "hedge of wild roses" which used to enclose it, is situated, like Däpung, at the foot of the mountains, and lies on the northern border of the Lhasa plain some 2 miles from the city (see plan, p. 330). This is the monastery which harboured the Japanese priest, Kawaguchi, three years ago, and for which several of the monks had been punished, though the convent refused to comply with the Dalai Lama's demand to deliver up their abbot as well. As the abbot had been notified that we were coming, his staff were ready at the gates (see photo opposite) to receive us, including the two proctors wearing the crested yellow cap like a Roman helmet, and each attended by a mace-bearer carrying elaborately embossed square iron rods (see photo) and a lictor with a chastising rod. It has a population of nearly 6000 monks. Passing through the gate, we found the monastery was quite a little town of well-built and neatly white-washed stone houses with regular streets and lanes, some of which recalled those of Malta (see photo, p. 373).

It is a monastic university, and consists of three colleges, or Ta-ts'ang,[1] one for the elementary teaching of the doctrine and ritual—this is the largest—another for friars who go about itinerating over the country, and the most select and smallest, the esoteric and mystical. All of these meet daily in the great Assembly Hall, which provides a joint temple for the

[1] Literally, "Residence of the Learners."

OUTSIDE THE GATES OF SERA MONASTERY.
Lamas and acolytes going to Lhasa.

THE TWO PROCTORS OF SERA WITH MACES AND LICTORS.
View inside the gate.

LANE IN SERA MONASTERY.

CHIEF TEMPLE IN SERA MONASTERY.

whole community. This is a very fine building (see photo, here), much larger than the Gyantsé temple. At one side of the door was a proclamation of the Dalai Lama in a roofed-in enclosure. The document was very artistically illuminated, with the celestial dog of China bearing the seal on a cushion (see photo, p. 413). In the verandah was a manuscript copy in Chinese, Mongolian, and Tibetan, of the hymn in praise of Potala which is carved on the verandah of the Lhasa "cathedral." The temple was of the usual kind already described, the walls covered with brilliant parti-coloured frescoes that outvied the most vivid patchwork quilts, whilst scrolls hung from the balconies and pillars. As service was going on, I was fortunate to secure a photograph of the ceremony (see photo, p. 401). On the roof of this temple is a summer house of the Dalai Lama, but the present Dalai, who was affiliated to the Däpung monastery, never resides in this one, but sometimes in the former. We then were shown over the several colleges, and some of the dormitories and kitchens, which were all fairly tidy and clean. Hundreds of the younger monks peeped from the windows and scampered round to corners to get a view; but everybody was very respectful and apparently friendly, and we were pressed to take tea, cake, and sweetmeats several times. The miraculous thunderbolt —a dumb-bell-like *Dorjê* (see cover)*—which is placed on the heads of pilgrims as a charm, at an annual festival here, was alleged by the Lamas to be at Potala, where it is kept locked up and only lent for use here for a few days during the New Year's festival. I got one of the most learned of these Sera monks to come to me daily to supply me with information on a variety of points, and found him to be an exceptionally well-educated man with intellectual powers of no mean order.

None of the Lamas teach the laity as in Burma and other Buddhist countries, nor do they preach to the

* On page i of the present edition.

people, but keep all their learning to themselves; the laity are thus forced to have their own schools with lay teachers. The pupils in the schools, monastic as well as lay, use as slates, slabs of black painted wood, dusted over with white chalk, on which surface the writing is done with a style. Some of the more accomplished Lamas are trained as painters, and others in caligraphy, embroidery, carving, etc.: whilst the more stupid ones are made to do the out-of-doors drudgery of hewing wood, drawing water, ploughing and harvesting. All pure Tibetans and Mongols may enter the Order, except the butcher outcastes and the half-breed progeny of foreigners who have married Tibetan wives. The young Lama then rises through ability or influence, but the appointment of abbot of the larger monasteries must be approved by the Amban.

On leaving this monastery, it was rather incongruous to find just outside the gate of a Buddhist convent a large butcher's bazaar, with the monks buying and carrying off pieces of flesh-meat. For animal flesh is a staple diet with the monks of Tibet (excepting the few who have taken the higher vows). The Lamas evade the Buddhist prohibition to take life, for this purpose, by employing the butchers to do it for them, whilst they assign to the butchers for doing this the position of outcastes, and do not permit any of them to enter the Order. When no butchers are available, it is usual for the Lamaist to drive the cattle over a precipice, or make the beast strangle itself.

The great monastic university of Däpung (pp. 328 and 329) was generally similar to Sera, but had four colleges, and the summer residence of the Dalai Lama, called the "Paradise Palace," a fine and commodious block of buildings, in which His Holiness spends a few weeks every year, as he is nominally a monk of this Lamasery. Below this monastery was a printing establishment. The four royal monasteries or "*Lings*,"[1] which used to supply the Regents who ruled during the minorities of the Dalai Lamas, are of the same general character as a section of the larger monasteries, but are more elaborately decorated, as they all have at various times been the residences of political prelates.

The temple of Ramoché, or the "Small Jo-k'ang," is attributed to the Chinese wife of the great King Srongtsan, and like the "cathedral" has a gilt roof and iron-ringed chains in front of its chief image; but it is in a very neglected and almost ruinous condition.

Following the holy "Circular Road" (see plan, p. 330) from here to the Temple of Medicine, we met, coming the other way, in the lucky direction, a straggling line of pilgrims and the devout of Lhasa, twirling their prayer-wheels and counting their beads. The majority are old and decrepit women, from which it might perhaps be inferred that the people do not think much of the next world until they are about to leave this one.

Only two or three were seen progressing by measuring their length on the ground by consecutive prostrations. Such zealots, who are generally of the type of the besotted mendicant "fakirs" of India, are said to make the circuit three, and even seven times, thus making over 40,000 prostrations, as the Circular Road is about 6 miles in circuit.

In a fine grove of grand old trees at the north corner of Potala hill, we passed the temple of the King of the Dragons on its islet, in a pool in whose abysmal depths he holds his court. He seems to be the same who is worshipped in the subterranean vault in the "cathedral," and here I secured a photograph of the Dalai Lama's elephant, which is dedicated to this Dragon and is considered a mascot.[2] The attendant

[1] Tängyä Ling, Kundä Ling, Tsemcho'g Ling, Tsamo Ling.

[2] See footnote, p. 342.

said that young dragons were to be seen in the water of the pool, but the animals he pointed out to me were newts or salamanders.

The Temple of Medicine, as seen from the north, crowns the summit of a high rocky pinnacle (see accompanying sketch), the further side of which sweeps almost sheer down to the river that laps its base; and here on the river-bank the face of the great limestone cliff is covered all over with thousands of brilliantly painted rock-sculptures of Buddhas and other divinities, forming a marvellous piece of varied colour. I was fortunate enough to have with me the materials for "colour photography," by which I secured photographs of this wonderful-hued cliff direct from Nature, and I am glad to be able to present here the result (see colour print, p. 424).* This striking picture-gallery of coloured bas-reliefs was evidently begun by the first Grand Lama, Lobzang, as it bears an inscription of his in its centre, and it is still being added to; a scaffolding was to be seen at one end where new images were being chiselled out of the rock. A painter resides in a hut below, who is constantly engaged in keeping the colours in repair. The soft limestone rock here is esteemed sacred and is scraped away by pilgrims to be swallowed or treasured as a talisman; the attendant offered me some for this purpose.

The high priest of the Temple of Medicine was waiting by appointment to receive our party of medical officers, and led us into the main room of the temple where the central image was appropriately "The Healing Buddha," the Tibetan Æsculapius, as man values health next to life, and Buddha in the Tibetan pantheon is made to take care of the body as well as the soul. As the god of Physicians, he is portrayed in the usual seated form of that saint, but holding a blue lapis lazuli bowl with a pomegranate-like drug in it. His

* In black and white in the present edition.

TEMPLE OF MEDICINE.

TEA CAULDRONS IN GREAT SQUARE, LHASA.

PHYSICIAN FEELING THE THREE PULSES.

image was surrounded by four others, which appeared to be canonised famous physicians.

This temple carried us back to the early ages of the Greeks when Medicine had its home in the sacred shrines. Here the Lamas combine the duties of doctor of the body with those of priest. At present there are fifty-four priests and three teachers. This institution was founded two and a half centuries ago by the Viceroy Sangyä (the same who concealed the death of the first Dalai Lama), who compiled for its use a text-book called "The Blue Jewel," with reference to the jewelled bowl which the Healing Buddha holds in his hands, and endowed the temple, and arranged that the sixty-four large monasteries of Tibet should each send hither one pupil.

The treatment of disease, though based in some measure upon a judicious use of the commoner simple drugs of the country, is, as was inevitable amongst so superstitious a people, saturated with absurdity. The Lamas follow the ancient Romans and Arabs in employing such things as fox's liver and hot blood. They believe that all poisons are neutralised and rendered innocuous when placed upon vessels of mussel shells or mother-of-pearl, hence such vessels are used in the preparation of some of their mixtures as well as by the rich when taking their draughts. They teach a crude sort of anatomy, not by dissection, but by means of a fantastic chart of the body ruled into minute squares in which the positions of the internal organs are marked. Curiously, they make the heart of a woman to beat in the middle of the chest, though that of a man is on the left; and they imagine that the red blood circulates on the right side of the body and the yellow bile on the left, and it is by feeling the six pulses on the wrists, the three red on the right and the three yellow on the left, that they are chiefly able to diagnose the malady, each pulse being supposed to come from a different organ. To show

how the pulses were felt a priest operated on another (see photo here), and as he sat down he amused us immensely by assuming a very superior knowing manner that must inspire his patients with a good deal of confidence, and contribute to many cures by "faith healing." I asked him to examine the pulse of one of us, and after much deliberation he pronounced him to be suffering from disease of the right kidney, as the pulse from that organ was weak.

Both the sick themselves and the Lama physicians rely more on the efficacy of prayers than on the pharmacopœia for recovery. Lamas are employed to read out lengthy litanies and offer sacrifice to the devils of disease. For this work a priest seldom receives more than fivepence (one silver *tangka*) for a full day's employment, which is the highest wage ever given to any workman.

The curriculum takes about eight years to master, and consists chiefly of committing chapters to memory. Very few of the priests are passed as proficient, and those who are, as well as those who fail, still remain residents of the temple, and never leave it for other towns or monasteries in the provinces, its learning being restricted to Lhasa. The sick poor are not attended, only those who can pay, and none come here for treatment; the priests visit the sick only when sent for. The school has no regular test examination for proficiency, and no certificate or diploma, so that it is neither a college as we understand it, nor an hospital.

Their chief text-book treats of the various common diseases, in quite a systematic manner, under the heads of symptoms, prognosis, and treatment; and has evidently been derived in part from Chinese and Indian sources. Their surgery naturally is of the most primitive kind; they seemed to have no instruments beyond the actual cautery, bleeding lancet, and a cupping horn. They were much impressed with Western surgery as seen in the dispensary opened at Lhasa by Dr Walton, and especially with the operation for cataract, and begged for a set of the instruments. As it would have been unsafe to give these without the necessary instruction, I persuaded one of the most intelligent priests to come with us back to Calcutta to be taught the Western methods of treatment in the Medical College, and he willingly consented, but was afterwards prevented coming by his senior Lamas.

I enquired especially about the treatment for smallpox, as it is one of the most deadly diseases in Tibet. Although the Chinese doctors in Lhasa employ inoculation for its prevention, the Tibetans trust to camphor with a few other aromatics and charms, and the priest wound up his account by saying, "and doing so you never get smallpox." As, however, both the high priest and his staff were badly pitted with the marks of that affection, I asked why they had not themselves avoided catching the disease by their vaunted method of prevention, to which impeachment they merely smiled. I enquired whether the Dalai Lama had escaped the bad epidemic of 1900, and they replied that he had not, but had nearly died of it, and is now deeply pitted by this disease—a flagrant comment on the boasted divinity of this God-in-the-flesh.

CHAPTER XVIII.

ORACLES AND SORCERERS.

"*That mendicant does right to whom omens, planetary influences, dreams and signs are things abolished; he is free from all their evils.*"—BUDDHA'S SERMONS.

THE craving to pry into the future, the desire to see behind the Known, is a widespread human frailty; but few attempt to gratify it except those primitive folk who have not yet realised the limitations of their powers over Nature. Every Tibetan believes as implicitly in the oracle as a guide in his daily affairs as ever did the ancient Greeks and Romans. He believes that the hermits in the mountains, and the monks in their cloisters can become adepts in the black art and foretell the future, banish delight, stay the storm, exorcise devils, raise spirits from the dead and conjure up to their assistance the demons of darkness. Many of the necromantic performances of the professional wizards recall the scene of the witches' cauldron in Macbeth. The people put much faith in astrology, imagining that Nature and the planets exercise direct and potent influence upon man's welfare, and that their evil effects are only to be foreseen and counteracted by the priests, a considerable proportion of whom become professional astrologers and prescribe ostensibly for the "benefit" of the laymen a large amount of costly ritual by which exactions from the laity the monasteries derive their chief means of livelihood.

The oracular forms of divination are, however, not dependent on astrology, but on demoniacal "possession," and are practised by the professional oracles and wizards in the capital, who are survivals of the old pre-Buddhist religion of the country with its black-hatted devil-dancers. These sorcerers dress up in the fantastic equipment of the old religion, with flags and tufts of wool on their head-dress, or with a ponderous metal cap, and a dragon coat with a breastplate, and working themselves up into a frenzy, dance, crying and howling, till they fall down on a seat "possessed," and then deliver an oracular reply. They have no literature, and utter their sayings orally. The leading oracles in Lhasa are the Nächung and the Karmashar.

The chief Oracle is attached to the principal state monastery, Däpung. For, notwithstanding its un-Buddhistic character, this gross form of heathen sorcery was so deeply rooted in the minds of the people that that crafty ruler, the first Dalai Lama, brought it into the order of the Lamas. In doing this, he was doubtless actuated, as were the Roman governors, by the obvious political advantages of having so powerful an instrument for the government service entirely under the control of the priests. The chief Soothsayer was accordingly admitted into the brotherhood, but not being a Buddhist he could not be permitted to reside within the sacred precincts, but was accommodated outside. The one attached to Däpung lives in a fine grove below that Lamasery, in what was originally a small hermitage or "Nächung," from which he takes his name. He is supposed to be possessed by the spirit of the great Mongolian King of the Demons, "The White *Pe*" (see photo, p. 383), who had been bound by the spells of the wizard St. Padma (see page 115) to guard the treasury of the first Lama monastery in Tibet, at Samyä, where he became incarnated, and marrying, continued to be manifested in his lineal earthly descendants until his transfer to Däpung, when he was forced to become celibate, thus leaving the appointment of his successor in the hands of the Grand Lama. His transfer was represented as miraculous, and is associated with the legend of a tree-spirit.[1]

The present Nächung high priest is a young man of twenty-two, and was believed to be in hiding in his temple when we went there. He is given a retinue of a hundred yellow-hatted monks, and a magnificent little temple with a palatial residence for himself and them. The golden roof of the Chinese pavilion, on its upper storey, is as fine as that of the "cathedral."

The monks received us with smiling affability and led us over the place. The buildings are arranged round a paved courtyard in which, beside a small chorten, a pair of incense kilns scented the air with their fumes. On two sides run two small galleries supported by red painted pillars on which were hung bits of ancient armour, chain and steel helmets and coats, bows, arrows, leather quivers and spears, and the walls are frescoed with cabalistic signs and monsters, with the heads of birds and beasts destroying the enemies of Lamaism. The principal title of this Chief Soothsayer is "Defender of the Faith [Lamaist];" and when he is approached for an augury he is addressed as: "To the exalted footstool, composed of the dead bodies of the infidels, on which rest the feet of the Great Defender

[1] The legend runs:—"A man in Lhasa was found to be possessed by the demon king, 'The white *Pe*,' and was seized and shut up in a box and thrown into the Kyi river. Now the Abbot of Däpung had prophesied the previous day: a box will float down the river, go, find it and seize it. The search party found the box and brought it to the spot where the Nächung oracle now is, and here they opened it, when lo! a great flame of fire came out and disappeared into a tree, and the dead body of a man was found in the box. By the prayers of the abbot the spirit consented to return to the body, and the resuscitated corpse had a small dwelling built for him at that spot where the identical tree, a gnarled old willow, is still pointed out."

THE STATE ORACLE, NÄCHUNG.

PICTURE OF THE MAGICIAN SPIRIT OF THE STATE ORACLE—(*Pekar*).

of Religion, the chief incarnation of the Almighty Conqueror of the Enemies in the three Worlds, the Lamp of Wisdom."

A broad flight of stairs leads up to the temple on the left, whilst overhead innumerable flags and streamers printed with spells droop from ropes stretching across the courtyard, and suggest washing-day on board ship (see photo here).

The temple stair is flanked by two great lions in tin, of Chinese pattern. The sanctuary itself is embellished with finer paintings and frescoes than any we had yet seen, and it was scrupulously clean. The verandah, about 50 feet long and 12 feet wide, was especially full of bright colour, and revealed on closer inspection the same theme, the myrmidons of the Devil King triumphing over the enemies of the Lamas. The floor was a smooth concrete of small stones, so highly polished as to reflect the painted frescoes bordered by skulls, cornices, and the scroll work of the massive doors.

The interior of the outer temple was of the usual kind; the frescoed walls and red pillars were hung round with silk banners, and Kakemono scrolls, to which warlike armour was here added. At the further end, between two large altars with six colossal figures, a brass gateway gave entry into the oracle-chamber, a small dark room, in the recess of which, behind a table altar on which burned the sacred fire, stood dimly the chair of the great Sorcerer covered with silk cushions, and upon it lay his robes and accoutrements, the great sword on the left, the magic breastplate, and his great brass cap loaded with gold, and covered by necklaces of precious stones (see photo, p. 386).

The demon who "possesses" the high priest is figured as that of a ferocious white monster enveloped in flames. It has three heads, six hands wielding weapons, and rides a white lion, attended by the Tibetan King of

Battle in chain armour, and by two harpies riding on a wild yak and a deer, whilst over its head are yellow-hatted Lamas. The high priest himself, we found, had escaped a few days before with the Dalai Lama, with whom he is on terms of great intimacy, as his oracular deliverances form an important factor in politics. It is he who indicates the place where a new incarnation of the Dalai Lama should be searched for on the death of the latter. His utterances, of which I have seen several, are usually couched in allegory with quite an oracular ring about them :—

The meek sheep should not try to imitate a furious bull. [A warning to an ambitious courtier.]

Even the nibbling rabbit can gorge itself to death. [Exhorting an official to give up peculation or he will come to grief.]

Father wolf secures the sweet flesh while sister fox gets the blame. [A warning that slyness does not pay.]

Be merciful to your riding horse. [Equivalent to our proverb of the goose and the golden eggs.]

There is no hope of fruit from a tree which has been robbed of its flowers by the frost. [Reply regarding some project.]

Though a stream has no claws it yet can dig a hole in the ground. [To reassure an aspirant.]

Regarding the Mission to Khambajong last year, this Oracle when asked whether it would reach Lhasa, declared that a British Mission would eventually come to Lhasa, not that one, however, but a larger; whilst the other, the Karmashar Oracle, replied more guardedly: "The English are like bubbles on water, here to-day, away to-morrow."

In the upper storey above the devil's temple the rooms were arranged for the worship of the Buddhas. The dormitories of the monks are beyond the temple further to the right, whilst the augur's chambers are in a neat little cottage in a high-walled garden in the grove to the north, in which grow some dwarf bamboos and a variety of pines and imported shrubs, and masses of gaudy hollyhocks, asters, and nasturtiums. The three rooms have polished wooden floors, and their neat lacquered furniture, refined taste, and cleanness suggested a dainty house in Japan, rather than one in inartistic Tibet. And as we came away the friendly monks presented us with some fine moss roses and other flowers.

The Karmashar Magician in the town is the oracle chiefly consulted by the common people, though he is also associated with Sera monastery, which he visits every autumn, and makes an augury for the current year which is placarded up on the walls of that monastery. As this year's augury referred to the British expedition, I have extracted some of its rather incoherent passages:

"I, the Devil, warned you from the beginning of the male iron-mouse year [1900 A.D.[1]] that the rays of the Sun [that is the Dalai Lama] are hidden by smoke, [but] if the servants be careful the vows will be preserved. The wise Tibetans [nevertheless] the hawk and the Hor tribe deemed my Devil's sayings as bubbles. But if the enemies who have come to our front be cleared away like the darkness of ignorance by wisdom, understanding, and true sense, the three jewels of the crown [will remain]. Watch for the general good of the world, and the religion. The darkness of the Devils will be clear in the sheep-year [1907 A.D.].

"*Hri!* At the altar of the great tutelary, let me see the things which are going to happen! I see (1) A magic circle; (2) A banner with a yellow top ornament; (3) A banner with a red top; (4) Cymbals; (5) A flag on a sheep's horn; (6) A bundle of tents; (7) One shoe; (8) A blanket tied with ropes; (9) A sword; (10) A heart on a goat's head; (11) Black peas, Indian grains; and two-thirds raw flesh. This prophecy is given by me, the doctrine holder, 'The Bird-headed One,' at the curdled milk festival held at Sera on the thirtieth day of the sixth month of the wood-dragon year."

[1] See Appendix I., p. 450.

This augury like a Pharaoh's dream is not, however, explained by the sorcerer until after the year has passed to which it relates; but several Lamas whom I asked to interpret it said that they understood it to mean that in the current year the chief actors and events would be: (1) The order of the Lamas; (2) The Dalai Lama; (3) The Tashilhumpo Grand Lama; (4) Notoriety or fame; (5) There will be war in the sheep-year [1907 A.D.]; (6) Many will encamp; (7) Not travel much; (8) Many dead bodies; (9) War; (10) Hearts out of place; (11) Plenty crops.

On my visit to the home of the Karmashar Oracle, I found that auguries were given every day, and several times a day if necessary, and some people were coming out who had been consulting the Seer. The temple is small, hung round with masks of devils and a large drum, the operator on which is the only assistant whom this soothsayer has. The Oracle chamber is a dark inner room, in the gloom of which, facing the door, the magician sits on a cushioned chair, with a heavy conical hat (see photo here) covered with jewels, breastplate on, shod in long Chinese boots, and wearing a sword by his side. I was fortunate to get a photograph of an applicant in the act of receiving a reply from the Oracle, which embodied some pithy and shrewd common-sense.

Before I left, the priest looked at me piercingly for an instant, and asked, "What is your age?" On my replying, he promptly retorted, "No! You are one year more; you are . . . ." Then I remembered that a few days before I had passed my birthday and had actually reached the exact age which he thus disclosed. With this oracular parting shot he vanished from our view into the gloom of his temple.

RECEIVING AN ORACLE.
At the Karmashar Magician's temple.

CHAPTER XIX.

THE PRIEST-GOD AND HIS PALACE.

As the young priest-god had fled with his evil genius, Dorjieff, we were able to penetrate into the recesses of his sealed palace, to his private apartments, and to the steps of his throne, around which had been woven a web of mystery and romance.

The mystery which enshrouded his origin is now unveiled, and we have seen how he became adored, as an earthly manifestation of the Divine Being, by about four million people. His spiritual influence outside Tibet only radiates to a few of the small Himalayan States where there are Lamas, and to Mongolia, although the latter has a Grand Lama of its own at Urga, the capital; it extends thus only over a very small fraction of the Buddhist world. For he is in no way recognised as the head of their Church by the Buddhists of Burma, Ceylon, Siam, China,[1] and Japan; but on the contrary, is looked upon by them as impure and extravagantly unorthodox, not so much on account of any doctrinal difference as because under his rule the ascetic system of Buddha has been carried to its most absurd excesses.

His superb palace that proudly crowns Potala Hill is well adapted for keeping up the illusion of his divinity. The sight of its fascinating piles towering

[1] The Lama temples at Peking and a few other towns in China are in the hands of Tibetan and Mongolian priests, not Chinese Buddhists, who profess a less impure form of the faith.

into the sky, with its golden roofs flashing from afar above the beautiful woods and surrounding hills, must strike awe and veneration into the hearts of the pilgrims, as they arrive from the barren deserts of the uplands, and it must seem to them to be, indeed, an earthly paradise.

On this building the Tibetans have lavished their utmost skill (see my photograph of it by the colour process, p. I).* It consists of a cluster of many residences, temples, tombs, reception and other rooms erected at different times. The palace of the old kings of Tibet built by the warlike Srongtsan, who founded Lhasa in the seventh century A.D., seems to be represented by the group of white buildings at the south-west corner (see plan of Lhasa); and doubtless gave it the fortified character, which it still retains. The great central block dominating the others, and called by reason of its purply-crimson colour, the "Red Palace," was built by the first Dalai Lama after usurping the temporal power, and was extended by his son, the Regent Sangyä, who did much for the welfare of the country, codifying the civil laws[1] and in other ways, in addition to founding the Temple of Medicine. The Capuchin missionaries who were his contemporaries in Lhasa spoke of him respectfully as "vir ingenii sagacissimi."[2] The "Red Palace" contains all the great temples, throne-rooms, and relic-shrines of former Grand Lamas, and on its roof stand the golden Chinese pavilions which form its glittering landmark.

Its hill is called "Potala," after the name of a rocky hill overlooking the harbour at Cape Komorin, on the extreme tip of the Indian continent, which the Indians fancied was the end of the world, and on which was placed the mythical abode of the Buddhist God of Mercy, which the Lamas identified with the Com-

[1] Dang-shel melong *g*nyer *g*chig-pa.

[2] Giorgi, p. 329.

* In black and white in the present edition.

GROUNDS OF POTALA PALACE.

THE VATICAN OF TIBET.
Potala Palace from the north-west.

NORTH ENTRANCE OF RED PALACE.

NORTH GATE OF POTALA PALACE.

passionate Spirit of the Mountains that the Dalai Lama alleged had become incarnate in himself.

On nearer approach, the castle of the Tibetan Pope is seen to be a great fort about a mile in circumference, surrounded by a loopholed wall on three sides, and on the other—the northern—defended by the precipitous crags whence the buildings sweep up in a bold scarp. This northern side is pierced by a gateway, through which we entered. We rode more than half-way up the hill to the great circular bastion which from below suggests the Vatican (see photo here). At this point, the so-called "Horse Stage," we found ourselves at the foot of a long flight of stairs, as here it is necessary to dismount. Here we were met by the Great Chamberlain (see photo, p. 430, in which he stands next to the General), also a Grand Councillor (to the extreme left in the same photo). A zigzag of over a hundred steep steps took us under the dark crimson walls of the "Red Palace," which loomed threateningly above us. The entrance gateway was rather mean, and screened by a torn curtain (see photo, p. 389); it was for those who had the private *entrée*, and not the usual pilgrims' entrance. The paved narrow court inside was lined by guards' quarters and store-rooms several storeys high, and through a lane of these buildings, where we were watched by supercilious groups of officials in yellow- and cherry-coloured uniforms, we turned to the left to the north door of the castle (photo, p. 389), now guarded by some British and Indian soldiers of our escort, some of whom also accompanied us on our exploration of the interior.

The outside of the palace is substantially built of roughly hewn stone, and pierced by many windows, most of which were fitted with sunshades suggesting the Italian pattern.

Inside was a labyrinth of gloomy narrow passages

and low-ceilinged corridors, as in a mediæval castle in Europe. To the left, along a dark corridor lit by lamps and torches, was the New Throne Room, a spacious large hall about 20 yards each way, with a surrounding gallery, and lit by a skylight, its beams and walls finely picked out in pleasing bright colours and frescoes. Along its northern wall behind the throne, which was an open simple frame-work, were displayed under iron gratings many of the treasures and votive offerings of the pilgrims, whilst above it hung horizontally like a great sign-board a complimentary "card" presented by the last Chinese Emperor, Tungchi (1862-1875 A.D.), bearing the following inscription in Chinese and Tibetan :

> "The best Saviour [may his] blessed light pervade all directions."[1]

The Old Throne Room is to the west of this one, nearer the entrance door, through more dark corridors. It is of similar appearance to the other, and here Buddha's vice-regent, seated as in frontispiece, holds his court and blesses by his touch the pilgrims who throng hither to worship him. Only the heads of the Lamas and of the higher classes are directly touched by His Holiness' hand; for the great unwashed he uses a tassel at the end of a sceptre. This apartment had been reported to contain a picture of the Emperor Chenlung, but it was not here at our visit. The throne of the Living Buddha, "The Precious Victor of Death," is placed at the western end, in front of the foot of the colossal mausoleum called "The Ornament of the World,[2] enshrining the bodily relics of his predecessor

[1] This is the translation of the Tibetan inscription : "*h*drin *m*ch'og *h*p'rin las 'od kyi p'yogs kun Kyab." The Chinese inscription, Mr Wilton informs me, has several meanings, of which one can be generally similar to the above Tibetan rendering.

[2] Dsamling gyän.

and former "embodiment," the first Dalai and founder of the priest-kingship. The throne is a simple daïs raised about 3 feet from the ground, open in front for a seat of fine cushions, and surrounded on the other three sides with a framework of thin batons. It was noteworthy that above the supporting lion insignia of "Sakya, the Lion," the plinth of the seat was ornamented with the simple diaper-worked flowers like marguerites which decorate the ancient marble seat of the Master at Buddh Gaya under the fig-tree where he first became "Enlightened."

The base of the great relic shrine behind the throne is richly adorned with gold and inlaid with precious stones, and the steps of its plinths are used as altars for the countless votive-offerings of princes for ages, and wreaths of pearls and other jewelled necklaces hang from its upper structure, which can be seen towering up some 40 feet overhead. To see the top of this monument we followed the pilgrim track up a maze of seemingly never-ending terraces of dark stairs and corridors, where we longed for a string to guide us, and had to keep in close touch with each other to avoid losing our way. At last we emerged under the top storey into a well-lighted court, around which ran pillared galleries with stately corridors (see photo, p. 392), leading from the residential chambers of the Grand Lama to the Chapel Royal, and to the top of the relic shrines under the four golden pavilions which mark their position on the roof. In these corridors were posted stately court attendants, and Lamas, with quite the dignified bearing of courtiers, moving softly to and fro on the thick carpeted floors.

The gorgeousness and finish of the decorations here surpassed any we had yet seen, and were worthy of the royal residence of the ruler of the destinies of a people. Colonnades of crimson pillars support elaborately carved beams, and panelled ceilings embellished with a brilliant mosaic of pleasingly blended hues and frescoes painted with the delicate detail of miniatures on ivory. The richness of the colouring, and the lavishly elaborate golden scroll-work on the massive doors, recall the temples of Nikko. Painting in Tibet is decorative rather than artistic, as we understand the term, for it aims at beautifying the surface with pigments, and employs mostly rich and intense hues, the effect of which is heightened by a free use of gold, silvery white, and dark blue, whilst the figures are always in stiff conventional attitudes without perspective, and clearly based on Chinese models. In their chromatic composition the Tibetans use freely, side by side, the "primary" red, blue and gold with green also, and less often the other "secondaries," the purple and orange; yet in the subdued light of the interiors there is seldom an unpleasant harshness of colouring and contrasts.

The finest of these glorified doors are opened to give pilgrims a glimpse of the relic-shrines of the early Grand Lamas, and the finest of all these glimpses is that of the gorgeously jewelled top of the first Dalai Lama's tomb (see photo, p. 396). This tomb,[1] as we have seen, is of colossal dimensions, and springs from the throne-room below; but all the others, although of the same *chorten*-like model (see figure, page 231, and photo, p. 208), spring from the floor of the room on the corridor on which we were now standing. Although there are three other sets of tomb chambers, only two are occupied, that next the great Dalai's being empty, whilst the others enshrine the bodies of the third and fourth succeeding Dalai Lamas. The reason for the absence of the second Dalai is, as will be remembered (p. 32), that that

[1] Erected by the Regent Sangyä over two centuries ago, and said to have been sacked of its ornaments by the Jungar Tartars a few years later. See pp. 33, 187 footnote, and Appendix V., p. 468.

CORRIDOR IN GRAND LAMA'S PALACE, POTALA.

THE GRAND LAMA'S PROMENADE (on the Roof of Potala Palace).

The Golden pavilion on the left crowns the Mausoleum of the first Dalai Lama, and the sunken court is the skylight of the old throne-room.

young reprobate, born of vicious parents, was deposed and murdered on account of his dissolute conduct, and his body thus appears to have been dishonoured by exclusion from the royal tomb. None of the four subsequent Grand Lamas has any relic-shrine here, nor any of the four who preceded the first Dalai, and who were unpossessed of temporal power; thus Nagwang, the first Pope King, and inventor of the myths of the divinity of the Dalai, still dominates the whole in death.

Opening from these beautiful corridors is the Chapel Royal, for Potala is a monastery as well as a palace, and accommodates 500 monks, of which the Dalai Lama himself is the abbot, and clad in ordinary Lama's robes conducts here the church services. The chapel has the same general appearance and arrangement as the temples already visited and described, but the furnishings, images, and paraphernalia of worship are richer. One of the altars contains a very finely executed image of solid gold of the Lord of Mercy (see photo, p. 400), of whom the Dalai poses as the incarnation. Here the chief duty of the priests is to provide relays for the routine recital of prayers for the long life of His Holiness; and in this service, at the time of our visit, they were droning their chants and sprinkling in front of his image holy water from the mystic vase of ambrosia or deathless nectar, adorned with a stopper topped by a brush of peacocks' feathers. This silver vase was of the usual rough Tibetan make, and not the one which was lately sent him from Paris. [1]

[1] This Paris-made one was described by M. J. Deniker in the *Century Magazine* for February 1904 as follows:—It has roughly the appearance of a candlestick, of which the platter is silver gilt. From this rises the "boumbe," carved from a large piece of coral, and on this, like the flame of a candle, rests an oval of chased leaves in lapis lazuli. In the centre, seated on a lotus flower of white chalcedony, is the figure of the god Amitabha, the "Boundless Light," the emanation of Adi-Buddha, who in Buddhist Lama's

On the flat roof above the temples and relic-shrines is the promenade of the Grand Lama (see photo here), where, surrounded by his satellites, he takes his exercise amidst one of the finest panoramas in the world; and from that lofty perch looks down as a god upon the upturned faces of his worshippers, 500 feet below him, whose muttered chorus of "Hail to the Jewel [Grand Lama] in the Lotus Flower!" (*Om ma-ni pad-me Hung!*) has literally the identical sense of our Pater Noster—Our Father who art in Heaven![1]

In this restful panorama, a vast bird's-eye view of the valley of Lhasa and its noble hills, scarcely a hum from the life below breaks upon the stillness. The plain stretches out as a great land-locked sea, with wavelets of green copses, amongst which peep, like ships cosily at anchor on its bosom, the tops of the "cathedral," the town houses, and the cottages beyond with their smoke curling to the sky, and from its green borders purple capes and promontories shoot boldly up into the dark blue, snow-streaked peaks fading away into soft azure in the distance.

We descended by the great front staircase, the

religion is the source and cause of all things. Amitabha is supposed to be incarnated in the person of Panch'en Rim-po-ch'e, a sort of supplementary Dalai Lama who lives at Tashi-lhumpo, in Southern Tibet. The figure is in coral, and above it on the point of the oval is a moon in chalcedony, a sun in yellow-stone, and a flame of coral, symbolising the radiance of wisdom. On each side of the platter is a silver-gilt Chinese Royal dragon; but these can be detached, and the writer of the article suggests that they are put in or taken out according to whether any representative Chinaman of importance happens or not to be present at the ceremony where the Tse-boum is used. It is a beautiful piece of workmanship, and was entirely the work of Parisian artisans; and so great was the desire to have the symbolisms correct that one of the Dalai Lama's high priests came to Europe to find artists to carry out the design. The large pieces of coral used came from Leghorn, and the high priest went there himself to procure them.

[1] The lotus flower is the symbol of heavenly birth.

outward zigzag of which gives the castle its diamond-shaped band when seen from the front (photo, p. 1). At first we plunged again through a maze of dark corridors, past dungeon-like vaults suggestive of instant chains and torture for anyone who disputed the will of the priestly autocrat in the rooms above. Here is said to be hoarded the wealth of a Government which never issued a budget; and amongst other treasures the golden lottery vase presented by the Chinese Emperor, from which the Amban in great state, surrounded by all the assembled Lama abbots, draws forth with a pair of tongs the name of the new Dalai Lama from amongst slips inscribed with the names of the approved candidates for the new incarnation, on the death of the living Buddha.

Over these vaults, in the luxuriously furnished apartments, in the north-east corner of the "Red Palace" overlooking the town, are the residential rooms of the "Victor of Death," whose present embodiment has spent here twenty-seven out of the twenty-eight years of his life. During his joyless infancy, unbrightened by the society of other children, his mother is permitted to reside for two years in a lower building, in order to prevent contaminating by her presence the holy atmosphere that surrounds her son, as Buddhism gives woman a low place in its system. The father, on the other hand, however poor and low-born he may be (the father of the present one was a wood-cutter), is ennobled and given a palace to reside in, with the Chinese title of "Duke" (*Kung*), and a button and peacock's feather to his hat of the second highest mandarin, and is known to the populace as "The Father of Buddha."

At the age of eight he was ordained as a monk and head of the Church, and at eighteen he seized the reins of State, so that for the past ten years he has been here as absolute an autocrat in his small way as the Tsar.

The government of Tibet is called "The Central Governor" (*Depa zhung*), and nominally consists of a council of four ministers or "Lotus feet [of the throne]" (*Shapé*),[1] of whom three are laymen and one a monk, under the presidency of the Dalai Lama or the Regent. These ministers are appointed by the Amban, who is said to sell the post to the highest bidder. Certainly he did not allow the crafty Chief Secretary to take his place in succession to the genial old Ta Lama, who had been deposed since our arrival in Lhasa, for the reason, so said the Nepalese Consul, that the Secretary had not yet paid the Amban for the appointment. This council, which sits in Lhasa, conducts most of the routine business of the State and appoints the various officers for the districts (see p. 165). Most of the superior ones, including the Jongpöns, are Lhasa men, who are sent for a three years' tour of duty and then return to the capital to give a personal report, on which they are transferred to a new charge. For large and exceptional measures there is summoned a "General Assembly" (*Tsong du*), consisting of a large number of lay and cleric subordinate officials. This Assembly reports its views and decisions to the *Shapés* in council with the Dalai or Regent.[2]

The Pontiff himself is accessible to those who have complaints, and freely shows himself to his worshippers. His usual form of address for letters and memorials is:—"To the pure toe-nails of His Holiness, the Victor of Death, the Granter of every Wish, the Omniscient, All-Seeing Peerless One, the Protector, the Friend, and Patron of the Angels and all living things."

Under the windows of the Grand Lama's sitting-rooms we left the dark passages and descended into an

[1] Properly "*Zhabpäd.* Rockhill is inclined to derive it from *g*shag*s*, justice, and *d*pe, a model, although it is never spelt in that way.

[2] The so-called "General Assembly" deals with the smaller matters and does not seem to hamper much his actions in the larger.

TOP OF MAUSOLEUM OF THE FIRST DALAI LAMA IN POTALA.
Called The Ornament of the World.

open paved court bordered by a gallery, in which sacred dances and plays are held for the amusement of His Holiness. The buildings were crumbling to decay, but some of the frescoes on the walls were being re-painted and the walls replastered. Beyond this we descended past the immense kitchens, and out on to the great staircase, where we obtained good views of the front of the building. The colour of the "Red Palace" is a dingy crimson, from an ochrey red earth which is used to paint it. The great "coats of arms" emblazoned on its walls are the mystic spell of its royal occupant, and the "Wheel of the Buddhist Law" supported by two couchant deer, symbolising Buddha's first preaching of his doctrine in the "Deer Forest"[1] at Benares.

Farther down we passed the lodge of the "Treasurer of Offerings,"[2] who receives gifts for the Lama Pope, and gives in return a small clay seal impressed in relief with a dragon-thunderbolt and a spell, which is treasured in an amulet as a charm. He also sells relics of His Divinity's dress and person as talismans.[2]

At the foot of the great staircase stands a tall monolith, a counterpart of the one outside (see photo, p. 336), but bearing no inscription. To this is fixed the lower end of the great rope for the "Flying Spirits" at the festival of the New Year, the upper end of the rope being tied to the topmost roof of the palace, over 500 feet above, and down this terribly dangerous incline

[1] Sarnath.

[2] These include shreds of his vestments, also nail parings and other bodily relics. By special enquiry on the spot, I elicited that the present-day custom confirms the report published in the *Dictionnaire Infernal* by M. Collin de Plancy of Paris in 1825:—"Ses excrémens sont conservois comme des chose sacreés. Après qu'on les a fait sécher et réduire au poudre, on les referme dans des bôites d'or enrichies de pierreries, et les envoie aux plus grand princes comme de saints reliques. Son urine est un elixir divine propre a guérir toute espéce de maladie."

slides an acrobat, carrying good luck for the incoming year amidst the huzzas of 50,000 people. The man who personates the flying spirit belongs to a class of professional acrobats. He rides a wooden saddle, and encases his body in thickly padded vestments to counteract the friction of the rope. Taking his stand on the top of the palace, he throws a libation of wine and dough images of men and animals to the devils and then slides down the rope, sometimes sitting astride as on a horse's saddle, at other times flying with the saddle under his breast. Although he travels down with terrific speed, and the dangers of being killed or lacerated by the friction are great, he seldom suffers accident, the present performer having accomplished the feat for several consecutive years. Its object is to confer good fortune on the Grand Lama and his country, and the "Flying Spirit" appears to take the part of a good angel[1] rather than a scape-goat, as he is fêted and does not flee into retirement.

In the great courtyard, at the foot of the staircase, are housed the lay servants, the stables, granaries, the printing-house, a mint and foundry for casting images and bells, the prison, also large store and lumber rooms. Here it is said is locked away the only wheeled vehicle which was in Tibet until our *ekka*-carts came. It is a four-wheeled elegant phaeton, which the King of Nepal purchased in Calcutta a few years ago and sent as a present to the Grand Lama, by whom it was never used but treasured as a curiosity, for he generally travels in a sedan-chair.

The great public gateway of entrance and exit,

[1] This practice, which recalls the Hindu "Hook-swinging Festival" of Jagarnath, used to be common in the north-western end of the Himalayas, in Garhwal, where it was witnessed and described under the name of "Barat" by Dr Moorcroft about a century ago as a protection against cholera plagues.—*Travels in the Himalayan Provinces*, i. 17, *et seq.* It was afterwards suppressed by the British Government on account of the fatal accidents which attended it.

through which we now passed, has a bifurcating curved passage under the massive walls, over 30 feet thick, which seems modelled after the outer ceintures of the Peking city gateways. Through its dark portals we emerged on to the open lawn and the gardens in front, where several old decrepit men and women were dreamily turning their prayer-wheels and muttering the Grand Lama's mystic formula, as they glanced devoutly up to the towering red walls emblazoned by the legend "Hail to the Jewel [Dalai Lama] in the Lotus Flower," the narcotic against all the miseries of this life and the passport to Paradise.

CHAPTER XX.

TEA WITH THE REGENT, RULER OF TIBET.

When the terror-stricken Dalai Lama was preparing to flee, about a week before we reached his capital, he summoned to his aid the venerable Cardinal of the yellow sect. This dignitary, on hurrying from his country seat to Potala, was surprised and annoyed to find that his saintly master had incontinently fled, and had left behind him his seals of office and a letter in which he appointed the Cardinal to act for him as Regent,[1] face the Mission in his stead, and settle up the dispute as best he could. The choice did great credit to the young Dalai's judgment; for the Regent has proved himself a man of strong character and sound sense, and one of the very few Lamas who are worth anything at all as statesmen.

This Cardinal has his seat at the old monastery where the founder of the yellow-cap sect, Tsong-khapa, began his great reform in the fifteenth century, and founded that sect which two centuries later seized the temporal government. As the occupant of Tsong-khapa's old chair at Gahldän monastery, he receives the title of "Holder of the Gahldän Throne,"[2] or "The Precious Enthroned,"[3] and exercises spiritual authority over the three great State monasteries, and also over the whole of the yellow-cap

[1] Gyal-tsab. [2] Gahldän 'kri 'dsin-pa.

[3] 'Kri [pronounced Tī] Rimpoch'é.

ALTAR IN POTALA, IN CHAPEL OF AVALOKITES'WARA.
(The images and lamps are of solid gold.)

THE RULER OF TIBET.

HIGH MASS IN THE TEMPLE OF SERA AT LHASA.

order. He, like his predecessors[1] in this chair, is not one of the so-called "reincarnated" Lamas but of natural birth, and was appointed to the office by reason of his superior reputation for profound scholarship—as this quality is understood in Tibet. The office is tenable for seven years, of which he has already run four. His private monkish name is "The Noble-minded Banner."

It was fortunate for Tibet that she had schooled in her cloisters such a strong man for this emergency. When he appeared on the scene, he took in the situation at a glance, and with business-like promptitude set about to make the best of it. Deeply imbued with the pacific principles of Buddhism, and its horror of sacrificing life, he galvanised the lagging councillors into quickened action, and soon got matters into train for the speedy signing of a treaty of peace.

As I was desirous of meeting him to solicit his help in several researches I was making, I wrote to him asking for an audience, inditing my letter with his formal title of: "The Glorious Sun of Learning, the Understander of the Doctrine and the Precepts." In reply I received the following missive:—

"Unto The Honourable, The Great Physician.

"You are welcome to come to see me here to-morrow morning at the middle of the forenoon.[2]—From The Precious Enthroned One, on the second day of the eighth month of the Wood-Dragon Year."

Accordingly, on the next day, I set out for his

[1] His immediate predecessor was the Bodhisat Chöp'el of Däpung monastery, who died before he had held the post for one year. This one is a friar of Sera, and one of his chief duties is to lecture the massed Lamas at the great New Year festival at Lhasa on the thirty-four lives of Buddha (that is, Buddha's own life and his thirty-three legendary previous ones).

[2] Ts'ading.

residence, which was temporarily not in Potala, but in the wealthy monastery of Muru at the north-east corner of Lhasa, famous for its teaching of the occult and black art, and also as containing the printing establishment for the treatises of Transcendental Wisdom.[1] It is a fine building, kept in excellent order and repair, and is surrounded by a high wall along which runs a deep cornice of stone slabs, with the "God of Wisdom" and other divinities with their spells carved in low relief, and all brilliantly painted.

I was received at the gate by some smiling Lamas, who, saying that I was expected, invited me to enter, which I did without any military guard, leaving my escort of British soldiers[2] at the gate, out of respect to the sacred character of the building and to show my confidence in its high occupant.

Inside, facing the gate, was a long block of dormitories three storeys high, strongly built of stone, with many windows and pierced by a broad passage, lined by large prayer-barrels. This passage gave entry into the grand square, a spacious paved courtyard about 80 yards broad, brightened with pots of blooming marigolds, chrysanthemums, stocks and asters. On the further side of the square stood the temple, and round the other three sides ran the residential rooms with a projecting wooden verandah, in which stood clusters of staid monks.

A procession of shaven-headed acolytes in their claret robes was passing into the temple with blare of trumpets, beat of hand drums, and clashing cymbals,

[1] The *'Bum* or "100,000 Mystic Sermons." The printing house with the wooden blocks for printing these books adjoins the Gya Bum *Chorten*, which is said to derive its name from these treatises, though the priest of the new temple built in 1891 beside the *Chorten* tells me that the name meant the 100,000 images of Tsong-khapa which originally were plastered over the surface of the monument.

[2] Royal Fusiliers.

and I peeped in to see the service going on there. The interior was of the general type, but the paintings and frescoes were in better preservation than usual, and the earnest, devotional demeanour of the young Lamas spoke well for the discipline of this monastery. The monks sat facing each other (see photo here) in rows on each side of the aisle, as in a choir. The drums were in the second row, and held aloft by their stem above the head like a standard. The abbot at the end of the aisle on his raised throne blended with the life-sized images of the gods upon the altar. The larger pillars of the colonnade, painted a glowing scarlet, consist of a cluster of beams clamped together, doubtless owing to the absence of sufficiently large single beams in the local woods; but the fluted effect is pleasing. For a course of refreshment of hot soup-tea, the service was interrupted for a few minutes during which several neophytes poured out the tea from large kettles into the wooden saucers which each of the seated Lamas produced from his pocket, and after drinking its contents, licked clean and replaced in his pouch.

The chants often take the form of a monologue litany with alternating responses thus:—

Priest. "There has arisen the Illuminator of the World! The Protector of the World! The Maker of Light who gives eyes to the world, which is blind, to cast away its burden of sin!"

Congregation of Monks. "Thou hast been victorious in the fight! Thy aim has been accomplished by Thy moral excellence! Thy virtues are perfect! Thou shalt satisfy men with good things!"

P. "Gotama (Sakya) is without sin! He is out of the miry pit. He stands on dry ground!"

C. "Yes! He is out of the mire; and He will save [by his teaching] other animated beings that are carried off by the mighty stream."

P. "The living world has long suffered the disease

of corruption. The Prince of Physicians is come to cure men from all diseases!"

C. "Protector of the world! By Thy appearance all the mansions of distress shall be made empty! Henceforth angels and men shall enjoy happiness," etc., etc.

. . . .

P. "To Thee Whose virtue is immaculate, Whose understanding is pure and brilliant, Who has the thirty-two characteristic marks complete, and Who hast discerning memory of all things and foreknowledge."

C. "Reverence be to Thee! We adore Thee, bending our heads to our feet."

P. "To Thee Who art clean and pure from all taint of sin, and celebrated in the three worlds! Who being possessed of the three kinds of knowledge givest animated beings the eye to discern the three stages of emancipiation from sin!"

C. "Reverence be to Thee!"

P. "To Thee Who with tranquil mind clearest the troubles of evil times, Who with loving-kindness teachest all living things to walk in the path designed for them!"

C. "Reverence be to Thee!"

P. "Saint! Whose heart is at rest and Who delightest to explain the doubts and perplexities of men! Who hast suffered much for the good of living beings! Thy aim is pure! Thy practices are perfect!"

C. "Reverence be to Thee!"

P. "Teacher of the four truths Who rejoiceth in salvation! Who being Thyself free from sin desireth to free the world from sin!"

C. "Reverence be to Thee!"

Another young priest of the Regent's retinue now came forward and conducted me to the apartments of his master, situated on the topmost storey, to which we ascended by many twists and turns and stoopings to avoid the beams of low doorways, up to an open verandah. Here I was offered a chair, upholstered with Chinese brocade, and asked to wait for a few moments, as His Excellency was engaged with a high State official. The Regent had no guard, though he will doubtless have one as soon as our force withdraws, as he is *de facto* King of Tibet,[1] since the Chinese have deposed the Dalai Lama on account of his refusal to return. Presently out came the dignified senior abbot of Däpung, who might be called a Bishop, a man of fine presence and winning manner, accompanied by one of the State Councillors, who bowed me a salutation in passing; and I was ushered through two halls, frescoed with sacred pictures, into the presence of the Regent.

He sat cross-legged, Buddha-wise, on a cushion, at the end of a long dimly-lit room with a low table in front of him; the light from a small latticed window falling on his features gave him a statuesque appearance in the gloom (see photo, p. 400), whilst his face, directed towards me, wore a fixed sphinx-like expression, resembling that of the Buddhas on the frescoes around him. When I advanced up to him over the thick-piled Tibetan carpets, he held out his hand to be shaken, and, without rising, motioned me with a bow to be seated on a side cushion by his right hand.

In appearance he is quite the ascetic—an old rather wizened man of sixty-five with shaven crown, and garbed simply in the monkish ruby-coloured woollen robe, his yellow hat hanging on a peg near by. Of average height, he has strong but rather stern features, a broad thinking brow, long oval face, clear steady eyes, a firm mouth, and a rather bulbous large nose—his worst feature, which gives him a somewhat unprepossessing appearance on first sight—a powerful chin, and grave sonorous voice. Such is the present Ruler of Tibet.

On the table stood his drinking cup filled with tea, a bundle of State papers, which he placed in a pigeon-hole, and a few other articles, including a stationary praying-wheel, which is turned like a spinning-top by twirling its

[1] He has the title of Gyalpo or "*King*" of Tibet, which is now restricted to Lamas—*Desrid* (vulgarly *Desi*) being the title of a lay Regent.

upper stem (see photo here). Behind him stood his two Lama attendants, a young functionary as a sort of aide-de-camp and orderly, and his cupbearer of extraordinary appearance, who leered all the time under his heavy brows, with the look and bearing of a low-born serf. Ranged round the room, the walls of which were covered with fine frescoes, were a few cupboards containing books and implements of worship, amongst which were some handsomely worked silver and gilt censers (see photo here), and the hangings were of Chinese silk and satin embroidered chiefly with dragon patterns. The pervading appearance was that of the study of a saintly recluse rather than the room of a temporal governor.

After we had sat a few minutes in the decorous exchange of compliments, during which I apologised for having come empty-handed without the customary presents, having nothing suitable to offer—which he kindly said was of no consequence—tea was brought in, and as we talked about various matters, his reserve thawed, he became more communicative, and we struck up quite a friendship. Some State officials called on urgent business, on which I made a move to go; but he would not consent to this, and pressed me to stay, thus giving me an opportunity of seeing the vigour and speed with which he transacted his business; he would listen to some official visitor, put a few rapid questions quietly, and, making up his mind on the spot, issue concise orders in a few words, and then turn to me with a pleasant smile to resume the conversation on which he had become interested.

Talking of the religion of the country, he had heard, he said, of the interest I took in his creed. Then looking fixedly at me for a moment, he leaned forward across the table with a searching gaze, and asked slowly: "Are *you* a Buddhist, or are you not?" I replied that I was not, *but*, as Christians, we had very much in common with

TABLE PRAYER-WHEEL.

INCENSE CENSERS.

TI RIMPOCHÉ, THE REGENT, RULER OF TIBET.

Cardinal of the Lamaic Church,
with his two attendants.

the teachings of Buddha. He enquired eagerly: "Is Buddha mentioned in your Christian Scriptures?" to which I had to reply in the negative. But I said he would see how similar in many ways were the two creeds when I told him that the mainspring of Christ's doctrine was "peace and goodwill to men," as was Buddha's; that Christ had said, "Love your neighbour as yourself," "Love your enemies, and do good to them that hate you, and despitefully use you and persecute you," and that our Christian commandments were of exactly the same number as Buddha's decalogue, and all of them were couched like his in the negative form—"thou shalt not" do so and so—and that many of them were identical in their substance.

On this he exclaimed bitterly, smarting under the defeat inflicted on his country by our troops: "The English have no religion at all!" And on my enquiring why he thought so, he replied deliberately and emphatically: "Because I *know* it! Because I *see* it for myself in the faces and actions of your people! They all have hard hearts, and are specially trained to take life and to fight like very giant Titans who war even against the Gods!" I was bound to admit that a military expedition was an inconvenient object-lesson in practical Christianity, and urged that it was not a fair test, as war stirred up the worst passions in men's hearts; and after all we did not want the war, that it was his people who had always fired the first shot; besides, they too had trained their men as well as they could to take life in war. "It is not only your military, but *all* your people, even those who are not military; you are *all* the same, except [here he added somewhat apologetically, probably out of deference to my feelings] you doctors, of whose humane work I have heard; but all the others are utterly devoid of religion!"

I assured him that the people of England spend enormous sums of money on religion, and everywhere have built beautiful churches, several hundreds of which are much finer and more costly than any temple in Tibet, and that the commentaries and other books on our religion would fill enormous libraries, many times larger than those of the Tibetan monasteries, and that their priests were real ecclesiastics, preaching to and teaching the people, unlike the Lamas, who never teach the people but keep all their education within their order, and are therefore not ecclesiastics. Hereupon he answered with a fine scorn: "But what is the good of all these buildings, and all these books and teachings, if the people do not read them, or, in any case, do not practise their maxims?" As he was so hopelessly biassed, I could only reply that I hoped he would judge us more generously when he knew us better, and that he might discover that, because of our superior strength in war, we could now afford to exercise the Christian principle of showing mercy to the weaker.

On hearing that Buddha was not mentioned by name in our Scriptures, he did not evince a great desire to know more about other salient points of Christianity, but seemed interested in hearing that one great point of difference was, that man was to be saved, not by his own merits, but by the saving grace of God, his sins being atoned for by the sacrifice made by Christ. This was quite foreign to all his conceptions, as he had been educated in the strict traditions of Buddhism with its ethical doctrine of retribution or *karma*, which teaches that each soul has to work out its own salvation, and to counterbalance by a corresponding number of good deeds all his accumulated misdeeds before the latter are forgiven by the inexorable "Judge of the Dead."

It was interesting to find him asserting that the objections of the Tibetans to our coming were more religious than political, though he could not reconcile this with the extensive admission of Mahomedans into the city. Regarding Hindus, he said these differed but little from Buddhists, and their scriptures contained references to Buddha by name as one of the deities to be worshipped. They both were striving to reach the same goal, and any apparent opposition and divergence in their course was merely occasioned by their seeking their object from different directions and by different paths; and to illustrate this, he drew a diagram similar to one which the Shata Shapé had drawn for my information. In a circle representing the world, a dot is placed in the centre to indicate the common destination to which the Hindu and Buddhist set out from opposite sides within the circle; but missing their objective in a mist, they each swerve considerably to one side, and so chance to meet one another below the goal, each travelling different ways. Whereupon the Hindu asks the Buddhist where he is going, and is told: "To the great goal"; to which the Hindu responds: "You are going the wrong road, as I too am going there." But in reality both are wrong, or rather, both are right, and when the mists lift they will find the haven quite near to them. This delightful allegory recalls Clough's poem about the two homeward-bound ships that met only once in the long voyage:—

"One port methought alike they sought,
One purpose hold where'er they fare,
O bounding breeze and rushing seas,
At last, at last, unite them there."

In this way the Lamas explain the essential differences between themselves and the Hindus.

Regarding the so-called "Mahatmas," it was important to elicit the fact that this Cardinal, one of the most learned and profound scholars in Tibet, was, like the other learned Lamas I have interrogated on the subject, entirely ignorant of any such beings. Nor had he ever heard of any secrets of the ancient world having been preserved in Tibet: the Lamas are only interested in "The Word of Buddha," and place no value whatever on ancient history. No Lama, he added, nor even any of the great monasteries in Lhasa, the greatest in all Tibet, possessed, he was certain, any account of the ancient history of India, the land of Buddha himself, beyond such fragments as were to be gleaned from the orthodox scriptures of which every monastery has a copy. Books about ancient history had only an interest for the laity, the old nobility, and lay officials who were concerned in mundane matters. This declaration of the Cardinal was confirmed by all the enquiries made by myself and by that Tibetan student, Mr David M'Donald, of all the Lamas most likely to know, and by actual examination of many of the large libraries. The result of these enquiries shows that the Lamas seem to possess no historic works, except the quasi-authentic chronicles of their own kings and monasteries subsequent to the seventh century A.D., when their language was first reduced to writing, and a few fragmentary histories of India during its Buddhist period compiled from Indian and Chinese sources during the Middle Ages, with possibly a few Indian Buddhist manuscripts of the same age.[1] There is thus, I am sorry to say, little hope to hold out to those who fondly fancied that the lost secrets of the beginnings of the earliest civilisation of the world, anterior to that of Ancient Egypt and Assyria, which perished with the sinking of Atlanta in the Western Ocean, might still be carefully preserved in that fabulous land which is no longer wholly "Unknown."

[1] These are likely to be, if at all, at Tashilhumpo and Sakya monasteries in Western Tibet, and at Samyä, the first monastery ever built in Tibet, in the Lower Tsangpo Valley.

Amongst other matters, I asked His Excellency if he would permit that clever young student of the Temple of Medicine to come back with us to Calcutta, to learn our Western methods of treatment for the benefit of the people of Lhasa; and he frankly said that he should be very pleased if this could be arranged. He requested me to write down for him my name in English characters.

All through this conversation he pressed me to take more tea, and insisted always on the cup being filled up as some of it was sipped, which I tried to escape doing as much as possible, for it was "the buttered tea," and not very palatable to my taste, although he drank it with evident relish; the biscuits and sweets were better. The tea-cups were little bowls of modern Chinese porcelain. In the intervals of our conversation would sometimes be heard the deep tones of the organ-like music, and the drone of the priests' chant in the distant temple, in keeping with the pervading sanctity of our surroundings.

On my rising to come away he also rose, and as he did so, I asked if he would be kind enough to come into the well-lighted verandah so that I could take a photograph of him as a memento of my visit. He smilingly consented, and in this way I secured the picture facing page 407. And so we parted, with a firm grip of the hand and a cheery good-bye, he promising to send me certain information that I wanted, and I carrying away with me the remembrance of a noble personality.

CHAPTER XXI.

PEACE NEGOTIATIONS AND SIGNING OF THE TREATY.

"*The stick is greater than the King's command.*"—TIBETAN PROVERB.

AFTER arrival at Lhasa on the 3rd August, no time was lost by the Mission in trying to secure a speedy settlement with the Tibetans, in the form of a treaty. The Tibetan ministers were informed of the precise demands for an agreement, and given the fullest opportunities for negotiating; but none of them would assume any responsibility, fearing, as they alleged, the wrath of the Dalai Lama when he returned.

While they doubtless had some reason for dread on this account, it was clear also that with ostrich-like obstinacy they had not yet grasped the fact that the detested foreigner had come to dictate terms which he could enforce. On the contrary, they tenaciously clung to the idea that they could dictate terms, and would agree to none of those of the Mission. They proceeded to cut off the food of our troops, stopping supplies from the merchants in the town and the local monasteries, thinking thereby to drive us away. As the monastery of Däpung was conspicuous in this obstructive policy, and was known to have enormous surplus stores in its granaries, and refused to supply any of these even on full payment, a forage party was sent out on the 9th August under a strong escort, with the message that unless supplies were forthcoming they would have to be levied forcibly. Although the monks delayed for some hours coming to terms, General Macdonald,

MONKS BRINGING IN BAGS OF GRAIN AND FLOUR.

ILLUMINATED PROCLAMATION OF DALAI LAMA.

loth to abandon all hope of a peaceful settlement, did not resort to extreme measures, and was able to extract a large instalment of grain that day, and a promise to send the rest within a given time, which was faithfully carried out: another instance of how the semi-civilised, whilst appreciating kindness, worship strength. It was quite a remarkable sight to see the long string of monks from this monastery filing into camp laden with the bags of grain and flour thus extracted (see photo, p. 412).

The Amban, despite his promises to make the utmost of the suzerain powers in assisting in effecting a settlement—and he really did exert himself with this object—was nevertheless able to contribute little to advance matters. He wrote to the Dalai Lama advising him to return, and urged the General Assembly[1] to accede to the terms proferred; but this Assembly, which sat continuously, wasted its time in empty talk without any result, everyone refusing to assume authority.

In this deadlock there arrived the Cardinal, the *Ti Rimpoché*, from Gahldän monastery, and from the date of his coming, on the 14th August, negotiations may be said to have begun in earnest. He said that the Dalai Lama had left his seal with him, but without any authority to use it. He had sent off a deputation of Lamas to beg their august master to return, and within three days would know the result. This party reported that the Dalai had definitely refused to return, and had posted off with Dorjieff by the Tengri Lake[2] to Mongolia to seek protection from the Mongols. As this people have a Grand Lama of their own established at Urga (see map, p. 4),* they are not likely to give him a very cordial welcome, though he has a claim on their feelings, as he poses as the incarnation of their national hero Kesar. The Ti Rimpoché professed to be greatly

[1] Tsongdu.

[2] *Viâ* Reting monastery and Nagchuka.

* On page xxiii in the present edition.

indignant at the Dalai's desertion at this great crisis; and as it was now clear that negotiations must proceed without the Priest-God, he insisted on the National Assembly giving him authority to treat and to use the Dalai's seals, to which they reluctantly consented after a long discussion.

Empowered in this way, the Ti Rimpoché set about dealing with the articles of the proposed Treaty one by one, and as a proof of his desire to settle matters, released on the first day the two Sikhimese who had been sent out as spies at Khambajong, and had been seized and imprisoned. He also placarded the following quaint proclamation over Lhasa, imploring the people to abstain from any hostile acts which might jeopardise a settlement:—

"*Monks and Laymen in all the four directions of our Great Kingdom! Hear and understand!*

"After the war with England in 1888 the Chinese and English made a Treaty in which it was stated the matter would be settled later. But last year the English crossed the Khamba frontier with soldiers, and we sent men to negotiate, and conducted the negotiations with care and patience; but the English, acting in a high-handed manner, entered our territories, and so having no resource, war began and matters turned out badly. So the English came close and said a Viceroy had given orders, and they had no resource but to obey, and that if we did not oppose they would not fight. The Chinese, too, wishing only the good of the country, ordered us to make a settlement, and the Amban ordered us to withdraw all soldiers from the frontier and enter into relations with the English. But when we came to consider the conduct of the English, we found we had no resource but in war. Now it is the custom of all nations after war to make a Treaty, and although we were burning with anger, we considered the matter well in order to save the world from conflagration, and decided to act in accordance with our religious tenets. The English will act in accordance with the declaration they have made us, and we will act as Fate demands, having regard to our Buddhist faith. If war arises, men and animals will suffer, so we consulted carefully, and withdrew our soldiers for the sake of peaceful negotiations, and now are making a Treaty, with the Amban acting between us and the English. So you must all, monks and laymen, listen and behave properly, for bad men do not know what is for their benefit or hurt, and think they may quarrel and loot. Let none carry slanderous tales and so provoke a quarrel, let none forget the Buddhist faith and act for his own benefit, let none who does not understand the matter talk about it. We are on watch day and night whether you are speaking well or ill, and if we find you ill, we will kill or fine you as you deserve. We will not act without knowledge. We will watch you all, Chinese, Goorkhas, Bhutanese, and monks, and you should understand what is for your benefit."

It almost looked as if the temper of the Lamas was not going to be held in check by this proclamation, and as if the hope of a friendly settlement might at the last moment be disappointed. On the 18th August, a fanatical Lama, clad in chain armour, ran *amok* into the camp, and murderously attacked the first two officers he met, who happened to be medical officers.[1] This bloodthirsty Lama was hanged in view of the town, and it was clearly a solitary instance of homicidal madness, as no other assault happened. Both the Ti Rimpoché and the Amban called to express their distress on hearing of the outrage, and the Amban politely sent his cards for several mornings and an enquiry after the condition of the wounded officers. As illustrating the confidence inspired in the Tibetans by our soldiers, it should be noted that when this fanatic attacked these officers and some shots were fired at him, some Tibetan prisoners who were on a fatigue duty near by rushed to the nearest guard for the protection of our sentries.

[1] Captains A. C. Young and T. B. Kelly, I.M.S., the former of whom was savagely cut over the head and arm with a sword.

By the 1st of September every article was agreed to except the amount of the indemnity, and this too by a steady insistence was conceded on the 4th September, when the Ti Rimpoché called and said he was ready to sign the Treaty, agreeing to all the conditions in full at once, that very day, and added with emotion that he would seal it a hundred times over, if by so doing he could bring immediate peace to the country. As, however, several copies had to be made in the three languages, English, Tibetan, and Chinese, he was told it could not be ready for some days more, till the 7th August; on hearing which he was rather downcast, as he said the astrologers had ascertained that that day, the 4th, was a lucky day for signing, so also was the 5th, and even the 6th and 7th, but he should like it disposed of at the earliest date possible. This impatient haste was an agreeable change from the dilatory tactics of his predecessors, and the accommodating dates fixed by the astrologers showed how eager they were for peace.

Thus it happened that the 7th September 1904 saw the conclusion of the Treaty of peace and friendship between Great Britain and Tibet. It was done with great pomp and ceremony in the Dalai Lama's new Throne Room in the castle of Potala. The British Commissioner, attended by the other officers of the Mission and the military escort, rode in procession to the northern entrance of the fortress. Our troops lined the road all the way from the foot of the hill up to the great gate of the venerable Red Palace, which looked down grimly on the grand display. Inside also our soldiers formed a line extending across the courtyards to the palace door, and through it along the dark corridors to the Throne Room itself.

The scene in this great hall was very picturesque and impressive. The throne had been lifted behind the gallery pillars, and screened by a crimson silk curtain embroidered with a great five-clawed dragon, under the

PEACE DELEGATES.

Yatok Minister. Lama Minister (*Ta Lama*). Chief Secretary (*Tungyig*). Abbot representing the Three State Monasteries.

Emperor Tungchi's yellow presentation sign-board. In front of the curtain under this celestial board sat, on crimson-covered chairs, Colonel Younghusband, with the Amban on his left and General Macdonald on his right, and from these on either side curved round a semicircle of seated higher officials, the Mission and military headquarters' staff on the General's right, and the Regent, bareheaded, in monk's red garb, and the rest of the Chinese mandarins, in their dark blue gowns and peacock's feathered hats, on the Amban's left. The rest of the inner circle was formed by the row of bright amber-clad councillors facing the British Commissioner, each with a garnet-robed attendant wearing a Beefeater's hat, standing behind his chair, and the representative abbots of the three great monasteries tailing off to the gorgeously dressed Tongsa Penlop and the Nepalese Consul with their bodyguards. Outside this circle sat closely packed rows of other British officers, and outside these stood several deep the guard of honour, composed of British soldiers, Sikhs, Pathans and Goorkhas, with the brilliant-hued background of the frescoes on the walls and the bright mosaics of the beams and surrounding balconies. In the centre of the inner circle, on a table covered by the Union Jack, lay the Treaty ready for signature, and around it stood several monks and lay officials, the former bareheaded, in light ruby robes, and the latter in dark magenta, with fluffy yellow Tam-o'-Shanters, holding the seals and pads of ink for stamping the impressions, as no sealing wax is used. It was a marvellous blending of brilliant colour, of the sacred and the secular, of the East and West.

When all had taken their seats, a troop of Tibetan waiters brought in tea on lordly salvers, and plates of biscuits, sweets, and dried fruits, which were handed round, after which the Treaty was read out by a Tibetan clerk of the Mission. When this was done, Colonel Younghusband rose and asked the Tibetan authorities whether they were prepared to sign the document, and they all unanimously murmured their assent.

The Treaty was then unrolled; it was a long parchment scroll in three vertical columns, containing side by side the Tibetan, Chinese, and English versions. As, however, there were five copies, and each had to be signed, or rather stamped, with seals in seven different places, the operation occupied a long time. The lower ranked officials first affixed their signature stamps, the representatives of the National Assembly, then the monks of the three great monasteries, and the councillors. Then last but one was the Regent, and then the British Commissioner. Whilst the latter were affixing their signatures, the whole assemblage rose and remained standing. It was noticeable that the Regent, beaming with smiles at this consummation of his wishes, did not himself impress the great seal of the Dalai Lama on the Treaty, but touching this exalted stamp, commanded one of the monks to imprint it for him (see p. 448 for facsimile of seal which was impressed with vermilion ink).

After the signing of the Treaty, Colonel Younghusband, in a speech addressed to the Tibetan signatories, announced that England is now at peace with Tibet, and summarised the leading features of the situation: how the Treaty leaves the land, the liberties, and the religion of the Tibetans untouched; that it recognises the suzerainty of China, and does not interfere with the country's internal affairs, but confers increased facilities for trade with India; and that if they honestly kept the Treaty they would find the British as good friends as they had been bad enemies. This speech was translated sentence by sentence, the Tibetans nodding assent to it as it proceeded. As a first token of the good-will thereby established, the Commissioner announced that all the prisoners of war would be set at liberty. On the conclusion of this speech Colonel

Younghusband took farewell of the Regent, the Amban, and the others; and the procession re-formed and returned to camp, passing several groups of Lamas and laity, who stood respectfully by, as the completion of the Treaty within the sacred walls of Potala had created a deep impression on the people.

On the following day the prisoners on both sides were released. The Tibetans set free the survivors of those prisoners who had been chained in dungeons for befriending the British and Japanese subjects, Sarat Chandra and the priest Kawaguchi. The soldiers captured by our troops on being set free were given each a present of over six shillings, which must be a rather infrequent experience in warfare; certainly such treatment so astonished them that they remained kow-towing, grinning, and thrusting out their tongues for a long time before they attempted to leave, and always doffed their caps to us afterwards in the city. Presents of money, too, were largely given by the Mission to the monasteries and temples, and to the poor of the city and suburbs, nearly 10,000 of whom paraded one morning to receive the bounty—all these acts tending to promote and cement good feeling.

CHAPTER XXII.

RAMBLES ROUND LHASA.

THE signing of the Treaty, accompanied by the release of all the prisoners and distribution of largess, seemed to reassure the people and did much to dispel any lingering animosity. In this more friendly state of affairs we were able to go about the town freely and ramble over the suburbs, sketching and photographing, observing the customs of the people, and enquiring into points of historical, antiquarian, and general interest.

These outings led us daily along the sacred Circular Road, past straggling files of prayer-wheel spinners, thence through avenues of trees to the city, or out to the country beyond, passing gardens and orchards that supply the markets with vegetables and fruits, across parks, to the fields and shaggy stretches of woodland. The air was always delightfully free from dust, that plague of Gyantsé and Phari, and this was doubtless due to the heavy rain combined with the marshes and the far-reaching network of streamlets, which give to Lhasa its refreshing green and luxuriant vegetation. Although the sparkling streams are teeming visibly with lusty trout, no fishing may be done here, nor any killing of birds, from New Year's Day till the end of the seventh month by order of the Grand Lama, lest a transmigrated human life may be thus sacrificed. The banks of these numerous brooklets are a mass of blossoms of wild flowers trying to outvie

HARVESTING THE GRAND LAMA'S CORN.

SUBURBS OF LHASA.

KING OF THE DRAGONS.

MYSTERY-PLAY AT LHASA.

each other in gaudy tints, scented potentilla, magenta and blue daisies, scarlet arums, buttercups, primulas, and harebells. Up the valley the fields of ripening corn seem to stretch like a sea for miles, and lave the foot of the hills in yellow waves. In the Grand Lama's fields under Potala harvesters have commenced work, singing in light-heartedness, the women wearing garlands of yellow clematis (see photo here). A few fields are being ploughed by means of a primitive wooden ploughshare shod with an iron tip, that simply scratches the rich soil. Beside the comfortable farm-houses cattle are grazing, and under the cool shade of the adjoining clump of stately old willows ponies take shelter from the sun and flies. Turning towards the hills we find that the flatness of the valley has deceived us as to the breadth of cultivation; for we soon get beyond the irrigated tract which closely follows the river and its canals, whilst outside a sheet of white sand, the desert tribute of the crumbling granite hills, stretches for a mile or more up to the craggy foot of the mountains. The sandy hillocks are seldom wholly bare, but support a straggling growth of pink and yellow saxifrage and wiry tufts of grass amongst which burrow and scamper the tiny Pika mouse-hares.[1] The rushy morasses teemed with water-fowl, amongst which I noticed a pair of the huge red-capped Sarus crane[2] which the Japanese delight to paint.

The villas and better farmhouses are all built on the same plan, the buildings ranged round a central courtyard, the cattle being stalled underneath, together with the stores, and in the upper storey, fronted with a balcony and open verandah, are the human dwellings and cooking-rooms. Windows are conspicuously few and small, so as to keep out the winter cold and wind. There are no chimneys, but only a hole in the roof, so everything in the interior is more or less tanned by

[1] *Ochotona curzoni*, p. 482. [2] *Grus antigone*, p. 487.

the smoke; and even in the houses of the rich, a notched log often takes the place of the smaller stairs. Most of the gardens grow excellent potatoes, which are probably the produce of those which Warren Hastings with benevolent foresight instructed the Bogle Mission of 1774 to plant at every camp they halted at. Large turnip-like radishes were the commonest vegetable.

Near the foot of the hills might occasionally be seen the gruesome way in which the Tibetans dispose of their dead. A man carries the dead body doubled up in a sitting posture and tied in a piece of a tent or blanket, deposits it on the recognised place on a rock, and then he and the attendant Lama proceed to cut off the flesh in pieces, so that the vultures and ravens can devour it. As Manning quaintly puts it, when protesting against their close game laws: "They eat no birds, but, on the contrary, let the birds eat them."

The chief amusements of the men are horse-racing, wrestling, putting the stone, archery, quoits, dominoes, and a game like draughts called "Pushing the Tiger." They are fond of songs, accompanied by a guitar, flute or bell, and the women and men dance on planks as sounding boards, as in "hornpipes." Children indulge in kite-flying; the machine is of paper, without a long tail, and is called the "Kite, or Hawk-bird." Theatrical performances are very popular, and are held in the open air, in a street, or in a courtyard. They are given on the occasion of a festival, the general public being admitted free, at the expense of some well-to-do person. They are always enacted by the laity, never by Lamas, although most of the pieces are mystery- and sacred plays, usually former births of Buddha. There is always a large element of burlesque buffoonery in which the men, dressed up fantastically with monstrous grotesque masks representing infidels and malignant demons, go through a pantomime of clumsy antics and pirouetting — the words of the play being usually read from a book.[1] One of these plays, acted for the amusement of the Mission, was called "Lotus of Brilliant Light, The Merchant Prince." The performers are known as "Aché Lhamo," and the female parts are usually taken by women. It lasts for several hours each day and the spectators bring some work with them to spend the day, industriously spinning wool when not handling their prayer-wheels or beads. The Lhasaites, both poor and well-to-do, are much given to picnicing in the autumn under the trees, with their families; we often passed such parties. The nobles spend several weeks in tents in their summer gardens, because, as they allege, the houses become unhealthy at that season.

They are fond of dogs, and especially favour the mongrel breed between the Lhasa terrier and the Chinese spaniel. Few of the swarms of ownerless dogs that infest the streets are of this class, most of them being stunted and mangy mastiffs. The well-cared-for mastiff of the houses was usually a fine beast with a huge lion-like head and mane, often with a white breast patch, suggestive of a bear, and such frequently were called "Bear";[2] other favourite names for them were "Bull-bear,"[3] and "Supreme Strength";[4] the favourite name for small bitches is the equivalent of Mary.[5] The cats are not the tailless kind of China, but like those of Bengal, and bear the Indian name of "Byila," as apparently showing their foreign origin.

The different modes of salutation were curiously varied amongst the several nationalities. The Tibetan doffs his cap with his right hand (see photo, p. 446) and making a bow pushes forward his left ear and puts out his tongue, which seems to me to be an excellent example of the "self-surrender of the person saluting to

[1] For full details see my *Buddhism of Tibet*, pp. 515-565.

[2] Tomo.

[3] Pa-to (m ?); might also mean Dough or Putty.

[4] Rab-shugs.

[5] Dölma, see pp. 316 and 426.

the individual he salutes," which Herbert Spencer has shown to lie at the bottom of many of our modern practices of salutation. The pushing forward of the left ear evidently recalls the old Chinese practice of cutting off the left ears of prisoners of war and presenting them to the victorious chief. The Mongol, without removing his hat, bows low, placing both palms on the front of his thighs; though equals stretch out both hands, and seizing the other's, squeeze and then shake them. The Bhotanese, who often go bareheaded, take the end of their plaid from their shoulders and spread it out as if offering a tray of presents, and at the same time bow low. The Nepalese and Mahomedans make a salaam, bowing and touching their forehead with the palm side of the tips of their fingers, thereby screening their face for the moment from the sacred view of the person they salute.

There seems quite a craze for edict pillars in Lhasa; nearly a dozen appear to have been erected at various times,[1] and the Councillors mentioned that perhaps the recent British Treaty will be made the subject of another. Nevertheless the unwritten law of the people seems to take pre-eminence over all, according to the saying: "Religion's laws are soft as silken

[1] A list of some of these published in 1851 (Rockhill, *loc. cit.* p. 264) cites eleven inscriptions in the Chinese character: (1) Imperial autograph dated 60th year of Kangshi (1721) on the pacification of Tibet. It is in front of Potala. (2) Imperial autograph dated 59th year of Chenlung (1794) also in front of Potala. [These two are probably within the small Chinese temples on either side of the tall edict pillar, see photo, p. 336.] (3) Imperial autograph dated 1808 in Chiaching's reign; it is entitled "Tablet of the narrative of the devotional ceremonies of the P'uto' tsung-sheng temple"; it is N.E. of Potala near Mount Sera. (4) Tablet commemorating the victorious campaign against the Goorkhas, in front of the Jo-k'ang, dated 1793. (5) Tablet of the hall of the drill-ground signed by the Amban and the assistant Amban Ho Ning. (6) Tablet of the erection of a temple to Kuanti on Lupan Hill, dated 1793. (7) Tablet of the Double Devotion N.E. of the Jok'ang, dated 1793; this tablet records

SUNSHADES IN TENGYE LING, LHASA.

(Note the pots of flowers
on window-sills.)

References to the chief Deities and Saints in the Rock Picture Gallery at Lhasa.

On right of the central inscription, the upper large red image, holding a beggar's bowl, is *Amitabha*, or the "Buddha of Boundless Light" (pp. 31, 192), who is incarnate in the Tashi Lama (pp. 30, 192); the large blue-bodied one is the celestial mystic Buddha, *Akshobya*. Below Amitabha is *Tārā* or *Dölma*, the green Goddess of Mercy (pp. 209, 316), holding a lotus flower; and on a level with her are the "Three Defenders" of the Lamaist faith, the blue Thunder-bolt-holder *Vajrapāni* (or *Chagnadorjé*), *Avalokita padma-pāni* (or *Chänrasi*), and the God of Wisdom (*Mänjusri*) (pp. 85-86). Below this triad is *Tsongkhapa*, the founder of the Yellow-Cap Order (p. 400), with his two chief disciples, to the right of whom is a dark red-capped Sakya Lama. On the border of the inscription stands the eight-handed form of the Grand Lama as the Lord of Mercy (*Chänrasi*) (p. 23).

On left of inscription, on its border, is the mythical primordial wizard-Buddha, "The Indestructible" (*Vajradhara*), holding a thunderbolt (*dorjé*, see cover of book) and a bell; above him is a colossal carving of the historical Buddha, Sakya Muni, with the wizard priest, the Founder of Lamaism (p. 115), above his left shoulder. On the right of Vajradhara, *i.e.*, to the reader's left, is the God of Wisdom (*Manjusri*) with the uplifted flaming sword of knowledge.

André & Sleigh, Ltd.

PAINTED ROCK SCULPTURES AT LHASA.

ESCORTED PARTY VISITING LHASA CITY.

CHINESE PROCLAMATION DEPOSING THE DALAI LAMA.
It was being torn down by the populace.

thread, but strong; the King's laws are heavy like a golden yoke; but the Country's laws stand hard as iron pillars, and are inflexible."

One of the interesting old memories of Lhasa is the community of the Capuchin fathers that lived here for so many years about two centuries ago, and were given a tract of land where they built a chapel, to which the Grand Lama and the Governors seem to have paid friendly visits. I made repeated attempts to ascertain the site of this chapel[1] with absolutely no definite result, no vestiges of any such building, nor of even the traditions of any "White" Lamas, were elicited. The prevalence of Florentine window-sunshades in Lhasa (see photo here) is, I believe, probably a survival of those introduced by these old Italian fathers; nor did anyone seem to know anything of Moorcroft's reputed visit to the city as related by Huc.[2]

The old palace of the military governors of Lhasa near Ramoché temple, called Kangda Kangsar (No. 21 on plan), is of much interest. It was often visited by the Capuchin fathers two centuries ago. Though now unoccupied, it still is one of the most striking buildings in Lhasa on account of its solid stone walls four storeys high and unwhitewashed.

As to Friar Odoric's alleged visit, as the first European to enter Lhasa, it seems to me very doubtful whether the city he visited in the fourteenth century A.D.

the history of the assassination in the 15th year of Chenlung (1752) of the two Chinese Ambans Fu and La, and is a temple at Ch'ungsu Kang (it has been translated by Jametel in the *Revue d'histoire diplomatique*, No. 3, 1887, p. 446). (8) Treaty between T'ang Te'-ts'ung and the King of Tibet, in front of the Jo-k'ang. (9-11) Three tablets dating from the 59th year of Kangshi (1721), two on the top of the east slope of Potala, and one at the east foot, composed by military officials who participated in the great campaign. They seem to be those which are cut on the rock.

[1] It was on a piece of land called Shar gyud Na-gar, or Sha-ch'en Naga, which seems to have been near Ramoché temple.

[2] See p. 17.

could have been this one at all, as his description of the place is so different from Lhasa as we now find it. The good friar writes: "The city is all built with walls of black and white, and all its streets are very well paved."[1] Now none of the streets of Lhasa are paved, although plenty of stones are locally available for the purpose, and it seems unlikely that a city which was formerly "very well paved" should have so entirely given up this practice and left no trace of it. The only parti-colouring of walls now in vogue is the transverse band of dull maroon along the line of beams on the eaves. I saw hereabouts none of those vertically banded houses with stripes of blue, red, and white that were so conspicuous in the Gyantsé and Ralung valleys.[2]

The "Rock Gallery" pantheon of paintings, described at p. 376 and here reproduced by colour photography,* was frequently passed in our outings.

On the northern border of the town is a crystal spring by the roadside (see No. 32 on plan), about which a pretty legend is related, as to how the Chinese princess, who was born out of a tear shed by the Compassionate Spirit for the poor benighted Tibetans, was sent as a bride to the great King Srongtsan, but was prevented seeing him through the wicked spell of a rival. She built a bower by the side of this spring, and languished here for two years, and in her sadness made a guitar, on which she played so sweetly that the king, hearing her play one day, was at once freed from the witchery of the jealous rival and married the princess, and they two lived happily ever after. Her body is said to be enshrined in the temple of Ramoché,

[1] Yule's *Cathay, and The Way Thither*, i. 148. Here "dwells the *Abassi*, which in their tongue is the Pope." Odoric's visit was during the Sakya rule (p. 26) before the rise of the Lhasa popes.

[2] This style is stigmatised as unorthodox, and so may have formerly been prevalent in Lhasa and put down by the yellow-caps.

* In black and white in the present edition.

about 50 yards to the west of this spring. On the high-road to the west of Lhasa, midway to Däpung, is a small summer-house by the roadside, "The Home of Religion"[1] where the Grand Lama halts for tea on the way to and from that monastery.

The arsenal on the opposite bank of the river, in which the Indian mechanics worked, was a new building, little more than a shed running round a square. It contained several good lathes, of local make, for boring gun-barrels and manufacturing cartridges, and a brass-bound driving fly-wheel, also some saws, files, and other tools of English manufacture, a large number of partially-made breech-blocks, bayonets and cartridges, and a quantity of sulphate of copper, sulphur, graphite, and a few guns. Another and larger arsenal is said to lie about 4 miles off amongst the hills. The fourth "Royal" monastery of Tsemchok Ling is near the arsenal, but is very small and commonplace. The "mint" had none of its appliances visible at our visit.

Restaurants are plentiful over the town; two large ones adjoin the great square of the market-place, and seem mostly patronised by the Chinese. One of them could accommodate about a hundred people. In these places and in the private houses a good deal of beer is drunk, but not much drunkenness or brawling was noticed.

Considerable excitement was caused in the city on the 13th September by the Amban placarding a proclamation in which he deposed the Dalai Lama by order of the Chinese Emperor;[2] but it was speedily torn down by the populace (see photo, p. 425). It specified that the Tashilhumpo Grand Lama was appointed to carry on the religious administration until a final decision was made regarding the runaway.

[1] Chö-kyi k'ang, the *Ching-yüan* or "Garden of the Classics" of the Chinese. Compare Rockhill, *loc. cit.* p. 258.

[2] For text, see p. 500.

There are precedents, as we have seen, for the deposition of the Dalai by the Emperor of China; but it was doubted by the Tibetan officials whether the Tashi Lama would accept the position conferred on him by the edict, and subsequent events proved that they were right.

In the proclamation, the Emperor of China was entitled "The five times Excellent One." This reminded us that the arrogant chief of Paro in Western Bhotan appropriated this title to himself in addressing the British Commissioner, whom he termed merely "The *three* times Excellent Commissioner"; this was before our armed occupation of Phari and the Chumbi Valley had impressed him with a proper respect for our superior strength.

The fugitive Dalai Lama reached the capital of Mongolia, Urga (see map, p. 4),* on November 27th, 1904. His arrival there was described by a local correspondent of the *Warsaw Gazette*:—

"His baggage and that of his suite was carried by 200 camels. The people of Urga had long been expecting his arrival, and, notwithstanding the severe frost, the Chinese and Mongol authorities, the clergy, an escort of Chinese troops, and over 20,000 citizens went out of the town for several miles to meet him. His arrival was announced to the rest of the population by a salvo of artillery, and he took up his quarters in a palace specially prepared for him, where all the holy men and teachers of Urga usually hold their meetings, and which contains the most famous Buddhist temples. Many thousands of pilgrims are arriving from all parts of Mongolia from the country beyond Lake Baikal and from the Astrakhan steppes to do him homage. Among them is Erettuyeff, the chief Lama of Eastern Siberia, who has obtained the permission of the Russian authorities to join the pilgrims. Although the etiquette of the Dalai Lama's Court forbids him to receive Europeans, he has given a long audience to a Russian official sent to him by the Consul. Various reports are

* On page xxiii in the present edition.

current among the Mongols and Buryats as to the Dalai Lama's plans for the future. Some say that he will proceed to the Goose Lake, where is the chief temple of the Lamas in the Trans-Baikal, others that he is going to St Petersburg."

Before we left Lhasa the Amban was preparing for possible trouble from the slumbering volcano, on the withdrawing of our troops, as the presence of these had considerably aided in restoring his lost prestige. He was enlisting more men locally for his body-guard and had asked for an additional thousand armed men from China.

CHAPTER XXIII.

THE RETURN JOURNEY — EXPLORATION OF THE TSANGPO VALLEY, AND SNOWBOUND AT PHARI.

AFTER a residence of nearly two months at Lhasa, we left that city on the 23rd September 1904, the whole force striking tents and marching away.

The previous day a round of ceremonial farewell visits had been paid by the Amban, the Councillors and Chief Abbots, who visited the Mission and the General, and cordially shook hands also with all the officers of the Staff. Several of us received from the Nepalese Consul and the monasteries trifling presents of trays of sweets and other things, made up in Chinese bulky fashion to augment their apparent value, but expressive of the friendly feeling which had arisen during our stay at the Hermit City.

In the early morning of our departure I was surprised to find, sitting outside my tent, the venerable Lama of Sera monastery who had assisted me in some enquiries into his religion, and to whom I had already said good-bye. He had walked all the way from the Lamasery to bid me a final farewell, and to present a parting gift of a painted scroll and an embroidered scarf; and presently there came also the young Lama of the Temple of Medicine to express regret that he was not able to proceed to India, owing to certain obstacles having been placed in his way, but he still hoped to come later on.

As we were starting, the Regent rode up with two

STATE COUNCILLORS AND GENERAL MACDONALD.

The three Shapés. Chief Secretary (successor of Ta Lama). Chief Chamberlain.

THE JOINT-GOVERNORS OR JONGPÖNS OF PHARI FORT.

SAVAGE ABORS OF THE DIHONG (LOWER TSANGPO).

Photographed in the Lower Dihong Valley
by the author.

STRIPED WALLS OF MONASTERY.

attendants and bade General Macdonald farewell, presenting him at the same time with a small gilt image of Buddha as a souvenir. He thanked him for his humanity in sparing the temples and monasteries, and said that he would pray for his safe return to India, and hoped that when he looked at that effigy of Buddha he would always think kindly of Tibet. After saying this, and requesting me to write to him sometimes, the Ruler of Tibet, a courteous, cultured priest, a man of generous impulses, shook hands, and mounting his horse, rode slowly away, evidently depressed by the cares of State which now, at this crisis, must weigh heavily on his shoulders.

We reached the Iron Bridge ferry over the Tsangpo in three days, though doubtless in the future, when there are stern-wheel launches and shallow draught steam-boats running to Lhasa, for which the river seems practicable, the distance to that city should be covered in a day; whilst from the ferry here our post goes in two days to Gyantsé, which should be only about three days from the Indian plains, *viâ* Chumbi, by a light steam tramway. As there was an easier crossing at an upper ferry, 10 miles above the old Iron Bridge, where the river was only 120 yards wide, it was made use of this time, and the whole force was ferried over within three days.[1]

During this halt the prohibition against shooting was relaxed, and many pigeons, hares, and a few gazelle and wild sheep[2] fell to some guns and rifles

[1] On the way we passed two large monasteries, *Tak-k'u-pe* and Yangtsé, this latter a fine large monastery with an incarnate head Lama, a pleasant young man, who came out as we passed; it has a *chorten*, which is visited by pilgrims as a shrine (ch'o-k'or); and near by are two old *chortens* called "The Royal Vases of the Plain" (*T'ang gyal bum-pa*).

[2] The giant sheep (*O. hodgsoni* or *ammon*) and great stag are not found here, so I was told by the hunter of the place, who

for the pot, affording a pleasant change from Commissariat rations. In the alder woods here I obtained three new species of birds.[1] The general absence of bright colours in the plumage of the birds was remarkable; nearly all were dull and dark hued, probably for protective purposes, amongst the prevailing olive tints of the trees, though autumn was now brightening the coppices on the sombre hillsides with brilliant patches of orange and russet. The luxuriance of the wild flowers here surpassed anything I have seen in any alpine meadow, and covered the ground with their variegated blossoms, even so late in the season as the end of September. The cultivation, too, at this level, 12,100 ft. above the sea, was surprisingly rich, covering the greater part of the bottom of the valley, the fields forming a golden sea of waving wheat and corn about 2 to 3 miles broad from near the river-bank up to the foot of the hills, where the irrigation canals from the river weirs fed the plain. The cottars were just commencing their harvest, forming great stacks of sheaves on their threshing-floors, where lines of yaks were treading out the corn. Some of the villagers suffered from goitre.

Westward, some 4 miles off, rose almost sheer from the broad meadow bottom the two bold snowy peaks, about 20,000 feet high, which seemed to close the upper end of the valley of the Tsangpo. From this near point of view they stand up like a forked cone, one of the peaks being distinguished as the "Lord" and the other as "The White-Horned Lady."[2] This mass of rock, the northern end of the Kharo spur, thrusts to its north side the great river, which is forced to cut its way through a chasm

said that the nearest place for the former was the tract between the Yamdok and Rham lakes, and for the latter, as well as for wild yaks, the Changt'ang plateau above Lhasa.

[1] Appendix XI. p. 487.

[2] Jomo karra or Jora.

so precipitous that no road for traffic can go this way to Shigatsé and the Upper Tsangpo Valley.[1] The detachment, therefore, of our party which was going *viâ* Shigatsé to open up the trade mart in N.W. Tibet as provided by the new Treaty, at Gartok on the Indus (see map, p. 40) to the east of Simla, under Captain Rawling, had to proceed to Shigatsé by way of Gyantsé and travel thence over 1000 miles behind the Himalayas, up into the bare desert plateaus, past the source of the Tsangpo, near the great Manasarowar Lake and sources of the Sutlej River, a region which I have twice visited, from the Almora and Garhwal Himalayas. As no Europeans have previously traversed the greater part of this barren valley above Shigatsé, this party should obtain some interesting geographical information about Mount Everest and Dhaulagiri and the trade routes from Nepal, though they will not touch the great gold-field region, Tok-jalung, which lies much further east, in the direct Lhasa-Ladak route *viâ* the Tengri Lake.[2]

With the new experience we have gained, we are now able to realise better than before the true

[1] The Amban and Dalai Lama usually go to Shigatsé by a road which strikes off at Toi-lung Bridge, in the Kyi valley.

[2] Captain Rawling's party, which included Captains Ryder and Wood, R.E., of the Survey Department, rapidly performed their adventurous journey and crossed into the Simla district on 24th December 1904. It appears that the Miriam-La (the watershed between the Brahmaputra and the Sutlej) was crossed so far back as 26th November. There was bad weather, with snow, but the pass was easy, though 16,600 feet above sea-level. A lake with no outlet was seen, and then the great Manasarowar Lake itself was reached. Here the work of exploration was, of course, full of attraction, for the controversy regarding this sheet of water is a very old one. Captains Ryder and Wood went to the outlet, and found there was no flow. A rise of 3 feet would have been necessary for the stream to run, but the Tibetans agreed in declaring that in the rains and when the snow melts, *i.e.* for some four months of the summer season, there is always an outflow. About a mile down the channel in the direction of the next lake, known as the Rakas Tal, a hot

physical features of this great central valley, which with its side glens may be called the real Land of the Tibetans, where the Tibetans dwell, in contradistinction to the surrounding lofty desert tableland of the Changt'ang and the frozen uplands which are unfitted for permanent habitation. This Tibet Proper is situated off the plateau altogether, and lies some 2000 to 9000 feet below it, on the terraces along its southern border, and within the deep rugged ravines there, that have been hewn out of the sides of the great plateau by the rivers which rise thereon, or in the adjoining snowy ridges which border or traverse it. Lying in these more genial regions, it descends to boldly sculptured, well-wooded valleys, with fertile meadows and scenery which recalls the Swiss Alps. Lhasa and Shigatsé thus occupy sheltered nooks upon the eroded shoulders or buttresses of the great plateau within the upper limit of trees (see physical map, p. 40).

It is, however, the Lower Tsangpo Valley, below this ferry, which is the most interesting and important, both from an economic and a geographical point of view. For the Tsangpo, the central river of Tibet, is now proved almost beyond doubt to be the upper source of the great Brahmaputra river of Assam,[1] and

spring was found, and the lake which was frozen over had no outflow. The Tibetans stated that a stream used to run from it in past years. The chief results of the exploration were to show that there was no higher peak than Everest visible to the north, and to place the source of the Sutlej far more to the west than has been usually believed. When the party visited Gartok they found only a few dozen people in winter quarters, their houses being in the midst of a bare plain. In the course of the journey to the British frontier, the party crossed the Ayi-La (18,400 feet), the cold being intense as snow was falling. The Sutlej there flows through very broken country, with ravines 2000 feet deep.

[1] For some additional proofs, see my article in the *Geographical Journal* (p. 258), 1895, which shows that the river-name is sometimes spelt by the Tibetans *Ts'ang-pu*, which is the literal equivalent of the Indian word *Brahmaputra*, which means "The Son of Brahma," the Creator.

along its banks therefore would be the natural inlet to this country from the Indian plains, whilst in the Lower Tsangpo Valley would seem to lie the richest and most genial tract of Tibet, resembling Kashmir in appearance, and giving access to the gold-mines east of the Yamdok Lakes (see route-map at end); but at present the greater part is unoccupied by the Tibetans, mainly on account, it is alleged, of the savage cannibal tribes who live there, and who absolutely cut off all communication between Tibet on the one hand and Assam on the other (see map, p. 40).

This *terra incognita* has never yet been penetrated even by the Tibetans, and the lower part only by one of the Survey spies who was sent to throw into the river marked logs of wood to prove the continuity of the Tsangpo with the Assam river. There is something pathetic in the way in which this well-planned experiment miscarried. This brave fellow, "K.P.," did his dangerous part in this trans-frontier exploration, which Kipling calls "The Great Game." Pushing his way through the forests infested with cannibals, and after thrilling adventures and escapes, he threw in the marked logs; but there was no one watching for them below in Assam, as meanwhile the officer in charge of the experiment had got fatally frost-bitten in the snows of Kangchenjunga. As this explorer, "K.P.," a naturalised Tibetan of the Sikhim Himalayas, was afterwards for several years in my service, and accompanied me on the present expedition, I elicited from him a vivid picture of this great "Unknown Land" below the Iron Bridge and the Lhasa river, which is of so much interest and importance that I may insert it here.

A short distance below this Lhasa ferry, the central valley of the Tsangpo becomes more and more wooded with every mile it descends. In this attractive part of the great Tsangpo Valley, with its countless tributary valleys running down from snowy peaks that cut the sky-line on either side, the great central river, about half a mile wide, flows tranquilly, a navigable stream, for about 100 miles, after which, although it becomes more rapid in places, it still is crossed by rude boats for a long way further down. Its banks are fringed with open grassy meadows several miles broad, dotted scantily here and there with hamlets and monasteries, as the settlements lie mostly in the level bottoms of the valleys, though some of the Lamaseries and hermitages nestle up the pine-clad bases of the bold side valleys. The scenery altogether is more of the kind we associate with the European Alps than with the outer Himalayas, where the settlements are perched on the summits of the mountains, from whence the stupendous depth of the valleys is quite depressing.

Already at about 50 miles below the Lhasa ferry it is fairly thickly wooded, and at 30 miles still further down the scenery must rival Kashmir, and has good roads "like the roads about Darjeeling." The resemblance to Kashmir is all the more striking as the broad central hollow here seems almost like a lake-valley. The great Tsangpo river, seeking its outlet to the southern sea, is hemmed in on the south by the giant Himalayas, and is forced to flow behind the whole length of the southern half of that range before it can find a passage through the rocky barrier. For over 100 miles below the Lhasa ferry the Tsangpo is a placid stream flowing south-east with the trend of the Himalayas, and so gentle is its current that long boat journeys are made up and down for distances of 200 miles or more. It still seems to retain something of this character for the next 100 miles further down along the district of Takpo, beyond which, at the Kongbu district, its course is barred by a bluff ridge running to the north-east, which appears to represent the last link of the chain of the main axis of the Himalayas. This bends the river northwards for about 80 miles till it reaches a depression near the end of the chain, through which, gathering its waters into a narrow torrent, it rushes down southwards in a series of rapids, precipitating itself over a cliff about 100 feet in depth, cutting and boring its way so deeply through the rocks that about 100 miles below these falls it is said to go quite out of sight, until it emerges in the Abor[1] country on the plains of Assam near Sadiya, where it is the chief feeder of the Brahmaputra, and is known by its Abor name of Dihong. For, although the absolute continuity of the Dihong and Tsangpo has not been actually traced throughout, the identity of these two rivers is now generally accepted.

The finest scenery and climate in the Central Valley appear to lie above the falls, beginning about 80 miles below the Lhasa ferry, and continuing for over 200 miles past the Takpo district with its gold mines (see route-map) to Kongbu; and this tract, although possessing good soil and pastures, is scarcely inhabited, apparently through fear of the wild tribes. In Kongbu wild peaches and apricots are so abundant that the pigs are fed on them, and a wild grape is also mentioned. One of the conspicuous peaks here is quaintly described as a "high slender snowy mountain, like a white column of cloud rising in the sky."

Of the falls, which seem to lie in about 29° 36′ N. latitude and 94° 47′ E. longitude (see map, p. 40), I attach a copy of a drawing of them made for me by a Tibetan artist, a native of the place, which is interesting amongst other things as showing bamboos there, also that the Tibetans with their inveterate superstition place a demon inside the falls.

Below the falls, Tibetan influence, which has been gradually dwindling as the valley descends, ceases

[1] For details regarding these Abors and adjoining tribes, see my "Tribes of the Brahmaputra Valley," *Jour. Bengal Assoc. Soc.* Part iii. 1900.

FALLS OF THE TSANGPO RIVER.
(*From a Tibetan drawing.*)

altogether after a few miles. The wild ravines below this point never did belong to Tibet, and its few hamlets do not bear Tibetan names. The country here is inhabited (if you can call a country "inhabited" which has only about one person to the square mile) by a sprinkling of savage cannibal tribes called by the Tibetans "Lalo" (*i.e.* savages)[1] and Chingmi.[2] They are allied to the Abors and Nagas of Assam, with whom they are more or less conterminous. Indeed, this part of the Tsangpo Valley for the next 100 miles downwards is already within our political sphere of influence from the Assam side, and is marked as such on some of our maps, although it has never yet been occupied by us, owing to the bitter hostility of these wild tribes and the dense forest of its lower section, through which, however, Mr Needham has penetrated a short distance.[3] The climate soon begins to get warm below the falls. About 20 miles or so farther down, Explorer K.P. and others state that it is sufficiently hot to grow rich patches of rice, cotton, millet, "apples," and plantains; silkworms abound in the woods and fish in the rivers. The forest becomes ranker with tangled undergrowth and brakes, among which roam many deer, tigers, and the lordly "Mithan" (*Bos frontalis*); but the atmospheric dryness—and this is a great point—is attested by numerous "Cheer" pines (*Pinus longifolia*), which cannot exist on the damp,

[1] The "Black Savages" (*Lalo* or *Glak-lo Nagpo*) are said to eat their prisoners of war, and at their marriage festivals kill and eat the mother of the bride if no other person is forthcoming.

[2] These latter are described as being like the Lepchas; those around the Tsari mountain call themselves "Pakchat siri," and supply most of the baskets used in Lhasa.

[3] The Abor expedition of 1894 followed up the Dihong to a point about 100 miles above Sadiya, where the river appeared to flow from an almost westerly direction, and the country beyond was seen to consist of rolling downs, almost free from heavy forest. As a result of this expedition the subsidy or "blackmail" to the Abors was withdrawn.

dripping Indian side of these southern Himalayas. The track along the river here is reported by Explorer K.P., who is the sole authority for this region (as no Tibetans ever penetrate so far), as being "difficult" at times owing to cliffs. By experience I have found that K.P. tended to minimise the difficulties of mountain tracts; so that until this lower valley is surveyed by Europeans its difficulties cannot be estimated properly. The sides of the valley are cool, and every gradation of temperate climate should be found in the lateral valleys, most of which run up to high peaks.

It is the tract below the temple of Samyä,[1] Chetang, some 80 miles down from the Lhasa ferry, which possesses the most magnificent climate and varied scenery, and is the most fertile; and in it are few or no spots of any consequence which are generally esteemed sacred. Besides, comparatively little of this part of the country seems actually occupied by the Tibetans. In the remaining two-thirds of this basin belonging to Tibet, there are perhaps not more than 5000 Tibetans all told. This estimate excludes a peculiarly isolated settlement called Lower "Po" in the north-eastern corner, which, owing to an intervening ridge, seems to have its outlet lower down. The history of this settlement, as lately ascertained by Mr Rockhill when he passed to the north of it in Tibet, is interesting as showing how this country may be developed under more civilised influences.[2]

Reluctantly we turned our backs on the fascinating secrets of this unexplored valley, and climbed out of the trough of the Tsangpo into the Yamdok basin by the Dok Pass (16,800 feet), which was generally

[1] Samyä monastery contains the State treasury and gold from the mines. Near this is the thriving village of Chetang, or "The Plain of Peaks," with about fifty Nepalese and Chinese shops at a large ferry.

[2] Appendix XV. p. 503.

EASTERN TIBETAN OF KHAM.

CEMETERY OF BRITISH WHO FELL AT GYANTSÉ.
(On river bank under the Fort.)

WHEEL OF LIFE IN VESTIBULE OF GYANTSÉ TEMPLE.

similar to the neighbouring though slightly lower pass by which we had come (Kamba, 16,500 feet).

From this high ridge we enjoyed magnificent panoramas in the clear crisp atmosphere. Away to the east rose a snowy peak which probably was Tsari, to the north the snow-capped Nyän-chan Tang, which shut the inland sea of Tengri from view, to the south the dominating mass of Nöjin Kang Sang above the Kharo Pass; but no vestige of the Chumolhari range or of the dome of Kula Kangri to the east was visible. The conical peak which the Littledales saw from Tengri Lake, on the southern horizon, must, I feel sure, have been Nöjin Kang Sang with its satellites.

The great Yamdok lake was as blue as ever, surrounded by its bare hills, which were now bleaker even than before, the frost and snow having killed off all the grass and wild flowers, the withered remains of which rusted the hill-sides. The weather fortunately was splendid, not a speck in the cloudless sky and little wind; but the nights were very cold, 10 degrees below the freezing-point, showing that we had not left Lhasa a day too soon. Another striking instance of the early onset of winter was the total absence of all small fish along the shores of the lake at Palté and Nagartsé and in the small feeder streams.[1] The wild ducks, and geese, and other waterfowl which had swarmed there in thousands had nearly all deserted this inland sea for warmer climes, and several V-shaped flights of them could be seen leaving their summer haunts for the south:

> "When inclement winters vex the plain
> With piercing frosts or thick descending rain,
> To warmer seas the cranes embodied fly."

On either side of the Kharo Pass the snow lay

[1] The only place in which fish were seen was at the incoming stream from Yarsig.

decidedly deeper than when we had crossed two and a half months previously, having fallen, doubtless, at the time when we were having such heavy rain in Lhasa. This additional snow enhanced the beauty of the overhanging cornices on the sheer ice-walls. The Ralung valley also was already in its black winter garb.[1] With our arrival at Gyantsé, which we now called "the half-way house," we got again into touch with the telegraph, and felt we were getting near home.

At Gyantsé a few days' halt was made to pick up the heavy baggage and the warm clothing, such as it was after surviving the vicissitudes of the last winter's rough life, to repair the cemetery (photo here),[2] and to leave a small escort and a year's supplies for Captain O'Connor, who was remaining as Trade Agent under the new Treaty, with Captain Steen I.M.S. as resident surgeon.

From here, our march back to India was immensely facilitated by the excellent cart-road which had been constructed by the hands of our troops of the posts along the line of communications. The sepoys of each of these posts made a section of the road on either side of their little fort, and these sections when linked up together formed a grand trunk road, which extended for over 100 miles across the plateau, all the way from Gyantsé to the Himalayan ravines south of Phari; and along it streamed every day convoys of more than 800 carts, pouring in food supplies for the large force at the front and to stock the Gyantsé garrison. These carts, indeed, contributed in no small degree

[1] The pass over the top of this valley west of the Kharo leads us to the Rong Valley. It was explored, and found to be 16,750 feet high, and as easy as the Kharo. It is called "The Nape of the Ravines" (*Nya-rong*), and was a double pass over two ridges. The first village beyond the pass is Takra.

[2] The Expedition had sixteen engagements and skirmishes, with 202 casualties, including twenty-three British officers, of whom five were killed at and around Gyantsé.

to the military success of the Expedition, and more than justified General Macdonald's foresight in importing them at such pains over the mountains from India (p. 151); for it is not too much to say that it would have been impossible, after the breakdown of the yak transport through murrain, to have got up sufficient supplies in time for the advance and return from Lhasa, but for this *ekka* train. The road also, thus quickly extemporised for these carts, is already for most of the way a good driving road for mail-carts and "tongas"; and the superstitious Tibetans, when looking at its smooth path bordered by low walls of stone and its line of steel telegraph posts stretching away and disappearing on either horizon, may well be excused for regarding it with wonder and awe. In this road our pioneers and sepoys have certainly left their mark upon Tibet.

The return from Gyantsé over the bleak uplands was without incident as far as the Tang Pass, through the main chain of the Himalayas, where, as we crossed under the lofty crest of Chumolhari, a blinding blizzard suddenly swept down upon us, making it a painful struggle for everyone to reach Phari before nightfall. At night the cold inside the tents was 27° Fahr. below the freezing-point, and during the night our troubles were increased by a heavy snowfall of over 3 feet, which buried up our tents, numbers of which collapsed in the middle of the night, half smothering their occupants, and, completely obliterating the road, held us snowbound. It looked as if the terrible ice-giants of the Himalayas were determined that we should not bring away too pleasant recollections of Tibet and our invasion of their icy realms. But that the storm should have happened just when it did, on the very eve of our leaving those regions, was unfortunate, as one more day's march would have taken us down into the tree zone.

Next morning the camp was a wondrous sight. In many cases the men remained beneath their fallen tents half suffocated, but too cold and tired to get up and erect them again. The yaks lay placidly embedded in the snow, as in caves, from which only their black heads powdered with snowflakes projected; and dirty Phari stood transformed, for once spotlessly pure and white. We now realised why the Phari people dread having snow added to their many discomforts, and had appealed to us not to fire guns near Chumolhari, as it caused snow to fall.

A dash was made on the second day to escape into the Chumbi valley, as the snow had slightly melted and in case more should fall, as our stock of food would only last a few days at the most. Special precautions were taken to guard against snow-blindness. Although 20,000 pairs of green and smoked goggles had been issued at the beginning of the expedition, it was now found that a large proportion of the men, with the customary improvidence of soldiers, had thrown away or carelessly lost their eye-preservers. Each of these men was now made to tie a dark bandage over his eyes as a protection. As our army sallied forth from Phari that morning over the spotlessly white plain, with the pure cone of Chumolhari towering supreme over all, it recalled the retreat of Napoleon from Moscow, and we only hoped it would not prove as disastrous. The sun shone out brightly, and its glare reflected from the satiny sheen of the melting snow was so dazzling as to be almost blinding, even to the eye protected by dark-coloured glasses. Every one tramped on painfully with bent head through the deep snow, shading his eyes at intervals with his hand, and possessed by the one thought, to escape snow-blindness. After about five hours' march we got beyond the edge of the white plain, and entered the ravine leading down to the frozen Dot'ag, and below this the snow grew rapidly thinner as we descended, till by the time we reached Gaut'ang, the grateful sight of its black pines well justified to us its name of "The Meadow of Gladness," and here everyone ere nightfall was enjoying the luxury of roaring log-fires, on the snow under the pines.

In the morning it was found that about 200 of the men were snow-blind, and it was pathetic to see them led helplessly along by their fellows. As showing the protective power of the glasses, it was comical to see one of our number, who had lost one of the glasses of his eye-preservers, was snow-blind in that eye only, and marched along with it bandaged up. Every one of us had his face severely blistered and burned by the terrible glare from the snow, so much so that it peeled and was painfully tender for a week or more, so that the usual morning salutation of "How's the head?" with reference to the headache from the great altitudes, was now exchanged for "How's the face?" The nose was especially burned, and those who most escaped this infliction were the few who wore motor-masks.

Chumbi was reached the next day, and in its genial climate all had a rest for a day or two. The people were busy harvesting, and were tying up the sheaves on tall poles to preserve them against the damp, as one observes in Norway. It was sad to see how the rich harvest of rupees reaped by the thousands of our Nepalese coolies was being wasted in gambling. Oblivious of everything around them, they sat in excited groups tossing up the silver coins and playing games of chance, parting with their unusually high but hard-earned wages recklessly.

We emerged from Tibet over the deep snow-drifts of the Nathu Pass, whence we descended to the Indian plains through the beautiful wooded gorges of the Sikhim Himalayas, where the sands of Lamaism are fast running out, and the prayer-wheel is being expelled by the Trident of the Brahmans and the Cross of the

Christians. As our returning waves of dusty humanity toiled across the strip of open plain to the railway at Silliguri, we were able to pause for a last look backwards, up to the towering edge of the icy table-land from which we had come, and to think, before we threw off the harness of war, what had been achieved by the laborious toil of this unique Expedition to the Roof of the World.

The earthly paradise of "The Living Buddha" is no longer the centre of fabulous conjecture. Its ring fence of mysticism has been penetrated, and the full glare of Reality has dispelled the mirage of spurious marvels that gathered over this Far Eastern Mecca during its long centuries of seclusion. Its doors are now thrown freely open to the trader, and even to the adventurous tourist who may wish to penetrate the old-world romance that still clings to it. Many hundred miles of good roads have been made and vast tracts of the country mapped out; and if in the new facilities for communication with the outside world the light of civilisation should dissipate the dense mists of ignorance and unhealthy superstitions that cruelly harass the people, it would indeed be a blessing to The Hermit Land, whilst politically the Expedition has vindicated British prestige in the eyes of the world for the protection of India at a timely moment, and opened a new chapter in the History of Asia.

On the other hand, it must be acknowledged that the devil-worship and superstition which have been brought so prominently before the reader seem to demand an apology from one who has been in some measure identified with the study of "Northern" Buddhism. Why is it that we find here, in the citadel of one of the great religions of the world, so little which a traveller from Europe can appropriate or approve? Is the system wholly degenerate? Are the tares, which spring up instead of wheat in a barren soil, the effect

PEASANTS OF CENTRAL TIBET.

upon the ancient enlightenment of a thousand years of barbaric decadence? Will the dead bones among which we have been rummaging, amid the solitudes of the world's roof, never again live? Shall we Westerners when we obtain possession write no cheerful resurgance over their immemorial shrines?

In the world growth and decay go on side by side. The movement of the human spirit is, "One shape of many names." What meets the eye is not always a sure indication of character. The Catholic organisation, for example, was in the twelfth century sunk into apparently hopeless decay, yet in a few years we had Dante, and a century or two later the Renaissance. If a learned Tibetan were to attend a wee Free Kirk service in the Highlands, or in that lovely forbidden region of the Clyde, the island of Arran, he might be quite right in thinking it no better than some of the most degraded observances of his friends at home; but would certainly not be justified in concluding that Scotland was sunk in ignorance and in the practice of a peculiarly malignant form of devil-worship. Were we to carry out the evangelical precept, that the true way to judge a religion is by its fruits, are we sure that the rulers of India would better abide the test than the poor peasants of the Tibetan hills?

For my part, I approve the extremely practical method of my friend, the Cardinal of Lhasa, and am further of opinion that there was much point in his enquiry as to whether Buddha is mentioned in the sacred books of Europe. Would not a knowledge of the religions of Asia on the part of the fathers of the Catholic Church have saved that institution from the degeneration which befell it so soon after the disappearance of its immortal founder? The recent vogue of Buddhism in Europe has been held to betoken a latitudinarian indifference. It may be that it is a sign rather of a new illumination, showing that Christians are at length beginning to understand the Word of the Master, who was in truth much nearer akin to Buddha than to Paul or Augustine or Luther, or any of the others who have proclaimed themselves to be in a special sense His followers and interpreters.

In short, the real mind of Tibet seems to me to be more authentically expressed in the words of the Cardinal of Lhasa than in the superstitions of the monks and people. And I would fain believe that the mission of England is here not so much to inter decently the corpse of a decadent cult, as to inaugurate a veritable dawn, to herald the rise of a new star in the East, which may for long, perhaps for many centuries, diffuse its mild radiance over this charming land and interesting people. In the University, which must ere long be established under British direction at Lhasa, a chief place will surely be assigned to studies in the origin of the religion of the country.

SEAL OF DALAI LAMA.
(In square Indian characters, full size impression.)

SEAL OF TASHI LAMA.
(Full size impression.)
It bears in modern Indian characters the word "*Mangalam*," which is the equivalent of the Tibetan "Tashi."

APPENDICES

SCIENTIFIC RESULTS AND NOTES TO THE TEXT.

APPENDIX I.

TIBETAN YEAR-CYCLES.

THE Tibetan system of reckoning time is of a mixed Western and Chinese origin. It is by the twelve-year and sixty-year cycles of Jupiter which have been derived through India from the West, but with the substitution of some Chinese astrological terms for the Indian, the Tibetans having derived their chronological system mainly from India with their Buddhism in the seventh century A.D. The twelve-year cycle, in which the year is named after the twelve zodiacal beasts (see last column of Table), is only used for short periods. For longer times and general use these twelve animals are combined with the five elements of the Chinese, namely, wood, fire, earth, iron, and water, and each of these elemental bodies is given a pair of animals, the first being considered a male and the second a female; and it is by giving a realistic meaning to these several animal-elements of the year with reference to those of the birth year of the person, and the time in question, that the astrologer-Lamas concoct an endless variety of repulsions and attractions requiring costly rites to be performed by the priests to neutralise their evil influences. I here append for reference a list of the cycle-years of the more recent past and near future :—

Year A.D.	Tibetan Era. Cycle No.	Cyclical year.	Year-name.	Year A.D.	Tibetan Era. Cycle No.	Cyclical year.	Year-name.
1862	XIV	56	Water-Dog.	1895	XV	29	Wood-Sheep.
1863	,,	57	,, -Hog.	1896	,,	30	Fire-Ape.
1864	,,	58	Wood-Mouse.	1897	,,	31	,, -Bird.
1865	,,	59	,, -Ox.	1898	,,	32	Earth-Dog.
1866	,,	60	Fire-Tiger.	1899	,,	33	,, -Hog.
1867	XV	1	,, -Hare.	1900	,,	34	Iron-Mouse.
1868	,,	2	Earth-Dragon.	1901	,,	35	,, -Ox.
1869	,,	3	,, -Serpent.	1902	,,	36	Water-Tiger.
1870	,,	4	Iron-Horse.	1903	,,	37	,, -Hare.
1871	,,	5	,, -Sheep.	1904	,,	38	Wood-Dragon.
1872	,,	6	Water-Ape.	1905	,,	39	,, -Serpent.
1873	,,	7	,, -Bird.	1906	,,	40	Fire-Horse.
1874	,,	8	Wood-Dog.	1907	,,	41	,, -Sheep.
1875	,,	9	,, -Hog.	1908	,,	42	Earth-Ape.
1876	,,	10	Fire-Mouse.	1909	,,	43	,, -Bird.
1877	,,	11	,, -Ox.	1910	,,	44	Iron-Dog.
1878	,,	12	Earth-Tiger.	1911	,,	45	,, -Hog.
1879	,,	13	,, -Hare.	1912	,,	46	Water-Mouse.
1880	,,	14	Iron-Dragon.	1913	,,	47	,, -Ox.
1881	,,	15	,, -Serpent.	1914	,,	48	Wood-Tiger.
1882	,,	16	Water-Horse.	1915	,,	49	,, -Hare.
1883	,,	17	,, -Sheep.	1916	,,	50	Fire-Dragon.
1884	,,	18	Wood-Ape.	1917	,,	51	,, -Serpent.
1885	,,	19	,, -Bird.	1918	,,	52	Earth-Horse.
1886	,,	20	Fire-Dog.	1919	,,	53	,, -Sheep.
1887	,,	21	,, -Hog.	1920	,,	54	Iron-Ape.
1888	,,	22	Earth-Mouse.	1921	,,	55	,, -Bird.
1889	,,	23	,, -Ox.	1922	,,	56	Water-Dog.
1890	,,	24	Iron-Tiger.	1923	,,	57	,, -Hog.
1891	,,	25	,, -Hare.	1924	,,	58	Wood-Mouse.
1892	,,	26	Water-Dragon.	1925	,,	59	,, -Ox.
1893	,,	27	,, -Serpent.	1926	,,	60	Fire-Tiger.
1894	,,	28	Wood-Horse.	1927	XVI	1	,, -Hare.

APPENDIX II.

POINTS REACHED BY PREVIOUS MODERN TRAVELLERS.

THE nearest points to Lhasa reached by these respective explorers were :—Mr Rockhill, in 1892, penetrated to the N.E. of Tengri Lake, about 110 miles, or a week's journey N. of the city. M. Bonvalot and Prince Henry of Orleans, in 1890, reached the Tengri Lake, 95 miles N. of Lhasa. In 1891, Captain Bower arrived at Garing Lake, about 200 miles N.W. of the holy city. In 1892, Miss A. Taylor seems to have reached Nagchuk'a, about twelve days' journey from the Capital. In 1893, M. Dutreuil de Rhins and his companion insinuated themselves as far as the S.E. corner of Tengri Lake, about 70 miles or 5 days' journey from Lhasa. Dr Sven Hedin, in the guise of a Buriat Mongol, and a modest following with only four Cossacks as an escort, succeeded in reaching a spot 150 miles N.N.W. of Lhasa, about half a month's journey from the sacred city.

APPENDIX III.

CONVENTION BETWEEN GREAT BRITAIN AND CHINA RELATING TO SIKKIM AND TIBET.

Signed at Calcutta, 17th March 1890.

[Ratifications exchanged at London, 27th August 1890.]

English Text.

Whereas Her Majesty the Queen of the United Kingdom of Great Britain and Ireland, Empress of India, and His Majesty the Emperor of China, are sincerely desirous to maintain and perpetuate the relations of friendship and good understanding which now exist between their respective Empires; and whereas recent occurrences have tended towards a disturbance of the said relations, and it is desirable to clearly define and permanently settle certain matters connected with the boundary between Sikkim and Tibet, Her Britannic Majesty and His Majesty the Emperor of China have resolved to conclude a Convention on this subject, and have, for this purpose, named Plenipotentiaries, that is to say:

Her Majesty the Queen of Great Britain and Ireland, His Excellency the Most Honourable Henry Charles Keith Petty Fitzmaurice, G.M.S.I., G.C.M.G., G.M.I.E., Marquess of Lansdowne, Viceroy and Governor-General of India.

And His Majesty the Emperor of China, His Excellency Shêng Tai, Imperial Associate Resident in Tibet, Military Deputy Lieutenant-Governor;

Who, having met and communicated to each other their full powers, and finding these to be in proper form, have agreed upon the following Convention in eight Articles:—

Article I.

The boundary of Sikkim and Tibet shall be the crest of the mountain range separating the waters flowing into the Sikkim Teesta and its affluents from the waters flowing into the Tibetan Mochu and northwards into other rivers of Tibet. The line commences at Mount Gipmochi on the Bhutan frontier, and follows the above mentioned water-parting to the point where it meets Nipal territory.

Article II.

It is admitted that the British Government, whose Protectorate over the Sikkim State is hereby recognised, has direct and exclusive control over the internal administration and foreign relations of that State, and except through and with the permission of the British Government, neither the Ruler of the State nor any of its officers shall have official relations of any kind, formal or informal, with any other country.

Article III.

The Government of Great Britain and Ireland and the Government of China engaged reciprocally to respect the boundary as defined in Article I., and to prevent acts of aggression from their respective sides of the frontier.

Article IV.

The question of providing increased facilities for trade across the Sikkim-Tibet frontier will hereafter be discussed with a view to a mutually satisfactory arrangement by the High Contracting Powers.

Article V.

The question of pasturage on the Sikkim side of the frontier is reserved for further examination and future adjustment.

Article VI.

The High Contracting Powers reserve for discussion and arrangement the method in which official communication between the British authorities in India and the authorities in Tibet shall be conducted.

Article VII.

Two Joint-Commissioners shall, within six months from the ratification of this Convention, be appointed, one by the British Government in India, the other by the Chinese Resident in Tibet. The said Commissioners shall meet and discuss the questions which, by the last three preceding Articles, have been reserved.

Article VIII.

The present Convention shall be ratified, and the ratifications shall be exchanged in London as soon as possible after the date of the signature thereof.

In witness whereof the respective negotiators have signed the same and affixed thereunto the seals of their arms.

Done in quadruplicate at Calcutta, this 17th day of March, in the year of our Lord 1890, corresponding with the Chinese date, the 27th day of the second moon of the 16th year of Kuang Hsu.

(L.S.) (Signed) LANSDOWNE.

(L.S.) Signature of the Chinese Plenipotentiary.

APPENDIX IV.

CLIMATE AND METEOROLOGY.

I AM indebted for the following records of temperature to Captain T. B. Kelly, I.M.S. They were taken with the utmost care inside a double-fly Cabul tent, with the door-flap half open in order to show the actual temperature to which the men were subjected to. Other observations out of doors at the same time and in the same locality, taken by myself and others, are placed within brackets, and these comparative observations showed that the tent temperatures differed from the outside ones by an average of about 4° Fahrenheit only. The maximum temperatures refer to the camp opposite which they are shown, the minimum to the previous camp. The thermometers used were tested by fresh ones from the Survey of India, and found to agree with these to within a fraction of a degree. The elevations, when not recorded by the Survey Department, were taken by aneroids controlled by hypsometer.

The lowest temperature recorded was −26° F., or 58° below the freezing point at Chugya, an encampment on the Tang Pass. At the posts of Tuna and Phari, night temperatures of −17° F. and −15° or 47° and 49° of frost were repeatedly reached. At this elevation of about 5000, the normal minimum temperature in January is probably about 22° F. In the Arctic regions much lower temperatures were experienced by Nansen and the *Discovery*, the former recording 89° F. of frost, and the latter, in May 1903, 100° F. of frost; but these explorers were sheltered in warm ships, whilst in the Tibetan expedition, the men, who were mostly natives of the tropics, had to be out in the open air, and marching under these rigorous temperatures, so that it is a matter of congratulation that they entirely escaped any disaster such as befell the Russians in the Turkish War of 1877, when the 24th Division lost over 6000 men in a snowstorm in crossing the Skipka Pass on the 18th to 20th December, and 2000 men of General Gourko's were frozen to death in the same storm.

In the Chant'ang desert, Captain Bower found in 1891, during September, at elevations between 15,000 and 17,000, that the temperatures at daybreak ranged between 19° and 29° F.; during October, between 21° and 15° below zero; and during November between 2° and 15° below zero. There was, in fact, uninterrupted frost at daybreak throughout the last five months of the year, while in October and November the thermometer fell to 47° below freezing point. Snow, which fell frequently even in July and August, was of daily occurrence from September onward, while heavy rain constantly occurred, and the country was cut up by deep water-courses.

Date.	Place.	Elevation in feet above sea-level.	Minimum temperature in Fahrenheit degrees.	Maximum temperature in Fahrenheit degrees.	Remarks.
1903					
Nov. 6	Sivok	500	64*	78	* At Silliguri (397 ft.)
,, 7	Riang	620	64	82	
,, 8	Tarkhola	900	61	83	
,, 9	Rangpo	1,200	57	86	
,, 10	,,	,,	56	84	
,, 11	,,	,,	55	85	
,, 12	Pakyong	4,450	51	71	
,, 13	,,	,,	50	74	
,, 14	,,	,,	49	71	
,, 15	,,	,,	48	71	
,, 16	,,	,,	48	70	
,, 17	,,	,,	47	69	
,, 18	,,	,,	49	68	
,, 19	,,	,,	48	68	
,, 20	,,	,,	48	70	
,, 21	,,	,,	49	73	
,, 22	,,	,,	49	69	
,, 23	,,	,,	50	73	
,, 24	,,	,,	55	70	Thunderstorm and wind.
,, 25	,,	,,	52	64	
,, 26	,,	,,	52	65	
,, 27	,,	,,	53	61	
,, 28	,,	,,	51	70	
,, 29	,,	,,	51	61	
,, 30	,,	,,	50	58	
Dec. 1	,,	4,450	47	62	
,, 2	Rorot'ang	1,660	46	72	
,, 3	Lingtam	3,960	54	76	
,, 4	Jeyluk	8,760	40	44	

Date.	Place.	Elevation in feet above sea-level.	Minimum temperature in Fahrenheit degrees.	Maximum temperature in Fahrenheit degrees.	Remarks.
1903					
Dec. 5	Gnatong	12,210	38	36	
,, 6	,,	,,	23	42	
,, 7	,,	,,	15	42	
,, 8	,,	,,	16	40	
,, 9	,,	,,	16	40	
,, 10	,,	,,	19	49	
,, 11	,,	,,	23	34	
,, 12	,,	,,	21	40	
,, 13	,,	,,	14	38	
,, 14	,,	,,	14	43	
,, 15	,,	,,	16	44	
,, 16	,,	,,	21	51	
,, 17	,,	,,	24	47	
,, 18	,,	,,	23	46	
,, 19	,,	,,	22	44	
,, 20	,,	,,	20	53	
,, 21	,,	,,	16	46	[Phari – 9½ minimum.]
,, 22	,,	,,	16	44	[Phari – 7° minimum.]
,, 23	Langram	12,150	17	42	
,, 24	Rinchengang	9,370	15	52	
,, 25	Chumbi	9,780	34	51	
,, 26	,,	,,	23	56	
,, 27	,,	,,	18	60	
,, 28	,,	,,	17	59	
,, 29	,,	,,	20	58	
,, 30	,,	,,	20	63	
,, 31	,,	,,	20	57	
1904					
Jan. 1	Tongshong	12,200	18	52	Clear, windy S.W. after sunset.
,, 2	,,	,,	24	57	Half-gale S.W. at night. Calm in day.
, 3	,,	,,	23	54	Calm and clear.
,, 4	,,	,,	25	54	,, ,,
,, 5	Kamparab	14,300	– 21 (– 22)	31	Above tree line. Calm, clear.
,, 6	Phari	14,570	– 14 (– 20)	33	Calm, clear.
,, 7	Chugya	14,650	– 3 (– 26)	30	S. wind, slight, clear.
,, 8	Tuna	14,950	– 8 (– 12)	28	Calm, clear.
,, 9	,,	,,	– 7 (– 11)	42	Bright, cloudless.
,, 10	,,	,,	– 5 (– 8½)	40	,, ,,
,, 11	,,	,,	+ 3 (– 1½)	35	Calm. Wind after 11 A.M.
,, 12	,,	,,	– 4 (– 4)	35	Calm, clear. S.W. wind afternoon.
,, 13	,,	,,	– 5 (– 1½)	48	Half-gale. S.W. wind and sand.
,, 14	,,	,,	– 3 (– 6)	52	Clear, calm. S.W. wind later.

Date.	Place.	Elevation in feet above sea-level.	Minimum temperature in Fahrenheit degrees.	Maximum temperature in Fahrenheit degrees.	Remarks.
1904 Jan. 15	Tuna	14,950	− 11 (0)	48	Cloudy, calm.
,, 16	,,	,,	− 4 (− 8)	51	Calm, clear.
,, 17	,,	,,	+ 2 (− 4)	45	Calm, clear, half-gale. S.W. wind afternoon.
,, 18	,,	,,	+ 17 (+ 12)	49	Stormy, S.W. wind; dust and sand.
,, 19	,,	,,	+ 11 (+ 5)	44	Stormy, snow on hills, S.W.
,, 20	,,	,,	+ 8 (+ 5)	48	Calm, clear.
,, 21	,,	,,	+ 2 (− 2½)	55	Windy, S.W., and sand.
,, 22	,,	,,	+ 1 (− 3)	57	Calm, clear.
,, 23	,,	,,	+ 4 (− 3½)	55	,, ,,
,, 24	,,	,,	+ 2 (− 4)	43	Windy, S.W., and dust.
,, 25	,,	,,	+ 5 (− 1½)	42	,, ,,
,, 26	,,	,,	− 2 (− 6)	45	Calm, clear, morning. Windy and dust, afternoon.
,, 27	,,	,,	+ 13 (+ 7½)	48	Gale from S.W., cloudy.
,, 28	,,	,,	+ 9 (+ 3½)	43	Windy, S.
,, 29	,,	,,	+ 4 (− 1)	41	Windy.
,, 30	,,	,,	+ 7 (+ 1)	32	Snow from 5-10 P.M., 2 ins., with wind.
,, 31	,,	,,	+ 4 (− 1)	15	Snow, 1½ ins., S. wind.
Feb. 1	,,	,,	+ 2 (− 1)	19	Cloudy, with heavy gusts wind. No snow.
,, 2	,,	,,	− 4 (− 10)	34	Calm, clear. Cloudy in afternoon.
,, 3	,,	,,	− 3 (− 8)	48	Calm, clear.
,, 4	,,	,,	− 3 (− 7)	31	Heavy clouds, S.W. and W.
,, 5	,,	,,	+ 1 (− 3)	33	Slight snow at 9 P.M.
,, 6	,,	,,	− 3 (− 7)	45	Clear, moderate wind, S.
,, 7	,,	,,	+ 6 (+ 1)	48	Calm, clear.
,, 8	,,	,,	+ 3 (− 1½)	49	,, ,,
,, 9	,,	,,	+ 6 (+ 2)	52	,, ,,
,, 10	,,	,,	+ 8 (+ 1)	49	Calm morning. Wind and dust afternoon.
,, 11	,,	,,	+ 11 (+ 5)	50	Fine morning. Wind N.E. afternoon.
,, 12	,,	,,	+ 7 (+ 2)	49	Calm, clear.
,, 13	,,	,,	+ 5 (− 3)	50	,, ,, morning. Wind and dust afternoon.
,, 14	,,	,,	+ 10 (+ 4)	42	,, ,,
,, 15	,,	,,	+ 4 (− 1)	46	Wind and clouds afternoon.
,, 16	,,	,,	+ 14 (+ 8)	37	Snow all round, but none at Tuna.

Date.	Place.	Elevation in feet above sea-level.	Minimum temperature in Fahrenheit degrees.	Maximum temperature in Fahrenheit degrees.	Remarks.
1904 Feb. 17	Tuna	14,950	+13 (+8)	32	Half-gale, S., and clouds.
,, 18	,,	,,	+9 (+3)	34	Wind and clouds; snow all round, but none at Tuna.
,, 19	,,	,,	+6 (+2)	35	,, ,,
,, 20	,,	,,	+6 (−2)	43	Calm, clear; clouds later.
,, 21	,,	,,	+11 (+3)	46	Cloudy, moderate wind, slight snow.
,, 22	,,	,,	+6 (0)	49	Calm, clear; clouds, S.W.
,, 23	,,	,,	+10 (+4)	50	Slight snow at night. Wind after 3 P.M.
,, 24	,,	,,	+8 (+2)	56	Calm, clouds to S.W.
,, 25	,,	,,	+15 (+10½)	53	Calm.
,, 26	,,	,,	+25 (+21)	54	Cloudy, S.W. (warmest night).
,, 27	,,	,,	+15 (+8)	46	Windy and cloudy. Slight earthquake at 11.20 A.M. Snow to W. afterwards.
,, 28	,,	,,	+14 (+8)	49	N.E. wind. S.W., snowy clouds.
,, 29	,,	,,	+14 (+8)	51	Calm, clear morning. Windy afternoon.
Mar. 1	,,	,,	16 (−8½)	50	Fine, calm, clear morning. Cloudy afternoon and light snow.
,, 2	,,	,,	+15 (−5)	43	Calm, clear morning. Wind S. afternoon.
,, 3	,,	,,	+12 (−5)	46	Calm, clear morning, wind and clouds.
,, 4	,,	,,	+17 (−12)	46	Calm, clear morning and day; 2 in. snow during night.
,, 5	,,	,,	+14 (−8)	38	Calm, clear morning and day.
,, 6	,,	,,	+16 (−11½)	45	Clear but windy (S.W.) and dusty.
,, 7	,,	,,	+19 (−14)	46	Half-gale, S. all day.
,, 8	,,	,,	+14 (−8)	44	Calm and clear morning. Strong S. wind afternoon.
,, 9	,,	,,	+15 (−9½)	45	Light snow fell early morning, later calm and clear. Snow again 7.10 P.M.
,, 10	,,	,,	+10 (−5⅘)	34	Cloudy and windy, snow early morning, and a little during day.

Date.	Place.	Elevation in feet above sea-level.	Minimum temperature in Fahrenheit degrees.	Maximum temperature in Fahrenheit degrees.	Remarks.
1904 Mar. 11	Tuna	14,950	+5 (−5)	40	Fine morning. Wind and clouds afternoon, snow later.
,, 12	,,	,,	+14 (−6)	34	Snow early morning. Calm and clear later.
,, 13	,,	,,	+10 (−3)	37	Calm, clear morning. Usual wind afternoon.
,, 14	,,	,,	+7 (−1)	39	Clear morning, cloudy afternoon, snow at 5 P.M.
,, 15	,,	,,	+12 (−7)	50	Gale S.S.W. all day. Clouds.
,, 16	,,	,,	+10 (−3)	54	Clear, calm day.
,, 17	,,	,,	+14 (−8)	53	Clear, but squally from S.W., clouds later.
,, 18	,,	,,	+18 (−13⅘)	51	Clear, windy.
,, 19	,,	,,	+11 (−5)	49	Clear, windy.
,, 20	,,	,,	+20 (−14)	49	Wind S.W. Dusty.
,, 21	,,	,,	+17 (−13)	56	Half-gale S.W. Dust storm.
,, 22	,,	,,	+16 (−12)	56	Light wind S. Clear.
,, 23	,,	,,	+18 (−13)	50	Clear, but moderate wind S.W.
,, 24	,,	,,	+16 (−10½)	46	Calm, clear morning, later wind and clouds, 1½ in. snow 6 P.M.
,, 25	,,	,,	+9 (−2)	52	Calm, clear day.
,, 26	,,	,,	+15 (−9)	56	Calm, clear day. Clouds and heavy wind at night.
,, 27	,,	,,	+15 (−10⅘)	53	Calm, clear morning. Dust storm afternoon.
,, 28	,,	,,	+21 (−13½)	51	Calm day, cloudy all day.
,, 29	,,	,,	+14 (−9)	52	Light wind S., cloudy part of day.
,, 30	,,	,,	+16 (−11)	56	Clear morning, moderate wind and dust.
,, 31	,,	,,	+26 (−23)	51	Snow early morning, 1 in. Clear, calm day.
Apr. 1	,,	,,	+24 (−21)	48	Calm, clear day.
,, 2	,,	,,	+25 (−23)	44	Cloudy, with moderate wind, and light fall of snow.
,, 3	,,	,,	+15 (−12)	58	Calm, clear day.
,, 4	Guru	14,900	+23 (−20)	50	Calm, clear day, mountains overclouded.
,, 5	Chalu	,,	+18 (−9)	48	Calm day, some clouds. Snow in afternoon and night.

Date.	Place.	Elevation in feet above sea-level.	Minimum temperature in Fahrenheit degrees.	Maximum temperature in Fahrenheit degrees.	Remarks.
1904 Apr. 6	Kala Lake	14,700	+26 (−21	52	Cloudy, windy morning and evening. Calm day.
,, 7	Mangtsa	14,400	+17 (−12½)	54	Clear, calm morning. Wind S. afternoon.
,, 8	Beyul (near)	,,	+26 (−14)	55	Clear, calm morning.
,, 9	Kangmar	13,900	+30 (−26)	58	Calm, cloudy morning. Clear day.
,, 10	Saogang	13,500	+32 (−29)	50	Cloudy morning, snow during day. Fine evening.
,, 11	Gyantsé	13,200	+31 (−28)	56	Calm, clear morning and day.
,, 12	,,	,,	+31 (−25)	62	Calm, clear morning. Wind during day.
,, 13	,,	,,	+30 (−22)	69	Calm, clear morning. Windy and dusty day.
,, 14	,,	,,	+33 (−31)	64	Cloudy morning, snow on hills. Storm at 7 P.M.
,, 15	,,	,,	+29 (−18)	59	Windy and dusty day.
,, 16	,,	,,	+27 (−22½)	68	Calm, clear morning. Wind and dust after 1.30 P.M.
,, 17	,,	,,	+31 (−24)	62	Cloudy, windy morning and day.
,, 18	,,	,,	+29 (−21)	63	Clear, windy morning. Calm day.
,, 19	Dote	13,450	28	60	Calm, clear day.
,, 20	Kangmar	13,900	31	58	Calm, clear day after windy night.
,, 21	Mangtsa	14,400	29	46	Calm, clear morning. Windy and cloudy afternoon.
,, 22	Kala Lake	14,700	26	76	Calm, clear morning. Gale S.W. evening.
,, 23	Dochen	14,900	25	69	Fine morning. Half-gale S., with snow evening.
,, 24	Tuna	14,950	21	55	Snowy morning. Calm, clear day.
,, 25	Phari Jong	14,570	25	52	Calm, clear morning. Light E. wind day.
,, 26	Gaut'ang	12,360	29	55	Calm, cloudy morning. Clear day.
,, 27	Chumbi	9,780	39	73	Calm, clear day.
,, 28	,,	,,	50	66	Rain almost all day, fine mist, with heavy showers.

Date.	Place.	Elevation in feet above sea-level.	Minimum temperature in Fahrenheit degrees.	Maximum temperature in Fahrenheit degrees.	Remarks.
Apr. 29	Chumbi	9,780	40	65	Cloudy morning. Light rain afternoon.
,, 30	,,	,,	39	67	Calm, clear day.
May 1	Chumbi	,,	47	65	Cloudy morning. Rain afternoon. Thunderstorm night.
	Gyantsé	13,200	33		Cloudy, slight snow and hail.
,, 2	Chumbi	9,780	40	54	Cloudy morning. Light rain during day
,, 3	,,	,,	36	76	Calm, clear morning. Moderate S. wind afternoon.
,, 4	,,	,,	37	68	Calm, clear morning. Cloudy and windy afternoon.
,, 5	,,	,,	45	55	Rainy morning and day.
,, 6	,,		44	58	Cloudy morning. Rainy afternoon.
,, 7	,,	,,	44	64	Clear, calm day.
,, 8	,,		47	64	Cloudy, rainy morning. Fine afternoon.
,, 9	,,	,,	47	67	,, ,, ,,
,, 10	,,	,,	36	69	Fine, clear day.
,, 11	,,	,,	45	67	Rainy morning, and most of day.
,, 12	,,	,,	43	65	Clear, calm morning. Heavy rain afternoon.
,, 13	,,	,,	45	63	Rain 11-2 P.M. Rest of day fine.
,, 14	,,	,,	48	62	Cloudy, with light showers.
,, 15	,,	,,	49	64	Showery day.
,, 16	,,	,,	51	71	Showery morning. Fine day.
,, 17	,,	,,	49	74	Light showers at intervals.
,, 18	,,	,,	50	72	Clear morning. Heavy rain afternoon. Snow, 12,500 ft.
,, 19	,,	,,	36	71	Clear, calm day.
,, 20	,,	,,	37	72	,, ,, ,,
,, 21	,,	,,	39	68	,, ,, ,,
,, 22	,,	,,	44	68	,, ,, ,,
,, 23	,,	,,	46	68	Fine morning. Thunder and heavy rain afternoon.
,, 24	,,	,,	45	64	Showery.
,, 25	,,	,,	49	61	Showery, but, on the whole, fair.

Date.	Place.	Elevation in feet above sea-level.	Minimum temperature in Fahrenheit degrees.	Maximum temperature in Fahrenheit degrees.	Remarks.
May 26	Chumbi	9780	44	68	Showery.
,, 27	,,	,,	77	61	Rain all day.
,, 28	,,	,,	46	60	,, ,,
,, 29	,,	,,	52	66	Rain to 10.30. Cloudy, windy afternoon.
,, 30	,,	,,	52	60	Cloudy morning. Fine afternoon.
,, 31	,,	,,	50	71	Calm, clear day.
June 1	,,	,,	49	62	Cloudy, no rain.
,, 2	,,	,,	49	71	,, ,,
,, 3	,,	,,	50	72	Fine, clear day.
,, 4	,,	,,	54	71	Rain early morning. Fine day.
,, 5	,,	,,	49	72	Fine, bright day.
,, 6	,,	,,	51	74	Fine day. Showery evening.
,, 7	,,	,,	49	76	Clear, calm day.
,, 8	,,	,,	50	74	,, ,,
,, 9	,,	,,	48	67	Cloudy morning. Clear, calm day.
,, 10	,,	,,	49	68	Cloudy day, no rain.
,, 11	,,	,,	50	79	Calm, clear day.
,, 12	,,	,,	51	79	Fine morning. Rainy afternoon.
,, 13	Gaut'ang	12,360	54	64	,, ,,
,, 14	Kamparab	14,300	50	60	Rain almost all day.
,, 15	Phari Jong	14,570	39	60	Cloudy. Rain in afternoon.
,, 16	,,	,,	39	76	Fine, clear day, with a few light showers.
,, 17	Tang La	14,950	38	67	Calm and clear.
,, 18	Tuna	14,956	35	62	,, ,,
,, 19	Dochen	14,900	38	67	Clear, moderate S. wind.
,, 20	Kala Lake	14,700	45	69	Calm and clear.
,, 21	Samanda	,,	44	68	Calm and clear day. Light shower afternoon.
,, 22	Kangmar	13,900	45	81	Calm and clear day.
,, 23	,,	,,	47	83	,, ,,
,, 24	,,	,,	43	82	,, ,,
,, 25	Sdogang	13,500	49	74	,, ,,
,, 26	Gyantsé	13,200	55	82	,, ,,
,, 27	,,	,,	50	81	Heavy rain afternoon.
,, 28	,,	,,	48	83	Rainy morning. Fine, clear afternoon.
,, 29	,,	,,	50	84	Fine, clear day.
,, 30	,,	,,	50	92	Fine, clear day. Thunder-storm afternoon.
July 1	,,	,,	50	102	Fine morning. Thunder and rain after 3 P.M.

Date.	Place.	Elevation in feet above sea-level.	Minimum temperature in Fahrenheit degrees.	Maximum temperature in Fahrenheit degrees.	Remarks.
July 2	Gyantsé	13,200	42	99	Cloudy morning. Thunder, but no rain afternoon.
,, 3	,,	,,	42	98	Clear morning. Light shower afternoon.
,, 4	,,	,,	40	102	Clear, calm day.
,, 5	,,	,,	46	104	,, ,,
,, 6	,,	,,	48	104	Cloudy morning. Fine, clear day.
,, 7	,,	,,	49	102	Clear day, with squalls.
,, 8	,,	,,	48	102	Clear, calm day.
,, 9	,,	,,	40	103	,, ,,
,, 10	,,	,,	46	104	,, ,,
,, 11	,,	,,	51	105	Fine morning. Rainy afternoon.
,, 12	,,	,,	51	83	Rainy morning. Cloudy afternoon.
,, 13	,,	,,	46	88	Fine, but some clouds.
,, 14	Kotang	14,000	45	64	Showers during day. Rainy night.
,, 15	Shatöd (Taklung)	14,200	44	61	Cloudy morning. Heavy rain afternoon.
,, 16	Ralung	14,500	42	70	Cloudy morning. Fine, clear day.
,, 17	Kharo La	16,300	36	69	Fine, clear, calm day.
,, 18	Zara	16,000	29	66	Clear, calm day. Rain at night.
,, 19	Nagartsé	15,000	36	78	Fine, clear day.
,, 20	,,	,,	38	84	,, ,,
,, 21	Yasig	14,950	41	64	Cloudy, rainy morning. Hail afternoon.
,, 22	Palte Jong	,,	38	68	Rainy morning. Fine afternoon.
,, 23	Demalung	,,	43	79	Rainy morning. Rain and hail afternoon.
,, 24	Kampa Barji	12,200	41	87	Cloudy morning. Fine, clear day.
,, 25	Chaksam Ferry	12,100	51	92	Rainy morning. Fine, clear day.
,, 26	,,	,,	50	95	Fine, clear, calm day.
,, 27	,,	,,	50	98	,, ,,
,, 28	,,	,,	49	96	,, ,,
,, 29	,,	,,	52	95	,, ,,
,, 30	,,	,,	49	98	,, ,,
,, 31	Jang	12,150	54	87	Light rain, early morning. Cloudy afternoon.
Aug. 1	Nam	12,210	52	98	Cloudy morning. Calm, clear day.

Date.	Place.	Elevation in feet above sea-level.	Minimum temperature in Fahrenheit degrees.	Maximum temperature in Fahrenheit degrees.	Remarks.
1904 Aug. 2	Tilung	12,240	56	78	Cloudy, windy morning. Rain in afternoon.
,, 3	Lhasa	12,290	47	95	Rain morning and evening. Cloudy day.
,, 4	,,	,,	58	85	Rainy morning. Clear afternoon.
,, 5	,,	,,	51	88	Calm, cloudy morning. Rain afternoon and night.
,, 6	,,	,,	49	87	,, ,,
,, 7	,,	,,	48	87	Calm, rainy morning. Fine afternoon.
,, 8	,,	,,	49	89	Calm, cloudy morning. Fine afternoon.
,, 9	,,	,,	44	92	,, ,,
,, 10	,,	,,	46	88	Calm, cloudy morning. Heavy rain afternoon.
,, 11	,,	,,	48	85	Rain morning. Thunderstorm evening.
,, 12	,,	,,	46	81	Rainy morning. Fine afternoon.
,, 13	,,	,,	51	84	,, ,,
,, 14	,,	,,	52	87	Calm, cloudy morning. Fine afternoon.
,, 15	,,	,,	50	92	Showery morning. Calm, clear day.
,, 16	,,	,,	52	87	Calm, clear day. Storm and rain 8 P.M.
,, 17	,,	,,	47	80	Rain morning. Calm, cloudy day.
,, 18	,,	,,	42	82	Calm, clear day.
,, 19	,,	,,	38	83	,, ,,
,, 20	,,	,,	42	91	Calm, cloudy day. Rain at night.
,, 21	,,	,,	49	84	Showery morning, cloudy day. Storm 8 P.M.
,, 22	,,	,,	49	88	Calm, cloudy day. Storm and rain 7.30 P.M.
,, 23	,,	,,	50	80	Rain morning. Cloudy day. Storm at night.
,, 24	,,	,,	49	82	Rain morning and evening. Cloudy day.
,, 25	,,	,,	51	89	Cloudy morning. Showery day. Storm at night.
,, 26	,,	,,	49	83	Showery morning. Clear day. Rain and mist 8 P.M.
,, 27	,,	,,	47	86	Calm, cloudy day. Storm at 8 P.M.

Date.	Place.	Elevation in feet above sea level.	Minimum temperature in Fahrenheit degrees.	Maximum temperature in Fahrenheit degrees.	Remarks.
Aug. 28	Lhasa	12,290	49	84	Showery morning. Thunderstorm 8 P.M.
,, 29	,,	,,	50	85	Calm, cloudy day.
,, 30	,,	,,	50	85	Showery morning. Cloudy day.
,, 31	,,	,,	50	86	,, ,,
Sep. 1	,,	,,	48	89	Calm, cloudy morning. Clear day.
,, 2	,,	,,	50	84	,, ,,
,, 3	,,	,,	46	89	Calm, cloudy morning. Clear day. Showers evening.
,, 4	,,	,,	52	86	Showers morning and evening. Fine day.
,, 5	,,	,,	47	85	Cloudy day. Thunder and rain 8 P.M.
,, 6	,,	,,	46	80	Rain all day, off and on.
,, 7	,,	,,	43	78	Rain morning and evening. Fine, calm day.
,, 8	,,	,,	46	76	Showery morning and evening. Fine, calm day.
,, 9	,,	,,	43	86	Showery morning. Stormy evening.
,, 10	,,	,,	46	75	Clouds and shower.
,, 11	,,	,,	36	76	Clear, calm weather.
,, 12	,,	,,	33	78	,, ,,
,, 13	,,	,,	31	77	,, ,,
,, 14	,,	,,	33	76	Clear, calm day. Cloudy evening.
,, 15	,,	,,	42	70	Cloudy. Calm.
,, 16	,,	,,	40	80	Cloudy and showers.
,, 17	,,	,,	38	84	Clear, calm morning. Cloudy evening.
,, 18	,,	,,	44	79	Clear, calm day.
,, 19	,,	,,	48	79	Clear, calm morning. Cloudy day.
,, 20	,,	,,	44	83	Cloudy. Showers.
,, 12	,,	,,	44	82	Cloudy morning. Fine day.
,, 22	,,	,,	47	78	Calm, clear.
,, 23	Nethang	,,	40	76	,, ,,
,, 24	Nam	12,210	44	84	Calm, clear morning. Light showers evening.
,, 25	Chusul	12,100	48	65	Cloudy, with light showers afternoon.
,, 26	Chaksam	,,	47	69	Cloudy. Showery day.
,, 27	Upper Ferry	12,250	41	72	Cloudy. Showery morning. Fine day.
,, 28	,, ,,	,,	39	82	Clear, calm.
,, 29	Palté Jong	14,950	37	77	,, ,,
, 30	Nagartsé	15,000	30	75	,, ,,

The *Rainfall* was not accurately gauged; but at Gyantsé, in the Yamdok Basin, and at Lhasa about 30 inches must have fallen during the summer and early autumn. At Yatung in the Chumbi Valley the average of three years' observations of the rainfall by the Imperial Chinese Customs Officer was 57·01 inches, whilst at Gangtok, in the adjoining district of Sikhim, the average of four years was 146·36 inches.

Snow fell at Gyantsé in every month of the year, 2 feet fell on the Kharo Pass so early as the 9th of August.

At Shigatsé the weather was reported to be as follows: In May cloudy and gusty, but no rain; in June rain set in from middle of month preceded by strong east winds, and continued all July and August; in September the rain lessened, but it still remained very cloudy; in October the rain stopped, and cold east winds set in at 11 A.M., reaching their height at 2 P.M. and declining till 5 P.M., and being absent during the night and morning; in December and January violent cold winds blew so terrifically from three to four hours every day that no one moved out till the wind stopped. Snow seldom fell at Shigatsé over 1 foot.

APPENDIX V.

SACK OF LHASA IN 1710 A.D.[1]

THE horde of Euleuth Tartars which achieved the feat of sweeping down upon Lhasa from across the great Changthang desert plateau, nearly two centuries ago, belonged to the eastern or "Jungar" branch of the tribe, which occupied the district known as Jungaria or Sungaria, between the highlands of Mongolia and the lowlands of Turkestan (see maps, pp. 4 and 40). These people were by instinct marauders, and it was in the depression in the mountain chains here that the devastating hosts of Genghis Khan advanced westwards. It now forms part of the Chinese "New Province" (Sin-Mong), along with Chinese Turkestan and that portion of Kansu north of the Gobi desert. The chief, Tse Wang Rabdan, advanced in person with an army to Sining in Kansu (see map, p. 40) to secure the person of the infant Dalai Lama; and sent his brother (or cousin), Chereng Donduk, with 6000 men, accompanied by several thousand camels, most of which carried provisions, but some had swivel guns, which were discharged from their backs. This army reached the district south of Tengri Lake in good condition and without loss. Between that lake and the capital they found a Tibetan force of 20,000 men drawn up to oppose their progress; but few of them being soldiers the advance of the camel corps and the noise of the swivel guns put the whole force to flight, and the Tibetan General was killed. After this the Euleuths met with no opposition, and entered the holy city without firing a shot. They pillaged the temples and monasteries, and sacked the Dalai Lama's new red palace on Potala hill, and several towns in other valleys, and, according to their own accounts, returned with their spoil to their homes. But the Chinese version of the affair states that these invaders were driven out and their chief killed by the avenging army of the Emperor Kangshi. For further particulars, see Mr D. Boulger in the *Nineteenth Century*, July 1904, and Sir H. Howorth's *History of the Mongols*.

[1] This date is given in Tibetan history as 1717 A.D.

APPENDIX VI.

POPULATION OF TIBET, AND CAUSES OPERATING TO KEEP IT DOWN.

THE population of Tibet is very small in proportion to the size and resources of the country, and probably does not exceed 1,500,000. The exact number is not exactly or approximately known, even to the Government of the country itself. The only general census which appears to have been taken was one by the Chinese in 1737, which gave—

	LAMAS.	LAITY at 5 per family.
Central Province (U) . .	302,500	602,190
Western Province (Tsang) .	13,700	33,760
	316,200	635,950

This total of about 1,000,000 does not include the populous eastern and Chinese districts of Kham, which Mr Rockhill, who has twice visited those parts, estimates at about 300,000, and in addition those pastorals of the North-Western province and the Changt'ang nomads. The most densely populated tract is the eastern border on the Chinese frontier, after which comes the Lhasa or central province, with Tsang or the western.

There seems to be no doubt that its population is dwindling. Not one-half of the arable ground is cultivated, and one sees everywhere evidence of the shrinkage in abandoned tracts of former cultivation. The cause of this decrease is chiefly the enormous tax of celibate Lamas which the present priestly government extracts from the people, about one out of every two males; and to a lesser degree the practice of polyandry and promiscuity, decimating epidemics of smallpox and bad administration. Wherever Mr Rockhill and the Indian Survey spies have estimated the population, the figures are always much inferior to those given in the censuses by the Chinese officials fifty to a hundred years before. (See Rockhill, *Jour. Roy. As. Soc.* xxiii. 14.) Excessive infant mortality must also account for some of the loss, owing to the rough, exposed life led by the Tibetans; though excessive altitude of itself has a marked tendency in this direction, as has been, I am told, the distressing experience of the Moravian missionaries in Ladak, where the cemetery is filled with infant graves, few or no children having survived their second year.

APPENDIX VII.

CHARM FOR KILLING THE ENEMY.

THE Magic Circles which were found drawn at Gyantsé monastery for killing us as the "Enemy," comprised the seven circles of the following magical weapons and implements:—(1) Stones and other Missiles; (2) Boats for attack by the river; (3) Fire; (4) Swords; (5) Hurricanes; (6) Thunderbolts; and (7) Arrows.

The incantation used with these is accompanied by a barbaric sacrifice to the devils on the principle of sympathetic magic, and the old-world custom of sticking pins into an image of one's enemy. The book of directions for this begins:—"Hail to the wise God! The requisite materials for killing one's enemy are: An axe with three heads, the middle a pig's head, the right a bull's, the left a snake's. On the pig's head place a lamp, and in its mouth the image of a man in wheaten dough. The upper part of the man's body is black, the lower red. On the side of the upper part draw the eight planets, on the lower the twenty-eight constellations, the eight Chinese trigrams (*pa-kwa*), the nine-figured magic square, the claws of the Roc, the wings of an eagle and a snake's tail. Hang a bow and arrow on his left side and load him with provisions on the back, an owl's feather on the right and a crow's feather on the left; stick a piece of poison tree on his head, and surround him with swords on all sides, and place a red wall on the right, a yellow on the left, a black in the middle. Then sitting in quiet meditation recite! *Hung* this axe with a bull head will repel all the sorceries of the Bon, the snake will repel all pestilences thrown at us, the pig will repel all the sorceries of the earth spirits, the lamp will repel the spirits of the air. O axe! pierce the hearts of the hosts of the enemy!"—and it proceeds on in this fashion.

APPENDIX VIII.

ANALYSIS OF SALINE EARTH, ETC., FROM YAMDOK AND RED GORGE.

I AM indebted to the kindness of the Chemical Examiner, Bengal, for the following interesting analysis of specimens which I sent to him :—

Saline Efflorescence from Red Gorge.

Moisture	12·86 per cent.
Insoluble Matter . . .	6·75 ,,
Oxide of Iron ($Fe_2 O_3$) .	0·83 ,,
Calcium Carbonate . .	11·54 ,,
Sodium Carbonate . .	36·98 ,,
Sodium Chloride . . .	30·12 ,,
Sulphuric Anhydride Phosphoric Anhydride } .	1·42 ,,

N.B.—The large proportion of common salt, nearly one-third of its weight, is noteworthy.

Tufaceous Concretion from Hot Springs in Red Gorge.

Moisture	0·30 per cent.
Insoluble Matter . . .	6·61 ,,
Oxide of Iron . . .	2·45 ,,
Carbonate of Lime . .	90·64 ,,

Saline Earth from Shores of Yamdok Lake.

Moisture	1·12 per cent.
Organic Matter . . .	4·63 ,,
Insoluble Matter Clay and Sand, etc. } .	78·38 ,,
Ferric Oxide (Fe O) . .	10·67 ,,

Oxide of Lime (Ca O) . .	1·80 per cent.
Sulphuric Anhydride . .	2·46 ,,
Chlorine and Phosphoric Anhydride . . .	0.94 ,,

[*N.B.*—The absence of borax and common salt is remarkable.]

Weed from Yamdok Lake.

Contains no Iodine.

Water from Yamdok Inland Lake.

Dissolved Solids	22·4 parts per 10,000.
Chlorine	·71 ,,
Free Ammonia	·0035 ,,
Albuminoid	·0224 ,,
Nitrogen as Nitrates . . .	·07 ,,
Hardness Clark's Scale :	
Total	7·5
Permanent . . .	2·5
Nitrates	Present
Nitrates	Absent
Sulphates	Present

APPENDIX IX.

GOLD IN TIBET.

THE regions beyond the Himalayas have from time immemorial been credited with possessing vast sources of gold. The Greek legend which placed here the Gold Digging Ants was probably based on the assumption that the precious metal was so abundant that it was to be found on anthills. The inhabitants of the Altai, to the north, were the "Griffins" who guarded the gold. These stories may have arisen from the fact that all the great rivers flowing from the lofty tableland brought down in their sand grains of gold, not only on the Indian side, but to Burma and China, in the Yangtse, "the River of Golden Sand," and other valleys.

Large gold mines undoubtedly exist in Tibet, but their extent cannot be ascertained until that country is fully explored by Europeans. At present the metal is mined at several places over a tract of some 300 miles in length, on the Changt'ang desert to the north-east of Lhasa, the principal workings being at Thok Jalung to the east of Simla in N. lat. 32° 24′ 26″ and E. long. 81° 37′ 38″.[1] Another auriferous tract is to the south-east of the Yamdok Lake on the north of Bhotan, at the source of the Subansiri or "Golden" River of Assam, in the lower reaches of which are many colonies of gold washers. There seems to be another reef, a few days' journey due east of Lhasa, and from this latter source, the Nepalese Consul informed me, the best gold comes, and rich deposits are known to exist in Lit'ang further east. The gold is found in nuggets as well as in spangles and dust; but the Tibetans are careful to leave the nuggets intact or to replace them if disturbed, under the belief that they are

[1] Captain Rawlings visited this neighbourhood last year (1903).

living and are the parents of the spangles and gold-dust, which latter would disappear were the lumps removed. I made enquiries regarding the alleged gold and silver mines on the hill of Sera monastery, but could find no trace or tradition of them; if they formerly existed, they must have been closed for many years. In the valley to the west of Sera, up which runs the road to the Tengri Lake, silver ore is said to be found in small quantities at Dogbdepu, one day's journey off under the Pemba Pass. Silver and mercury come from Litang and Batang in the far east, districts which are now annexed by China (see map, p. 40).

APPENDIX X.

TRADE—IMPORTS AND EXPORTS.

THE value of India's trade with Tibet is at present under a quarter of a million sterling per annum.

As illustrating the character of the imports from India, the following articles passed into Tibet through Yatung during the first quarter of 1899:—

Mirrors, 34,496; needles, 960 lbs.; spectacles, 2214 pairs; Assam silk, 3846 yards; Chinese silk, 10,889 yards; umbrellas, 2000. And who will say that the Tibetans neglect their toilet when it is seen that 720 lbs. of soap and 6694 towels crossed the border in three months? The bulk of the trade, however, was in cotton goods, of which passed 174,794 yards; blue piece-goods, 97,846 yards; printed and fancy, 39,305 yards; cambrics, 262,048 yards; woollen cloth goods, 21,710 yards in 1899. Among the curious articles of import we find imitation gold-foil valued at Rs.7130; amber, Rs.1090; 79 maunds (1 maund= 80 lbs.) of incense, and 97 maunds of paints; peacocks' feathers, 9 maunds, and amongst the miscellaneous articles kerosene oil, clocks, and watches. The chief export is the renowned sheep's wool, which in three out of the last four years has reached well over 15,000 maunds, and this year tops the record with 15,981 maunds. There is a big drop in the export of woollen cloth, from 8262 yards in 1898 to 818 yards in the present year, and fox skins also fell from 5920 in 1898 to 420 in the present year. The export of musk reached 2801 tolas; and yaks' tails have increased to 316 maunds.

Shawl-wool, or "*Pashm.*"—I enquired why this valuable commodity was not exported *viâ* the Chumbi and Nepalese Passes, as it must be available in quantities across the border here, and was told that it was partly because no demand had been made for it at this end of Tibet, and partly owing to the Kashmiris having a monopoly of the trade in Upper Tibet, whence they export it all by way of Rampur on the Sutlej, Kashmir and Ladak, and canvass for it chiefly in the tracts adjoining there. In Southern Tibet, however, most of this important product, the felted silky underwool, which should amount to hundreds of tons annually, is wasted, as the Tibetans do not know its great value, and do not collect it from either the yak when shedding its winter coat in spring, or the goats and sheep.

Tea is one of the chief imports that interests India, as the Tibetans are a nation of inveterate tea-drinkers; the annual consumption of Chinese tea amongst the lay population has been estimated at 11,000,000 lbs., in addition to the subsidy from the Chinese Emperor to the monasteries of about 8,000,000 lbs. a year. The aspirations of Assam and Darjeeling tea-gardens, which adjoin the doors of Tibet, to share in this trade is very reasonable; and under the new Treaty, if prohibitive duties are removed, India may succeed in wresting a large portion of this traffic from China, and the supply of a much better and wholesome article than the Chinese tea-bricks (or *Dum*), which consist of a hard block of tea-leaf and crushed twigs mixed with a strong extract of the boiled leaves, and compressed in moulds. The process of manufacture of these bricks is well known. The cakes weigh about $4\frac{1}{2}$ lbs. each, and being in such universal demand and fairly portable and uniform in size, they pass current as money at their market value. In Lhasa the commoner qualities are of two kinds, *Chupa* or "tens," because they cost 10 *tankas* each or Rs.$\frac{10}{3}$; and *Gyepa*, or "eights," costing 8 *tankas* or Rs.$\frac{8}{3}$, but the market price is usually higher than this. These coarse kinds are for making buttered tea, which is the staple drink. For unbuttered tea, which the wealthier classes drink, a much better quality is used called *Dut'ang*, at Rs. 6 to 8 a brick. Already I am informed enterprising tea-planters in the Dovars have commenced the manufacture of tea-bricks for the Tibetan market, as the "brick" is the only form of tea which the Tibetans will buy. A profitable trade might be developed by bartering tea-bricks for "*pashm*" or shawl-wool, as Mr Hennessy suggested many years ago.

In *Lhasa* the imports arrive mostly in December, and the

caravans leave in March before the rivers become flooded. From China come silks, carpets, porcelain and tea-bricks. From Mongolia, leather, saddlery, sheep and horses, with coral, amber, and small diamonds from European sources. From Kham, perfumes, fruits, furs, and inlaid metal saddlery. From Sikhim and Bhotan, rice, musk, sugar-balls and tobacco. From Nepal, broadcloth, indigo, brasswork, coral, pearls, sugar, spices, drugs, and Indian manufactures. From Ladak, saffron, dried fruits, and articles from India.

In the market at Lhasa opium sold for its weight in silver. The exports from Lhasa are silver, gold, salt, wool, woollen cloth, rugs, furs, drugs, musk. By the Nepal, Kumaon and Ladak routes go borax, gold and ponies; Patna in Bengal is the chief mart for the Nepal trade. Dewangiri and Udalgiri for Assam, and Darjeeling and Kalimpong for Sikhim and Chumbi.

The rug and carpet industry of Gyantsé is capable of large development were a demand to arise for the products, which are as fine a quality as any in the Orient. In the pine-forest of Kongbu are said to be large sulphur deposits which suggest possibilities for match-factories.

APPENDIX XI.

THE FAUNA OF CENTRAL AND SOUTH-WESTERN TIBET, WITH DESCRIPTIONS OF NEW BIRDS, FISH, ETC.

THE circumstances of our journeyings in Tibet were not so favourable as we should have wished for observing the natural history of the country, as we were "held up" beleagured at Gyantsé during the summer months, and for the rest of the time, until the return march, shooting and independent roaming were practically prohibited for military reasons. It is hoped, however, that the following notes may afford useful indications of the fauna of the country we traversed, and form a basis for a more detailed record hereafter.

Zoologically, Tibet and the stupendous southern spurs of its tableland running down into Upper Sikhim and Chumbi, over which we passed, lie within the Palæarctic region,[1] where it adjoins the Oriental, so that a few of the animals of the latter region, especially of its Indo-Malayan province, ascend into the Palæarctic region, to about 10,000 feet elevation, in addition to these birds which migrate to Tibet in the breeding season. As regards the vertical distribution of animals, the climate of Tibet may be divided roughly into—

Temperate, including Lhasa and Shigatsé,	9,000 to 12,500	ft.	above sea-level.
Subarctic, up to limit of trees . .	12,500 to 16,000	,,	,,
Arctic	above 16,000	,,	,,

The more obvious Game animals in the Chumbi Valley, in its lower temperate portion (9000-12,500 feet) are Tragopan

[1] Wallace, following Sclater and other naturalists, divides the surface of the globe, zoologically, into six great regions, viz. (1) The *Palæarctic*, including Europe, Africa north of the Sahara, and Asia north of the great wall of the Himalayas; (2) the *Ethiopian*, comprising the rest of Africa with

pheasants in the pine and rhododendron woods, blood pheasants amongst the greenish licheny rocks, and "monāl" on the uplands. On the Lingmo meadow (11,200 feet) solitary snipe, woodcock, and water-fowl are found and everywhere snow-pigeons and blue rocks; whilst in the forest roams the great stag or *Shao*, and on the upper hills musk-deer. In Upper Chumbi, Phari and Khangbu, above the tree-limit, about 14,500 feet, are found on the hills herds of blue sheep (*Nawa* or *Bharal*), and sometimes a few giant sheep (*Ovis hodgsoni*), necessitating much stalking and climbs of 2000 to 4000 feet; and on the plains and in ravines gazelle which at first were so easily approached that you could ride slowly up to within 300 yards of a herd, and then dismount and stalk them in the open, like black buck. On the plateau and intervening tracts from Tuna (14,950 feet) onwards to Gyantsé (13,200 feet), and thence to Lhasa (12,290 feet), were numerous gazelle, woolly hares, Tibetan partridge, water-fowl, and sand-grouse, in addition to a solitary lynx and fox, whilst near the snow-line were *Bharal*, occasional giant sheep, snow-cock, and an occasional musk-deer and snow-leopard.

Mammals.

Monkeys: Tibetan—*Teu*. No wild ones were found, though several small tailless monkeys from Bhotan were kept as pets in Lhasa.

Carnivora were numerous and varied, as evidenced by the skins everywhere for sale; but, being largely nocturnal in habits, were seldom seen.

Woolly Tiger (*Felis* sp.), T.—*Stag-gung*. Several skins of this beast were in the Lhasa bazaar as well as that of the ordinary tiger (*Stag*, pronounced 'Tāk'), the former reported to be from the eastern ravines, and the latter from the Lower Tsangpo.

South Arabia and Madagascar; (3) the *Oriental*, consisting of India, Southern China, Burma, Siam, and the Malay Peninsula and the adjoining islands of the Archipelago; (4) the *Australian*, comprising Australia, New Zealand, and the remaining south-eastern islands of the Malay Archipelago, etc.; (5) the *Nearctic*, and (6) *Neotropical*, approximately corresponding to North and South America. In his *Manual of Palæarctic Birds*, Mr H. E. Dresser extends the southern limits of the Palæarctic region down to the Himalayas above 6000 feet.

Ounce or Snow Leopard (*F. uncia*), T. — *Gzig* or *Zik*, Nepalese, *Tharua*. Near the snow-limit, it feeds on the blue sheep and musk-deer. Its tracks were frequently seen in the snow.

Lynx (*F. isabellina* v. *lynx*), T.—*Yi* or *Dbyi* or *Ee* was shot on several occasions on the rocky hillsides at Tuna, Kangmar, etc. The skin varies much in tint, probably seasonal change, ranging from pale hair brown to silvery white in the winter coat.

Of other wild cats, skins of the following three were several times obtained in the Lhasa bazaar: (1) Pallas's Lynx (*F. manul*), T.—*Yi-ch'ung* or *Tsokde*, (2) Clouded Leopard-cat (*F.* sp.), T.—*Sa-chuk*, (3) Brown-shouldered Tiger-cat (*F. nigrescens*), T.—*Pungmar*. A brindled wild cat was shot at Yamdok in October by Major Iggulden, and was identified for me by Mr O. Thomas as *F. manul*. Skins of the following cats were also on sale at Lhasa: Civet (*? Vivera melanurus*), T.—*Sa-chong;* Spotted Civet (*Prionodon particolor*), T.—*Zik-chung;* and a tree cat (*Paradoxurus laniger?*), T.—*Chya-zik*.

Wolf (*Canis laniger*), T.—*Chāng-go*. On the plateau but uncommon. The specimens shot near Phari were of a light grey colour.

Jackals were reported to have been at Lhasa infesting the cemetery there until a few years ago, but none were seen by us.

Otter, T.—*Chu Sram*. One was seen on the banks of the Tsangpo and another on the bank of the stream at Phari, but none were secured.

Fox, T.—*Wah*. Two species were met with on plateau; *Vulpes flavescens*, of which I shot one on the flanks of Chumolhari, near Phari (17,000 feet), with a fine brush; and *V. ferrilatus*, smaller, with a shorter tail. This latter species extends to Lhasa.

Weasels and Martens. The weasel at Gyantsé seemed to be *Putorius tibetanus*, T.—*Shub-ji*. Skins of the following were got in the Lhasa market: martens (*Mustela* sp.), T.—*Te-mong;* two kinds of sable, a brown and a golden brown (*Putorius* sp.?), T.—*Bulak'a;* and an ermine (*Putorius erminea?*).

Badger (*Meles* sp.), T.—*Dum-pa*. This is a very common

and cheap skin, and comes chiefly from the warmer district of Kongbu below 10,000 feet.

Cat-bear or Racoon (*Ailurus fulgens*), T.—*Wag dong-kar*, or "the white-faced fox," is found in Chumbi Valley above 9000 feet, extending into Sikhim and Bhotan. Another much larger species called "Panda" (*A. melanoleucus*), of piebald black and white, is said to inhabit Eastern Tibet.

Bears. The black hill bear (*Ursus tibetanus*), T.—*Tom*, was common near Chumbi. The brown bear (*Ursus arctus*), T.—*Demo* or *Mi-de*, "the man devil," frequented the upper woods, above 12,000 feet. A skin of *U. pruinosus* was obtained in Lhasa similar to one shot by Major Bower; it was of the size of the brown bear, of a dark brown with a whitish band over nape and neck, and was said to have come from the Lower Tsangpo. A "white" bear, called "*Tik Dom*," was reported by the surveying Pundit of 1872 to infest the hills around the Tengri Lake, near the Khalambu Pass, and to commit great havoc amongst cattle.

Hare, Woolly (*Lepus oiostolus*), T.—*Rigong*, was very common all over the plateau, and especially in the ravines on the edges of the plains.

Marmot (*Arctomys himalayanus*, Hodg.), T.—*Abra* and Gomchen or "the Hermit." This large species with short tail was occasionally seen with burrows near the snow-line. It is about the size of a poodle, and is called by the natives a "wild dog." It emits a pungently offensive smell, so is not eaten; but its fat is in great repute as an external application in rheumatism.

Pika or mouse-hare (*Lagomys ochotona curzoniæ*), T.—*Chipi*. Is very common on all the plateaus from Gyantsé to Lhasa.

Mice.—Neither the field nor house mice which were seen appeared to be new, and no squirrels were observed.

Deer.—The great Tibetan stag (*Cervus affinis*), T.—*Shao*, was found in considerable numbers at an elevation above 10,000 feet in the Chumbi Valley (p. 137), which is its western limit; for it is not found in Sikhim, although the fact of the first specimen of its horns having been picked up in Sikhim gave the name of this latter country to this fine stag. Its fur is thick and coarse, almost like that of the musk-deer. The heads bought at Lhasa had enormous brow-antlers, and were said to come from the Lower Tsangpo and Bhotan. I obtained in the Tsangpo Valley a magnificent head of Thorold's Stag (*C. albirostris*) which was brought from the Changtang plateau, north of Lhasa, and is 8 inches longer than the record pair in Ward's *Records of Big Game.*

Musk-deer (*Moschus moschiferus*), T.—*Lawa*, were met with occasionally all the way from Chumbi to Lhasa in the upper wood zone. Actively hunted for their "pods," which are in great demand as a medicine, they are shy. Both sexes are destitute of horns, but the males have long tusks in the upper jaw, with which they dig the frozen ground for roots.

Gazelle (*Gazella picticaudata*), T.—*Gawa* or *Goa.* Was very common on all the plains and in the ravines. The herds often approached close to villages. The flesh was excellent eating. Two of those I shot had horns 13½ inches long, but several were obtained over 14 inches in length. The white patch around the base of the tail, which gives the animal its scientific name, often revealed their presence in the distance.

Antelope (*Pantholops* v. *Kemas hodgsoni*), T.—*Chiru.* None were seen, and the people did not appear to know of any, although Hooker mentioned having found them to the west of Tuna. Numbers of their horns were used as supporting prongs for Tibetan muskets. This, or the "Takin," which is reported from the Lower Tsangpo, was probably the "unicorn" of Huc, though it is doubtful whether this antelope extends so far east.

Giant Wild Sheep (*Ovis hodgsoni*), T.—*Nyän.* This colossal sheep, which is nearly allied to *O. ammon*, was occasionally seen and shot at elevations above 16,000 feet on the northern flanks of the great chain of the Himalayas, between Khambagong and Tuna. I saw some on the Yamdok Hills above Rham Lake and Ralung.

"Blue" Sheep (*O. nahura*), T.—*Nawa, Nao* or *Napik*, the *Bharal* of Indians. These were common all over the upper mountains between the limit of trees and the snow-line (13,000 to 17,000 feet). Old males leave the females in June and live by themselves. Both sexes have horns, those of the females being very small and depressed, and only slightly recurved. The bluish-grey coat of the old males has a band of rich black on the lower part of the neck and chest and along the flanks, with white over the chest. They had the usual habit of grazing always near rocky ground for retreat, and of posting sentries when feeding. Few of them had large horns; the largest shot was under 27 inches. Their flesh was good eating. At the Tsangpo ferry the lambs had horns about 2 inches long in August. The horns of this sheep were a favourite offering on the cairns at the top of passes.

Wild Yak (*Poephagus grunniens*), T.—*Dong*. No living specimens of these were seen, but the stuffed skins were hung up as scarecrows in several of the verandahs of the doors of temples and forts. The animal is said to be found no nearer to Lhasa than the border of the Changtang plain, several days' march to the north of the city. The domesticated yak is of course the chief beast of burden.

Wild Ass (*Equus hemionus*), T.—*Kyang*. These were very numerous on all the large open uncultivated plains at Tuna, etc. They roamed about in troops of half-a-dozen to a score or more. I saw in the month of April solitary animals, evidently males, several miles up the mountains. They move very swiftly when disturbed, and were said by the Tibetans to be untameable; but at Lhasa we found three tame ones (see p. 355), one of which was safely landed in England in January 1905, as a present to the King from General Macdonald. In size and appearance they are more like mules than asses. The colour was generally a light rusty brown above, contrasting with the pale fawn of the lower parts and legs. They are unstriped, with the exception of a thin dorsal line of brownish black from the mane to the tail. In winter the hair is said to become rougher and more reddish, assimilating the colour to the withered grass. The wild Dromedary (*Camel bactrianus*), T.—*Ngargöd*—is reported to occur on the plateau to the north of Lhasa, near Nagchuka.

Birds

As summer visitors, during the breeding season, most of the ducks and geese which visit India in the winter months were found, and in addition several other migratory birds, of which I understand Captain Walton took detailed notes for publication. The permanent residents varied in size, from the magnificent Lammergeyer (*Gypaetus barbatus*), T.—*Glag*, with a wing-spread of 9 feet, down to tiny flower-peckers. This huge, bearded vulture, sailing gracefully in the sky, was a constant feature in the landscape all the way to Lhasa. The bird, in company with the great Vulture (*? Gyps himalayensis*), T.—*Göd* or *Cha-göd*, were the common carrion feeders on the carcasses of the dead transport yaks, which lined the track across the plateau.

Of other birds of prey at Gyantsé and Lhasa, were Pallas's sea-eagle (*Haliaetus leucoryphus*), some falcons, hawks, kites and owls, including the Hobby (*Falco subbuteo*); Kestrel (*Cerchneis tinnunculus*), T.—*Pin-kyur-ana* (onomatopœic for its call); the European Sparrow-hawk (*Accipiter nisus*), T.—*Ucham;* Black-eared Kite (*Milvus melanotis*), T.—*Nelé;* Eagle Owl (*Bubo ignavus*), and the Owlet (*? Syrnium nivicolum*) T.—*U-ko.*

Of Perchers (*Insessores*), Swallows (*Hirundo rufula*) and Crag-Martins (*Ptyonoprogne rupestris*) were widely distributed, and Sand-Martins (*Cotile riparia*), and a Swift (*Cypselus ? affinis*) were frequent. No Kingfishers, Cuckoos, or Woodpeckers were observed, but a Wryneck (*? Iynx torquilla*) was found in the Dalai. Lama's plantation at Lhasa in early September, after the yellow Wagtails had passed. Hoopoes (*Upupa epops*) were everywhere common.

The Raven (*Corvus corax*), T.—*Ulak*, after its call, was the most widely diffused, as it was the commonest of all the birds, and was found on the highest passes. They were the familiar scavengers in camps and villages, and very tame. The Magpie of Tibet (*Pica bottanensis*), generally like the English bird but larger, was common everywhere within the tree zone. I saw some Jays, and what seemed to be starlings, but did not secure any. The red-billed and -legged Chough (*Pyrrhocorax graculus*) T.—*Kyung-ka*, or "the phœnix-mouthed"—was found everywhere from 10,000 feet upwards; and the Brown Ground Chough (*Podoces humilis*) was equally common on the plateau.

Larks.—The Calandra (*Melanocorypha maxima*) and the Horned Lark (*Otocorys elwesi*) were found on the loftiest uplands. The Common Skylark (*Alauda arvensis*) was met with on all the lower plateaus, and the Grey Titmouse (*Parus cinereus*) in the woods.

Laughing Thrushes were found in most of the thickets in Upper Chumbi, above 10,000 feet, and were chiefly *Trochalopterum affine*, and a few *Garrulax leucolophus* and *G.* (?) *waddelli* (Ibis, 1894, p. 424), and *Dryonastes cærulatus.* In the Tsangpo Valley I obtained two new species, at 12,000 feet, the descriptions of which by Mr Dresser are given below. Several Flower-peckers were seen in the woods at Gyantsé and Lhasa.

Warblers.—Amongst the willow groves *Phylloscopus affinis* was common, and a specimen of the beautiful Cobalt Warbler of Severtzoff (*Leptopœcile sophiæ*) was shot by Captain Walton at Gyantsé.

Shrikes of two species were found by me, one of which proved to be a new species, as described by Mr Dresser below. The fire-tailed Minivet (*Pericrocotus brevirostris*) was observed at Gyantsé.

Redstarts (*Chimarrhornis leucocephalus*) were found as high as Phari: and on the plateau Gyantsê to Lhasa (*Ruticilla hodgsoni*, and *R. rufiventris*); also the Hill Robin (*Tarsiger chrysceus*).

Thrushes.—The black-throated Ouzel (*Merula atrigularis*), the red-naped *M. ruficollis*, and in summer the Desert Wheatear (*Saxicola deserti* v. *atrogularis*).

Finches. — The gorgeous scarlet "Sepoy" (*Hæmatospiza sipahi*) T.—*Ka-byu* was occasionally seen near Pharï. On the plateaus three mountain species were common (*Montifringilla blanfordi*, *ruficollis*, and *adamsi*). Rose-finches (*Propasser*, *pulcherrimus*, and *Carpodacus severtzovi*). The Twite (*Acanthis brevirostris*) was common. Sparrows, the ordinary (*Passer montanus*), also the cinnamon-coloured (*P. cinnamomeus*). Wagtails.—The two Indian forms were common during the summer.

Pigeons were everywhere represented on the upper plateaus and near villages by the Himalayan blue pigeon (*Columba rupestris*), whilst the so-called "snow" pigeon (*C. leuconota*) was most common in the lower ravines. In the groves and thickets about Gyantsé and Lhasa, the Oriental turtle-dove (*Turtur orientalis*) was common.

Game birds.—The Monāl Pheasant (*Lophophorus refulgens*) T.—*Chamdong*, was common in Chumbi over 10,000 feet; also the Blood Pheasant (*Ithagenes cruentus*) T.—*Semo*, amongst the greenish lichen-covered rocks in the same locality. On the bare uplands the Snow Cock (*Tetraogallus tibetanus*), T.—*Hrak-pa*, was common over 15,000 feet, and occasionally also was found there the Snow Partridge (*Lerva nivicola*). The ordinary Partridge (*Perdix hodgsoni*) was extremely common, especially in the ravines on the edge of the plateau. Sand-grouse (*Syrrhaptes tibetanus*) were found in the Gyantsé valley and shores of the Kala lake. The great Crane (*Grus antigone*) was seen at Lhasa. Snipe of two kinds were shot—the Solitary (*Gallinago solitaria*) and a few Pintail (*G. stenura*) in the Lhasa marshes, where Coots (*Fulica atra*), Red-shanks (*Totanus calidris*), and Moor-hens (*Gallinula chloropus*), also two Terns (*Sternus* sp.) were common, and on the larger lakes a Gull. Ducks, T.—*Dàm-cha*, and geese of most of the species which emigrate in the winter to India were found. The common Goose was the bar-headed (*Anser indicus*). The Ruddy Sheldrake or Brahmany Duck (*Casarca rutila*) was breeding all over the country. The Mallard (*Anas boscas*), Pintail (*Dafila acuta*), Wigeon (*Mareca penelope*), Gadwall (*Chaulelasmus streperus*), Shoveller (*Spatula clypeata*), White-eyed Pochard (*Nyroca ferruginea*), Tufted Pochard (*Nyroca fuligula*), were common, also Teal (*Nettion crecca*) and Garganey or Blue-Winged Teal (*Querquedula circia*), Goosanders (*Merganser castor*) were shot at Lingmo plain, Phari, and Gyantsé; large flights of geese passed Gyantsé northwards in April, making apparently for the Tengri Lake. No Swans were seen, but the people said that they were occasional visitors, probably the Whooper (*Cygnus musicus*).

NEW BIRDS.

THE following three new birds collected by me in September 1904, in the Tsangpo valley of Tibet, near the Chaksam Ferry, at an elevation of 12,100 feet, have been kindly described and figured by H. E. Dresser, Esq., F.Z.S., *Proc. Zool. Soc.*, 17th January, and *Field*, 21st January 1905.

"**Babax waddelli.** Waddell's Striped Laughing Thrush.—Adult male, Tsangpo Valley, Tibet, 25th September. Upper parts dull ashy grey, each feather with a broad central blackish stripe, the rump slightly less striped than the rest of the upper parts; wings blackish brown, most of the feathers narrowly margined externally with ashy grey; tail blackish brown, much graduated, under parts somewhat paler and more narrowly striped than the upper parts. Total length about 12·60 inches, culmen 1·40, wing 5·10, tail 6·50, tarsus 1·70.

"The nearest ally to this species is *Babax lanceolatus*, from which, however, it differs considerably, being larger (wing 5·10 against 3·75, tail 6·50 against 5·0), and, as will be seen by the above description, it differs considerably both in colour and markings."

Habits.—This bird is called by the Tibetans "Téh-Téh" in imitation of its call. It frequents poplar and alder thickets remote from villages. It is gregarious in groups of eight to ten; but not so active or secretive in its movements as the Babblers. Its iris is a dull orange, and the soft parts leaden.

"**Garrulax tibetanus.** Tibetan Laughing Thrush.—Adult male, Tsangpo valley, Tibet, 25th September. Upper parts dark brown with a tinge of ochraceous, the crown slightly darker, lores and a patch through the eye, with the ear-coverts black; quills blackish, externally margined with slate or dark lavender grey; wing coverts like the back; tail graduated, blackish, broadly tipped with white; under parts rather paler than the upper parts; a broad white stripe below the eye, and a few white feathers above the eye; under tail-coverts and lower flanks chestnut red. Total length about 10·50, culmen 0·90, wing 4·50, tail 6·40, tarsus 1·50.

"From *Garrulax sannio* (Swinhoe), its nearest ally, this species differs in having the upper parts much darker and more uniform in colour, the crown not chestnut brown, the under parts darker without any white or ochraceous on the belly, and the tail is not uniform in colour, but has a broad white terminal band."

Habits.—It is called "the Lady" (*Jomo*) by the Tibetans. It occurs in the alder and poplar thickets alongside the Babax, and also in the copses close to the villages. It has the characteristic habits of a Babbler in marked degree, roving in groups of eight or more, chattering noisily, with its fluty call of *Whoh-hee! Whoh-hee!* It is always on the move, scampering along the branches, and is very secretive, seldom showing itself, and flying very low across a clearance to the next cover. Its iris is dull crimson, and soft parts dark slaty.

"**Lanius lama**. Tibetan Shrike. — Adult male, Tsangpo valley, Tibet, 26th September. Head, nape and upper parts generally dark plumbeous, much as in *Lanius algeriensis;* a narrow line across the forehead, the lores and a broad band through and behind the eye deep black; lower rump and upper tail-coverts rufous; wings black, the inner secondaries and larger wing-coverts narrowly margined with dull white; tail uniform blackish brown, rather pale at the extreme tip; under parts white, the breast, flanks, and under tail-coverts washed with rufous fawn. Total length about 10·10 inches, culmen 0·83, wing 4·30, tail 5·0, tarsus 1·12.

"*Lanius schah* appears to be the nearest ally to the present species, but this latter has only a narrow black line across the forehead, the upper parts are much darker, and it has no rufous on the back or scapulars, but only on the upper tail-coverts, and no trace of an alar speculum."

Reptiles and Amphibia.

No trustworthy evidence of the occurrence of Snakes was elicited. I saw newts twice in the neighbourhood of Lhasa (pp. 328 and 376), but failed to secure any. Of the two species of Lizards which I found in the Tsangpo valley, one is new, and is named by Mr Boulanger *Alsophylax tibetanum* (to be described in the *Annals and Magazine of Natural History* for April 1905), and the other was *Phrynocephalus theobaldi.* The Frogs belonged to a well-known species, *Rana pleskei*, some of the specimens of which had a dorsal stripe which was wanting in others.

Fishes.

The Carp from the Yamdok lake proved to be a new species, which has been named by Mr C. T. Regan of the British Museum, to which I sent specimens:—

Gymnocypris waddelli. Yamdok Carp. — It is not a new genus as might have been supposed from the long isolation of Yamdok lake, but belongs to one which was found by Russian explorers in North-Eastern Tibet. It is figured at page 306, where the variety in its spot-markings is noticeable, and is to be described in the *Annals and Magazine of Natural History* for April 1905.

INSECTS.

Five or six species of Butterflies and Moths were common on the plateau. The four species which I caught at Lhasa were identified by Mr Heron of the British Museum as (1) *Chrysophanus phlœas, stygianus*, Butler; (2) *Lycœna ariana*, Moore; (3) *Colias fieldii*, Mén. form *xenodica*, Felder; (4) *Plusia gutta*, Guence. Near Phari the silvery spotted tortoise-shell Queen of Spain, Fritillary (*Argynnis latona*, Lin.) was found; several species of brilliant-hued Dragonflies were common in all the ditches, also Lady-Birds; and there were several species of Ants and Spiders, whilst large black Mosquitoes were a pest at Lhasa. I found a black Scorpion a few miles below that city, and it was identified as *Scorpio hardwickii*.

APPENDIX XII.

GEOLOGY.

A GENERAL view of the stratification of the rock-formations as observed along our route across the axis of the Himalayas to beyond the Tsangpo, and the great disturbance suffered by the earth's crust in the upheaval of that mountain chain, are indicated in the following sketch.

In the outer Himalayas up to the Chumbi, the general arrangement is, as was first noted by Sir Joseph Hooker, the pioneer explorer of Sikhim:[1] the sedimentary rocks, the slates and shales,[2] with coal-bearing strata of the Lower Tista Valley, give place about 2000 feet up to gneiss and mica schist, which forms the mass of the Himalayas, whilst the core of the highest peaks is granite. These sedimentary rocks seem to have been formed in greater portion before the great upheaval, and from the detritus brought down from a pre-Himalayan range here (probably gneissic); for they are extensively crumpled and contorted at their junction with the massive gneiss of the present range. In the shales at Rorot'ang (p. 72) a copper ore (pyrites) is worked by a Nepalese lessee in mines in a dark greenish soft shale banded with quartzite.

In the Chumbi valley our track (see altitude profile - chart, p. 62) led up the drainage line coming from the north, directly at right angles to the axis of the main chain. We started from the gneiss at Chumbi, and found interesting evidence in favour of the new view of the formation of this rock. Its stratified or

[1] *Himalayan Journals*, ii. 156, 177. For geological sections across Northern Himalayas, see the article by Lieut.-Col. Godwin-Austen. *Proceedings*, Royal Geog. Soc., 1884.

[2] The so-called "Daling" shales which predominate consist of *Phyllites*. —Mallet, *Memoirs and Records*, *Geological Survey of India*, vols. iii., etc.

laminated character was formerly attributed to the sedimentary action of water upon the detritus of granite rocks, but it was difficult to reconcile this agency with the location of this rock. In the Chumbi valley the blasting operations exposed fresh sections of the rocks, which illustrated the conversion of crystallised granite into flaky gneiss and mica-schist by mere pressure on the crystals through the enormous weight of rock overlying it. Under this crushing stress, the rounded black grains of the granite can be seen in all stages of the process of horizontal compression; some are flattening out into ovals and further down into the fully stratified structure of gneiss; and where the proportion of mica is greater it assumes the foliated structure characteristic of mica-schist. Much of the lower gneiss was rich in garnets of poor size and quality.

The passage from the gneiss into the upper sedimentary rocks occurred about 15 miles to the south of the main axis of the Himalayas, as indicated by the line of the highest peaks, and coincided almost exactly with the upper limit of trees and shrubs, namely, at the old lake meadow of Dot'ak. Here, at the line of a great fault, the gneiss suddenly ended, and gave place to reddish and yellow strata of slates and claystones, which had been deposited in the bed of the great ocean which formerly rolled here before the rising of the Himalayas.

The lower beds of this marine mud are unfossiliferous, but across the Tang Pass, beyond the main axis of the chain, on the chalky limestone hill of Tuna, are found encrinitic fossils and nummulites similar to those found by Sir Joseph Hooker in the Cholamo plain in a corresponding position some 50 miles further along, to the west; and still further west at Khambajong were found ram's-horn-like Ammonites, and various large bivalves, like oysters, penhandle-like Belemnites of Jurassic age, such as are found in the trans-Himalayan valley of the Sutlej and in Ladak, showing the existence of a sea here probably in the tertiary period. Here, however, there has been so much disturbance of the strata that it is very difficult to make out the sequence of the deposits, such as is clearly seen in the adjoining basin of Cholamo on the west. On the moraines of Chumolhari blocks of granite testify to the structure of that peak.

At Kangmar as the Red Gorge is neared, the shaly rocks become redder, and some hot springs here[1] testify to the

[1] See p. 189.

existence of latent volcanic action here. Although only two or three hot springs are noticed near the road here, along the right bank of the stream for 6 miles, all the way down to the Red Gorge, shaggy masses of waving confervoid growth cover the stones, and the people say that this part of the river never freezes over. For several miles here the bed of the valley is covered by calcareous tufa[1] and the hollows are white with patches of a saline efflorescence.[2]

The Red Gorge itself is formed by the rounded dome-shaped shoulders of massive granite.

At Gyantsé the rock is chiefly a gritty limestone banded with white sulphate of lime, and occasionally quartzite.

Above Gyantsé the shales becomes much darker in colour, but never carbonaceous; towards the Kharo Pass they are occasionally contorted. At Ralung the valley opens out in a wide shallow saucer shape of the glacier type.

In the Tsangpo gorge the rock at the ferry is a dark compact granite with very little quartz.

In the Lhasa valley, the granite, on the other hand, which intrudes into the shale and dark bluish limestone, is remarkably coarse-grained, consisting of masses of almost pure quartz with the felspar widely scattered through it. This coarse granite is further noteworthy in containing embedded in its structure large boulder-like masses of the charred fossiliferous limestone rock through which the molten granite had burst. The rock at Lhasa itself was chiefly limestone with numerous intrusive veins of granite.

In the Lhasa bazaar were to be got a few chalky fragments of fossils brought from the Tengri or "Celestial" Lake,[3] 80 miles north of the city, and sold as medicines and charms. This lake contains fish, and fresh-water shells are found on its shores, as well as fossil shells from its chalk beds, which are considered not older than the Cretaceous period.[4] No fossil fish or reptiles have been found.

[1] See pp. 189 and 472 for analysis. [2] See p. 472 for analysis.

[3] Near its northern border is a small lake called "The Borax" (*Bul*) lake, which is 6 miles long, and a commercial source of that substance.

[4] Mr W. Oldham, in *Man. Ind. Geol.*:—A specimen of *Omphalia trotteri* was brought to Calcutta by Pandit A.-K. Old palæozoic Devonian fossils were found by the Abbe des Mazures near "Gouchou" in Eastern Tibet (*Comptes Rendas*, LVIII. [1864], 878).

For the following interesting account of the section through the rocks between Chumbi and Gyantsé, I am indebted to Lieutenant R. Lloyd, I.M.S:—

"Until I reached Dot'ak I saw no sedimentary rocks except gneiss and schist, which might be pre-Cambrian sedimentaries with granite intrusions; but just as one comes to Dot'ak plain these older rocks end and an old limestone rock appears, the junction of these two series is unfortunately a fault fracture. This can be seen very well if you stand between the commissariat shed and the river and look south down the valley. The fault is easily seen as the older rock is dark in colour, in contrast from the light brown sedimentary. I could find no fossils of any sort in the sedimentary rock. I should suppose it was probably carboniferous. Unfossiliferous sedimentaries extend as far as Tuna.

"I had no opportunity of examining Chumolhari, but it looks from its outline to be composed of a centre of some reddish granitoid rock, with old sedimentaries and slaty rocks around it composing the lesser peaks. The centre has weathered out with a rounded outline, while the lesser peaks are jagged.

"On the other side of the Tang La one can see on the left-hand side (to the west) a line of low hills of a yellow colour. These I had a good look at, and obtained several fossils of a cretaceous age. These rocks are very little crushed. They slope to the north-west at an angle of about 30, and are a good deal faulted in places, but are not contorted. They consist of two series: above, a series of yellowish or light brown limestones, in which I found the fossils; and below, a grit or coarse sandstone of the same colour. This shows the structure known as "filose bedding," indicative of shallow water deposit, while the limestone indicative of deeper water being above it proves, I think, a subsidence during the deposit of these rocks prior to the great upheaval.

"These rocks lie all along the road to Guru, and to the south and west of Tuna. They are the only rocks which I could certainly assign a date to. Hayden had obtained similar fossils to mine, and agreed with me that they were cretaceous.

"I obtained a few fossils near Kangmar, at least two species of Crinoids from that extraordinary section between the post and the village on the other side of the river from the road. These were, I think, Liassic species; but might have been Carboniferous.

The white rock in that section is deposited calcium carbonate, to my great surprise, as from Kangmar it looked like granite intrusion. I could find no fossils around Gyantsé. The Red Gorge is, of course, a huge intrusive mass of granite."

No useful minerals were noticed, nor anything geologically of economic importance, all the way up to Lhasa. The sources of cinnabar, cobalt, tin, silver and gold (see pp. 474, 475) are said to be many days' journey to the north and to the east of that place.

APPENDIX XIII.

TEXT OF THE TIBETAN TREATY.[1]

Preamble.

The Tibetans having paid no heed to China's counsels, and having failed to conform to the conditions of the treaty signed at Calcutta between China and Great Britain in the sixteenth year of Kuang-hsu (1890) and the treaty of the nineteenth year (1893), owing to their containing terms of ambiguous and objectionable character, Great Britain, finding it necessary to take action on her own account, appointed Colonel Younghusband, a high Boundary official, as plenipotentiary to arrange a satisfactory basis with the Imperial Resident Yu for all matters that required settlement. Great Britain and the Tibetans having now agreed upon ten clauses in connection with the objectionable and doubtful points of the treaty of the sixteenth year, and the Chinese Imperial Resident Yu having duly examined the same treaty, it may accordingly be signed and sealed. After the conclusion of the treaty between China and Great Britain the inhabitants of Tibet shall not violate the terms. This is because the Tibetans failed entirely to conform to the terms of the treaties made in the sixteenth and nineteenth years between China and Great Britain owing to their containing much that was unsatisfactory and objectionable, so that Great Britain specially appointed Colonel Younghusband as plenipotentiary in frontier affairs to proceed to the frontier and negotiate. Unexpectedly hostilities were again committed, thus causing a rupture of amicable relations, but negotiations have now been opened and ten clauses definitely agreed upon, in order that upon completion of the treaty and the sealing of the same by the Dalai Lama, as head

[1] This is as published by Dr Morrison of Peking.

of the Yellow Priesthood, and Colonel Younghusband, the Boundary Commissioner, peace may hereafter be secured.

Article I.

The Tibetans hereby agree, in accordance with the first clause of the treaty of the sixteenth year, to re-erect boundary stones at the Sikhim frontier.

Article II.

The Tibetans hereby agree to establish marts at Gyantsé and Kotako (Gartok) in addition to Yatung, for the purpose of mutual trading between the British and Tibetan merchants at their free convenience. Great Britain will arrange with Tibet for the alteration of all objectionable features in the treaty of the nineteenth year of Kuang-hsu, and as soon as this agreement shall have been completed, arrangements shall be made at Yatung, Gyantsé and Gartok accordingly. The Tibetans having agreed to establish markets at Yatung, Gyantsé, and Gartok, merchandise purchased by Tibetans from India may be transported along existing routes, and arrangements may be made for opening marts in future at other prosperous commercial places.

Article III.

With regard to any objectionable features of the treaty of the nineteenth year requiring alteration separate arrangement may be made, and Tibet will appoint a Tibetan official having plenipotentiary authority to confer with the British officials for their alteration.

Article IV.

No further Customs duties may be levied upon merchandise after the tariff shall have been agreed upon by Great Britain and the Tibetans.

Article V.

On the route between the Indian frontier and Yatung, Gyantsé, and Gartok no Customs stations may be established. Tibet shall repair any dangerous passes on the road in order to facilitate merchants travelling thereon and the prevention of difficulties. Tibet shall appoint native officials at these three places, and the officials appointed by Great Britain at these places shall have their correspondence with the Imperial Resident and other Chinese officials forwarded through the above-mentioned native officials. Similar officials shall be appointed at other flourishing places which may be opened to trade and the same course adopted.

Article VI.

Tibet having disobeyed the treaties and insulted the Commissioner by the wrongful commission of hostile acts, shall pay Great Britain an indemnity of 5,000,000 dollars equivalent to Rs. 7,500,000 (£500,000),[1] payable in three yearly instalments; the first payment to be on 1st January 1906. When the time arrives Great Britain will first notify the Tibetans as to the place at which payment shall be made, or whether receipt may be taken thereof at the Tibetan temple at Darjeeling.

Article VII.

For performance of the conditions comprised in Articles II., III., and IV. for opening trading stations, and in the sixth clause relative to the indemnity as security for the punctual discharge of its obligations on the part of Tibet, British troops will continue to occupy the Chumbi Valley for three years, until the trading places are satisfactorily established and the indemnity liquidated in full. In the event of the indemnity's not being paid, England will continue in occupation of Chumbi.

Article VIII.

All forts between the Indian frontier and Gyantsé on routes traversed by merchants from the interior of Tibet shall be demolished.

Article IX.

Without the consent of Great Britain no Tibetan territory shall be sold, leased, or mortgaged to any foreign Power whatsoever; no foreign Power whatsoever shall be permitted to concern

[1] This amount was afterwards reduced by the Home Government to one-third of this amount.

itself with the administration of the Government of Tibet or any other affairs therewith connected; no foreign Power shall be permitted to send either official or non-official persons to Tibet, no matter in what pursuit they may be engaged, to assist in the conduct of Tibetan affairs; no foreign Power shall be permitted to construct roads or railways or erect telegraphs or open mines anywhere in Tibet. In the event of Great Britain's consenting to another Power constructing roads or railways, opening mines or creating telegraphs, Great Britain will make a full examination on her own account for carrying out the arrangements proposed. No real property or land containing minerals or precious metals in Tibet shall be mortgaged, exchanged, leased, or sold to any foreign Power.

ARTICLE X.

The Boundary Commissioner Jung and the Dalai Lama will sign and seal this treaty on the 22nd day of the 7th moon of the Tibetan calendar, being the 1st day of September 1904 of the English calendar. Of the two versions, English and Tibetan, the English text shall be regarded as authoritative.

APPENDIX XIV.

DEPOSITION OF THE DALAI LAMA BY THE CHINESE.

The following is the text of this proclamation issued by the Amban:—

"This notice is posted by Lu Amban on receipt of a reply telegram on the 5th September. The rank of the Dalai Lama is temporarily confiscated, and in his place is appointed Teshi Lama. For over 200 years Tibet has been feudatory to China, and the Dalai Lama has received much kindness from this great Kingdom, but in return did not remain to guard his Kingdom. On account of his not regarding the interests of the faith the gods and guardian spirits became angry. He also allowed his subjects to act as they pleased. Moreover, he gave no orders to settle the Sikkim-Tibet boundary outstanding for over ten years, and although orders were given to him to settle the matter quickly, he paid no attention, but collected soldiers from various parts and made war. Then, being defeated and great troubles having arisen, instead of protecting the country and his subjects, he ran away to a distant place in an unknown country. During the war thousands and tens of thousands of Tibetans were slain, and those who ran away and were unable to fight were reproached by him. The teacher of the Dalai Lama, the late Regent, and with him the Amban, had desired peaceful solutions, but the present Dalai Lama, out of jealousy, caused the death of many people, and thus caused much grief to the people of Tibet, and listening to bad advice heavily punished the Regent. In the case of the Shapé Paljordorje the Dalai Lama reported him to the Amban, who reported the matter to the Emperor, and the Shapé was punished. As to the other Shapés, if they deserved punishment, it should have been done, in accordance with the custom of nations, but the Dalai Lama, although he sent a representation to the Emperor, nevertheless of his own accord punished them severely, and then being appeased set them free, thus paying no regard to the Emperor, nor to law or justice. These various crimes show him not to be a man who should not be punished, and so being a man of evil mind, and having oppressed all his subjects and robbed them, it appears that his Ministers cannot hold him in much regard, as he has transgressed the laws of the Buddhist faith, thus causing disturbance to great Powers. He has been denounced, and so has reaped the fruits of his ill-doing, and all will thus receive satisfaction. You should all, Chinese and Tibetan officials, soldiers, peasants, laymen and monks, take this notice to heart in future, Tibet being feudatory to China. The Dalai Lama will be responsible for the Yellow Cap faith, and monks will only be slightly concerned with official matters, while the Amban will conduct all Tibetan affairs with Tibetan officials, important matters being referred to the Emperor. The Dalai Lama will not be permitted on his own option to intervene in civil affairs. All must understand, and not transgress these orders."

APPENDIX XV.

FERTILITY OF THE PO DISTRICT OF THE LOWER TSANGPO.

THE following particulars regarding this almost unknown rich district of Lower Tibet bordering Assam, and showing how these tracts may be developed, were elicited by Mr Rockhill:—

A detachment of 500 Chinese soldiers who were being sent from Sze-chuan to Nepal during a war with the latter country (in 1793 or more recently) lost its way in Lower Po or "Po-" mä. Here they were so captivated with "the beauty and fertility of the country that the men decided to go no further and to make it their home. They married women of the country and greatly prospered, and their descendants still occupy the land. . . . While Po-tö (or 'Upper Po') is under the rule of Lhasa, Po-mä is independent in fact, it being under the nominal control of a high Manchu officer stationed at Lhasa who is known as 'Envoy to the Savage Tribes' or 'Third Amban.' Po-mä is visited by Lao-Shan and Yunnanese traders, and it carries on a large trade with Derge, Jyade, and Lhasa. The horses of Po-mä are famous throughout Tibet, and its leather-work, iron-work, and jewellery, as well as the products of its looms, are celebrated and in great demand. The products of the soil are varied and of excellent quality, and altogether this country would seem to be the most fertile spot of Tibet." And Mr Rockhill elsewhere remarks: "The best workmanship I have seen in Tibet is that of Po-mä. That region apparently supplies all Eastern Tibet with delicacies: it is the land of promise of Tibet."

This thriving settlement is said to connect with the fine central section of the Tsangpo valley through the Upper Po District (which is skirted on its north by the post road), and also at Kongbu with the post road to Eastern Tibet and the Yangtse, so that it could be traversed from India to China by a route which would steer altogether clear of Lhasa, its sombre uplands and its most holy places. This, of course, presupposes the practicability of a road up the Dihong. The direct route up the eastern branch of the Brahmaputra, through the Mishmi country, is the natural overland line of communication between India and China, but this would not pass through Tibet, which would be left to the north of it. This natural overland route between China and India crosses several parallel ridges, three or four thousand feet high, which divide the valleys of the Brahmaputra, Salwin and Mekong from the rich valley of the Yangtsé.

APPENDIX XVI.

ITINERARY—FROM CALCUTTA TO LHASA.

THE elevations were taken by an aneroid controlled by hypsometer on several occasions.

STAGES.	ELEVATION above sea-level.	DISTANCES.		REMARKS.
		Inter-mediate.	Total.	
Silliguri .	397	...	...	14 hours rail from Calcutta.
Sivok . .	500	11	11	In gorge of Tista River.
Riang . .	625	12	23	
Tarkhola .	900	13	36	At 4½ miles cross Tista Bridge (710 ft.), which is 18 miles from Darjeeling and 5 from Kalimpong.
Rangpo .	1200	6	42	In Native Sikhim. Here leave Tista Valley.
Rorot'ang .	1660	8	50	
Lingtam .	3960	10	60	At Rongli (2590 ft.) begins steep climb.
Jeyluk .	8760	7	67	
Gnatong .	12,210	8	75	
Kuphu .	13,200	8	83	Cross Tuko Pass (13,550 ft.) at 5 miles.
Langram .	12,150	6	89	Cross Jelep Pass (14,390 ft.) at 4 miles into Tibet.
Rinchengang	9370	4	93	Pass Yatung at 2 miles.
Chumbi Camp	9780[1]	4½	97½	Pass Chumbi Valley (9530 ft.) at 3 miles.
Lingmo .	11,200	7	104½	Passing Chorten Karpo at 3½ miles, and Galingk'a at 4 miles.
Gaut'ang ("Gautsa")	12,360	5½	110	
Dot'ak. .	13,550	5	115	
Phari . .	14,570	12	127	Passing Khamparab Bridge at 3½ miles. 30 miles from Chumbi.

[1] Fixed trigonometrically by Capt. Ryder, R.E.

Stages.	Elevation above sea-level.	Distances.		Remarks.
		Inter-mediate.	Total.	
Chugya .	14,650	3½	130½	
Tuna . .	14,950	15½	146	Passing Tang Pass (15,200 ft.) at 4½ miles.
Dochen .	14,900	12	158	Guru at 8 m., and along Lake [Rham.
Kala Lake.	14,700	12	170	
Mangtsa .	14,400	10	180	
Kangmar .	13,900	12	192	Here direct road to Lhasa, *viâ* Nyeru and Gobzhi.
Saogang .	13,500	15	207	
Gyantsé	13,200	15	222	Large mart. 124½ miles from Chumbi and 94½ from Phari.
Kotang .	14,000	10½	232½	
Lungmar .	14,200	13½	246	Leave Nyeru River at Gobzhi at 7½ miles.
Ralung .	14,500	8	254	
Kharo Pass (below)	16,300	10	264	
Zara . .	16,000	7	271	Over Pass (16,500 ft.).
Nagartsé .	15,000	12	283	On Yamdok Lake.
Yasig . .	14,950	11	294	
Palté . .	14,950	5	299	
Demalung.	14,950	11	310	
Kamba Partsï	12,200	6	316	In Tsangpo Valley, across Kamba Pass (16,500 ft.), or Dok Pass (16,800 ft.).
Chaksam Ferry	12,100	7	323	
Jang . .	12,150	10	333	In Kyi (Lhasa) Valley.
Netang .	12,210	13	346	
Tilung Bridge	12,240	7	353	Here best road to Shigatsé.
Lhasa .	12,290	6	359	137 miles from Gyantsé, 231 miles from Phari, and 261 miles from Chumbi.

APPENDIX XVII.

DIARY OF THE CHIEF EVENTS OF THE EXPEDITION

1903

July 7.—First British Mission under Col. F. E. Younghusband arrived at Khamba Jong.

Oct. 3.—British Government authorised military occupation of Chumbi Valley, and advance to Tibet.

Dec. 11.—First British Mission withdrawn from Khamba Jong.

„ 11.—Second Mission, with Colonel Younghusband as Commissioner escorted by military force under General Macdonald, left Gnatong.

„ 12.—Jelep Pass crossed, and Tibet entered.

„ 19.—Phari occupied.

1904

Jan. 8.—Tuna occupied.

Mar. 31.—Fight at Guru Wall four miles north of Tuna. 300 Tibetans killed.

April 5.—Chalu reached.

„ 6.—Fight at Samada, thirteen miles from Kala Lake.

„ 7.—Mission arrived at Salu.

„ 9.—Langma (two miles north of Kangmar) reached.

„ 10.—Fight in Red Gorge south of Gyantsé.

„ 11.—Mission reached Gyantsé.

„ 12.—Gyantsé Fort surrendered.

May 6.—Tibetans from Shigatsé attacked Gyantsé.

„ 6.—Tibetans defeated at Kharo Pass.

„ 19.—Tibetans driven out of post north of Gyantsé.

„ 20.—Fight at Gyantsé.

„ 26.—Phala village, about ½ mile from Gyantsé post, stormed.

„ 30.—Tibetans attack Gyantsé.

1904

June 2.—Phala attacked by Tibetans.

„ 7.—Kangmar post attacked by Tibetans.

„ 16.—Tibetans ambuscaded Sikhs.

„ 25.—Skirmish near Gyantsé.

„ 26.—Fight at Niani monastery near Gyantsé.

„ 28.—Fight at Tsechen monastery near Gyantsé.

July 1.—Tongsa Penlop arrives at British camp to assist in making peace for which Tibetan delegates arrive.

„ 3.—Peace negotiations broken off. Tibetans ordered to evacuate Jong by July 5.

„ 6.—Jong stormed and captured by General Macdonald.

„ 8.—British force reached Dongtsé unopposed.

„ 10.—British forces reconnoitred to Penam Jong, near Shigatsé, which was found unoccupied. Tibetans fled to Shigatsé.

„ 14.—Advance from Gyangtsé to Lhasa begun.

„ 18.—Forced the Kharo Pass.

„ 19.—Arrived Nagartsé on Yamdok Lake where negotiations reopened.

„ 24.—Crossed Kampa pass to Tsangpo Valley.

„ 25.—Crossing of Tsangpo commenced. (Major Bretherton drowned.)

Aug. 3.—Arrived at Lhasa.

„ 8.—Demonstration against Däpung monastery.

„ 20.—Arrival of Cardinal, the Ti Rimpoché.

Sept. 4.—Treaty agreed to.

„ 7.—Treaty signed.

„ 23.—Leave Lhasa.

Oct. 17.—Troops snow-bound at Phari.

„ 25.—Detachment of Lhasa column arrived at Silliguri railway terminus.

PART OF ENGLAND ON THE SAME SCALE.
LONDON
SHEERNESS
Reigate
R. Medway
MAIDSTONE
Tunbridge Wells
BRIGHTON
HASTINGS
89°
90°
30°
29°
28°
27°
88°
C E N T
Chamnamring
Shang-shung
Bon temple
Hotspring
SHIGATSE
12,400
TASHILHUMPO MONASTERY
Penam
Shalu
Hermitage
Dongtsé
Tsechen
GYANTSE
May 5. July 6
Hermitages
Nyarong
Mt. Nöjin
24,000
Kharo P.
May 6
July 18
Ralung
Sakya Monastery
From Nepal
Nanyi
Gabzhi
Red Gorge
Apr. 10
Hot Springs
Kangmar
Wall, Apr. 7
Salu
Samada
Apr. 6
16,200
Khamba Jong
13,800
Kala
Chalu
Lapchi Monastery
Dochen
Guru
Spring
Rham
Mar. 31
Kula Kan
24,740
Chorten Nyima
18,650
Donkia P.
18,100
Tuna
Jan. 6
Tang P.
Chumolhari
24,000
Tango
Lachen
Hot Spring
Khungbu
PHARI
Lachung
Kangchenjunga
28,150
Thangkar P.
Chungthang
Gautsa
Dotak
Pempa P.
Punakha
Lingmo
Chinese Wall
Camp
Chumbi
Rinchengang
Yatung
Dec. 13
Paro
Tashi
Jelep P.
14,390
Wall
Gantok
Gnatong
Lingtam
Rangpo
Rongli
Pedong
Kalimpong
3,918
DARJEELING
7,160
Riang
Sivok
Chalsa
D O A R S
Lakhi
Baxa
Hantupara
SILIGURI
397
Route of Bogle, Turner & Manning
B E N G A L
N E P A L
S I K K I M
B H
William Stanford & Company, Ltd.

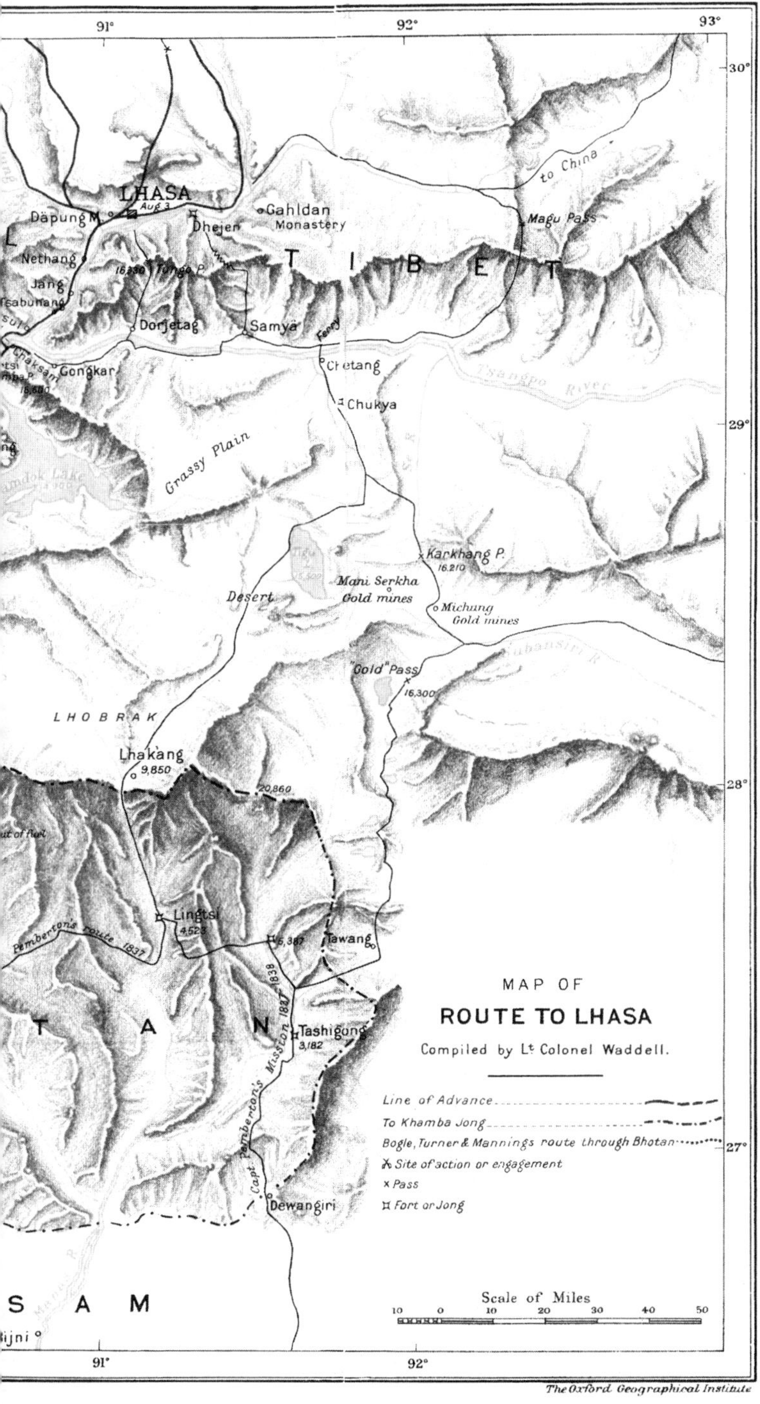

The Oxford Geographical Institute

INDEX.

* In black and white in the present edition.

C

* In black and white in the present edition.

D

E

F

G

H

L

M

* In black and white in the present edition.

* For new locations of all maps, see page xxii.

N

O

Q

R

S

* In black and white in the present edition.

* In black and white in the present edition.

T

* In black and white in the present edition.

* In black and white in the present edition.

U

V

* In black and white in the present edition.
†On page xxiii in the present edition.

* In black and white in the present edition.

Z

A CATALOG OF SELECTED

DOVER BOOKS

IN ALL FIELDS OF INTEREST

A CATALOG OF SELECTED DOVER BOOKS IN ALL FIELDS OF INTEREST

DRAWINGS OF REMBRANDT, edited by Seymour Slive. Updated Lippmann, Hofstede de Groot edition, with definitive scholarly apparatus. All portraits, biblical sketches, landscapes, nudes. Oriental figures, classical studies, together with selection of work by followers. 550 illustrations. Total of 630pp. 9⅛ × 12¼.
21485-0, 21486-9 Pa., Two-vol. set $25.00

GHOST AND HORROR STORIES OF AMBROSE BIERCE, Ambrose Bierce. 24 tales vividly imagined, strangely prophetic, and decades ahead of their time in technical skill: "The Damned Thing," "An Inhabitant of Carcosa," "The Eyes of the Panther," "Moxon's Master," and 20 more. 199pp. 5⅜ × 8½. 20767-6 Pa. $3.95

ETHICAL WRITINGS OF MAIMONIDES, Maimonides. Most significant ethical works of great medieval sage, newly translated for utmost precision, readability. Laws Concerning Character Traits, Eight Chapters, more. 192pp. 5⅜ × 8½.
24522-5 Pa. $4.50

THE EXPLORATION OF THE COLORADO RIVER AND ITS CANYONS, J. W. Powell. Full text of Powell's 1,000-mile expedition down the fabled Colorado in 1869. Superb account of terrain, geology, vegetation, Indians, famine, mutiny, treacherous rapids, mighty canyons, during exploration of last unknown part of continental U.S. 400pp. 5⅜ × 8½. 20094-9 Pa. $6.95

HISTORY OF PHILOSOPHY, Julián Marías. Clearest one-volume history on the market. Every major philosopher and dozens of others, to Existentialism and later. 505pp. 5⅜ × 8½. 21739-6 Pa. $8.50

ALL ABOUT LIGHTNING, Martin A. Uman. Highly readable non-technical survey of nature and causes of lightning, thunderstorms, ball lightning, St. Elmo's Fire, much more. Illustrated. 192pp. 5⅜ × 8½. 25237-X Pa. $5.95

SAILING ALONE AROUND THE WORLD, Captain Joshua Slocum. First man to sail around the world, alone, in small boat. One of great feats of seamanship told in delightful manner. 67 illustrations. 294pp. 5⅜ × 8½. 20326-3 Pa. $4.50

LETTERS AND NOTES ON THE MANNERS, CUSTOMS AND CONDITIONS OF THE NORTH AMERICAN INDIANS, George Catlin. Classic account of life among Plains Indians: ceremonies, hunt, warfare, etc. 312 plates. 572pp. of text. 6⅛ × 9¼. 22118-0, 22119-9 Pa. Two-vol. set $15.90

ALASKA: The Harriman Expedition, 1899, John Burroughs, John Muir, et al. Informative, engrossing accounts of two-month, 9,000-mile expedition. Native peoples, wildlife, forests, geography, salmon industry, glaciers, more. Profusely illustrated. 240 black-and-white line drawings. 124 black-and-white photographs. 3 maps. Index. 576pp. 5⅜ × 8½. 25109-8 Pa. $11.95

THE BOOK OF BEASTS: Being a Translation from a Latin Bestiary of the Twelfth Century, T. H. White. Wonderful catalog real and fanciful beasts: manticore, griffin, phoenix, amphivius, jaculus, many more. White's witty erudite commentary on scientific, historical aspects. Fascinating glimpse of medieval mind. Illustrated. 296pp. 5⅜ × 8¼. (Available in U.S. only) 24609-4 Pa. $5.95

FRANK LLOYD WRIGHT: ARCHITECTURE AND NATURE With 160 Illustrations, Donald Hoffmann. Profusely illustrated study of influence of nature—especially prairie—on Wright's designs for Fallingwater, Robie House, Guggenheim Museum, other masterpieces. 96pp. 9¼ × 10¾. 25098-9 Pa. $7.95

FRANK LLOYD WRIGHT'S FALLINGWATER, Donald Hoffmann. Wright's famous waterfall house: planning and construction of organic idea. History of site, owners, Wright's personal involvement. Photographs of various stages of building. Preface by Edgar Kaufmann, Jr. 100 illustrations. 112pp. 9¼ × 10. 23671-4 Pa. $7.95

YEARS WITH FRANK LLOYD WRIGHT: Apprentice to Genius, Edgar Tafel. Insightful memoir by a former apprentice presents a revealing portrait of Wright the man, the inspired teacher, the greatest American architect. 372 black-and-white illustrations. Preface. Index. vi + 228pp. 8¼ × 11. 24801-1 Pa. $9.95

THE STORY OF KING ARTHUR AND HIS KNIGHTS, Howard Pyle. Enchanting version of King Arthur fable has delighted generations with imaginative narratives of exciting adventures and unforgettable illustrations by the author. 41 illustrations. xviii + 313pp. 6⅛ × 9¼. 21445-1 Pa. $5.95

THE GODS OF THE EGYPTIANS, E. A. Wallis Budge. Thorough coverage of numerous gods of ancient Egypt by foremost Egyptologist. Information on evolution of cults, rites and gods; the cult of Osiris; the Book of the Dead and its rites; the sacred animals and birds; Heaven and Hell; and more. 956pp. 6⅛ × 9¼. 22055-9, 22056-7 Pa., Two-vol. set $21.90

A THEOLOGICO-POLITICAL TREATISE, Benedict Spinoza. Also contains unfinished *Political Treatise*. Great classic on religious liberty, theory of government on common consent. R. Elwes translation. Total of 421pp. 5⅜ × 8½. 20249-6 Pa. $6.95

INCIDENTS OF TRAVEL IN CENTRAL AMERICA, CHIAPAS, AND YUCATAN, John L. Stephens. Almost single-handed discovery of Maya culture; exploration of ruined cities, monuments, temples; customs of Indians. 115 drawings. 892pp. 5⅜ × 8½. 22404-X, 22405-8 Pa., Two-vol. set $15.90

LOS CAPRICHOS, Francisco Goya. 80 plates of wild, grotesque monsters and caricatures. Prado manuscript included. 183pp. 6⅜ × 9⅝. 22384-1 Pa. $4.95

AUTOBIOGRAPHY: The Story of My Experiments with Truth, Mohandas K. Gandhi. Not hagiography, but Gandhi in his own words. Boyhood, legal studies, purification, the growth of the Satyagraha (nonviolent protest) movement. Critical, inspiring work of the man who freed India. 480pp. 5⅜ × 8½. (Available in U.S. only) 24593-4 Pa. $6.95

ILLUSTRATED DICTIONARY OF HISTORIC ARCHITECTURE, edited by Cyril M. Harris. Extraordinary compendium of clear, concise definitions for over 5,000 important architectural terms complemented by over 2,000 line drawings. Covers full spectrum of architecture from ancient ruins to 20th-century Modernism. Preface. 592pp. 7½ × 9⅝. 24444-X Pa. $14.95

THE NIGHT BEFORE CHRISTMAS, Clement Moore. Full text, and woodcuts from original 1848 book. Also critical, historical material. 19 illustrations. 40pp. 4⅝ × 6. 22797-9 Pa. $2.50

THE LESSON OF JAPANESE ARCHITECTURE: 165 Photographs, Jiro Harada. Memorable gallery of 165 photographs taken in the 1930's of exquisite Japanese homes of the well-to-do and historic buildings. 13 line diagrams. 192pp. 8⅜ × 11¼. 24778-3 Pa. $8.95

THE AUTOBIOGRAPHY OF CHARLES DARWIN AND SELECTED LETTERS, edited by Francis Darwin. The fascinating life of eccentric genius composed of an intimate memoir by Darwin (intended for his children); commentary by his son, Francis; hundreds of fragments from notebooks, journals, papers; and letters to and from Lyell, Hooker, Huxley, Wallace and Henslow. xi + 365pp. 5⅜ × 8. 20479-0 Pa. $5.95

WONDERS OF THE SKY: Observing Rainbows, Comets, Eclipses, the Stars and Other Phenomena, Fred Schaaf. Charming, easy-to-read poetic guide to all manner of celestial events visible to the naked eye. Mock suns, glories, Belt of Venus, more. Illustrated. 299pp. 5¼ × 8¼. 24402-4 Pa. $7.95

BURNHAM'S CELESTIAL HANDBOOK, Robert Burnham, Jr. Thorough guide to the stars beyond our solar system. Exhaustive treatment. Alphabetical by constellation: Andromeda to Cetus in Vol. 1; Chamaeleon to Orion in Vol. 2; and Pavo to Vulpecula in Vol. 3. Hundreds of illustrations. Index in Vol. 3. 2,000pp. 6⅛ × 9¼. 23567-X, 23568-8, 23673-0 Pa., Three-vol. set $37.85

STAR NAMES: Their Lore and Meaning, Richard Hinckley Allen. Fascinating history of names various cultures have given to constellations and literary and folkloristic uses that have been made of stars. Indexes to subjects. Arabic and Greek names. Biblical references. Bibliography. 563pp. 5⅜ × 8½. 21079-0 Pa. $7.95

THIRTY YEARS THAT SHOOK PHYSICS: The Story of Quantum Theory, George Gamow. Lucid, accessible introduction to influential theory of energy and matter. Careful explanations of Dirac's anti-particles, Bohr's model of the atom, much more. 12 plates. Numerous drawings. 240pp. 5⅜ × 8½. 24895-X Pa. $4.95

CHINESE DOMESTIC FURNITURE IN PHOTOGRAPHS AND MEASURED DRAWINGS, Gustav Ecke. A rare volume, now affordably priced for antique collectors, furniture buffs and art historians. Detailed review of styles ranging from early Shang to late Ming. Unabridged republication. 161 black-and-white drawings, photos. Total of 224pp. 8⅜ × 11¼. (Available in U.S. only) 25171-3 Pa. $12.95

VINCENT VAN GOGH: A Biography, Julius Meier-Graefe. Dynamic, penetrating study of artist's life, relationship with brother, Theo, painting techniques, travels, more. Readable, engrossing. 160pp. 5⅜ × 8½. (Available in U.S. only) 25253-1 Pa. $3.95

ILLUSTRATED GUIDE TO SHAKER FURNITURE, Robert Meader. All furniture and appurtenances, with much on unknown local styles. 235 photos. 146pp. 9 × 12. 22819-3 Pa. $7.95

WHALE SHIPS AND WHALING: A Pictorial Survey, George Francis Dow. Over 200 vintage engravings, drawings, photographs of barks, brigs, cutters, other vessels. Also harpoons, lances, whaling guns, many other artifacts. Comprehensive text by foremost authority. 207 black-and-white illustrations. 288pp. 6 × 9. 24808-9 Pa. $8.95

THE BERTRAMS, Anthony Trollope. Powerful portrayal of blind self-will and thwarted ambition includes one of Trollope's most heartrending love stories. 497pp. 5⅜ × 8½. 25119-5 Pa. $8.95

ADVENTURES WITH A HAND LENS, Richard Headstrom. Clearly written guide to observing and studying flowers and grasses, fish scales, moth and insect wings, egg cases, buds, feathers, seeds, leaf scars, moss, molds, ferns, common crystals, etc.—all with an ordinary, inexpensive magnifying glass. 209 exact line drawings aid in your discoveries. 220pp. 5⅜ × 8½. 23330-8 Pa. $4.50

RODIN ON ART AND ARTISTS, Auguste Rodin. Great sculptor's candid, wide-ranging comments on meaning of art; great artists; relation of sculpture to poetry, painting, music; philosophy of life, more. 76 superb black-and-white illustrations of Rodin's sculpture, drawings and prints. 119pp. 8⅜ × 11¼. 24487-3 Pa. $6.95

FIFTY CLASSIC FRENCH FILMS, 1912–1982: A Pictorial Record, Anthony Slide. Memorable stills from Grand Illusion, Beauty and the Beast, Hiroshima, Mon Amour, many more. Credits, plot synopses, reviews, etc. 160pp. 8¼ × 11. 25256-6 Pa. $11.95

THE PRINCIPLES OF PSYCHOLOGY, William James. Famous long course complete, unabridged. Stream of thought, time perception, memory, experimental methods; great work decades ahead of its time. 94 figures. 1,391pp. 5⅜ × 8½. 20381-6, 20382-4 Pa., Two-vol. set $19.90

BODIES IN A BOOKSHOP, R. T. Campbell. Challenging mystery of blackmail and murder with ingenious plot and superbly drawn characters. In the best tradition of British suspense fiction. 192pp. 5⅜ × 8½. 24720-1 Pa. $3.95

CALLAS: PORTRAIT OF A PRIMA DONNA, George Jellinek. Renowned commentator on the musical scene chronicles incredible career and life of the most controversial, fascinating, influential operatic personality of our time. 64 black-and-white photographs. 416pp. 5⅜ × 8¼. 25047-4 Pa. $7.95

GEOMETRY, RELATIVITY AND THE FOURTH DIMENSION, Rudolph Rucker. Exposition of fourth dimension, concepts of relativity as Flatland characters continue adventures. Popular, easily followed yet accurate, profound. 141 illustrations. 133pp. 5⅜ × 8½. 23400-2 Pa. $3.50

HOUSEHOLD STORIES BY THE BROTHERS GRIMM, with pictures by Walter Crane. 53 classic stories—Rumpelstiltskin, Rapunzel, Hansel and Gretel, the Fisherman and his Wife, Snow White, Tom Thumb, Sleeping Beauty, Cinderella, and so much more—lavishly illustrated with original 19th century drawings. 114 illustrations. x + 269pp. 5⅜ × 8½. 21080-4 Pa. $4.50

PLANTS OF THE BIBLE, Harold N. Moldenke and Alma L. Moldenke. Standard reference to all 230 plants mentioned in Scriptures. Latin name, biblical reference, uses, modern identity, much more. Unsurpassed encyclopedic resource for scholars, botanists, nature lovers, students of Bible. Bibliography. Indexes. 123 black-and-white illustrations. 384pp. 6 × 9. 25069-5 Pa. $8.95

FAMOUS AMERICAN WOMEN: A Biographical Dictionary from Colonial Times to the Present, Robert McHenry, ed. From Pocahontas to Rosa Parks, 1,035 distinguished American women documented in separate biographical entries. Accurate, up-to-date data, numerous categories, spans 400 years. Indices. 493pp. 6½ × 9¼. 24523-3 Pa. $9.95

THE FABULOUS INTERIORS OF THE GREAT OCEAN LINERS IN HISTORIC PHOTOGRAPHS, William H. Miller, Jr. Some 200 superb photographs capture exquisite interiors of world's great "floating palaces"—1890's to 1980's: *Titanic, Ile de France, Queen Elizabeth, United States, Europa,* more. Approx. 200 black-and-white photographs. Captions. Text. Introduction. 160pp. 8⅞ × 11¾. 24756-2 Pa. $9.95

THE GREAT LUXURY LINERS, 1927–1954: A Photographic Record, William H. Miller, Jr. Nostalgic tribute to heyday of ocean liners. 186 photos of Ile de France, Normandie, Leviathan, Queen Elizabeth, United States, many others. Interior and exterior views. Introduction. Captions. 160pp. 9 × 12. 24056-8 Pa. $9.95

A NATURAL HISTORY OF THE DUCKS, John Charles Phillips. Great landmark of ornithology offers complete detailed coverage of nearly 200 species and subspecies of ducks: gadwall, sheldrake, merganser, pintail, many more. 74 full-color plates, 102 black-and-white. Bibliography. Total of 1,920pp. 8⅝ × 11¼. 25141-1, 25142-X Cloth. Two-vol. set $100.00

THE SEAWEED HANDBOOK: An Illustrated Guide to Seaweeds from North Carolina to Canada, Thomas F. Lee. Concise reference covers 78 species. Scientific and common names, habitat, distribution, more. Finding keys for easy identification. 224pp. 5⅜ × 8½. 25215-9 Pa. $5.95

THE TEN BOOKS OF ARCHITECTURE: The 1755 Leoni Edition, Leon Battista Alberti. Rare classic helped introduce the glories of ancient architecture to the Renaissance. 68 black-and-white plates. 336pp. 8⅜ × 11¼. 25239-6 Pa. $14.95

MISS MACKENZIE, Anthony Trollope. Minor masterpieces by Victorian master unmasks many truths about life in 19th-century England. First inexpensive edition in years. 392pp. 5⅜ × 8½. 25201-9 Pa. $7.95

THE RIME OF THE ANCIENT MARINER, Gustave Doré, Samuel Taylor Coleridge. Dramatic engravings considered by many to be his greatest work. The terrifying space of the open sea, the storms and whirlpools of an unknown ocean, the ice of Antarctica, more—all rendered in a powerful, chilling manner. Full text. 38 plates. 77pp. 9¼ × 12. 22305-1 Pa. $4.95

THE EXPEDITIONS OF ZEBULON MONTGOMERY PIKE, Zebulon Montgomery Pike. Fascinating first-hand accounts (1805–6) of exploration of Mississippi River, Indian wars, capture by Spanish dragoons, much more. 1,088pp. 5⅜ × 8½. 25254-X, 25255-8 Pa. Two-vol. set $23.90

A CONCISE HISTORY OF PHOTOGRAPHY: Third Revised Edition, Helmut Gernsheim. Best one-volume history—camera obscura, photochemistry, daguerreotypes, evolution of cameras, film, more. Also artistic aspects—landscape, portraits, fine art, etc. 281 black-and-white photographs. 26 in color. 176pp. 8⅜ × 11¼. 25128-4 Pa. $12.95

THE DORÉ BIBLE ILLUSTRATIONS, Gustave Doré. 241 detailed plates from the Bible: the Creation scenes, Adam and Eve, Flood, Babylon, battle sequences, life of Jesus, etc. Each plate is accompanied by the verses from the King James version of the Bible. 241pp. 9 × 12. 23004-X Pa. $8.95

HUGGER-MUGGER IN THE LOUVRE, Elliot Paul. Second Homer Evans mystery-comedy. Theft at the Louvre involves sleuth in hilarious, madcap caper. "A knockout."—Books. 336pp. 5⅜ × 8½. 25185-3 Pa. $5.95

FLATLAND, E. A. Abbott. Intriguing and enormously popular science-fiction classic explores the complexities of trying to survive as a two-dimensional being in a three-dimensional world. Amusingly illustrated by the author. 16 illustrations. 103pp. 5⅜ × 8½. 20001-9 Pa. $2.25

THE HISTORY OF THE LEWIS AND CLARK EXPEDITION, Meriwether Lewis and William Clark, edited by Elliott Coues. Classic edition of Lewis and Clark's day-by-day journals that later became the basis for U.S. claims to Oregon and the West. Accurate and invaluable geographical, botanical, biological, meteorological and anthropological material. Total of 1,508pp. 5⅜ × 8½.
21268-8, 21269-6, 21270-X Pa. Three-vol. set $25.50

LANGUAGE, TRUTH AND LOGIC, Alfred J. Ayer. Famous, clear introduction to Vienna, Cambridge schools of Logical Positivism. Role of philosophy, elimination of metaphysics, nature of analysis, etc. 160pp. 5⅜ × 8½. (Available in U.S. and Canada only) 20010-8 Pa. $2.95

MATHEMATICS FOR THE NONMATHEMATICIAN, Morris Kline. Detailed, college-level treatment of mathematics in cultural and historical context, with numerous exercises. For liberal arts students. Preface. Recommended Reading Lists. Tables. Index. Numerous black-and-white figures. xvi + 641pp. 5⅜ × 8½.
24823-2 Pa. $11.95

28 SCIENCE FICTION STORIES, H. G. Wells. Novels, *Star Begotten* and *Men Like Gods,* plus 26 short stories: "Empire of the Ants," "A Story of the Stone Age," "The Stolen Bacillus," "In the Abyss," etc. 915pp. 5⅜ × 8½. (Available in U.S. only)
20265-8 Cloth. $10.95

HANDBOOK OF PICTORIAL SYMBOLS, Rudolph Modley. 3,250 signs and symbols, many systems in full; official or heavy commercial use. Arranged by subject. Most in Pictorial Archive series. 143pp. 8⅛ × 11. 23357-X Pa. $5.95

INCIDENTS OF TRAVEL IN YUCATAN, John L. Stephens. Classic (1843) exploration of jungles of Yucatan, looking for evidences of Maya civilization. Travel adventures, Mexican and Indian culture, etc. Total of 669pp. 5⅜ × 8½.
20926-1, 20927-X Pa., Two-vol. set $9.90

DEGAS: An Intimate Portrait, Ambroise Vollard. Charming, anecdotal memoir by famous art dealer of one of the greatest 19th-century French painters. 14 black-and-white illustrations. Introduction by Harold L. Van Doren. 96pp. 5⅜ × 8½.
25131-4 Pa. $3.95

PERSONAL NARRATIVE OF A PILGRIMAGE TO ALMANDINAH AND MECCAH, Richard Burton. Great travel classic by remarkably colorful personality. Burton, disguised as a Moroccan, visited sacred shrines of Islam, narrowly escaping death. 47 illustrations. 959pp. 5⅜ × 8½. 21217-3, 21218-1 Pa., Two-vol. set $17.90

PHRASE AND WORD ORIGINS, A. H. Holt. Entertaining, reliable, modern study of more than 1,200 colorful words, phrases, origins and histories. Much unexpected information. 254pp. 5⅜ × 8½. 20758-7 Pa. $5.95

THE RED THUMB MARK, R. Austin Freeman. In this first Dr. Thorndyke case, the great scientific detective draws fascinating conclusions from the nature of a single fingerprint. Exciting story, authentic science. 320pp. 5⅜ × 8½. (Available in U.S. only) 25210-8 Pa. $5.95

AN EGYPTIAN HIEROGLYPHIC DICTIONARY, E. A. Wallis Budge. Monumental work containing about 25,000 words or terms that occur in texts ranging from 3000 B.C. to 600 A.D. Each entry consists of a transliteration of the word, the word in hieroglyphs, and the meaning in English. 1,314pp. 6⅞ × 10.
23615-3, 23616-1 Pa., Two-vol. set $27.90

THE COMPLEAT STRATEGYST: Being a Primer on the Theory of Games of Strategy, J. D. Williams. Highly entertaining classic describes, with many illustrated examples, how to select best strategies in conflict situations. Prefaces. Appendices. xvi + 268pp. 5⅜ × 8½. 25101-2 Pa. $5.95

THE ROAD TO OZ, L. Frank Baum. Dorothy meets the Shaggy Man, little Button-Bright and the Rainbow's beautiful daughter in this delightful trip to the magical Land of Oz. 272pp. 5⅜ × 8. 25208-6 Pa. $4.95

POINT AND LINE TO PLANE, Wassily Kandinsky. Seminal exposition of role of point, line, other elements in non-objective painting. Essential to understanding 20th-century art. 127 illustrations. 192pp. 6½ × 9¼. 23808-3 Pa. $4.50

LADY ANNA, Anthony Trollope. Moving chronicle of Countess Lovel's bitter struggle to win for herself and daughter Anna their rightful rank and fortune—perhaps at cost of sanity itself. 384pp. 5⅜ × 8½. 24669-8 Pa. $6.95

EGYPTIAN MAGIC, E. A. Wallis Budge. Sums up all that is known about magic in Ancient Egypt: the role of magic in controlling the gods, powerful amulets that warded off evil spirits, scarabs of immortality, use of wax images, formulas and spells, the secret name, much more. 253pp. 5⅜ × 8½. 22681-6 Pa. $4.50

THE DANCE OF SIVA, Ananda Coomaraswamy. Preeminent authority unfolds the vast metaphysic of India: the revelation of her art, conception of the universe, social organization, etc. 27 reproductions of art masterpieces. 192pp. 5⅜ × 8½.
24817-8 Pa. $5.95

CHRISTMAS CUSTOMS AND TRADITIONS, Clement A. Miles. Origin, evolution, significance of religious, secular practices. Caroling, gifts, yule logs, much more. Full, scholarly yet fascinating; non-sectarian. 400pp. 5⅜ × 8½.
23354-5 Pa. $6.50

THE HUMAN FIGURE IN MOTION, Eadweard Muybridge. More than 4,500 stopped-action photos, in action series, showing undraped men, women, children jumping, lying down, throwing, sitting, wrestling, carrying, etc. 390pp. 7⅞ × 10⅝.
20204-6 Cloth. $19.95

THE MAN WHO WAS THURSDAY, Gilbert Keith Chesterton. Witty, fast-paced novel about a club of anarchists in turn-of-the-century London. Brilliant social, religious, philosophical speculations. 128pp. 5⅜ × 8½. 25121-7 Pa. $3.95

A CEZANNE SKETCHBOOK: Figures, Portraits, Landscapes and Still Lifes, Paul Cezanne. Great artist experiments with tonal effects, light, mass, other qualities in over 100 drawings. A revealing view of developing master painter, precursor of Cubism. 102 black-and-white illustrations. 144pp. 8⅜ × 6⅜. 24790-2 Pa. $5.95

AN ENCYCLOPEDIA OF BATTLES: Accounts of Over 1,560 Battles from 1479 B.C. to the Present, David Eggenberger. Presents essential details of every major battle in recorded history, from the first battle of Megiddo in 1479 B.C. to Grenada in 1984. List of Battle Maps. New Appendix covering the years 1967–1984. Index. 99 illustrations. 544pp. 6½ × 9¼. 24913-1 Pa. $14.95

AN ETYMOLOGICAL DICTIONARY OF MODERN ENGLISH, Ernest Weekley. Richest, fullest work, by foremost British lexicographer. Detailed word histories. Inexhaustible. Total of 856pp. 6½ × 9¼.
21873-2, 21874-0 Pa., Two-vol. set $17.00

WEBSTER'S AMERICAN MILITARY BIOGRAPHIES, edited by Robert McHenry. Over 1,000 figures who shaped 3 centuries of American military history. Detailed biographies of Nathan Hale, Douglas MacArthur, Mary Hallaren, others. Chronologies of engagements, more. Introduction. Addenda. 1,033 entries in alphabetical order. xi + 548pp. 6½ × 9¼. (Available in U.S. only)
24758-9 Pa. $11.95

LIFE IN ANCIENT EGYPT, Adolf Erman. Detailed older account, with much not in more recent books: domestic life, religion, magic, medicine, commerce, and whatever else needed for complete picture. Many illustrations. 597pp. 5⅜ × 8½.
22632-8 Pa. $8.95

HISTORIC COSTUME IN PICTURES, Braun & Schneider. Over 1,450 costumed figures shown, covering a wide variety of peoples: kings, emperors, nobles, priests, servants, soldiers, scholars, townsfolk, peasants, merchants, courtiers, cavaliers, and more. 256pp. 8⅜ × 11¼. 23150-X Pa. $7.95

THE NOTEBOOKS OF LEONARDO DA VINCI, edited by J. P. Richter. Extracts from manuscripts reveal great genius; on painting, sculpture, anatomy, sciences, geography, etc. Both Italian and English. 186 ms. pages reproduced, plus 500 additional drawings, including studies for *Last Supper, Sforza* monument, etc. 860pp. 7⅞ × 10¾. (Available in U.S. only) 22572-0, 22573-9 Pa., Two-vol. set $25.90

SIR HARRY HOTSPUR OF HUMBLETHWAITE, Anthony Trollope. Incisive, unconventional psychological study of a conflict between a wealthy baronet, his idealistic daughter, and their scapegrace cousin. The 1870 novel in its first inexpensive edition in years. 250pp. 5⅜ × 8½. 24953-0 Pa. $5.95

LASERS AND HOLOGRAPHY, Winston E. Kock. Sound introduction to burgeoning field, expanded (1981) for second edition. Wave patterns, coherence, lasers, diffraction, zone plates, properties of holograms, recent advances. 84 illustrations. 160pp. 5⅜ × 8¼. (Except in United Kingdom) 24041-X Pa. $3.50

INTRODUCTION TO ARTIFICIAL INTELLIGENCE: SECOND, ENLARGED EDITION, Philip C. Jackson, Jr. Comprehensive survey of artificial intelligence—the study of how machines (computers) can be made to act intelligently. Includes introductory and advanced material. Extensive notes updating the main text. 132 black-and-white illustrations. 512pp. 5⅜ × 8½. 24864-X Pa. $8.95

HISTORY OF INDIAN AND INDONESIAN ART, Ananda K. Coomaraswamy. Over 400 illustrations illuminate classic study of Indian art from earliest Harappa finds to early 20th century. Provides philosophical, religious and social insights. 304pp. 6⅝ × 9⅝. 25005-9 Pa. $8.95

THE GOLEM, Gustav Meyrink. Most famous supernatural novel in modern European literature, set in Ghetto of Old Prague around 1890. Compelling story of mystical experiences, strange transformations, profound terror. 13 black-and-white illustrations. 224pp. 5⅜ × 8½. (Available in U.S. only) 25025-3 Pa. $5.95

ARMADALE, Wilkie Collins. Third great mystery novel by the author of *The Woman in White* and *The Moonstone*. Original magazine version with 40 illustrations. 597pp. 5⅜ × 8½. 23429-0 Pa. $9.95

PICTORIAL ENCYCLOPEDIA OF HISTORIC ARCHITECTURAL PLANS, DETAILS AND ELEMENTS: With 1,880 Line Drawings of Arches, Domes, Doorways, Facades, Gables, Windows, etc., John Theodore Haneman. Sourcebook of inspiration for architects, designers, others. Bibliography. Captions. 141pp. 9 × 12. 24605-1 Pa. $6.95

BENCHLEY LOST AND FOUND, Robert Benchley. Finest humor from early 30's, about pet peeves, child psychologists, post office and others. Mostly unavailable elsewhere. 73 illustrations by Peter Arno and others. 183pp. 5⅜ × 8½. 22410-4 Pa. $3.95

ERTÉ GRAPHICS, Erté. Collection of striking color graphics: *Seasons, Alphabet, Numerals, Aces* and *Precious Stones*. 50 plates, including 4 on covers. 48pp. 9⅜ × 12¼. 23580-7 Pa. $6.95

THE JOURNAL OF HENRY D. THOREAU, edited by Bradford Torrey, F. H. Allen. Complete reprinting of 14 volumes, 1837–61, over two million words; the sourcebooks for *Walden*, etc. Definitive. All original sketches, plus 75 photographs. 1,804pp. 8½ × 12¼. 20312-3, 20313-1 Cloth., Two-vol. set $80.00

CASTLES: THEIR CONSTRUCTION AND HISTORY, Sidney Toy. Traces castle development from ancient roots. Nearly 200 photographs and drawings illustrate moats, keeps, baileys, many other features. Caernarvon, Dover Castles, Hadrian's Wall, Tower of London, dozens more. 256pp. 5⅜ × 8¼. 24898-4 Pa. $5.95